A Clever Base-Ballist

A Clever Base-Ballist

The Life and Times of
John Montgomery Ward

Bryan Di Salvatore

PANTHEON BOOKS, NEW YORK

Library of Congress Cataloging-in-Publication Data

Di Salvatore, Bryan.
A clever base-ballist : the life and times of John Montgomery Ward /
Bryan Di Salvatore.
          p.   cm.
Includes bibliographical references and index.
ISBN 0-679-44234-0
1. Ward, John Montgomery, 1860–1925.   2. Baseball players—
United States—Biography.   I. Title.
GV865.W363D5 1999
796.357'092—dc21
[B]   98-54189

Random House Web Address: www.randomhouse.com

Book design by Dutton and Sherman

Printed in the United States of America
First Edition

2 4 6 8 9 7 5 3 1

A Deirdre, ma radieuse fleur sauvage

It is also instructive to examine a strange game played by Berber tribesmen of Libya. The game is unique. It is played by one tribe, a tribe further distinguished from other Berbers by a remarkable incidence of blond hair. *Ta Kurt om el mahag,* "the ball of the pilgrim's mother," struck its discoverer, an Italian anthropologist, as a sort of elementary baseball. There is a home base, a base to run to, a pitcher, batters, and fielders. The captain is allowed three strikes, the others only two. A caught fly retires the side. The game has numerous terms that the Berber players themselves cannot explain. The game is, moreover, played without the toga-like *barracan* that is almost never doffed except for ceremonial occasions. No one can say for sure how the game came to North Africa or what exactly it signifies, but the likelihood is that it was brought by Germanic invaders centuries ago and that it contains the vestiges of a primitive rain ceremony now meaningless even to the Berbers.

Allen Guttman, *From Ritual to Record*

Contents

Part III

Part I

A youngster, perhaps sixteen or seventeen years old, was once playing ball . . . as he caught or threw the ball, we shouted together, "What rhythm! what modesty of manner, what skill!" Whatever he said or did, gentlemen, he seemed a miracle of beauty. Never before have I heard of or seen such grace.

—Athenaeus, *Deipnosophistae* I, 15

One

A Light Bit of a Boy

JOHN MONTGOMERY WARD was handsome, slender, slim-hipped—five feet eight inches tall, in cleats. As an eighteen-year-old rookie pitcher for the 1878 Providence Grays of the National League of Professional Base Ball Clubs, he weighed 140 pounds. Over the course of his seventeen-year major league career, he filled out some, gaining fifteen or twenty pounds.

Baseball players during the nineteenth century—the sport's gawky, vituperative adolescence—came, as they do now, in all sizes. Ward was smaller than the likes of Boileryard Clarke, Jumbo McGinnis, Big Dan Brouthers, Silver Flint, Big Dave Orr, Cupid Childs, Chief Zimmer, Fatty Briody, Adonis Terry, Podge Weihe, Chicken Wolf, Pud Galvin, Candy LaChance, Hick Carpenter, and Eagle Eye Beckley. In turn, Ward dwarfed a few players himself: Dummy Hoy, for one, Doggie Miller for another, as well as Shorty Radford, Wee Willie Keeler, Trick McSorley, and Buttercup Dickerson.

But when all is said and done, Ward—give or take an inch here and a few pounds there—was about the same size as many of his fellow base-ballists, including Ubbo Ubbo Hornung, Lip Pike, Ice Box Chamberlain, Lady Baldwin, Germany Long, Oyster Burns, The Only Nolan, Monkey Hotaling, Bid McPhee, Bug Holliday, Crab Burkett, Dupee Shaw, Tido Daly, Nig Cuppy, Hunkey Hines, Dude Esterbrook, Dirty Jack Doyle,

3

Blondie Purcell, Count Campau, Yank Robinson, Patsy Tebeau, Cannon-ball Morris, and Bald Billy Barnie.

His shoulders sloped dramatically. He was fair-skinned and high-cheeked, his face at once stalwart and delicate. He had a broad nose—in some photos it looks as if it had been broken, though there is no record of such an injury. His ears, large as playing cards, jutted boldly. His eyes were blue—pale, by some accounts. By the time of his death, in 1925, when he was sixty-five years old—gentleman farmer, successful lawyer, and first-rank golfer—he had a weathered, scoured look. All those afternoons in the summer sun.

His hair was light—the color of sand—and sometimes his eyebrows disappear in photographs. As a boy his hair was long. As a grown-up, he wore it neither long nor short. Sometimes he parted it on the left, sometimes on the right. In one photo, taken when he was fifty years old, he parts it more or less in the middle. He never lost his hair: it was thick and straight in his youth; later, when he was famous and rich, it looked as if it wanted to swoop and bank modestly, but had been brilliantined into submission.

There's an early photograph of Ward, taken in his home town of Bellefonte, Pennsylvania. He is perhaps nine years old, eleven at most, with a lingering of baby fat. He wears a heavy dress jacket with comically wide lapels. Those ears have outpaced the rest of him, as a puppy's paws do the puppy. His eyebrows are thick, bold as diacritics. He is not smiling—there exists no known likeness of him smiling—but Ward's visage here is a different thing from unsmiling. His small thin mouth, curving downward, suggests some pure and deep-seated misery.

How much should we read into this? If in fact he was eleven, and the year 1871, and the photo taken after May 1—the day his father died—his lost-boy look passes without comment. But let's assume he was ten. If it was spring or summer or fall, he would rather have been outside playing baseball—a sandlot boy with cheeks of tan—than sitting in J. W. Moore's studio. If it was winter, he would rather it were spring, summer, or fall, so he could be out playing ball. And how he loved to do so! He tells us so himself, in his 1888 book, *Base-Ball: How to Become a Player:*

Base-ball cannot be learned as a trade. It begins with the sport of the schoolboy, and though it may end in the professional, I am sure there is not a single one of these who learned the game with the expectation of making it a business. There have been years in the life of each during which he must have ate and drank and dreamed base-ball. It is not a calculation but an inspiration.

In another Bellefonte studio portrait, Ward is sitting next to his friend, neighbor, college chum, and teammate, Ellis L. Orvis. Orvis would become a locally prominent judge and town bastion. Even at the time of the photograph—it is 1875 or thereabouts and Ward is fifteen years old, Orvis about eighteen—Orvis looks poised, judicial. He is dressed in a handsome, well-fitting dark suit. One hand rests on his leg, the other against his vest. He looks as if he has sat for many portraits and knows he will sit for many more.

Not John Ward. He looks like every teenager who has been roped into yet another episode of damn foolishness by a doting parent. Sit up straight, Monte! See how Ellis does it?

Ward's light-colored jacket has those familiar immense lapels. The jacket fits him like a question: Whose was it originally? It drapes around his shoulders as if he were an amputee; it rides over his wrists as if he were trying to keep his hands warm. Like Orvis's, Ward's legs are crossed, but his hands, instead of resting on his thighs, grip them like talons. Ward's head is enormous, so disproportionate to the rest of his reedy self that we can't but wonder if the boy suffered from a terrible malady. He did not.

A team photo, the first of many, shows the Pennsylvania State College nine—"Champions of Center County"—in 1875. There's Frank Keller, who, like Ellis Orvis next to him, became a judge. There are the Calder boys, Charles and A. Russell, sons of the college president—Charles died in 1880, A. Russell became a metallurgist. There's Frank Knoche, whose father owned a music store in Harrisburg, which Frank inherited. Joseph Stull—he's the one whose long skeletal face reminds us of a tubercular poet—became an attorney in Salt Lake City.

Five of the State College boys are holding bats, cradled like rifles. The team has scraped together money for uniforms: caps, shirts, what we would all recognize as baseball pants, the sort that end just below the knee, and striped hose. They also wear ties—knotted like cowboy bandannas. Ward wears his differently—it trails down his chest like a modern-day necktie.

That's Ward, on the far left. One large ear is visible—if Ward had been born one hundred years later his schoolyard name would have been "Dumbo." He's holding a bat near the knob and leaning back slightly, against Frank Keller's bat, and he has his arm over Frank Knoche's shoulder. Again, how disturbingly sad Ward looks. Of course no one looked exactly lighthearted in photographs back then. Having one's picture taken was a rare, prolonged, and solemn business in 1875, and people approached a portrait session as we might the altar rail or a radiology lab.

But this stillness, this *melancholy* of young John Ward is of a different order entirely. He looks beaten, limp, distracted, bowed. His mouth is in collapse. Maybe the boys had just lost a game, or John had gone hitless at the plate and played like a muffin in the field. No, he looks more crestfallen than that. The photograph was taken less than a year after his mother's death from pneumonia. In all likelihood, the camera happened to catch him midstride down a dark alley of memory. Whatever the cause, if we were to pick from this long-ago pack of local heroes the one most likely to kill himself, we would guess Ward, and guess wrong.

Look at how tiny he is—bantamlike. How like a cathedral choirboy. Ward is the one whose voice hasn't broken; the one who has yet to shave. In baseball, size is, often as not, incidental to talent and effectiveness—and Ward was brilliantly talented and effective. What Ward did, in the parlance of sport, was put up numbers—numbers we will get to shortly. But there was much more to Ward the ballplayer than statistics.

Baseball of yore was a quicker, more dashing, arguably more deft game than baseball now. The ball was more crudely manufactured, became softer sooner, and remained in play longer—home runs were rare. The infields were lumpy, the outfields spacious and topographical. Runners tended to advance no more than one base or two at a time. Speed was important. Bunts were important. Base-stealing was important. Fielding prowess was more important than life itself. Players, for years, played gloveless. By the late 1880s many had donned what we would describe as fingerless golf gloves. (Fielding errors were common as spit and despite the lack of home runs, scores were quite often very high.)

Ward was the sort of player that other players appreciate as a team-mate and curse as an opponent. Whether he was pitching or playing the infield or outfield, he was a hustler, a scrapper, a playmaker, a gamer, a thinker, an analyzer. He beat you invisibly as often as he beat you visibly. In *Base-Ball: How to Become a Player* he expounds on the importance of the sport's vital edges: pickoffs, relay throws, brushback pitches, drawing the infield in or moving it out, hit-and-run plays, signals—all common-place today, but in 1888 only aborning. There were, statistically, better fielders than Ward, but the man who ranges wide—as Ward did—and gets his hands on more balls than average—as Ward did—often ends up com-mitting more errors than a stay-at-home Joe. Ward, in the field, was the guy who always seemed to be in the right place at the right time. He was the one who held a possible double down to a single by deflecting the ball as it left the infield; the one who placed himself far enough out on the out-field grass or close enough to home plate to relay the throw to home quick as a ricochet. He was the one who directed his teammates to move right, left, in, out—playing the percentages, thinking, thinking, thinking.

Offensively, he drove teams to drink. Clean hits were fine, but in those error-thick days, making contact was often as effective. Say it's the bottom of the ninth and Ward's team, down by a run, has its last at-bats. The opposing pitcher is tired. He gets one out. Ward steps into the box. The pitcher tenses; knows Ward's reputation for damage; knows he has to retire him. Ward watches the pitches; doesn't swing at the balls; fouls off the strikes. He makes the pitcher work. Work, work, work. More fouls. More work. Finally, Ward gets his pitch and hits the ball toward shortstop. Off he runs, like the wind itself. The nervous shortstop hurries his scoop and his throw. Ward's on.

The pitcher can't concentrate on the next batter—not with Ward dancing and stretching his lead from first. SSSSS! Ward steals second. SSSSS! Third. An easy fly to right. Ward tags up and beats the throw home. The game's tied.

He was always, it seemed, on base. If the infielders crept in, he would hit the ball sharply. If they cheated back, he'd push the ball softly. If Ward played on today's springy artificial turf, he'd have been the one to invent the chop stroke, slamming the ball hard onto the carpet, and running safely to first while the infielder waits, helpless, for the ball to fall toward earth.

What a nervous-maker was John Ward! What a pesky bastard!

He was very conscious of his size. He described himself in an 1886 article for *Lippincott's* magazine as "only a light bit of a boy," and the base-ball he played and championed was the baseball of a small man. In his 1888 book, *Base-Ball*, time and again he takes potshots at larger players, to the point of denying them, meanly, post-game refreshment and off-season leisure.

> A thin, nervous person, worn out with the excitement and fatigue of the day, will find [alcohol] a genuine tonic. . . . The "beefy" individual, with plenty of reserve force, needs no stimulant and should never touch liquor at any time. . . .
>
> The amount of work necessary to keep a player in the proper form must be determined in each particular case by the individual himself. If he is inclined to be thin a very little will be enough . . . while if prone to stoutness he may require a great deal. . . . [Heavy use of weights] is not good for any one, but especially is it dangerous for ball players. They do not want strength, but agility and suppleness.

Ward then applies his prejudice to other positions:

> Of all the players on a base-ball nine, the pitcher is the one to whom attaches the greatest importance. . . . Speaking first of the physical requirements, I will not discuss the question of size. There are good pitchers of all sizes . . . though naturally a man of average proportions would have some advantages.
>
> Next . . . comes the catcher. . . . Here again the size of the candidate seems not to be of vital importance . . . more important than size are pluck and stamina. . . .
>
> Second base is the prettiest position to play of the entire in-field. . . . the position requires a very active player, and for this reason, too large a man would not be desireable. . . .
>
> A short-stop should be a player of more than ordinary suppleness and activity. . . . he must be possessed of some intelligence and a wit. . . . Brains are as much a necessity in base-ball as in any other profession. . . .

Outfielders, Ward went on, must have, above all else, strong arms, good eyes, the ability to "start quickly and run fast," good judgment, and a strong, accurate arm. Not once does he suggest size or general strength as an advantage on the greensward. In fact, the only size-specific position, in his opinion, is first base, which, he concedes almost as an afterthought, "demands a tall man."

But defense is only half of baseball. Later, in *Base-Ball*'s sagacious chapter on batting, Ward enthusiastically dismisses the supposed advantages of brute strength, championing instead brains and guile—"cleverness," in the era's parlance.

> The hardest hit will sometimes go directly into the waiting hands
> of a fielder, while a little "punk" hit may drop lazily into some
> unguarded spot. . . . There are two classes of good batters, [one
> that makes] a decided *swing* [while for the other] the motion is
> more of a *push*. . . . A great fault with many batters is that they
> try to hit the ball too hard. This is especially true of the younger
> players, the "colts," as they are called. A young player with a
> reputation as a hitter in some minor league, goes into a big club
> and at once thinks he must hit the ball over the fence. The result
> is that he doesn't hit it at all, and unless he corrects his fault, he
> goes on "fanning the atmosphere" until he is handed his
> release. . . .

There would, of course, come many other team photos after that first one of the college nine: Ward with the Providence Grays, with the New Yorks and the Brooklyns of the National League, with the Brooklyns of the Players' League, and, during the off-season of 1888–1889, with a barnstorming team, the All-Americas, which traveled the globe to great American fanfare.

Ward, in the great majority of them, makes a point of differentiating himself from his teammates, just as he did in his college-team photo. If his teammates face toward the left, he faces to his right. If they face to the right, he will gaze to the left. If they are looking straight ahead, he will face half-left or half-right. His reluctance to face the camera directly may have been vanity—that nose, those ears. But why the contrariness?

There was about Ward a whiff of regency, of reserve, of arrogance, of high—or at least higher-than-you—purpose. He was, from his earliest professional baseball days, more of the boardroom than the barroom. He did not smoke. Unlike many of his teammates, he drank only in moderation, for the most part. Unlike almost all of his teammates, he maintained a rigorous off-season training program, in gymnasiums and in the countryside, where he loved to hunt. During his periods as team captain—a position equivalent to the modern manager—he was something of a martinet. His demands for total concentration, total dedication, made his captaincies generally short-lived affairs often characterized by player discontent. Upon his retirement in 1894, the sporting press dubbed him "The Little Duke of the Diamond" and "Prince Imperial."

Despite his twitchy, dust-raising style of play, he was never dubbed Pepper, Flash, Scooter, or Sparky. He was never even Jack. To call Ward "Jack" would have been as unseemly, as unthinkable, as calling FDR "Del." He was never quite one of the boys.

After his death, he was eulogized by the baseball world in this manner:

"The greatest competitor this country has ever known."

"Brilliant . . . concentration that was remarkable . . . speed, brains, skill, courage and the will to go the entire route."

"A scholar . . . [who] knew all the 'rules and tricks of the diamond' . . . [and maintained a] high standard of professional conduct."

"Strategist without a superior."

"No brainier player ever trod a diamond."

"Sharp-witted and quick of thought and action."

"Easily the most valuable player on the team . . . [with] an o'erweening desire to win."

"Rattling good."

"Handsome, aggressive. . . ."

"Versatile. . . ."

"One of the most forceful brains the game has ever known. . . ."

He was admired, applauded, cheered to the echo. He was embraced. But he was never *loved*.

During the years Ward played in the major leagues, from 1878 through the 1894 season, baseball cards were invented and became very popular. Most were published by tobacco companies, which included them in the packages of their products. Other, larger cards—called cabinet cards—were also popular. Fans collected these and placed them here and there—often on parlor mantels—for decoration, the way people put postcards and cartoons on their refrigerators today. Two of these are the most reproduced photos we have of Ward.

They were taken in the mid-1880s, when Ward was with the National League New Yorks. They were taken indoors, with self-consciously ennobling backgrounds. One shows Ward leaning against an ornately sculpted stone vessel of some sort—it is waist high, garlanded with pudgy cherubs. Ward's arms are crossed in front of his chest—as if he were posing foot-up on a deer he had just shot—and he looks to his right, his head slightly raised, as if he is considering something graceful and pleasing.

In the other, Ward, standing, holds a bat. The painted canvas backdrop depicts a narrow bridge over a creek. How handsome Ward looks! How confident! How slim! How gallant! How women's hearts must have throbbed when they saw this superb athlete at the height of his talent! Ward was, in fact, a lady's man of no small measure, and a ballpark favorite of women fans. In this photo, he seems to know it very well indeed.

There is a third card, one that catches Ward in an uncharacteristically silly mood. He is lying, belly-down, touching the base into which he has just "slid." In many of these staged action shots, the subject of the photograph is the infielder, who indicates that he has successfully tagged the runner out by holding up an index finger to the camera. In Ward's photo, *he* is the one holding up his finger—showing that he has successfully eluded the tag. The fellows are putting a twist on things, taking the mickey out of themselves. Ward might as well have been making rabbit ears behind a teammate's head.

During the last several years of his life, Ward could be found in one of four places: his law office, the golf links, the hunting fields, or his farm. Here's a shot of him on his Long Island land. He's lying on the ground, propped up on one elbow, looking at his favorite hunting dog, a golden retriever named Bob. Ward is wearing a tie, a hunting jacket, plus-fours and one of those soft caps newsboys in old movies wear when they scream "EXTRA!" Bob looks fat and sassy and well-loved and John Ward looks relaxed and proud of Bob.

An action shot taken in 1904 shows the sportsman playing golf, dressed in white shoes, white summer-weight pants, a long-sleeved striped shirt, and a white wide-brimmed sun hat. Behind him the windows of the Fox Hills, New Jersey, clubhouse are open to the breeze, and a young caddy, in knickers and cap, watches as Ward follows through—mightily, stylishly—after his drive. He looks perfectly at ease out there where the swells spend so many of their afternoons.

A later photo shows Ward, fifty years old, in his Manhattan law office in 1910. He's been retired from baseball for sixteen years. He has happily remarried—his new wife, Katherine Waas, is a handsome, athletic woman. He is successful in his new profession. He is a five-handicap golfer who runs with and sometimes beats the best players in America and Britain. His suit is perfectly tailored. His silk handkerchief rises owl-eared from his breast pocket. He has gained a few pounds, but he is still trim, fit. Under one eye, age lines are evident. His mustache is modest, suitable for a man of his stature: rich, honorable, smart, tenacious. We would have to search high and low to find a man better suited to the part of successful attorney.

Between the 1881 and 1882 baseball seasons—he was pitching for the Providence Grays then—Ward traveled west with some other ballplayers. The men hunted and fished in Idaho before heading to California, where they stayed in the Bay Area for a fortnight or so, touring and playing with some California ball clubs. Though the return trip east was "long and tiresome," according to the sporting press, the men—especially Ward and the Grays' first baseman, Jerry Denny—reported to the team in "admirable physical condition."

But what a surprise Ward had in store for the fans! He had grown a mustache. It was the talk of the town. For the rest of his playing days the mustache was quite the ornament. Sometimes he waxed it as straight to point as an artist's brush. Sometimes he shaped it into a moderately yoked handlebar.

In adopting this facial hair, Ward—twenty-one years old at the time—was following fashion, as young men do. He must have thought his new adornment made him look older, more mature, more dashing, more *manly*. In fact, however, compared with the boisterous, aggressive mustaches—some of them real hedges—of many nineteenth-century baseball players, Ward's was, at best, tentative, nominal. It looks, on his smooth young face, retrofitted, *purposeful*, as precocious and self-conscious as a new Easter suit.

Ward was inducted into baseball's Hall of Fame in 1964. His plaque there—his neighbors are Casey Stengel, Pud Galvin, and Ted Williams—is rendered most unfortunately. Maybe the artist that year was inept, or having a bad day, or feeling his oats. Maybe he didn't like what he knew of Ward. Whatever the reason, Ward's bronze-colored, three-dimensional likeness renders him wild-eyed and bee-stung-puffy, the opposite of elegant. And oh, that mustache that meant so much to him! The artist has one side nicely following the contours of Ward's mouth, but the other half stiff as a hunting dog's tail—pointing boldly and unnaturally into space. Ward, in Cooperstown, looks as if he is eternally signaling a left turn.

There's one last photograph we need consider. It's a team shot of the 1884 National League New Yorks and it tells us more about Ward, at least Ward the ballplayer, than any other. Four of the eleven players sit, the rest stand, on the grass at the side of a diamond. The uniforms are simple and typical: the blouses have pointed collars and button up the front; the belts are wide; the only insignia is a widely spaced "N Y" across the chest; the caps are striped.

The uniforms look roughly used. So do the ballplayers. They look exhausted and angry—as if they had just finished a shift in the mine, the woods, the foundry, the paint factory, the railroad; as if they could eat nails and spit out the rust. They look like a team from the penitentiary or a posse about to head out after the varmints who assaulted the schoolmarm.

Look closely at Ward. That's him standing at the far left. He leans against a bat, its business end on the ground. His other hand hooks his belt. His head is not turned this time! He's looking straight to the camera. He is squinting. His nose looks broken. Those ears. "Yeah," he seems to be saying to the photographer, "My ears stick out. You want to make something of it, you son of a bitch?"

This is the essential ballplayer Ward: Ward when he hadn't the time to gussy himself up; Ward as he must have looked as he made his living between the foul lines where, for a few hours most spring, summer, and fall afternoons, in cities across America, for seventeen years, the rest of the world fell away and nothing mattered but the contest at hand.

TWO

Not a Summer Snap

I N THE BEGINNING, John Ward was a pitcher. He threw right and batted left. After a few years in the National League, his arm went bad and he trained himself to be a pure position player: in turn an outfielder (for a while, to rest his right arm, he threw with his left!), a shortstop, and a second baseman. He was a team manager for the best part of seven seasons. He was twice, briefly, a team owner. He almost bought the New York Giants in 1895. In 1909 he very nearly became president of the National League.

Since 1871 there have been seven major leagues: the National Association, the National League, the American Association, the Union Association, the Players' National League, the American League, and the Federal League. From the 1871 season through the 1998 season, exactly 15,000 men have played major league baseball. Though their total exceeds 15,000 because many players—like John Ward—both pitched and played a "position," 6,965 major leaguers can be considered as pitchers primarily and 8,718 as batters primarily.

John Ward won more games than all but 179 of those 6,965 pitchers.

His winning percentage was higher than all but forty-seven of them.

He allowed fewer walks per game, and fewer earned runs (those not scored via errors) per game than all but three of them.

He allowed fewer baserunners per game than any of them.

He pitched major league baseball's second perfect game.

He once pitched an eighteen-inning shutout.

He scored more runs than all but sixty-four of those 8,718 batters.

He hit safely more times than all but 163 of them.

He stole more bases than all but twenty-six of them.

His strikeout percentage was lower than all but thirty-two of them.

He pitched major league baseball's second perfect game.

He pitched an eighteen-inning shutout.

One year, he won forty-seven games.

Another year, he won thirty-nine games.

Of the thousands of books written about baseball, perhaps one is indispensable—at least for the more factual-minded sort of fan. It is called *Total Baseball* and its subtitle is *The Official Encyclopedia of Major League Baseball*. The book in recent years has grown to the size of a cathedral Bible. The fourth edition, published in 1995, is 2,552 pages long. Some of those pages are taken up by team histories, lists (managers, coaches, umpires, owners and officials, Negro League players), and all-time records. There are essays on baseball in Canada, spring training, women in baseball, the evolution of the diamond. Another is on phantom ballplayers (those who, despite never existing or never having played, somehow found their way into box scores and statistical rolls). Pacer Smith, for example, never played in 1877 for either Chicago or Cincinnati—instead, it was Harry W. Smith. And it wasn't, as had been previously thought, George Gray in the outfield at the end of May in 1903 for the Pittsburgh Pirates. Instead, it was *two* other fellows, Ernest Diehl and Romer Grey. (Pacer Smith, by the way, was executed in 1895 for the brutal murder of his own child. Romer Grey was Zane Grey's brother.)

The bulk of *Total Baseball*, however, is devoted to the year-by-year records of those 15,000 major league baseball players. The players are given equal treatment, whether they batted once or played for twenty-four years. Most of the numbers run down the pages under column headings as familiar—to baseball fans at least—as the months of the year:

G AB R H 2B 3B HR RBI AVG OBP SLG W L SO ERA

But in *Total Baseball*—whose researchers pore over baseball performances as scholars do over the Talmud—strange and wonderful new statistics have taken root: PRO+, for example, and SBR, OOB, PD, and many others. The purpose of these formulations is a noble one—the marriage of the quantitative and the qualitative. Many of these new categories are complicated ones to derive. Take "batting runs," for example. Batting runs, according to *Total Baseball,* are those runs "contributed beyond [or below] what a league-average batter or team might have contributed." The batting runs formula is derived, in part, by calculating

> the run values for each offensive event. [Run values] change marginally with changing conditions of play . . . and they differ slightly up and down the batting order (a homer is not worth as much to the leadoff hitter as it is to the fifth-place batter; a walk is worth more for the man batting second than for the man batting eighth), however these differences have been averaged out historically in the figures below.
>
> $$Runs = (.47)1B + (.78)2B + (1.09)3B + (1.40)HR + (.33)(BB + HB) - (.25)(AB - H) - (.50)OOB$$

The rest of the explanation takes a full column—and the batting runs explanation is not the most complicated one in *Total Baseball*—not by a long shot.

Anyway, statisticians have figured out methods for ranking the performances of all those 15,000 baseball players—be they position players or pitchers—from the best to the worst, from Day 1 to Yesterday. These categories, called total (player or pitcher) ratings, take into account not just batting runs, but adjusted batting runs, as well as fielding runs and base stealing runs (minus, naturally, a positional adjustment). These are all divided by runs per win. A similar number of statistics are used to rank pitching performances.

This sort of research is, for most mortals—including baseball fans—too weird and mystifying for words. But the results are fascinating and—if we have faith—exquisitely accurate. (Babe Ruth, for example, ranks as the best player who ever lived.)

According to these calculations, of those 15,000 men who have ever played major league baseball, John Ward ranks as the 435th-best position player and the 163d-best pitcher. If we make no distinction between position-playing and pitching, and combine, basically, all the individual-player numbers in all of baseball for all of history—a process that, granted, is a little bit like mating giraffes and robins—John Ward is the 228th-best player of all time.

But John Ward's place in baseball history—one that until the last twenty years or so was one of confounding obscurity—is based only in part on his abilities as a player.

For a strange, brief period, the half-decade that ended after the 1890 season, John Ward was the most important man of his profession. He led a revolt of his fellow players, the workers, against baseball's front office, its board of directors. Had that revolt succeeded, the history of baseball—at least the history of baseball's contentious player-owner relations—would have taken a very different course.

What led Ward to his position of leadership in the Brotherhood of Professional Base Ball Players and to his founding of the Players' National League was, in part, his lifelong awareness that professional baseball was not just a sport. As he reminded players and fans alike in a reflective article in the *New York Clipper* newspaper in 1896, two years into his retirement,

> [Baseball] is not a Summer snap, but a business in which capital
> is invested. A player is not a sporting man. He is hired to do cer-
> tain work, and do it as well as he possibly can.

In 1890, John Montgomery Ward persuaded his teammates—his colleagues, his co-workers, his brothers—to rise against team owners and the executives of the National League. To compare this war, which became known as the Brotherhood Revolt, to the American Revolution or the Civil War, would be hyperbolic, profane. The Revolt was more analogous to the War of 1812. Both struggles were brief; neither struggle is much remembered today; both were acts of attempted reclamation and both would-be reclaimers—the British and the players—lost, but not before, briefly, storming the capital and setting it afire. For that short and not necessarily glorious time, Ward's executive skills, his shrewd mind, his honest and clear-eyed habits, his temperance, his foresight, and his rhetorical skills caused him to be the most discussed—reviled, applauded—man in America and, as far as the members of the Brotherhood were concerned, the most *needed* man in baseball.

There is, among baseball historians, and there was, among contemporary observers sympathetic to Ward, a tendency to see the man through rose-colored lenses: as a brainy St. George slaying the capitalist dragon, or as a hard-hitting Moses leading the poor, plodding, oppressed, thickheaded mass of ballplayers toward some economic promised land.

Fine. Give Ward credit—the fight, the journey, was perilous—but give the rest of the men credit as well. Ward was the right man for the job—the only man, in fact—and he was an extraordinarily shrewd, inspiring leader. He was very clever, certainly, but it was the players who listened to him and rose—loudly, raggedly, sometimes reluctantly—almost to a man, against a corporate system they saw as oppressive and emasculating. That system was embodied in the National League of Base Ball Clubs, which they felt picked their pockets, put saltpeter in their sidemeat, and gave them shameful financial beatings if they dared misbehave. Ward led, but the players were perspicacious enough to choose him and to follow his lead.

Ward the distant, Ward the arrogant, Ward the immaculate, Ward the fussy, Ward the sniffy, Ward the hard-nosed, was also Ward the trustworthy. The players, rough-and-tumble and streetwise, would never have followed into the frightening economic unknown anyone they considered weak, frivolous, selfish, or unmanly.

But follow him they did: the strong and the weak, the carefree and the cautious, the Catholic and the Protestant, the Irishman and the Englishman, the Italian and the German, the Aussie and the Cornishman, the infielders and the outfielders, the pitchers and the catchers, the bold and many of the timid, the college boys and the farm boys, the cynical and the naive, the ants and the grasshoppers, the cakes and the lulus, the crooks and Christians, the soaks, the squabs, the dandies, the droobs . . . Nearly every mother's National League son. The beasts of the kingdom.

Three

An Unfavorable Impression

J OHN MONTGOMERY WARD.

He hated that mouthful of a middle name; laid off it like an oh-and-two sucker pitch.

In court documents, personal correspondence, telegrams, business letters, letters to the editor, the dispatches he sent to the sporting weeklies, and most of the articles he wrote for *Lippincott's, Cosmopolitan*, and *Collier's*—he was John M. Ward. Only rarely did he allow his full name to fly boldly: most dramatically, on the title page of *Base-Ball: How to Become a Player,* published in 1888. At that time Ward was an established, worshipped, blazing star of America's favorite sport, playing in America's largest city. He was confident, mature, a celebrity; the husband of a popular actress; a feisty, hard-running, hard-sliding veteran; the captain of his team, a leader of manly men! Only then would he allow himself to be identified trinominally in public.

Family lore has it that he hated his middle name even as a child—especially as a child; he thought it effeminate. Adding to his self-consciousness was the fact that besides being a small, slight lad, he was a coddled one—the light of his protective, strong mother's eye. This was common knowledge in tiny Bellefonte, whose schoolyards and sandlots were as rawly intolerant as they were, and are, everywhere else. It is difficult not to feel sympathy for a red-blooded lad burdened with such a tinkly, fragile handle as Ward's.

He kept the name under wraps after he had left the schoolyard, and even the college diamond. He kept it as much of a secret as he could during his three-year *battue* of tank-town ball teams, and later, as a young adult, albeit a professional athlete of the highest caliber. He had every reason to do so. Post–Civil War America was a rowdy, chest-thumping place and John Ward's was an especially rowdy, chest-thumping profession, one with little truck for a Boy Named Sue.

From the 1870s through the early 1900s, professional base-ballists had a generally rotten reputation—though one that became, slowly, less so as the old century became the new. They were, these ballplayers, according to conventional wisdom, little more than simian rakehells: drunken, boisterous, whoring louts—ones that *played* for their living. (The general disdain may be attributed in part to America's anti-Irish sentiment during the Gilded Age. Irish surnames accounted for about 36 percent of big league rosters in 1885.)

This odor was exaggerated, certainly, but strong enough that baseball magnates felt they had a problem on their hands. Consequently, much of nineteenth-century baseball's corporate energy was expended in public relations: sanitizing baseball's reputation on the field (where fights, arguments, dramatic tantrums, and cheating were common), in the stands (where gamblers and rowdies sat), and off the field (where players' idle hands found the devil's work). Magnates and league officials essentially devoted themselves to wooing the middle and upper classes.

Ballplayer deportment was a topic of endless debate during the last century. In 1896, a *Buffalo Times* survey (whose comprehensiveness and accuracy is unknown) countered traditional views by finding that former big league players were nothing if not solid citizens, working as firemen, policemen, contractors, restaurateurs, cigar dealers, evangelists, hotelkeepers, delivery men, farmers, politicians, bookmakers (not bookies), sportswriters, merchants, brick masons, engravers, boilermakers, artists, glassblowers, orange growers, theatrical agents, motormen, and lawyers.

As long as a decade earlier, in 1886, John Ward took it on himself to refute his fellow ballists' poor reputation. In "Notes of a Base-Ballist," published in *Lippincott's* magazine, he anticipates the *Times* poll's findings.

It is still a more or less popular belief that ball-players are an improvident and even dissipated set. This is not true. . . . It has

been my fortune to meet all kinds of people, and I say unhesitat-
ingly that I believe ball-players *as a class* to be as well behaved as
any other in the community. Furthermore, if honesty, generosity,
courage, integrity, and true politeness, which is a kindly regard
for the feelings of others—if these, coupled with a full physical
development, are manly attributes, then do I know some ballplayers who may rank as representative men.

Ward goes on to strike preemptively at those who would find his
claims remarkable:

I make these statements boldly, in full appreciation of the fact
that they will convey a shock to the credulity of many. The reason for this misconception is not difficult. A private individual
may indulge in a lark, and it will pass unnoticed. But let a ballplayer be guilty of the same, and it is at once seized upon as a
subject for gossip. It is exaggerated and distorted, until finally it
bears little resemblance to the original offence. Then, again, an
entire nine is usually charged with the indiscretions of one. The
public reasons from the individual to the class.

All this ardor is well and good, but both the *Times*'s and Ward's
accounts must be recognized as ploys. Buffalo town, then, as now, was
never quite able to secure big league status. The poll can be seen as propa-
ganda—an attempt to persuade local residents of the advantages of supporting major league baseball. Ward's agenda was more personal. If
baseball faltered through a tainted reputation, his livelihood would falter
as well. Further, Ward was already seeking public support for players' labor
concerns—something made easier if the players' behavior was not suspect.

Finally, we must remember that these spirited documents were reac-
tive. If something does not need refuting, there is no need for refuters.

Ballplayers did have an unsavory and not entirely undeserved reputation, even if, "as a class," as Ward so adroitly put it, they were solid,
well-behaved young men. (Robert Todd Lincoln, for example, after his
daughter married a ballplayer, was so appalled that he vowed not to rest
until he had "destroyed their marriage.")

Now, put yourself in young John Ward's place on the eve of his professional career. It's summer 1877, and you've ridden all night in the smoking car (known as the Sullivan Sleeper) from central Pennsylvania to try out with a couple of Philadelphia teams. You've played a little semipro ball; you know you're good, but you may be just a big fish in a small pond. If you can hang on in Philly, your future is bright; fail and you're another grandstanding yokel who trips on the county line.

What happened next was so fraught with anxiety for Ward that, as part of his *Lippincott's* article, it became one of the few autobiographical anecdotes he ever penned. Unfortunately, he did so in a maddeningly bland way:

> On my arrival [in Philadelphia I] learned that the Athletics were
> to play that afternoon. . . . I was put in to pitch. . . . If some one
> of the Athletic players had spoken a word of encouragement, I
> am sure I would have felt more at ease. But even they looked me
> over in a half-critical, half-indifferent way that made me wish I
> was home. . . . I thought my appearance had made an unfavor-
> able impression.

Let's recast that hot afternoon. You are seventeen, a nervous country mouse and a bit of a swellhead. You step on the field, ball in hand, for warm-ups. If you make the team, someone else will be given a ticket home. You know this. The others know this. Forget all the myths you've heard about baseball's agrarian roots, for myths they mostly are. The team you are trying out for is made up mostly of tough city kids who have grown into tough adults: the kind who would nickname nonsmoking, nondrinking, nonswearing Charles Baldwin "Lady," or the deaf-mute William Ellsworth Hoy "Dummy," or dark-complexioned George Cuppy "Nig," or reedy James Holliday "Bug."

You're not a Nig or a Dummy or a Bug or a Lady. But you are a whelp. A jug-eared, willowy, peach-fuzzed, overreaching punk. A college boy to boot! With a middle name that . . . Comin' at you, Percy. Watch your back, darling. Let's play a little chin music for our sweet fancy boy. Here Lily! Give us a kiss, sister! Don't muss your skirt M O N T G O M E R Y!

So. John M. Ward it was.

Two other John Wards played major league baseball during Ward's career: one, who had no recorded middle name, was born in East St. Louis and pitched eight innings for Providence in 1885; John E. Ward, born in Washington, D.C., got one single in four at-bats for Washington in 1884. There have also been an Aaron Lee Ward, a Chuck, a Piggy, a Gary, a Jim, a Rube, a Jay, a Joe, a Hap, a Kevin, a Pete, a Preston, a Turner, a Chris, a Duane, a Colby, a Dick, and a Colin Ward. None were kin to John Montgomery.

What, however, about Aaron Montgomery Ward—founder of the famous retail empire? Was he kin? Yes, but not so you'd notice, and not so John Ward noticed, for he never mentioned the connection in his lifetime—at least in print. John Montgomery and Aaron Montgomery were distant cousins. Their great-grandfathers—Aaron's was Captain Israel Ward and John's was Josiah Ward—were brothers. Aaron, named for his grandfather, was an obscure teenager whose family had settled in Niles, Michigan, when John Montgomery was born. John was named, according to family lore, for some Bellefonte-area friends of his parents.

John Ward's full name, as singular as it is, has caused no end of confusion down through the years in baseball circles. As recently as 1963, the year before Ward was inducted at Cooperstown, Lee Allen, then historian of the Baseball Hall of Fame, was convinced that "John" was a nickname given Ward by James Mutrie, the manager of the National League New Yorks. Allen, citing an 1880s newspaper account, said that Mutrie, a rookie manager in 1883, did not recognize Ward—who had himself just arrived from Providence—and called out during a pre-season practice, "Hey, you, John." The story melts in early sunlight, however, as Ward, by then, was already one of baseball's best-known players.

Allen, who in 1963 was busy tracking down biographical information on nineteenth-century ballplayers, was not alone in his confusion. In the course of his research, Allen corresponded with John Fleming, the grandson of one of Ward's cousins. Fleming, an itinerant sportswriter, was a great admirer of his talented kinsman, and had, as a young boy, even met him on a few occasions. Fleming, after gently correcting Allen's misinformation about Ward's name, quickly offered a conflicting, equally spurious theory: Ward, Fleming wrote, had been christened simply John and had later for some reason given himself the nickname Montgomery. Fleming soon realized his mistake.

(The greater Fleming-Ward clan has always had a penchant for confusing nomenclature. One of John Ward's cousin's sons was named Montgomery Ward Fleming. The full name of one of Montgomery Ward Fleming's sons—John Fleming, the sportswriter—was John Montgomery Fleming. He, in turn, named one of his sons Montgomery Ward. On a more creative note, John Montgomery Ward had an uncle named Philo and a nephew named Algernon.)

Perhaps the most persistent misconception about Ward is that he was known as Monte during his playing days. Monte, in fact, was a childhood nickname only. He was Monte to his Bellefonte friends and to his family. He was John or Johnny or Johnnie to his teammates. He was John or Johnny or Johnnie and John M. to sportswriters. He was Mr. Ward, publicly, to his second wife. We don't know what he was to his first wife, the actress Helen Dauvray—probably Johnny. He was shortstop Ward. He was captain Ward. Briefly, in 1890, he was referred to in the sporting press as "John Montgum."

On two momentous occasions he was none of the above. When the sports and drama weekly, the *New York Clipper*, printed, along with the week's other games, the box score of Ward's first major league game, in 1878, his name appeared as "Wood." Just shy of forty-seven years later, on a one-page public document, he was listed as Mr. James Montgomery Ward. The document was the Georgia Board of Embalming Transportation of Corpse Permit, required to send Ward's body from Augusta to Long Island for burial.

Four

Every Window-Pane Blazed with Golden Light

ONE DAY EARLY in the nineteenth century, a man named Stephen Ward left Morris County, New Jersey, and struck west. He was a great-great-grandson of Lieutenant John Ward, who had migrated from England to Branford, Connecticut, in 1648. Around 1816, the thirty-six-year-old Stephen fetched up in south central New York—about ten miles south of Owego, near Binghamton, and a mile or so north of the Pennsylvania state line—in an area that became known as Wait's Settlement. Stephen's wife was Lydia Anable, whose family had come from England to America in 1623.

Ward, a farmer, was known as "Captain," for reasons unknown. Captain Ward's offspring who survived childhood were called Abram, Charles, Lewis, Henry, James, Philo, Matilda, and Elizabeth. Only two of these—James and Philo—are essential to our story, but Abram had a way with names, and those of his sons and daughters—read in a row—sound like poetry: Elizabeth, Rhoda, Matilda, Philetta, Selim, Sabrina, Lydia, Ezra, Abby, and Ursula.

In the late 1830s, Stephen's sons James and Philo left the farm. James was about thirty. We don't know his age exactly—the census of 1850 has him born in 1810; his Bellefonte gravestone has him born in 1806. Philo was in his late teens.

Nor do we know why they left. Perhaps the family farm was failing. Perhaps the boys hated farming. Or perhaps James and Philo struck out for

25

the same reasons young men through the ages have left home: because they were curious and full of beans, and because to them the world was a large and exciting place, deserving of a look-see.

There were no railroads in the region at the time and the only roads were little more than tracks that followed river courses. As the boys traveled, they probably hooked up with some tree fellers, of whom there were many in the area. Tree fellers worked through the winter, in bands. Then, come spring and high water, they would lash their timber into large rafts to float down the Susquehanna River and its feeders toward the large markets on the way to the Chesapeake Bay.

Many young men found the arduous tree-cutting business—or at least the go-to-market part of the tree-cutting business—grand work. Think of it: drifting down the curving, swollen river, drinking whiskey, alternately sheltering in a crude canvas deck lean-to and pole-steering the clumsy raft. At night, the rafts—there was heavy traffic on the river—would tie up together and the raftsmen, glad to have survived another day, made party.

In 1839, the Ward brothers found themselves sixty miles south and ninety or so miles west of Owego, in the muscle-flexing town of Bellefonte, Pennsylvania, on the foreshore of the Allegheny Front, between the heaving Alleghenies themselves and the wide-sighing, eyebrow curves of the Big and Penn and Brush Valleys.

Bellefonte today (population 6,500) is an isolated and softly splendid place, and it must have been so in the 1830s: leafy and laced with clear flowing waters. It is also the sort of place that requires good brakes and strong legs: the terrain is as steeply and randomly irregular as an unmade bed. To get to the center of town, for example—where High Street meets Allegheny and divides, neat as a tuning fork, to run steep and narrow up past the War Memorial, the wide steps of the imposing courthouse, the old opera house, and the jail—you must descend and ascend at least twice, no matter the direction you've come.

Most of the town's knolls are anonymous, but some are not: Half Moon, Academy, Reservoir, Quaker, Jail, Molasses, Valentine, Bluestocking. Bluestocking Hill is where, during John Ward's time, the rich people lived, the merchants and lawyers and ironmasters—especially ironmasters, for Bellefonte was a town built around iron. On Bluestocking Hill, the air was fresher, the summer breezes brisker. This was very important in the early and mid-nineteenth century because Bellefonte then was a smoky place. Many of the town's businesses, big and small, required some sort of foundry. Today, the air is generally clean, but Bluestocking Hill, northwest of the town square, is still where the breezes are freshest, the porches are widest, and the richest—or at least best-landed—folks live. Below Bluestocking Hill, toward town, are more modest homes: narrow-porched, wood-framed, tight-clustered or stacked one above the other and clinging to their lots on the vertiginous streets like hardy plants. That's where John Ward spent much of his youth, in the shadow of Bluestocking Hill, in a modest frame house.

Downtown Bellefonte today is a settlement of robust, handsome buildings. Except when Penn State University plays football at home, a dozen miles to the west, Bellefonte is peaceful as a napping dog. It also has a high opinion of itself.

In 1799, the story goes, the town fathers pulled a fast one on the world. Centre County was about to be formed, and Milesburg, just to the north, was the logical choice as county seat because, among other things, it abutted on navigable water, Bald Eagle Creek. Bellefonte, on the other hand, could only claim Spring Creek, not navigable by anything much larger than a canoe. But before Milesburg knew what hit it, some Bellefontians loaded a small flatboat with furniture and other goods and dragged it by mule up Spring Creek. Then they dispatched a messenger to the state legislature, proclaiming that the freight season had begun—in Bellefonte. Bellefonte became the county seat and its histories generally treat the flatboat incident as one not of treachery, but of ingenuity.

Bellefonte residents, rich and poor, important and obscure, knowledgeable or merely talkative, are always claiming things about their town. The bow hunting is the best in the state; the trout fishing is the best in the state; the Italian food is the best in the state; the streets are the cleanest in the state and the fire department is the best in the state.

Bellefonte calls itself the "home" of seven governors, and has erected handsome historical markers to prove it—never mind that six of the seven governors are terminally obscure. It calls itself the home of the Mills Brothers singing group, though it was really only the home of the singers' father and grandfather. Bellefonte evidently supplied some of the cannonballs Commodore Perry used against the British in 1813, so it takes full credit for winning the battle of Lake Erie and, by implication, changing the course of American history. The song "After the Ball Is Over" was first sung publicly in Bellefonte. The Bellefonte Academy football team outscored its opponents by a score of 1362–56 over a three-year period. Those three years were 1924–1926—but to many Bellefontians it seems like yesterday.

The chorus goes on and on. A Bellefonte man commanded the guard at the execution of Lincoln's assassins. Parisian bookseller-publisher Sylvia Beach's father, Robert Sylvester Beach, taught Latin at the Academy. Madison, Kentucky, the fictional setting for David Morrell's Rambo books, is based on Bellefonte. Bellefonte had the state's largest swimming pool—an astonishing natatorium indeed, 322 feet by 80 feet. The model for Lady Liberty on the Morgan silver dollar was the second wife of Bellefontian Charles McCafferty. A synthetic lubricant invented by a Dr. Edwin Acheson, who attended Bellefonte Academy, inadvertently helped the Germans prolong World War I, when his factory in Belgium was captured.

The *belle fonte* of much of this lore is the town's resident historian, a kind and generous man named Hugh Manchester. Manchester holds, along with three thousand other six-degrees-of-separation tales about Bellefonte and the larger world, that Bellefontians, in one way or the other, were responsible for the Cracker Jack box, the electric light switch, the automatic voting machine, the Tom Collins, the naming of Miles City, Montana, and the success of the Wright brothers' first flight—this last had something to do with stolen copper wire.

"I'm convinced," Manchester maintains, "that if Jesus Christ came back to earth, he'd land in Bellefonte."

Back in the days of the Ward brothers, however, Bellefonte, like most of the United States, was scurrying around, too busy building for its future to trumpet its past. The town—its population was about one thousand in the mid-1830s—was an early player in Pennsylvania's mineral and metal industries: it had an abundance of timber, coal, limestone, and iron ore as well as an excellent water supply. By 1802 it had a jail; by December that year it had hanged its first murderer. By 1810 it had five pig-iron furnaces, four forges, and at least one iron mill. It acquired critical mass: iron begat wealth; wealth begat more wealth; more wealth begat influence and power. In 1853 the town fathers successfully petitioned the state legislature, beating out stiff competition from Pittsburgh and Philadelphia and several other counties, to build the Farmer's High School—precursor to Penn State University—in Centre County. But they didn't want it built in Bellefonte proper. The Presbyterians, who more or less ran things back then, thought that while higher education might well be a fine thing, at least a fine financial thing for the area, it was even more so as long as the town—Bellefonte was a place that forbade train whistles to be blown on Sundays—would not have to mingle with actual students.

James and Philo came to town, saw opportunity staring in their faces, opened a small machine shop where they made threshing machines, and began courting local girls.

Of Philo, there is not much to say. He married Hannah Hall and the couple had four children: Elizabeth, Augusta, George, and Isabella. Philo died of old age in 1904, when he was eighty-five, three years after Hannah. He had been an invalid for several years, and the Bellefonte paper, the *Democratic-Watchman*, called his death a "blessing, inasmuch as he was ready and waiting for the summons." Philo, the paper added—politely, vaguely—was a "very useful, progressive citizen" and a "conscientious Christian gentleman."

James's life was edgier and far more eventful and erratic than his younger brother's. By the time he died, in 1871, James had, for whatever his faults, suffered more than his share of the sort of heartbreak common to Americans during the middle years of the nineteenth century.

James's first wife, whom he married soon after his arrival in Bellefonte, was a young woman, Caroline ————. She died two years later at twenty-four after bearing James two children: William, who died when he was four, and Mary Caroline.

Mary Caroline—John Ward's half-sister—went to live with her grandfather, Stephen, in 1850, when she was about ten years old. Eventually she began working at a spa near Binghamton, New York, not all that far from Stephen's land. America, at the time, was obsessed with water cures. Between the 1840s and the 1880s, more than two hundred bathing spas were in operation. Spas were so popular they had their own magazine, *Water Cure Journal*, whose motto was "Wash and Be Healed."

The Binghamton spa—a very successful enterprise founded by a homeopath, O. V. Thayer, and his wife—featured "soft . . . saline-chalybeate" waters that were thick with the "great essentials for hydropathic purposes." Patients could choose from a variety of baths, including "Full, Half, Shallow, Douche, Eye, Ear, Nasal, Spray, Steam, Medicated, etc." There was little, it seemed, that could not be cured at the spa, which catered to invalids, convalescents, and those needing traditional or solar ray surgery—a process that removed all

> surface Affections, such as Moles, Mothers' Marks, Discolorations, Knobs, Fungoid Growths, India Ink Marks, Powder Marks, Cancer Warts, Congenital Naevi, Common Warts, etc., etc., only by the concentrated rays of the Sun, producing not a drop of blood, and leaving no permanent Scar.

The spa's specialty, however, was "diseases of women"—a category it did not elaborate on in its broadsheets.

While at the spa, Mary Caroline fell in love with Erastus "Rat" Goodrich, the blind son of Cyrus Goodrich, a neighbor of her uncle Henry. The couple migrated to Kansas in the 1880s and had two children. Mary Caroline died in 1907, in Topeka. Rat died in 1925, by then deaf as well as blind.

James married a second time. Ellen Moore was twenty-seven years old when she died, two years after the birth of her only son, James Moore, who himself would die at age twenty-five.

In 1849, the year following Ellen's death, James married for a third and final time. His bride, Ruth Hall, was twenty-three years old. She was the sister of Hannah Hall, Philo's wife. The Hall girls were the daughters of Jesse Hall and Mary Fury. Jesse Hall counted among his ancestors Lyman Hall, of Fairfield, Connecticut, a signer of the Declaration of Independence and later governor of Georgia. The Halls were an established and prominent Bellefonte family.

Of Ruth Hall's life before she married James Ward, we know little: Jesse Hall took his family somewhere in Ohio for several years, returning in 1838, the year Ruth turned twelve. Upon the family's return, Ruth, "being of a delicate constitution," began school "with a view to educating her for a teacher's life."

James and Ruth had three children: Ida, who died when she was one week old; Charles Lewis, born in 1855; and John Montgomery, born on

March 3, 1860, in a frame house on two acres of land along the Lewistown Pike—known today as Blanchard Street—a short mile southeast of downtown Bellefonte.

The week preceding John Ward's birth was one of rain and mild temperatures in the eastern quarter of America. The big rivers, including the Hudson and the upper Susquehanna, had yielded their ice covers, and river traffic had resumed, much to the relief of merchants and factors. The spring was not just early, it was also, by some accounts, brilliant. Even in sooty, far-off New York City, the new season produced at least one literary effusion: "Every window-pane blazed with golden light," a *New York Times* reporter observed,

> and glittering roofs and shiny domes and vanes proclaimed the vernal advent. Grate fires were permitted to smolder away in ashes. . . . Window-sashes were thrown up, and canary birds sung merrily in the sunshine. Men threw off their overcoats, and grass plots donned "Nature's green livery." . . . [L]ike butterflies, radiant in rich and varied raiment . . . ladies kept the retailers busy all day long, and nimble counter-jumpers arise this morning feeling much the worse for wear.

It was also the week an outbreak of typhoid fever raced through a school near Bellefonte; the year the *Democratic-Watchman* endorsed Stephen A. Douglas for president and warned its readers that there was "no greater curse to a community than a large, idle, vicious population of Negroes," a curse with which Bellefonte, the paper said, was "deeply afflicted."

Eighteen sixty was a leap year, and the *Democratic-Watchman* urged women to "commence making love to any gentlemen they may deem worthy of their hands, heart and fortunes," but only if they take on the obligations of earning a living and paying the bills. ("Why was Adam's wife called Eve?" the *Watchman* asked. "Because when she appeared, man's day of happiness was drawing to a close," it answered.)

The paper berated Bellefonte parents for not taking enough interest in their children's education.

It reminded "Profane Swearers" that taking the Lord's name in vain made them liable for an indictment of blasphemy and a fine not exceeding $100.

Thomas Fategan was sent to jail for twenty days for selling liquor without a license, and on Sunday, and to minors. Soloman Kauterman, Lot Struble, and Hunter Neil were all indicted for Fornication and bastardy.

Druggist P. P. Green advertised his "pleasant, safe and certain" worm expeller for twenty-five cents a bottle.

The stray red and gray heifer that appeared on the land of Abraham Woodring on February 2 had still not been claimed.

Elsewhere in the country, as in Bellefonte, the weather was unsettled, a mixture of dark clouds, silver linings, silver clouds, and dark linings. The Civil War would begin in a year.

People died by the hundreds every week in the cities—including "colored persons," who were listed separately. Nearly half of America's deaths were of children. Most deaths—of all ages—were from scarlet fever and lung diseases such as congestion and "inflammation of the lungs." People died of "softening of the brain," scrofula, "dropsy of the head," "inflammation of the liver," "inflammation of the brain," and childbirth. Children died of "teething."

Mail from Salt Lake took twenty-three days to get to Leavenworth, Kansas. New Orleans newspapers took four days to get to Washington, D.C. News and mail from the Sandwich Islands took at least six weeks to get to New York.

Billy the Kid was two months old.

American Indians, like Negroes, were considered taxonomically separate from white Americans, as this dispatch to the *New York Times* suggests: "Indians on the upper . . . frontier of Texas have commenced an open war upon the people."

The common American spelling of Haiti was "Hayti," of Puerto Rico "Porto Rico," and of Chile "Chili."

Newspapers carried ads by doctors who invited "especial attention to [a] means and method . . . for the safe, speedy, and permanent cure of stammering, by electricity."

Lucina Cordial, the Elixir of Love, was ever so popular. Its "action on the nervous system and reproductive organs, is most extraordinary, allaying all over excitement, and infusing into the nervous organization that degree of tension which is requisite to give the human system the enjoyment of its full powers, both mentally and physically."

If a dog bit someone, one method to determine if the dog was rabid was to take a deposit of calcium, called a madstone, from a deer's stomach and place it next to the bite. If the madstone stuck, the dog was rabid.

There was no such thing as Labor Day or the Dewey Decimal System or Yellowstone National Park or salmon canneries or the motto "In God We Trust" or popcorn or catchers' masks or fielders' gloves or pitchers' mounds.

The first base ever stolen during a baseball game—by Eddie Cuthbert of the Philadelphia Keystones, legend has it—was an event still three years away.

The first deliberate bunt—by Dicky Pierce of the Brooklyn Atlantics, legend has it—wouldn't be laid down for six years.

Williams defeated Amherst, 66–32, in the country's first intercollegiate baseball game eight months before Ward was born.

There were no Dodgers or Giants or Yankees or Cleveland Indians or Boston Red Sox or St. Louis Cardinals or Cincinnati Reds. There was no National League. There was no American League.

When John Montgomery was born, James and Ruth Ward had been living on the two-acre Blanchard Street property for a little over six years. They had bought the land in January 1854 and, in short order, built their home and two small outlying tenant houses.

The house—remodeled and added to—still stands today. It is an unremarkable, white, nicely shaded, deep-porched, two-story-plus-attic affair set well back from the road. The lawn is healthy and wide, the paved driveway bordered by a manicured hedge. Behind the house stand a basketball hoop, a white outbuilding, and a weathered barn.

Though the land across Blanchard has been subdivided and is lined with modest ranch-style homes, the old Ward place—where John spent his first few years—is surrounded on its side of the street by open fields. It remains, one hundred and forty-odd years since the Wards built it, comfortably removed from anyone's definition of "town." What a grand place it is—and what a grand place it must always have been—to sit on a long summer evening and watch the sun set over the rolling, sloping land to the west.

On the surface, all seemed well in 1860 on Blanchard: the healthy family of four in a prosperous Pennsylvania town; a Negro manservant named Samuel Ellis; good land for cultivation; the father engaged in honest trade, an entrepreneur; the sternly handsome and educated mother, daughter of an established local family.

But a cloud hung over the household of James and Ruth Ward. Between 1853, the year before the Wards moved to Blanchard Street, and 1871, the year of his death, James Ward was involved in no less than seven local court actions. They were civil suits, involving money that James had borrowed and not paid back. The Blanchard Street property was legally owned by Ruth (on the deed James is merely listed as her husband), which suggests that the couple was seeking protection from creditors as early as 1854. In the normal course of things, women at mid-century were, in a legal sense, nonentities.

What sort of man was he? Was he a drunk? Was he a petty criminal? Merely financially incompetent? Profligate and impetuous? We cannot know for sure—the trail we are forced to follow, though tantalizingly suggestive, is dim and cold, its few markers blurred into unreadable code.

James Ward first appears in local court dockets in 1853. He had borrowed $125 from one Benjamin Shrock (the last name is an approximation—the document is badly smudged). The note became due and Schrock, or his agent, sued Ward. Ward stipulated to judgment—that is, he didn't dispute the facts—and was ordered to pay. Evidently he did—no further record of the issue exists.

Four years later, in August of 1857, Ward was sued by A. S. Rine for repayment of $416.

A month later, on September 7, 1857, John W. Bapler sued Ward for the repayment of a $106 loan. Ward was unable to pay, so Bapler got the judge to issue a writ allowing him to go after Ward's assets. In addition to the $106 original sum, Ward had to pay an attorney's fee of $4.12½, a sheriff's fee of $1.80, and $1.18¾ to the prothonotary—a chief clerk of court.

Two more similar incidents are recorded—one in August 1865, in which Ward was sued for $70, and another in June 1866, for $55.01, a sum that was soon paid.

However, between the time of the Bapler affair and these last two minor judgments, there occurred a major episode, the most shameful of James Ward's less-than-illustrious business career. On the last day of January and on May 23, 1862, when John was two years old, James borrowed two sums—$1,112.15 and $87.50, respectively. The total sum is large, but the source of the loan is the troubling part. Ward, evidently unable to find anyone in town who would give him credit, was forced to borrow the $1,200 from his own wife. (Her family had evidently set up a small trust for her. We have no idea how willing or reluctant Ruth was to sign over the money.)

So, by 1862, James Ward was living in a house that was in his wife's name, had run afoul of angry creditors on several occasions—creditors who had been forced to take legal action to regain their money—and had finally dipped into his wife's trust fund. Further, sometime before, even Philo had decided to distance himself from his brother. Their partnership had ended. Philo evidently continued making threshing machines without James.

James seems to have borrowed the $1,200 for a partnership with one George Bayard, who owned a small foundry in town. The agreement between the two men called for James's staying on the homefront and managing the business while Bayard went to war as a member of the 148th Pennsylvania Volunteer Infantry. (He would eventually become a brevet lieutenant colonel.)

James ran the new business no better than he had any of his earlier ones. In 1865, when John was five years old, James declared bankruptcy. In August that year the Blanchard Street property was sold at a sheriff's sale. The buyer, John Hoffer, who owned a general store and was Bellefonte's prothonotary, paid only $25 for the property and buildings (and assumed Ward's debts).

As shameful as the public spectacle of a sheriff's sale must have been, we must put out of our mind any vision of a destitute Ward family left homeless and possessionless on the side of the road. The sale was, in fact, a prearranged affair—the best evidence being the very low price paid for the Ward holdings. As well, Hoffer, a prominent member of the German Reform Church who was described in his obituary as being "as free from guile as Nathaniel," was close to both the Wards and the Halls. Hoffer let James and his family continue to live on the Blanchard property for two years—and no doubt would have let them stay longer had not Ruth's family come to her rescue. (Hoffer, in fact, would become the legal guardian of John and his brother Charles upon Ruth's death in 1874.)

In 1867, the Wards moved to Bellefonte proper, into a modest home on the corner of Lamb and Ridge Streets, not far from Philo and his family, on a slope of Bluestocking Hill. The house was owned at the time by one of Ruth's sisters, Priscilla. (In 1870, in an act of family charity, Priscilla transferred ownership to Ruth—not, significantly, to James.)

In May 1871, when John was eleven, his father died of tuberculosis. James's obituary in the *Democratic-Watchman* was polite but brief. "Mr. Ward," the paper reported, "was highly esteemed by this community and was one of the kindest-hearted and most generous of men." Tellingly, there is no mention of James's profession or church affiliation—both all but obligatory elements of the paper's death notices.

By contrast, three and one-half years later, Ruth Ward's fade into death would be news for almost three weeks.

Five

God Knows She Was a Good Woman

N THE FALL of 1873, two and one-half years after his father's death, John Ward traveled a dozen miles southwest from Bellefonte to attend Pennsylvania State College—the recently renamed Farmer's High School. He was thirteen years old.

On the one hand, Ward's matriculation made him a rarity—at the time, fewer than 2 percent of American adolescents attended college. On the other, Ward's tender age was only slightly remarkable—fourteen- and fifteen-year-old college freshmen were commonplace at the time.

To understand how American colleges worked during the 1870s and 1880s, we must discard our present-day notions of ferocious placement competition, and rigid entrance requirements. Entering college—certainly one of the newfangled land grant colleges—was a perfunctory affair. Faculty might interview a prospective student personally, perhaps asking him to submit a short essay (in Latin or English), or merely act on the recommendation of the student's "sponsors"—his teacher, minister, or other prominent friend or neighbor. In some cases, the acceptance process was only a formality. In short, the era in which John Ward entered college was a buyer's—a student's—market. Institutions of higher learning were blooming like dandelions, a development that had begun in 1862 with the passage of the Morrill Act—better known as the Land Grant College Act.

The act was simplicity itself. Each state was given public lands (or land scrip) equal to 30,000 acres for each senator and congressman. The

37

states, in turn, could sell those lands as they saw fit, as long as they allotted 10 percent of the proceeds to buy land for colleges (or retain the original land) and invested the remainder in a perpetual endowment.

Congressman Justin Smith Morrill of Vermont, the bill's namesake, had been offering versions of the bill since 1848. His intentions were partially nationalistic—he wanted to

> lop off a portion of the studies established centuries ago as the mark of European scholarship and replace the vacancy—if it is a vacancy—by those of a less antique and more practical nature.

(All this was well and good, but what, legislators and citizens wanted to know, was to be the mission of these strange new schools? Were they to be citadels of abstraction or practicality? In Missouri, a trustee of the University of Missouri warned of the dangers of too much practicality, as the main purpose of a university was "to develop the social and mental nature of the students." To which lofty abstraction a member of the state board of agriculture replied, "That is good, but what are they going to do about hog cholera?"

The debaters—at least those advocating practicality—rose to hilarious rhetorical heights. One Ohio newspaper suggested the state college change its motto from "Learning and Labor" to "Lavender and Lily White." In South Carolina, one legislator noted that he had never seen a man able to "write a nice essay or make a good agricultural speech who could make corn enough to feed himself and a bob-tailed mule until the first day of March.")

Further complicating things were a distinct dearth of college-trained faculty in the country and a generally widespread skepticism about the value of mass "higher" education of any kind, let alone education for something as absurdly commensensical as teaching farmers how to farm (actually, the colleges were more interested in training agricultural scientists, whose research might aid farmers). In addition, in the minds of many young men, the idea of becoming a noble yeoman was hardly attractive. They, as often as not, yearned for the dash of the city rather than the mud- and shit-stained yokel's life. (As early as 1860, Horace Greeley addressed this issue, advising a young man who wondered whether a professional life was preferable to that of "tilling the soil" that "there are three times as many lawyers and doctors in the country as are needed, and, judging from the price of flour and beef, not half enough farmers.")

In many cases—certainly in the case of Pennsylvania State College—the new institutions were anything but instant successes. To attract students, they felt they had to open their doors ever wider, in part by easing what minimal entrance requirements were in place, offering students a "choice" of classes (what we know now as electives), and opening on-campus preparatory schools. As one scholar notes, the colleges, in effect, were saying, "Come, and we will do what we can."

John Ward's era, as far as institutions of higher learning were concerned, was a time of matriculatory fire sales, and the fledgling Pennsylvania State College was offering some of the deepest discounts in the land.

Enrollment at Penn State, never healthy, was down. The school was drifting, many thought, under the administration of President James Calder—generally considered neither dynamic nor inspirational—from its original land grant mission toward the shores of "classical" education. The faculty was undistinguished, and so were the students. Many had matriculated by default after previous expulsions, resignations, or rejections by private colleges such as Villanova, Lafayette, Penn, or Gettysburg. One historian of the college describes Penn State's Calder/Ward era as one during which the college "bottomed out and became an academic dumping ground."

Despite all this, John Ward, because of his age, probably had to be approved for acceptance. He was either briefly interviewed by President Calder or granted admission by recommendation. The Hall family might have recommended him, or John Hoffer or John Ellis—Orvis Ellis's father—or another Bellefonte citizen, several of whom were Penn State trustees.

The oldest joke about present-day Penn State University is that, by virtue of its location—far from any large city and essentially in the geographic center of the state—it is equally inaccessible from all points. Indeed, after the furious bidding war among several Pennsylvania counties during the 1850s, the legislature decided that Centre County's distance from such population centers as Philadelphia and Pittsburgh was an advantage rather than a detriment, not only because of the plentitude of farming land for the students, but because, out there at the corner of 40th and Plum, students would face a minimum of distractions.

The campus, in Ward's day, was effectively some land and one building: a limestone atrocity known as Old Main. (The current building, many times remodeled, is known, with an apparent lack of irony, as New Old Main.) It was five stories high, 240 feet long, 90 feet wide, and divided into lodging rooms, study halls, a library, classrooms, a chapel, laboratories, a kitchen, and a dining hall.

In photos, the building—looming, huge, rough, and isolated on virtually treeless land—looks like a mad scientist's private asylum. Even today, its presence overwhelmed by dozens of other buildings and its lines softened by exuberant foliage, New Old Main has about it the thick, angry, disproportionate look of a former inside lineman gone to drink.

During the nineteenth century, however, the building looked, additionally, tumorous. Attached to the back of Old Main was something known as the Shot Tower—a wooden, five-story series of walled platforms, connected to each floor of Old Main by short passageways, that served as privies. The addition's nickname referred to the then-current method of molding lead for gunshot by pouring molten metal through a sieve from a great height.

Freshmen enrolled in one of three "emphases": agricultural, scientific, or classical. The former two, certainly initially, were virtually identical, and included courses in general agriculture, algebra, geometry, bookkeeping, physics, geography, chemistry, botany, and (optionally) beginning Latin and Greek. Ward, however, registered for the classical emphasis, with its courses in Latin and Greek composition, the *Aeneid*, Xenophon's *Anabasis*, Cicero's orations, and Herodotus.

Beginning their sophomore year, male students took mandatory courses in military training—infantry, artillery, and cavalry tactics, and sabre exercise. These courses required uniforms consisting of "coat and pantaloons of cadet gray, and a black hat," which were available for about thirty dollars—a laborer's monthly wage—from M. C. Thackray of Philadelphia.

While there was no tuition—except for special fees for music courses—the cost of a year's schooling was hardly insubstantial, especially in an era of dollar-a-day wages:

$ 40 Fuel, lights, and general maintenance of public rooms.

$ 12 Room rent.

$ 24 Coal for rooms.

$ 5 Furniture—stove, bed, mattress, table, washstand, chairs. Students provided their own "amenities," such as carpets, mirrors, wash basins, pails, brooms, lamps, and bedding.

$160 Board, either on or off campus.

Ward, that fall of 1873, was one of twenty-five freshmen in an under-graduate population of fifty-eight (including a few women). There were, in addition, eighty-seven prep students. Of those 145 students, slightly more than one-third hailed from Centre County.

However precocious Ward was—and however tenacious he would prove in later life—he did not survive that first year at college. It was such a false start—one that even stern college officials realized was a mistake—that the year was effectively erased from his college records. The only extant notation of Ward's first year is telling. His name appears in the minutes of a faculty discussion, during the spring term of 1874, of "delinquent" students, including Mr. Thompson, who was reported behind with his compositions; Mr. J. J. Wallace, who was deficient in Latin; and Mr. Kaufman, behind in several studies. "Mr. Ward" was deficient in both Latin and composition. None of these underachievers, however, could match the record of George F. Jackman of nearby Lock Haven, deemed deficient "in everything."

Ward may have stayed on campus through that 1874 spring semester, or dropped down for some preparatory school remedial classes, or returned to Bellefonte to study on his own. Whatever he did, in the following term, the fall semester of 1874, Ward began his college career anew. Since the college's General Principle VI stated that "No Student is promoted to a higher class except on merit—the design being to make good scholars and not merely to grant degrees," Ward was once again a freshman, this time a member of the class of 1878. (This business of class affiliation was a very fluid one. In the Penn State team photo taken in 1875, Ward is listed as a member of the class of 1876. In the Alumni Record of 1906, Ward is listed as a member of the class of 1879. Since Ward never, in fact, graduated from Penn State, the matter is, finally, moot.)

Ward's second freshman year was to prove even less pleasant than his first. In December, four months after his reenrollment, his mother died. The public attention paid to Ruth Ward's last days was as ardent and impassioned as that paid to James Ward's passing had been perfunctory.

On November 27, 1874, the *Democratic-Watchman* announced, prematurely, that "Mrs. Ward is recovering." (Bellefonte's population was about 2,600 people, and there was no need, evidently, to identify "Mrs. Ward" further.)

A week later, however, the news had become dire.

We grieve to say that as we go to press it is thought that Mrs. Ward, assistant principal of the public schools, is about dying. She was taken very much worse on Wednesday night [the paper appeared on Fridays] and ere any of our readers see this item, she will probably be dead. She is . . . beyond the reach of human help.

The following week's paper confirmed the morbid prediction:

DEATH OF MRS. RUTH A. WARD
A Good Woman Gone

. . . We stated last week that Mrs. Ward was thought to be dying. . . . We are sorry to say that our fears were only too well founded, for ere the paper had reached its country subscribers on Friday morning, and in fact, before many of our town patrons had read it, she breathed her last. Death came to her relief a little after 10 o'clock on that morning, putting an end to a most painful and long-continued sickness. . . .

Mrs. Ward lay sick for almost five weeks. . . . Wednesday night of last week she lost consciousness and continued in that state until she died. It was the doctor's opinion that from that hour she became insensible to pain and passed into the dark valley relieved from the throes of mortal agony that must otherwise have possessed her. With her mental vision clouded, she entered the rolling flood of Jordon [sic], but with angel hands to bear her spirit up, what a glorious scene of rest and immortality must have burst upon her recovered and enraptured sense as she emerged on the other side!

But here let us stop. Our friend is dead. Her eyes are closed. Her lips are hushed. . . . Flowers, beautiful flowers are laid upon her breast, and the silver plate tells us when she was born and when she died. We look at the calm, still, pale, cold face—note the tasteful black dress and the white rusche about her neck—smooth the hair, kiss the forehead, and then we turn away. . . .

How vain and poor are words to express the feelings of the soul. But the raindrops that fell upon her coffin and into the open grave on that solemn Sunday afternoon were but typical of the flood of anguish that welled up from fountains of eternal sorrow in some few loving hearts. . . . The poor, whom she had so often succored, and the children with whom she so deeply sympathized were there to weep over her grave. . . . And so let her sleep.

There followed both a brief report of the cause of death—pyemia, described as a "sequel of Pleuro-peri-pneumonia," with a ghoulishly graphic description of the disease's symptoms—and an outraged editorial directed at Bellefonte's Presbyterian minister:

It is generally conceded that Rev. W. T. Wiley made a ninny of himself in his pulpit on Sunday last. He had been requested to give notice of the funeral of Mrs. Ward on that day at 2 o'clock, and took advantage of the opportunity to indulge in a tirade against Sunday funerals. He said he disapproved of them—that they were all wrong, and in effect advised the members of his congregation to abstain from showing their respect for an esteemed lady who had been a citizen of Bellefonte during the greater portion of her life.

We have just this to say: Whatever may be Mr. Wiley's views in regard to Sunday funerals, that was not the time to express them. The deceased could not have been buried on any other day. She died on Friday. It would have been hasty and indecent to bury her on Saturday, and it was not thought advisable to keep the corpse till Monday. . . . We are not surprised that many of his congregation retired from the church disgusted and angry, or that a distinguished citizen made a contemptuous remark, which the reverend gentleman would very much dislike to hear.

Whence comes this bitter opposition to Sunday funerals . . . ? Is his record so square and sinless in moral matters that he is shocked at the consignment of decaying mortality to the tomb on the Lord's Day? Let him be certain that his daily walk and conversation are just what they ought to be before he makes so much fuss over Sunday funerals.

(Wiley, who had led the Bellefonte Presbyterian Church since 1870, would leave town within two years of this stinging editorial.)

After reporting, at length, the hour and circumstances of her death and sketching, more briefly, Ruth Ward's teaching career and her ensuing tenure as assistant principal in Bellefonte, the *Watchman* continued:

[Mrs. Ward] infused much of her own vigor into all those about her. She was here—there—everywhere. The children all loved her and the various teachers admired and respected her manner and method of inspiring the pupils with her own enthusiasm. . . . To her scholars she was the greatest woman living, and to her *they* were the dearest children in all the universe. She sympathized in their little troubles, encouraged their budding hopes . . . inspired them with her own strength. . . .

Her illness was produced by too intense application to her duties and in the management of her household cares. She had sons whom she was trying to educate, and in her anxiety to get her youngest—a very promising boy—through college, she denied herself the help she ought to have had, overworked her poor body, caught cold, and plunged into a pleura-pneumonia from which she was unable to recover. Her sufferings were long and painful, but she was patient unto the end. She said to the writer of this that she trusted in God, no matter what the result might be. She would like to live for her family, for her school, for her friends, and to accomplish other good works. Looking at her two sons, who sat at the foot of her bed, she said, with her eyes full of tears, "These are my jewels—oh, how I love them; how I love them!"

God knows she was a good woman. She had had her troubles and had borne her share of the slanders which the world heaps on every brave heart that dares to do right, but she knew her duty and kept on. . . .

Under the burden of a martyred mother, Ward returned to Penn State for the 1875 spring term and somehow managed a very respectable showing.

Algebra ------------84   (the best of 12 students)
Composition ------82   (2d of 14)
Latin--------------89   (2d of 6)
Greek--------------80   (2d of 6)
Agriculture --------90   (best of 9)
Conduct -----------95   (good)
Geometry ----------80   (tied for 2d of 13)

Ward was evidently given a dispensation of sorts—the college recorded only his cumulative fall/spring grades, rather than sorting them into separate terms. As well, his sixteen absences—an extraordinary number—were deemed "excused."

The next semester—fall of 1875—sophomore Ward's strong academic performance continued:

Geometry ----------78   (best of class)
Greek--------------72   (3d of 3)
Latin--------------79   (best of 4)
Chemistry ---------73   (best of 11)
Infantry Tactics ---74   (5th of 9)

He followed suit the spring of 1876:

Chemistry------------75   (89 on exam—2d highest in class)
Thucydides ---------83/80   (best of 3)
Geometry ----------83/91   (best of 10)

Latin --------------------84/92   (best of 3)
Infantry Tactics ----89/94   (best of 9)
Composition ---------73   (middle of class)
Rhetoricals -----------85   (best of 9)

Additionally, he won the Orvis Prize for being the best sophomore mathematics student.

The next term—fall 1876—found Ward the worst student of ten in zoology and tied for the worst of ten in "Drill," but otherwise academically sparkling:

Livy----------------------------90   (best in class of three)
Evidences of Christianity----81   (best of 9)
Rhetoricals --------------------82   (best of 9)
Greek----------------------------79
Surveying ----------------------80   (2d of 9)
Military Efficiency -------------   (best in class)

However, by mid-February 1877—a month or so after the end of the fall term—John Ward's undergraduate career at Penn State ended abruptly and ignominiously.

Six

It Was Known That They Took Chickens

P ENNSYLVANIA STATE COLLEGE in the 1870s was a grim place. The institution was ruled by a fastidious, judgmental, ironbound faculty—a group that seemed far less eager to educate students in the classroom than to take dim views of their behavior outside of the classroom and to inflict appropriate punishment. Faculty meetings rarely concerned themselves with curricula. Instead, their agendas resembled criminal court dockets. The minutes reveal nothing if not a prurient interest in ferreting out student misdeeds and a gleeful enthusiasm in punishing those misdeeds.

Indeed, the most prominent section of the school's catalogues during Ward's years there—far more prominent than mere information about courses—was the school's code of behavior.

STUDENTS ARE REQUIRED:

1) To conduct themselves in an orderly and gentlemanly manner at all times
2) To be punctual in their attendance upon all College exercises
3) To observe neatness in dress at prayers, at meals and at recitations

4) To wear the prescribed uniform at Sabbath services, and at drill
5) To keep their rooms neat and clean
6) To present to the proper officer, three weeks before delivery, all literary productions designed for public performance

STUDENTS ARE FORBIDDEN:

7) To be absent during study hours from the building within which they room without permission
8) To make or receive visits which may conflict with proper attention to study
9) To use musical instruments during study hours
10) To possess or use any keys belonging to rooms which they have no right to enter
11) To enter the boarding or laundry departments without permission
12) To use tobacco in or about the College except in their own rooms, or to smoke in or near any College building or on detail
13) To throw matter of any kind from the windows or doors
14) To have pistols or discharge fire-arms in the building or on campus
15) To associate with students of the opposite sex during either session or vacation, without special permission of the President and the Preceptress
16) To continue any entertainment, or meeting, beyond 10 p.m.

These rules were strictly enforced. The institution's charter mandated that students would, during the daily three-hour labor detail, "perform all the labor necessary in the cultivation of the farm, and shall thus be instructed and taught all things necessary to be known by a farmer." This mandatory work-study program was quickly expanded in scope, and misbehaving students were assigned additional work stints as punishment.

In large part, college faculties focused so on discipline because discipline and moral rigor were deemed part and parcel of any worthy educational mandate. The faculty felt that its primary duty was the training of boys to become men. (Women, a tiny minority of most student bodies, were an afterthought.) Manliness—one of the more important concepts of late-nineteenth-century America—in the context of higher education, "meant power: the kind of power that one gained by a diligent wrestling with Greek grammar." (The classes—especially Greek grammar—must have been deadly. Lecturing, while not unknown, was hardly in vogue. Memorization and recitation were the order of the day. One scholar has described a typical mid-nineteenth-century classroom session as an "oral quiz, one hour in length, five times a week during the academic year.")

From this hairshirt approach, manly men, it was believed, would emerge. As one college president put it:

> *Men* are in demand [as students and citizens]—not *homines*, ani-
> mals that wear pants, but *viri*, plumed knights, with swords upon
> their thighs; scholars and specialists they may be, if back of
> scholarship and specialty there is manhood enough to bear up
> under them and put them to service.

The college air was thick with paternalism and patriarchy. Moral uprightness was the true goal of a college. (The president of Penn State during Ward's years, the Reverend James Calder, was also a professor of "Mental and Moral Science.") The faculty at Penn State met weekly—and often in extraordinary sessions—to discuss the appropriate response to unmanly, immoral students. The discussions and punishments were spirited.

On April 30, 1873, the faculty passed a motion to "take some action towards the detection and punishment of the parties who have for some days been disturbing and destroying the lamps in the hall." On June 19, the minutes record that

> Miss Leona Harlan [and a male student had] been detected in a
> secret meeting in a room in the 3rd Hall of the Ladies Dept.
> They were called in and questioned and both confessed to hav-
> ing had the meeting and gave many particulars—both . . .
> expressed sorrow for having disregard [for] the rules . . . both

deprived of the privilege of meeting persons of the opposite sex
and . . . of privileges of [extracurricular] Societies and reading
room for the remainder of the term.

Also on June 19, a student was fined $2.25 and sent on a six-hour
work detail for breaking windows. On December 4, a student left campus
without permission and was sentenced to a day's labor cleaning recitation
rooms. After a Halloween disturbance in 1875 (students often threw
fruit, fences, furniture and even animals from the fifth floor of Old
Main), the faculty became apoplectic after "each student had declared
that he was innocent of any participation in the mischief of last night
and knew of none who did participate." "Charge and specifications" were
brought against Edward Wood for insubordinate and disrespectful conduct. The offense consisted in throwing pebbles against the window
panes and "speaking and acting in a manner disrespectful to [school
authorities]."

Additionally, students were actively encouraged to inform on each
other. At one point the faculty adopted a resolution asking students to
"use their influence" to prevent "further misdemeanors" and to take a
pledge to "make known the names of any perpetrators and that this pledge
be required of incoming students for admission."

Perhaps the least savory aspect of punishment was the requirement
that guilty students publicly confess their misdeeds. For example, after
several meetings one November, the faculty voted that Chauncey York, a
sophomore from Sherman, Michigan, should sign and read in Chapel the
following confession:

> I hereby confess that I have been guilty of violating the Rules of
> the College in that I have on several occasions been absent from
> class without excuse, have neglected military duty, and have
> failed to prepare Essays as required. Furthermore I am censurable
> for not drilling on last Saturday and for the manner in which I
> replied to Prof. Downey when called upon to do so. Confessing
> and regretting this wrong doing I . . . promise to make up all
> work and henceforth faithfully perform all duties and keep all the
> "rules" of the institution.

It is not difficult to imagine where all this led. College students then were not essentially different from college students today—full of wing-stretching energy, a strong sense of immortality, and a healthy, inchoate disregard of petty authority. The draconian, persistent hounding by the faculty became little more than an amusing game of cat-and-mouse. Although the faculty's long arm reached out to nab campus miscreants democratically—as near as we can tell—the names of one particular group of students, members of the school's baseball club (including John Ward, but, notably, not Ellis Orvis), appeared in the minutes with alarming frequency.

By 1875, collegiate baseball—along with the noncollegiate amateur and professional game—was enormously popular, though generally more so among Eastern colleges than in Pennsylvania and the West, and most of all among those universities that now make up the Ivy League. Baseball and crew, in fact, were the only team sports in existence on many campuses.

By 1875 students had been playing baseball in one form or another for 120 years. Princeton had banned ball playing against the president's house—and levied a five shilling fine for violations—as early as 1761. A 1786 Princeton student recorded in his diary: "a fine day, play baste ball . . . but am beaten for I miss catching and striking the ball."

Oliver Wendell Holmes remembered playing ball in the 1820s, as did Henry Wadsworth Longfellow. The University of North Carolina, while banning several campus sports in 1799, allowed students to continue playing baseball. On July 1, 1859, Williams College and Amherst played each other in what is generally considered the first formal intercollegiate game. In 1870 the Harvard nine, after a forty-game regular season, embarked on an ambitious barnstorming tour against local teams and even some professional teams. (In 1876 Harvard defeated the professional Boston Red Stocking Club.)

At Penn State—whose first recorded athletic event was a sort of gymnastic competition in 1866—students formed the first baseball team, the Union Baseball Club, the same year. The faculty allowed that team to travel thirty miles east and play the Lock Haven town team.

During John Ward's undergraduate years, there were no formal intercollegiate competitions or leagues and certainly no overriding body such as the National Collegiate Athletic Association. A baseball club was exactly that—a club. It consisted of a few like-minded fellows and occasionally, at least in 1875, a few spectators. The best analogy to the 1875 Penn State baseball club today would be a sky-diving club, a kayaking club, or perhaps a rugby club.

Penn State base-ballists played each other, or organized interclass games or games with local amateur teams from nearby towns. Besides Lock Haven, Penn State played teams from Boalsburg, Philipsburg, Williamsport, and Bellefonte.

Some college teams had elaborate uniforms, others could afford only caps. Some college teams, like the well-heeled Harvards, amassed enough funding to take luxurious road trips during the summer. Others, like Penn State, could scrape together only enough for trips around their home county and some neighboring counties.

College nines financed themselves in a variety of ways. If their organization was social as well as athletic—the most common scenario—they followed in the footsteps of college boat clubs: membership dues, fines for any number of petty offenses such as profanity or missing meetings or practices. Sometimes clubs canvassed for subscribers, much as modern amateur softball and baseball teams establish war chests via outright business sponsorships or fund-raising raffles and the like. As well, teams allowed the informal passing of the hat through the stands. The colleges themselves provided almost nothing in the way of financial help and regarded their baseball teams—as well as literary and dramatic and oratorical societies—as bootstrap operations. Penn State indulged the young ballplayers to the extent of approving a petition to allot a part of campus for ball games—raw land that the club prepared themselves.

As is the case with many campus clubs, with their ever-shifting memberships, enthusiasm, energy, and organizational talent, some years these athletic teams thrived and some years they were moribund.

When John Ward got to Penn State, there was no "regular baseball organization" until the spring of 1875. A game he recalled seeing in 1873 was probably an intrasquad or intramural affair. To Ward its highlights were the pitching of a man named Foster, who had only one arm, and the hilarious occasion of outfielder Frank Keller's running after a fly ball and splitting his "very tight flannel trousers."

A studio portrait of
John Montgomery
Ward made in Belle-
fonte, Pennsylvania,
ca. 1870. *(Courtesy
of The Pennsylvania
State University
Archives)*

Ruth Ward, John Montgomery Ward's mother.
Date unknown. *(Maria Sinn)*

Ward and Ellis Orvis, ca. 1875. Orvis was a boyhood and college chum, and a teammate. (*Courtesy of The Pennsylvania State University Archives*)

The 1875 Pennsylvania State college baseball team for which Ward pitched. *Bottom row, left to right:* Ward, Frank Knoche, Jos. M. Stull, Louis W. Eldridge. *Middle row, left to right:* B. Frank Keller, Ellis L Orvis, A. Russell Calder. *Back row, left to right:* Chas. M. Calder, Henry Huff. (*Courtesy of The Pennsylvania State University Archives*)

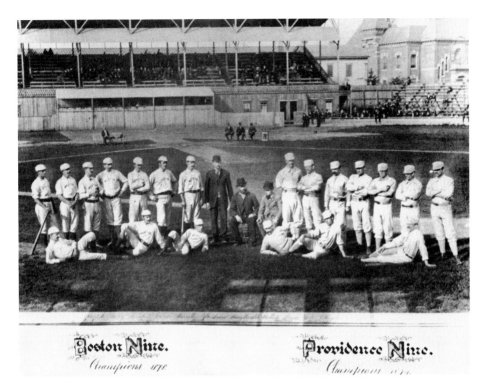

Boston Nine.
Champions 1878.

Providence Nine.
Champions 1879.

Top: The Boston and Providence teams at Providence's Messer Field. Boston had won the National League pennant in 1878. In 1879 Providence took the honors. The Providence team: *Reclining on grass, left to right:* Bobby Mathews, George Wright, Jack Farrell. *Standing, left to right:* Emil Gross, Tom York, Jim O'Rourke, Joe Start, Ward, Mike McGeary, Paul Hines. *(Baseball Hall of Fame Library, Cooperstown, N.Y.)* *Bottom:* A notice in the *Cincinnati Enquirer* for the July 15, 1878 game in which Ward made his major-league debut as a pitcher for the Providence Grays. *(Cincinnati Enquirer)*

BASE-BALL!

MONDAY, JULY 15.

PROVIDENCE vs. CINCINNATI.

TUESDAY, JULY 16,

CHAMPION BOSTONS
——VS.——
CINCINNATI.

Game called at 3 o'clock.
Trains leave Plum-street Depot at 2 and 2:30.
Admission 50c.; Children under 12 years 25c.   1t

JOHN M. WARD, Pitcher,

is one of the youngest and most promising players in the country, and, although but twenty years of age, he ranks second to none in his position. A Pennsylvanian by birth, he had attained considerable repute as the pitcher of an amateur organization of Williamsport, in that State, when he was induced to join the Athletics of Philadelphia, making his first appearance in the professional arena as the pitcher of that club in a game with the Hartfords on June 30, 1877, at Brooklyn. He did not remain long with the Athletics, however, but seceded to the Philadelphias, with whom he distinguished himself by his remarkable curve-pitching, puzzling completely his quondam associates in the first game they played, so that they failed to score. He next migrated to Janesville, Wis., where his pitching helped the semi-professional nine of that city to defeat the Chicagos, Alleghenys and Milwaukees by the respective scores of 5 to 3, 3 to 1, and 5 to 0. He concluded the season of 1877 by playing right-field and change-pitcher for the then newly-organized Buffalo Club. He pitched for the Crickets of Binghamton part of the season of 1878, and on their disbandment was at once engaged by the Providence Club, with whom he has remained ever since, and his effective pitching has greatly aided that nine in reaching its present premier position. His curve-pitching is very puzzling to most batsmen, although but medium-paced, he displaying much headwork, having a thorough command of the ball, and having no superiors in fielding in his position. He is also a very good general player, having filled the position of third-base remarkably well in some matches this season, and being a hard-hitting batsman.

A portrait and profile of Ward in the *New York Clipper*, September 6, 1879. During the *Clipper*'s heyday—the last three decades of the nineteenth century—an "oval biography" such as this was a high honor: the approximate modern equivalent would be a cover story in *Sports Illustrated* or *Time*. *(Transcendental Graphics)*

The 1884 New York National League team (before they became
known as the Giants). Ward is standing at the far left.
(*Baseball Hall of Fame Library, Cooperstown, N.Y.*)

Opening day of the 1886 National League season at the Polo Grounds, then
located at 110th Street and Fifth Avenue, the northeast corner of Central Park.
It's the bottom of the fourth inning, New York hitting. Charles Radbourn of
Boston pitches to Mickey Welch. Ward, wearing a sweater, is on deck. Note
how far behind the catcher the umpire stands. (*New-York Historical Society*)

Helen Dauvray in a scene from Bronson Howard's *One of Our Girls*, in which she played the lead. The play ran from November 1885 through May 1886. Dauvray married Ward in August 1887. She is about twenty-five years old in this photo. (*Hampden-Booth Theatre Library, N.Y.*)

Maxine Elliott in an 1895 publicity photo from either *Two Gentlemen of Verona*, *A Midsummer Night's Dream*, or *Twelfth Night*. Ward and Elliott (who was born Jessie Dermot) were lovers at the time of Ward's 1887 marriage to Helen Dauvray, and they probably continued their affair for some time thereafter. An enormously popular and successful actress, Elliott is twenty-six years old in this photo. (*Hampden-Booth Theatre Library, N.Y.*)

How to Become -A- Player

Base-Ball

WITH THE

Origin, History, and Explanation of the Game

BY

John Montgomery Ward

THE ATHLETIC PUBLISHING COMPANY

PHILADELPHIA

The cover of Ward's book, which was published in 1888 and became a great success. (*Transcendental Graphics*)

Ward in 1888, when, as a member of the New York Giants, he was
one of the highest paid and most popular baseball players in America.
Players of that era often posed for photographs that were then
included in packets of tobacco products—much as, years later,
chewing-gum companies would include photos with their products.
(*Transcendental Graphics*)

Ward, along with Frank Knoche of Harrisburg and Charley Shee of Philadelphia, got permission to build a field north of Old Main and spent several weeks digging base paths, a batter's box, and a pitching box, erecting a backstop, and leveling the field.

That 1875 team thrived. They declared themselves the Champions of Centre County by virtue of victories over Bellefonte and Philipsburg, and remained more or less intact through the spring and fall of 1876.

The lads spent much time together—as teammates do—both on and off campus. Despite the restrictions placed on off-campus travel, their occasional trips allowed them welcome time free of the immediate hoverings of school authorities. Without putting too fine a point on it, it was only a matter of time before various team members began succumbing to temptations.

In the spring of 1874, ballplayer Henry Huff, a preparatory student at the time, was given three hours' labor for ringing the college bell during recitation hours.

On October 11, the following term, another team member, William Reid, was found drunk on campus. After his swift dismissal, his fellow students petitioned the faculty for his reinstatement, saying that Reid was "truly penitent" for his misdeed and that in their humble opinion, the sentence was "too harsh and hastily imposed." The faculty disdainfully returned the petition, saying it was presented far too informally. The students then delivered a more "respectful" document. Reid was reinstated—on the condition that he disclose the name of the person who sold him the liquor. If Reid told the truth, his punishment would merely be a two-month "room arrest," extra work details, and term-long probation. If he lied, he would be expelled.

About the time of this decision, the baseball club as a group got into trouble after returning late from a game at Bellefonte. Though the faculty excused the tardiness, they soon regretted their leniency. Reid's confession revealed that he had bought his liquor during an earlier trip with the club, from three members of Penn State's opponent, Philipsburg.

A few days later, the Philipsburg club—unaware of Reid's confession—sent the Penn State club a letter proposing a game, on campus, at the end of the month. The faculty, with little comment, canceled the game "because of the immoral reputation" of the Philipsburg club.

On November 9, Henry Huff again ran afoul of the faculty. He and two other students were given thirty demerits each for a "rucus" in the laundry room. The boys had "interfered" with "clothing not their own" and used "improper language."

Toward the end of January 1875, Charley Shee, who had helped Ward create the campus ball field, was found guilty of "gross disobedience and willful avoidance of [mandatory campus] military duty." At the same time, Frank Keller, he of the split flannels and a future United States district judgeship, was reduced in military rank, given a public reprimand, assigned extra work details, and placed under room arrest for four months. He had been found drunk on duty.

The rest of the spring 1875 term was, for the renegades of the baseball team, quiet. In light of their evident reformation, the faculty, toward the end of May, allowed the team to travel to Lock Haven—thirty miles from campus—for a game with a local squad. The faculty's terms for this privilege, however, included a back-on-campus deadline and the submission of the names of the traveling squad for prior approval. Neither Charley Shee's nor Frank Keller's name was on the list, as they were still under room arrest.

There then follows a year during which the team was on its best behavior. Come May 13, 1876, however, team members had reverted to their wild and wicked ways. On that day James Stull—in the team photo he's the long-faced lad with a mustache and goatee—behaved in a "grossly disrespectful" manner toward his student drill leader.

Stull was expelled. He apologized. The expulsion became a mere dismissal. He apologized again, and was reinstated, though busted back to private.

Less than a week later, the baseball team naively asked permission to play a game in nearby Boalsburg. The faculty decided, quickly and without comment, that there would be no more road trips for the team that term. (Within a month, both Stull and Keller were given demerits for visiting the rooms of some coeds.)

Ward, though his name had not come up during the many trials and missteps of his fellow ballists, was probably more lucky than angelic. He had, in fact, once appeared on court dockets as a juvenile offender. In January 1871, Ward, his half-brother George, and six other young Bellefontians, "did steal take and carry away" a bushel of apples from John Orvis, Ellis Orvis's father.

The theft of apples was hardly heinous, but could not, Orvis and others evidently agreed, be ignored. While in most cases, punishment would have been a private matter—involving a woodshed and a leather strap—and likely was in this case, Orvis decided as well to "scare the boys straight" by threatening them with the long arm of John Law. The "legal action" was an ominous document—still on record in the Centre County Courthouse—that begins:

> The Grand inquest of the Commonwealth of Pennsylvania
> inquiring in and for the County of Centre, upon the oaths and
> affirmations respectively do present . . .

This single, mock-serious blemish on Ward's record was about to receive bad company.

That summer of 1876 Ward, whose baseball skills were already formidable, had hooked up to play some games with the Lock Haven town team. (Lock Haven was a much more avid baseball town than Bellefonte, whose fortunes rested with the Academy team, and the college team had disbanded for the summer.) On Saturday, September 30, Lock Haven met their archrival Williamsport in the third game of a scheduled five-game summer-long series. Williamsport had won the first two games, and Lock Haven, hoping to avoid a sweep, persuaded Ward to play for them. Ward agreed and did so—though he was already back in college. Despite Ward's notable play in the game, Williamsport pinned Lock Haven 7–4. For Ward, that was the least of his woes.

The faculty minutes of October 6, 1876, read in part as follows:

> Mr. Ward was reported by the President as having been absent
> from the College when permission had been refused him. [Upon]
> examination he confessed that he had gone to Williamsport to
> play in a match game of baseball, and that he had not gone gun-
> ning nor was in his room as he had previously stated. . . . It was
> moved [and carried] that Mr. Ward be suspended for the remain-
> der of the session.

(Other business at the meeting included the matter of William Calvin McCormick, a preparatory school student who had traveled to

Lock Haven without permission. Unlike Ward, he had not tried to deceive the faculty, so he received only demerits, not suspension, as a punishment.)

Ward was evidently a popular figure on campus. Students quickly presented the faculty with a petition asking that his case be reconsidered. The faculty agreed, but decided that a reduction in Ward's punishment would be "prejudicial to good discipline." Five weeks later, however, the faculty reconsidered their reconsideration. After Ward read a letter "expressing penitence for the offense which caused his suspension and asking that he be allowed to return in order to gain the advantage of reviews," his suspension was lifted.

Before the fall term ended, McCormick—he and Ward were evidently running buddies (though we don't know if their Lock Haven/ Williamsport trips were taken separately or together)—crossed the faculty again. The college kept two mules for plowing. One was docile, the other docile only if mounted from the right side. When mounted from the left— the normal side—it immediately began bucking. It was, among students, a traditional dido to force an unsuspecting underclassman to mount the second mule from the left for an initiatory ride of some sort. Evidently McCormick was the designated prankster—this or he had plans to lead the mule into and up the stairs of Old Main, another student activity—for he was convicted of "mule theft" and expelled until the spring term.

Toward the end of January, with the spring term just under way, the two-man gang of McCormick and Ward once again sprang into action. From the faculty minutes of January 26, 1877:

Mr. Ward and Mr. McCormick were reported to have been out of the building Thursday night. They first went to the church at Centre Furnace, and then up the road to Mr. Strous's, where they were seen . . . to enter the barnyard, and from the noise, it was known that they took chickens with which they returned across the fields to the College.

The young men were examined. . . . The report was denied. It was proven however that their statements were false. . . . It was moved that, in view of previous offenses of a similar kind, viz: of repeatedly leaving the institution without the permission of the

President, and of stating falsehoods before the faculty, now aggra-
vated by a pledge not to do so, voluntarily signed . . . for which
lesser punishments were awarded, but, as it appears, without
effect, and of strong suspicions, if not certainty, of having entered
a . . . shed and therein taking chickens, Ward and McCormick
are hereby dismissed from the Institution.

The town of Bellefonte immediately rallied behind Ruth Ward's son,
just as his fellow students had earlier. A citizen's group gathered signatures
on a petition asking the faculty to reconsider the case of Ward and
McCormick. The faculty voted to receive and discuss the petition. On
Saturday, February 17, the faculty met and, after due consideration,
adopted the following resolution:

> In view of repeated offenses by Mssrs. Ward & McCormick,
> and in view of their having been once before reinstated upon
> petition, the Faculty thinks that the respectful petitions of Belle-
> fonte Citizens in behalf of these young men cannot, without too
> great a sacrifice of discipline . . . be granted.

Two days later, John Orvis, an attorney and Ellis's father (and from
whom Ward and the others had stolen apples), wrote to the Reverend
James Calder, Penn State's president.

> I received to-day a letter from Mr. Buckhout, Sec. of the faculty,
> giving the result of the proceedings of the faculty on Saturday
> evening. . . . I am sorry for this result both on account of the
> young men and of the college. I am now fully satisfied of that
> which I have for some time feared: viz. that the college can never
> be made a success as a school until there is a radical change in
> the constitution of the faculty.
>   . . . I was chiefly instrumental in getting Mrs. Ward to send
> Monte up there. This I now regret, as I believe it has been a seri-
> ous wrong to him; as I have no doubt he would have gone
> through any other college without any difficulty.
>   . . . The great trouble seems to be, that the Faculty do not
> have the confidence or respect of but a small proportion of the

students. This causes large numbers to voluntarily leave, and others to conduct themselves as to be dismissed; and thus all the efforts of the friends of the College to fill the institution with students are unavailing. Instead of spending any more time and labor in canvassing for new students, we had better put forth our efforts to secure a Faculty that will possess both the disposition and skill to retain the students they do get.

The last Pennsylvania State College notation for John Ward consists of these words: "Left College." He was no longer a popular, award-winning undergraduate and mainstay of the college baseball team. He was a sixteen-year-old expelled liar and chicken thief.

Seven

To Travel
Had Been His Dream

I N THE WAKE of his expulsion, Ward expunged the incident, along with most of his youth, from his own accounts of his life. He never referred publicly to the expulsion, and only rarely referred to his undergraduate years or his Bellefonte years. We know about the game in which one-armed Foster and split-trousered Keller played on Ward's first day on campus, we know that the college nine played at the Centre County Fair in 1876, and we know that, by 1877, Ward had gained "some local reputation" as a ballplayer. But beyond this, his boyhood and adolescence are ciphers: we know nothing of his homelife; his relationship with his parents and extended family; his sorrow at his parents' deaths; his hobbies—if any—besides baseball; the locations of his Bellefonte sandlot fields; or even the identity of his Bellefonte sandlot teammates. In the few instances he did revisit his pre-professional life for readers, Ward manifested a willful inaccuracy. Sometimes, as in his 1886 "Notes of a Base-Ballist," he was merely vague: "In the spring of 1877 I was obliged, somewhat unexpectedly, to leave college." On other occasions he dons a fabulist's mantle. Montgomery Ward Fleming, John Ward's cousin (Fleming was the grandson of John's uncle Philo), recalled, some years after John's death, that "Uncle Monte" had made it clear that the only reason he had been "requested" to leave college was that he had "persisted in running away at week-ends to play baseball."

Ward told a much richer variation of his college expulsion to John Fleming, another cousin. In the early 1960s, during Fleming's correspondence with Hall of Fame historian Lee Allen, Fleming explained Ward's version thus:

> It seems that hazing wasn't confined to only freshmen [at Penn State] but kept up on something of a running feud basis. [Ward] lived in Old Main . . . on the third floor. The staircase made a complete turn with a landing between the floors. [Ward] had advance information that a group were coming to work him over. He rigged up a sandbag at the top of the stairs, holding it around the corner until he heard the boys coming. He waited until they had turned the corner and were on the flight of stairs above the landing before he let the sandbag go. His foes piled up haphazardly on the landing with some broken bones but no fatalities. . . . college officials took a dim view of the incident.

One thing is clear: Ward, upon his expulsion, badly needed a job. The proceeds from the sale, upon her death, of his mother's house—split between Ward and his brother Charles—had quickly been used up and Ward was determined to continue his education. He could have found immediate employment in Bellefonte, where he had a large, forgiving, generous support system. Instead he opted to take a job away from the fields of Bellefonte. Whether this was a unilateral decision on Ward's part we do not know, but by early spring, Ward set out as a drummer for a nursery. (With his customary revisionism, Ward says that he took to the road not only because of the demands of his pocketbook but because "to travel had been my dream.")

His choice of occupations was seriously flawed. His territory, northwestern Pennsylvania, was harsh, the economy sputtering, and his line of goods exotic: "With an agency for a bakery I might have found some trade," he wrote in "Ballist," "but strawberry-plants and fancy shrubbery are luxuries too easily dispensed with [in] that land of destitution and coal-mines."

The seventeen-year-old did not last long in sales. One late spring day he found himself in tiny Emporia, Pennsylvania. "Two hundred miles from home, among strangers, and without the price of a meal," he wanted only to "get back into civilization." His definition of civilization did not include Bellefonte, for he was "greatly chagrined" to find himself failing a second time in half a year. He befriended a railroad conductor, hitched a long night's ride in a caboose, and jumped off in Renovo—a narrow and isolated mountain town on the West Branch of the Susquehanna River. The town had been founded by the Pennsylvania Railroad to serve as a repair station—its name means "Restored" in Latin. Though today the town is still as death, in 1877 it was bustling and prosperous. Though only twenty-five miles north of Bellefonte as the crow flies, it was a full three hours by train—if a tight connection was made in Lock Haven.

Renovo (population 1,950) at the time had two baseball clubs: the premier nine, the Resolutes, and the scrub, "muffin" team, the Actives. According to Ward, there was a game scheduled for the afternoon he arrived. (Though he does not say which team was playing, it was surely the Resolutes.) Some of the local players recognized Ward and persuaded him to pitch. After the game, the Resolutes hired Ward to pitch for them for ten dollars a month and board.

While the job was a windfall—an entry-level semiskilled non-baseball position Ward could have found (clerk or amanuensis would have been likely candidates) would have paid him about a dollar or a dollar fifty per ten-hour day—Ward likely saw playing baseball as moonlighting, much as a schoolteacher today might play in a weekend dance band. The requirements for playing with the Resolutes would have been minimal—games twice a month (once a week, at most)—and a few evening practices a week. Ward probably planned to secure a day job, probably one with a baseball-friendly boss who would let him take game days off. Though he did not stay in Renovo long enough to do this, Ward was adamant that he saw professional baseball, at most, as merely a supplemental means to an end. In "Base-Ballist" he wrote that he had not the "faintest idea [as a teenager he] would be playing today. I intended to continue only until I should be able to find other employment." The sincerity of this recollection, unlike some others of Ward's, cannot be doubted. Less than a year after his arrival in Renovo, Ward, playing for a high-level minor league team and less than four months from a major league pitching debut, wrote to James Calder, president of Pennsylvania State College, asking for a "certificate of dismissal" (albeit without "reference" to his record at PSC). The reason for the request, Ward made clear, was that although he was still "playing ball . . . when I get enough laid by to see me through I want to complete my college education."

As handy as the Resolutes job was, the decision to play ball, even part-time, must have been a difficult one for Ward. He was the son of a mother who had died working to launch him into respectability, likely as part of the legal profession, and professional baseball, at the time, had much the same reputation that professional wrestling does today. As well, and perhaps more importantly, we cannot dismiss the possibility that Ward himself—despite his love for the game—was, in Renovo, still suffering some great psychic hangover, one that he, directly or indirectly, attributed to his college association with baseball and baseball players. He might well have made the same sort of never-again vow (and meant it just as sincerely) as have so many who have wakened to self-poisoned self-revulsion the morning after a long night in the wrong town.

But whatever Ward's conflicts about playing baseball, whatever his misgivings about not fulfilling his mother's ambitions for him, he did not allow them to override his own notions of practicality. When a Williamsport nine offered him a place on their premier team roster as well as a bigger paycheck, he had little trouble accepting the offer.

Williamsport, fifty-five railroad miles southeast, was a large and thriving town (population 18,000) and extremely serious about its baseball. It supported, besides its "A" team, on which Ward played, the High Boys, the Actives, the Red Stockings, the Brown Stockings, the Picked Nine, the Lumber City Nine, and the Star. The *Daily Gazette and Bulletin* regularly printed game scores from the region on the front page; the local ballpark, Herdic Field, had been retrofitted with barbwire to prevent "fence viewers" from catching a free game; sometimes paying crowds of 4,000 attended games.

The 1877 season had not been going well for Williamsport's "A" team. They had, toward the end of May, lost two games in three days to Sunbury before traveling to Renovo, where they lost again. This loss—at the hands of pitcher John Ward—to a mapspeck team likely caused Williamsport to offer him a job.

On Thursday, June 7, 1877, Ward, batting eighth, pitched his first game for Williamsport. He won, throwing a four-hitter against Sunbury. Two days later, Ward won again, throwing another four-hitter against Sunbury and scoring a run in the 6–3 victory.

Williamsport was ecstatic with its team's resurgence and urged one and all to witness the transformation for themselves.

> Thursday . . . there will be a game of base ball. . . . at 2:30 the
> youthful athletes will shy their castors into the ring. . . . members
> of both branches of the city councils and the school board are
> invited to be present to take lessons in scientific gymnastics.

Pitcher Ward was thermonuclear. In his next game he had a one-hitter going when, with the score tied at the end of nine innings, the visiting team had to return home and the game was called, as was common at the time, on account of "train time." On Wednesday, June 20, Ward threw yet another one-hitter, this time against Renovo, as Williamsport won 13–4.

The next day, ten men known as the Molly Maguires—a labor cabal within the Ancient Order of Hibernians who had been convicted of a series of terrorist murders in Pennsylvania coal mines—were hanged, six of them in Pottsville, only fifty miles southeast of Williamsport. Local newspapers had been filled for weeks with news of the region's labor unrest. Coalminers and railway workers had been in virtual revolt, protesting layoffs, pay reductions, "speed-ups," and anti-union intimidation by management. A good amount of ink and paper had, as well, been spent in covering the Molly Maguires' hopeless legal struggle. The papers reported the executions in great detail, including verbatim accounts of the condemned men's last words. The *Williamsport Daily Gazette and Bulletin*'s coverage was not sympathetic, ending with these words: "The evil they have done will live after them and the good will mostly be interred with their bones."

The day after the hangings, Ward beat Renovo again, 8–6, striking out thirteen.

A few days later, Williamsport was scheduled to play a game against an unnamed squad of Philadelphia "professionals." That team, however, had suddenly disbanded at Wilkes-Barre, so the Wilkes-Barre team came to play Williamsport instead. The game was called on account of rain after five innings, which was just as well for Ward. He was losing 6–0 at the time. Even so, the Williamsport paper defended the new phenom. Though he had pitched wildly, none of Wilkes-Barre's runs had been earned—instead, they were scored on errors, thanks to the "unaccountably bad playing" of the Williamsports.

The Williamsport "A" team's biggest game of the summer of 1877 was part of the town's Fourth of July celebration. They played before nearly 4,000 paying fans and won. Within days, possibly even hours, of the lucrative Independence Day gala, however, the team was bankrupt and John Ward out of a job. The team's business manager, his timing unimpeachable, had absconded with the team coffers. The man, Ward noted, "neglected to leave his address."

Eight

Cricket Is a Splendid Game— for Britons

I F, DURING THE YEARS between the end of the Civil War and the beginning of the twentieth century, a person had the slightest doubt there was no country on earth quite as great as America, and moreover, no people on earth quite as great as Americans, all that person had to do was ask a white American *his* opinion on the subject. He'd get an earful or three, he would. America started with the letter A and that was the first letter in the alphabet and the meaning of that was as plain as the nose on your face. The country's emerging, disproportionately powerful and increasingly vocal middle class—a huge majority of them of Anglo-Saxon heritage—were, in large part, mighty chauvinists. To them the world was more or less divided into regions of varying moral, political, spiritual, and economic inferiority with respect to America. There were the unspeakably backward heathens of Asia and Africa, the disorganized and volatile papists of Latin America, and the Europeans, most of them so badly provided for that they couldn't wait to leave and come to America. (Once here, these creatures ate strange food, spoke in indecipherable tongues, spread disease, and fomented labor unrest. The Irish were included in this group—being nothing but Europeans who happened to speak English.)

There were two special cases, however, countries that did not fit any of these categories: France and Great Britain.

If Americans neither loved nor respected France, they could not ignore it. Certainly, in large cities, its cuisine and general influence on fashions were becoming difficult to ignore. But—and here any American with a lick of sense had to admit—the moment one looked beyond the groaning board or the boudoir, France came up mighty short. It was not—at least the last time America looked—the sort of place that could build the Brooklyn Bridge, or invent the sewing machine or light bulb or telephone or cotton gin. Didn't they grow grain in France? Yes, in fact they did, and they had for a hell of a lot longer than we had—so how come they never came up with a mechanical reaper? The Statue of Liberty was inspirational, sure enough, but when all was said and done, it wasn't exactly *useful*. France was naughty. It was dashing. It was frivolous: brightly lit, but only in a twinkly sense. No, when you got right down to brass tacks, France wasn't . . . *manly*.

That left Britain-minus-Ireland. America had a troubled relationship with the United Kingdom, especially England: a love for it the size of Pennsylvania and an inferiority complex about it bigger than the olde land itself. On the one hand, England was the ancestral country for an overwhelming percentage of Americans, and, say what you will, one Englishman or English-American was worth any ten Wops or Polacks or Heinies or Micks or Hunkies or Greasers you could name. The English were a lot like us, or vise versa: Protestant, American-speaking, Irish-hating, horse- and yacht-racing, and hunting-, fishing-, and boxing-loving white men.

And they had their royals, a source of boundless fascination for Americans. (So many people attended a party for the Prince of Wales, the future Edward VII, at the Fifth Avenue Hotel in 1860 that a minor riot ensued outside. Inside, the throng was so large that the ballroom floor collapsed.)

On the other hand, Americans felt that the English found their former colonists, at best, *amusing*, and at worst, unruly, undependable, tobacco-spitting children. Many Americans bristled at this attitude and spent a lot of time, energy, and printer's ink asserting, promoting, and debating their country's superiority to Britain: touting America's political and cultural independence, its agility and innovation—in short, its bright shiny *newness*.

America's psychic relation to Britain was at once strutting, insecure, boastful, and homesick. On the subject of baseball and Britain, however, most Americans entertained few conflicts of opinion. When the subject of the sport came up—especially questions of its place in the world relative to cricket, and its origins—it elicited such shouts of nationalism, such screams of cultural independence, that any discussion quickly degenerated into tantrum.

Now, cricket was hardly unknown in America; in certain circles it was very popular. But the idea that England's lawn sport deserved the title of the American national game was not at issue by the late 1860s. The stakes were far higher than that. Baseball enthusiasts, magnates, and sportswriters were determined to prove that not only was baseball vastly superior to cricket and perfectly suited to America's vastly superior and more energetic *Zeitgeist,* but that baseball was, hands down, a purely American invention.

Indeed, the possibility, no matter how faint, that baseball, as some claimed, was not a native son, but instead some sickly bastard offspring of an English boy's game, cast a deep and chilling shadow across the brows of baseball's most vigorous promoters. If baseball was not "ours" and ours alone, the argument went, what apostasies might follow?

Albert Goodwill Spalding—one of America's first professional baseball players and a prime mover in the founding of the National League and the country's most wealthy and influential sporting goods magnate—could not let the baseball issue die. Even as late as 1911 he was still fulminating.

I claim that Base Ball owes its prestige as our National Game to the fact that as no other form of sport it is the exponent of American Courage, Confidence, Combativeness; American Dash, Discipline, Determination; American Energy, Eagerness, Enthusiasm; American Pluck, Persistency, Performance; American Spirit, Sagacity, Success; American Vim, Vigor, Virility. . . . its playing demands Brain and Brawn, and American manhood supplies these ingredients in quantity sufficient to spread over the entire continent. . . .

Cricket is a splendid game, for Britons. It is a genteel game, a conventional game—and our cousins across the Atlantic are nothing if not conventional. They play Cricket because it accords with the traditions of their country . . . because it is easy and does not overtax their energy or their thought. . . .

Cricket is a gentle pastime. Base Ball is War! Cricket is an
Athletic Sociable, played and applauded in a conventional,
decorous and English manner. Base Ball is an Athletic Turmoil,
played and applauded in an unconventional, enthusiastic and
American manner. . . . Base Ball, I repeat, is War!

Spalding's baseball accomplishments, while manifold, were bathed in
the caustic liquor of nineteenth-century monopolism. He was pompous,
button-busting, smug, clever, ruthless, and, especially in labor relations,
hypocritical in the extreme. Spalding was also, in his transatlantic sociological analysis of sporting preferences, far from the mark. Baseball won
out over cricket to become America's sport of choice for a variety of reasons, none of them having much to do with anything as mightily nebulous
as a "national character."

First, from Revolutionary times through most of the first half of the
nineteenth century, American boys, while certainly familiar with cricket
and sandlot-simplified forms of cricket, were on the whole excluded by
this country's adult cricketers from playing the grown-up game. The boys
instead turned to long-established "child's games"—baseball-like cricket
cousins such as "base" and "old cat." These popular proto-baseball
games—and baseball as we know it—would gain ascendency over cricket
and its dwindling and ever more elderly proponents as these once-
excluded boys became men and continued to refine the pastimes of their
youth rather than turn to the sport of their elders.

Second, baseball (informal baseball, as played by schoolboys) requires
much less space than cricket, and open space in urban areas, baseball's
most fecund nursery, was not easy to come by, even in the nineteenth century. As well, cricket grounds—by tradition—required level, pampered,
well-manicured fields. Baseball—certainly primitive baseball—did not.

Third, those cricket players living in America were, by and large,
snobs. If it was only broadly true that "Americans can't play cricket," it
was a reality that cricket clubs were extremely exclusive in both membership and field-access policies. As sporting missionaries, cricketers in
America were failures.

Fourth, baseball is vastly more participatory than cricket. In the
English game, a single batsman can stay at the plate for hours, while
novices, as often as not, are put out quickly. (A cricket batsman can act

defensively—he only runs when he feels he has a good chance of making it to the opposite wicket. In baseball terms, the cricket batsman can foul balls off forever. Of course, a baseball batter can do the same thing—with one exception: if he bunts foul with two strikes on him, this counts as a strikeout. Fouling off bunts—what a cricket batter effectively does during a defensive at-bat—is easier than fouling off full swings. One of baseball's most important self-adjustments was the adoption of the third-strike foul bunt rule, which prevented defensive batting.) Further, baseball players follow each other to the plate in relatively rapid progression. A "safe hit" means the next player gets his licks.

Baseball is a relatively quick game. Cricket matches can take an entire day, or several days, to complete. And in urban nineteenth-century America, time, like space, was an increasingly valuable commodity.

Finally, baseball was young and malleable. It could be adjusted; was open to suggestion, improvement, reform, invention. It traveled light on its feet. Cricket, on the other hand, was long-established, and burdened with time-honored rules and traditions. It was a regiment of redcoats to baseball's pelt-clad militiamen. At the risk of sounding like Spalding, restless Americans evidently preferred a game with which they could tinker.

Even more important to baseball's power structure than the game's inherent superiority were its origins. To prove that baseball was an American invention was, frankly, a difficult task—primarily because baseball was not an American invention so much as a series of American adjustments to a number of centuries-old games—most directly rounders, a child's game related to cricket and other games. But, by refusing to allow themselves to be confused with the facts, Spalding and others—John Ward included—overcame those difficulties with admirable dexterity.

The controversy about baseball's origins had become so heated, and so deadlocked, that in 1907 Spalding caused a blue-ribbon panel to be formed, one that would answer the question once and for all. The panel included two U.S. senators (one, Morgan Bulkeley, a former National League president), two other former National League presidents, and George Wright and Alfred Reach, former baseball stars who had entered the sporting goods business. The committee's report consisted essentially of three letters—Spalding's summary of their findings, a supporting letter of Ward's, and a minority dissenting opinion by sportswriter Henry Chadwick. Though any resemblance between the men's work and an investigation based on rigorous and disinterested research was coincidental, the commission's findings soon became part of American mythology.

Baseball, Spalding summarized, was invented by one Abner Doubleday in Cooperstown, New York, in 1839. Doubleday coined the term "base ball," he designed the diamond, he indicated the players' fielding positions. The game's rules and the field layout were not just suggested by Doubleday, but written down.

The cornerstone of the Doubleday theory was the testimony of one Abner Graves. Graves, a resident of the Cooperstown area in 1839, was a feeble elder in 1907 recalling events sixty-eight years old. But, even allowing that Graves's memory was infallible, which it wasn't—he muddles many biographical and geographical facts in his letters—Spalding's interpretation of Graves's letter is, let's say, somewhat detached from reality. (Graves makes no mention of a diamond, nor of positions, nor of the rules being written down, for starters.)

Other facts were conveniently overlooked, as well. In 1839, the year he was supposed to be lolling around Cooperstown changing the course of American leisure time, young Doubleday was, in fact, enrolled at West Point, where records do not show any leave time for the cadet. Nor was Spalding bothered by the fact that A. G. Mills, the commission's titular head and a lifelong friend of Doubleday's, had never heard the latter mention his "invention," or that the name "base ball" was, by 1839, well established. Even Ward, whose supporting letter says that he has no doubt whatsoever "but that baseball was a purely American game," disregards the Cooperstown/Doubleday business, mentioning a Col. James Lee, sixty years old in 1845, who remembered playing baseball as a boy.

If the Spalding commission's "American origin" theory was born of patriotism, so was the choice of Doubleday as baseball's founder: he was, in Spalding's view, an "ideal" American. Doubleday was a WASP. He was temperate, and a military exemplar: a West Point graduate, hero of the Mexican War and the Seminole uprising, and the man who—on his way to the rank of major general—supposedly aimed the first gun in defense of the Union at Fort Sumter. The choice of Cooperstown as baseball's ur-home field was patriotic as well, but only in that the upstate New York village was a paradigm of basic American values. Many nineteenth-century

Americans—as prone to nostalgia as modern Americans—were greatly troubled by what they felt was an increasing urbanism. Cooperstown, Spalding suggested, was the sort of place, the *only* sort of place, where America's national pastime could be invented: a rural, idyllic, unpolluted (by smoke or foreigners), and essentially nonindustrial village.

As crudely jingoistic as the debate of baseball's origins might seem, the sad part of the commission's conclusion—a version, really, of the immaculate conception—is that the actual roots of baseball, both its journey to America and its ensuing development, are much more fascinating. The best way to consider baseball's development, from its hoary ancestors through its baby-fat beginnings to its present adulthood, is to see it as an evolutionary continuum—spiky, lurching, spastic, potholed, speedy at times, glacial at others, dependent on precedent and serendipitous.

John Ward's 1888 book, *Base-Ball: How to Become a Player,* is part primer, part political philosophy, and part history essay. It begins with this sentence, a good example of Ward's graceful, Jamesian prose: "It may or it may not be a serious reflection upon the accuracy of history that the circumstances of the invention of the first ball are enveloped in some doubt."

He then cites Herodotus—who credits the Lydians with the invention of the ball—before racing through two dozen centuries of ballplaying history (Homer; William Fitzstephen, the twelfth-century English writer; Jane Austen's *Northanger Abbey;* and Joseph Strutt, who, in 1801, published the comprehensive *The Sports and Pastimes of the People of England*). Ward then settles down to prove—with tortured logic—that baseball was the "fruit of the inventive genius of the American boy." (The Strutt citation is fitting, since Ward's first page or so happens to be an overt plagiarism of Strutt's opening thoughts on ball games.)

Ward's familiarity with Strutt makes his insistence on the American genesis of baseball all the more curious, for even a cursory reading of the Englishman's history shows that baseball can be traced definitively back as far as the fourteenth century. Moreover, it was, without question, a descendant of a British game, one called stoolball.

The first generally accepted reference to stoolball appears in a 1330 poem by William Pagula, a vicar near Windsor, England, who instructed parish priests to forbid play of any kind within churchyards: "Bat and bares and suche play/Out of chyrche-yorde put away."

Stoolball may well have been, at one point, a form of simple "work-up." A batter stood before a three-legged stool. Another player pitched a ball to him. If the batter hit the ball—with a bat or, in some versions, with his hand—and it was caught by a fielder, the batter was out and exchanged places with either the fielder or another player. There was another way in which the batter could be put out: if the tossed ball hit the upturned stool. Stools were also known as crickets.

Stoolball was a game for maids and swains—a sort of publicly sanctioned spin-the-bottle. One late-seventeenth-century poem reads, in part:

> Down in the vale on a Summer's day,
> All the lads and lasses went to be merry,
> A match for kisses at Stoolball to play,
> And for cakes and ale, and sider and perry.
>
> CHORUS
> Come all, great small,
> Short tall, away to Stoolball

Another poem, "Stool-Ball, or the Easter Diversion," not only reiterates the game's amatory armature, but also suggests a clear evolution of equipment.

> Describe, my Muse, the annual play
> In which they waste the festal day . . .
> Obsequious youths their pleasure wait,
> Each proud to chase a lovely mate.
> At upper end is fixed the stool,
> In fam'd heroick games the goal;
> Not sacred tripod as of old,
> But quadruped of modern mold . . .
>
> Two genial parts the match divide,
> Proportion just on either side . . .

See at the goal Pulcheria stand
And grasp the board with snowy hand!
She drives the ball with artful force
Guiding through hostile ranks its course . . .

Where does the shame or crime appear
Of harmless romping once a year?

If, as seems likely, stoolball evolved into the adult game of cricket, several things had to happen. First, men had to realize the potential of the game's innate pleasure. Second, the new game would have to be adjusted, made, in a word, "manly." It is not at all difficult to imagine such a thing: narrow upright rods were substituted for the larger stool, to make the target harder to hit. And to minimize disagreement as to whether the rods had, in fact, been hit by a ball, horizontal pegs, or bails—which would fall to earth with any disturbance—were laid across the top of the rods.

Stoolball, cricket, and other variations of bat-and-ball games such as club ball, trap ball, and tip cat, were popular enough, at least in one instance, to bring down the wrath of clergy. Thomas Wilson, a Puritan authority of some local sort in the south of England, wrote, in 1700, of his disapproval of "Morris-dancing, cudgel-playing, baseball and cricketts" being played on Sundays.

In 1744, an Englishman, John Newbery, published *A Little Pretty Pocket-Book*, which included not only a woodcut of stoolball (with three players, including one at a nonstool "base") but a similar woodcut with an accompanying rhyme, under the heading "Base-ball."

The *Ball* once struck off,
Away flies the *Boy*
To the next destin'd Post,
And then Home with Joy.

An 1874 letter to the editor of the *London Times* referred, authoritatively, to a base-ball game played by Frederick, Prince of Wales, and his family, in 1748. But it is clear that the game was still primarily a children's game, and the play by the royal family was less "baseball" than some equivalent of church-picnic come-one-come-all informal softball.

A *Little Pretty Pocket-Book* appeared in America as a pirated volume in 1762 and went through many editions. It too contained a poem and woodcut illustrating "Base-Ball." One George Ewing, who wintered at Valley Forge with George Washington, mentions in his diary a game of "base" played by his fellow soldiers in the spring of 1778. Ewing's account of the game's existence is corroborated, at least anecdotally, by George H. Stoddard, who reported to the Spalding commission that his father, who had played "round ball" (another name for baseball) as early as 1820, had learned the game from his father, who had learned it from *his* father, who, family lore had it, did not consider the game a novelty in his youth.

(One of the stranger origination tales comes from France. In a book of boys' games, *Les Jeux des Jeunes Garçons*, published in Paris in 1810, is a description of *La balle empoisonnée*. In "poison ball," there were two teams of eight to ten children; four bases, one of them designated as "home"; a pitcher; a batter; a rule that a caught fly ball retires the batter; and, as was common in primitive baseball, a "soaking" rule, that is, a runner hit with a ball thrown by a fielder is out. Though the French game might have been nothing but a transchannel version of base- or stoolball, *Les Jeux*, according to some scholars, is "the first book . . . to contain the printed rules of a bat-and-ball base-running game.")

These primitive games had become so established that when William Clarke, in 1829, published *The Boy's Own Book* in London, he included a detailed section on the rules of a game called "rounders"—yet another variation on the game of "base." Five years after Clarke's book, a Boston firm published a similar guide to the rules of sport. Except for the name of the game—the Boston book changed "rounders" to "Base," or "Goal Ball"—the description of the American bat/ball game was identical to that given by Clarke.

Rounders/base had four bases (stones or posts) laid out in a diamond shape. Two sides—one "out" and one "in"—competed. A "feeder" pitched a ball toward a "striker" who tried to hit the ball. If he did—he had to hit it toward the fielders, otherwise the hit ball was considered "foul"—he ran clockwise around the bases. If a fielder caught the striker's ball—on the fly or after a bounce is not made clear—or "soaked" the striker as he ran between the bases, or if the striker swung three times without hitting the ball, the striker was out.

If rounders looked like a duck, walked like a duck, and quacked like a duck, many Americans—including Spalding and Ward—called it a partridge. The problem these men had with acknowledging rounders as baseball's sire seems to have been one not only of national but of masculine pride. Ward, in *Base-Ball: How to Become a Player* was insistent in pointing out that in *Northanger Abbey*, Austen's players were the *daughters* of Mrs. Morland and that Prince Frederick played with his *family* (with the strong implication that this included females). He also cited one English authority as saying, "There are few of us of *either sex* but have engaged in base-ball since our majority." (Austen's game, for the record, was most likely little more than a sort of ball-tag.)

The implications of all this cross-sexual girly-man ballplaying were quite clear to Ward:

> The fact that in the three instances in which we find the name [base] it is always a game for girls or women, would justify the suspicion that it was not always the same game, and that it in any way resembled our game is not to be imagined. Base-ball in its mildest form is essentially a robust game. . . . [It requires] an elastic imagination to conceive of little girls possessed of physical powers such as its play demands.

Unable to resist a final word, he continues:

> [As far as "soaking" a runner is concerned,] the ability to throw a ball with accuracy is vouchsafed to few girls, and if the change of innings depended upon this, the game, like a Chinese play, would probably never end.

Both Ward and Spalding felt that baseball was simply and irrefutably the offspring not of English rounders but of an American back-lot game of "cat" or "old cat." "Cat" had many variations, depending on how many people played (one old cat, two old cat, etc.), and was effectively a sort of hybrid of work-up and over-the-line (games—still played today—that require a minimum of two players), with a batter and a pitcher and a couple of bases, between which the runner, after hitting the ball, would run until thrown out. (The hoary English game of tip-cat, the likely ancestor of the "American" game, was identical to cat except that instead of a ball, a beveled peg was tipped into the air with the batter's foot before being hit with a bat.)

So Ward, Spalding, and company were wrong wrong wrong. Baseball, as common sense might dictate, was the product of centuries of evolution, local variations, and innovation, and had been played in America long before Abner Doubleday was even born. But for the sake of convenience—forgetting all the history above and forgetting, as well, a remarkable account, written in 1837, of a baseball-like game among Native Americans, and finally, forgetting that a group calling itself the Olympic Base Ball Club drafted a formidable constitution in 1837—our story of "modern" baseball begins in 1842, for that is when baseball was formally appropriated, and codified, for American adults.

Before that baseball was a backyard game, a lower-forty game, with very plastic site-specific and personnel-specific rules—rules that were passed along orally and changed constantly—a state of affairs familiar to any sandlot player.

Around 1842, first on open land on Manhattan's East Side—on 34th Street and Lexington Avenue, in the Murray Hill district, and later, as the city expanded and ate up vacant lots, across the Hudson in an area of Hoboken, New Jersey, known as the Elysian Fields—baseball took an irrevocable lurch toward modernity. There, in Manhattan and Hoboken, a group of like-minded young men began meeting after work with informal regularity to play baseball. Then, in 1845, they set themselves up formally as a social club: the Knickerbockers.

Before long, they wrote down a set of rules (which included such abstract concepts as foul territory and three outs retires the side). These rules are usually credited to Knickerbocker Alexander Cartwright, a young bookstore owner. In all likelihood they were baseball/Knickerbocker common law that Cartwright, one of the club's organizers and more enthusiastic members, drafted, amended, codified, submitted for approval, and had printed. (The Knickerbockers were not the first club of its kind in New York, just the best organized. In 1846 the Knickerbockers played the "New York Club," a very informal group that, by virtue of experience, among other things, handed the Knickerbockers their hats on a plate, 23–1.)

The Knickerbockers generally met a couple of times a week—the Elysian Fields had a small changing room—held business meetings and enjoyed dining and drinking together at a small hotel in lower Manhattan. They raised money through dues and an elaborate series of nominal fines for such things as speaking out of turn during meetings, tardiness or absence from practice, profanity, and disputing an umpire's call. Had they encouraged themselves to charitable acts, they might as well have been Kiwanis.

Most of the men were in their early thirties, and while only a few of them were wealthy, none were purely blue-collar. They were clerks, merchants, salesmen, or minor entrepreneurs—among them were a hatter, a U.S. marshal, and a sugar dealer. A few called themselves "gentlemen," which implied they lived on annuities. Though America at the time was hardly an industrialized country, and working hours were, by today's standards, extremely flexible, the Knickerbockers were clearly privileged—at least privileged enough to be able to knock off work early a couple of afternoons a week.

The exact nature of the Knickerbockers, and the dozen or more similar clubs formed in the next few years, is hard to convey to the modern sensibility. They were certainly not a service club, despite their elaborate attention to parliamentary procedure and their fondness for "sin taxation." Their facilities were too impermanent to consider them proper "country club" members. They were neither entirely a social group nor entirely an athletic group. Perhaps we should think of the Knickerbockers as a Downtown Businessmen's Association with a regular weekly gathering, or a group of former fraternity brothers who play softball or three-on-three basketball in a city league.

Even the rough analogy between a contemporary city league softball or basketball team and the Knickerbockers breaks down, however, because, oddly, the Knickerbockers for years weren't especially interested in outside competition. They played among themselves, usually on Mondays and Thursdays, for "exercise and enjoyment," as one of the original club members recalled it. "Once there [at the Elysian Fields] we were free from all restraint, and throwing off our coats we played until it was too dark to see any longer."

On a less Elysian note, we should remember that the Knickerbockers were a very exclusive club, a "voluntary association of sober, respectable Yankees" with a stern and irrevocable blackball system in place and set ideas as to the sort of member they wanted in their club. As well, the club had its share of internal conflicts. There seems to have been a distinct lack of enthusiasm for the athletic part of the program among certain Knickerbockers. Rounding up enough members to play a proper game was a constant struggle.

The attendance problem might have been a function of the Knickerbockers' odd attitude. Certainly, at the time of the club's inception, intrasquad games made some sense: there were effectively no other clubs against whom they could play. But this was soon to change. By the early 1850s, there were dozens and probably scores of clubs in the greater New York metropolitan area, each with ever more distinctive uniforms and names: Gothams, Eagles, Eckfords, Excelsiors, Atlantics, Eagles. The Knickerbockers, though, were slow to adapt to the idea of playing others. Instead, they divided their own membership into teams according to an elaborate system of attributes including social rank, athletic ability and, possibly, general affability. This system—an unstable melange of democracy, oligarchy, meritocracy, and popularity—was as unworkable as having new military recruits line up alphabetically by height. In a profound way, the Knickerbockers, it seems, were trying to have the best of both worlds: competition and cooperation. The center could not hold for long.

Inevitably, some clubs in the area began challenging each other to games. While the primary emphasis was still on sociability—invitations sent by mail, the host team treating the visitors to a post-game feast—little by little, actually very quickly, bragging rights became more important to many club members than mere sociability. The relatively jovial intraclub competitions gave way to less jovial, less decorous interclub competitions, which would, in turn, give way to full-pitched, rancorous games, no-holds-barred recruiting of players both above and under the table, barely covert shamateurism, and finally a dramatic split between amateurs and fully acknowledged professionals with high-stakes battles within each category.

As the number of baseball clubs increased, so did their entrance requirements—it was baseball's first real specialization. For example, the Eckfords were made up of shipbuilders. Though the Knickerbockers, of course, were exclusive in their own right, this new trend of "nonexclusive exclusivity" must have appalled the original members, those leisurely hobbyists, as thoroughly as William Faulkner's Snopeses appalled the Sartorises.

Robert F. Burk, in *Never Just a Game*, posits that this shift in membership philosophy can be seen as a response to two strong winds sweeping the country at the time: the first being what Burk calls a "softening" of traditional Protestant belief in predestination. That is, "success" and "status" (and therefore easier entrance into heaven), instead of being foreordained, could be acquired—or lost—or at least verified. Winning baseball games, clearly, was one indicator, albeit minor, of one's success and earthly status in the eyes of God.

The second wind, as Burke sees it, was secular. The "business" world was rapidly becoming more complex and cutthroat and sophisticated. Old-line "Yankees"—such as the original Knickerbockers—felt threatened by upstart industries and trades dominated by, as they saw them, opportunists from the "lower orders" (i.e., non-old-line Yankeees). These lower orders—whether they be immigrants or merely ambitious, less established Yankees—saw success on the ball field as an opportunity to gain entrance into that older, more established order. If, however, despite diamond success, entrance was not granted, the upstarts could still praise themselves and ridicule, and eventually ignore, the athletically inferior establishment.

This analysis is fascinating and entirely plausible. It seems somewhat overdrawn, however, as insight into how antebellum men actually felt about playing baseball. What was basically happening in the fifteen or so years before the Civil War began was this: a long-popular children's game—easy to learn, cheap to play, and great fun—had become popular with adults. The adults, with more resources, could play the game in places beyond their own backyards, places dedicated to the game. They also found that baseball was more fun—then, as now—to play competitively. Club championships are fun. Open city championships are more fun. Head-to-head series with the boys from the next village, the next town, the next city, the next county, the next state, are even more fun.

Homo ludens (playing man): what we are. *Homo agonistes* (competing man): what we are more.

Baseball spread across America like the smell of fresh-baked bread. By 1856 the most serious New York metropolitan teams played fifty-three-game seasons lasting from March to November. There were at least fifty teams in Manhattan, as well as another sixty youth clubs. By 1859, there were 130 teams in New Jersey, including 78 in Newark and Jersey City alone. In 1858, 1,500 people paid a hefty fifty cents each (a good part of a laborer's daily wage) to watch a game between New York and Brooklyn played on a Long Island race track.

Policemen formed teams. Firemen formed teams. Bartenders formed teams. Dairymen formed teams. Schoolteachers formed teams. Physicians formed teams. There were junior teams and teams in Syracuse, Albany, Buffalo, Philadelphia, Washington, D.C., Detroit, San Francisco, Los Angeles, New Orleans, Minnesota, Maine, and the Oregon Territory. (New England proper was playing a variation of baseball—the "Massachusetts" game—that still allowed, among other differences, "soaking." The Massachusetts version withered away.)

The Civil War generally spread baseball's gospel. The United States Sanitary Commission sanctioned the game, seeing it as a morale booster. Idle soldiers (of both armies) as well as their prisoners of war played the game whenever possible. Though sometimes the war's part in the diffusion of baseball is overstated, it takes little imagination to see how, after the fighting, as men returned home, or, more importantly, veered off to parts west for fortune and adventure, they would have brought baseball with them.

After the war's end, the game's glowing embers blew into a high flame. Allopaths played homeopaths; fat men (Jumbos) played lean men (Shadows) in Sharpsburg, Pennsylvania; bachelors played benedicts; maidens played "matrons." Yale University and other colleges played professional teams; the *New York Herald* played the *New York World*; New York bartenders played Providence bartenders; New York post office clerks played Park National Bank clerks; lawyers played doctors in Mexico City; actors played actors; actresses played actresses; actors played lawyers; syrup brokers played sugar brokers; the Ku Klux Klan played "nine carpetbaggers" in Fayetteville, Tennessee. Soldiers played civilians; sailors played soldiers; baseball players played cricket against cricket players and cricket players played baseball against baseball players; telegraph operators played railroad accountants; railroads played other railroads.

People played games in lakes, with fielders in knee-deep water and the pitcher and batter standing waist-deep; people played on ice skates and roller skates and bicycles and horses and snowshoes; Chinese teams played each other; in California, Digger Indian clans played each other;

the Dolly Vardens—"artistically dressed ladies of color"—played each other in "red and white calico dresses of remarkable shortness"; Negro teams played other Negro teams.

In Macon, Georgia, white prisoners were put in a special room to watch ball games in adjoining fields. When people got married the headlines sometimes read that the couple had "doubled up"—like oxen or unlucky baserunners. In 1883, in Fort Wayne, two teams played a game under lights; two thousand Philadelphians watched a game played indoors in 1888; fifteen hundred people watched an 1883 game between blondes and brunettes. Women played women all the time, thereby allowing reporters to write things like "With the exception of a mouse, there is probably nothing more dangerous than a base-ball flying through the air directly at some unprotected girl."

By 1888 people were already playing old-timers' games, under the rules of 1868. In what may be the weirdest game of the century, two teams "made up entirely of maimed men" played each other: the Snorkeys (each with one arm) versus the Hoppers (each with one leg). The *New York Times* could not withhold its admiration for these men, pointing out that all the members of both nines, "excepting Fay, Connors, Cahan and Bogan," were married, with children.

People were constantly trying to improve the game. One man proposed that, instead of runs, the winning team should be determined by the total number of bases reached by each team. Another futile campaign—this one by the century's most famous baseball writer, Henry Chadwick (who was the general for the vanquished baseball-came-from-rounders army)—argued that, since players in those days tended to stay close to their respective bags, the presence of a shortstop made the field uneven. He suggested a second shortstop, between first and second base. Bats flattened on one side were popular for a while.

In 1885, one W. Williams wrote to the weekly newspaper *Sporting Life* with a list of his inventions, each of which, he insisted, would "transform" the game. One was a paper bat, which, Williams said, was "more durable, of greater diameter of batting surface, of less weight, more elastic, [had] more friction on the surface and [was] less affected by water" than any other bat manufactured in the country. His second idea was an electric scoreboard; his third, fourth, and fifth ideas were electric signal systems that would alert the umpire, without the slightest inaccuracy, whether a ball was in the strike zone, whether a pitcher stepped out of his box, and whether the runner or the ball reached first base first.

Newspapers began running scores and game reports of teams all over the country as well as those of local teams. Box scores, which existed as far back as the early years of the Knickerbockers, became more and more refined. There were weekly sporting papers: the *Spirit of the Times; Porter's Spirit of the Times; Wilke's Spirit of the Times;* the *New York Clipper; Sporting Life; The Sporting News,* and the *American Chronicle of Sports and Pastimes,* as well as annual baseball guides such as Beadle's *Dime Base-Ball Player,* instruction books, board games, and baseball cards.

There grew up a huge sporting goods industry. An avid fan could buy any of seven types of scorebooks from the Spalding Company alone, ranging in price from ten cents to $3.00. Bats ($.15–$1.00) came in polished and unpolished models, plain or oiled, trademarked or plain, in ash, cherry, basswood, willow, or ash-and-willow models, for boys or for men. Uniforms went for anywhere from $7 to $20. After they were invented in 1875, catchers' masks came on the market. Spalding's company alone offered eleven different grades of balls: all the way from the "Official League Ball" for $15 a dozen, down through the King of the Diamond, the Grand Duke, the Eureka, the Rattler, and the Boss, to the lowly Nickel ball.

People had great fun naming their teams, just as musicians have fun naming their bands. There were Live Oaks, Joyfuls, Mutuals, Athletics, Browns, Standards, Alerts, Ironside, Domestic, Defiance, Dauntless, Acmes, Resolutes, Actives, Swift Foot, Red Hots, Bum Stingers, Hell Busters, Pill-Garlics, Ne Plus Ultra, Monumental, Experts, Quicksteps, Crickets, Flyaway, and Redemptor. There were High Boys, Young America (also a slogan of the Democratic Party), Asteroid, Mentor, Forester, Dreadnaughts, Romance (of Rome, New York), Nameless, Lifeguard, Amateurs, Misfits, the Nine Orphans, Black Nines, Ebony Nines, Colored Mutuals, and Buckeyes. In 1883 there were more than one hundred different teams named the Oscar Wildes.

By 1857, many baseball people thought the sport needed some sort of organization to monitor and regulate the exponentially growing number of teams. In 1858, the Knickerbockers, Gothams, Empires, and Eagles called for all metropolitan area clubs to convene at the Gothams' Bowery headquarters. The twenty-two attending clubs formed the National Association of Base Ball Players (NABBP). (In reality most of the members were from the Northeast and most of those from greater New York City.) The NABBP had one lasting legacy: it standardized the long-popular Knickerbocker rules, with two important modifications. The first mandated that the winning squad, instead of being the first to score twenty-one "aces," was the one outscoring the other after nine innings. The second was adopted after years of acrimony. Known as the fly rule, it abolished the previous "boyish" rule whereby a fielder could put a batter out by catching the ball either on the fly or after one bounce. Beginning in 1865, balls, to be considered outs, had to be caught on the fly. (This argument harkened back to the country's mixed attitude toward England. If cricket players were manly enough to accept the fly rule, so, by God, were Americans.) Another NABBP rule forbade players from catching balls using their hats, while another decreed that "colored" teams—defined as those with even one "colored person" on the roster—were excluded from Association play.

The Association also felt the need to proscribe certain rituals and behavior. For example, it prohibited the traditional practice of post-game banquets, saying they had become nothing but coffer-crippling excuses for drunkenness and rowdy behavior. (Though unstated, it is highly probable that the old-line "Yankees" saw this rule as necessitated by the inclusion of "others," especially the Irish, in baseball circles.)

But three other Association rules are much more telling. Any player found "throwing" a game would be expelled from his club. If a player quit a team, he would have to cool his heels for a month before playing for another team. Finally, no player, under threat of expulsion, could be compensated "directly" for play.

What these last three rules—almost entirely unenforceable and generally ignored—show us is that only sixteen years after the Knickerbockers' formation, competition had become so intense that teams, individual players, and, evidently, fans, were resorting to "ungentlemanly" behavior. Wagers were being made, bribes were being offered (and taken), and mercenary behavior was not uncommon. The prime tenets of "club" membership were quickly fading.

The Civil War accelerated this departure from the old ways. While teams would have soon enough begun using overtly acquisitive means to win games, the fact that hundreds of thousands of young men were far away fighting left a dearth of first-rate players on the home front. Those civilian teams still active—and there were many—struggled desperately to field respectable nines. It wasn't as if the war had halted all recreation. In 1862, for example, a "select nine" (an all-star team) from Philadelphia played a series of games against teams from Newark and New York, with attendance reportedly as high as 15,000. "Closed grounds"—those that controlled attendance—were springing up. Sometimes the games were advertised as charity events or all-star games, but soon even this white lie—who was to say that the empresarios and players themselves were not worthy objects of charity?—was abandoned.

A young pitcher for the Excelsiors, Jim Creighton, is usually credited as being the first professional. This is as unprovable as many other baseball firsts, including two others credited to Creighton: that he was the first "fastball" pitcher and the first of a long and noble line of pitching fudgers—he snapped his wrist and bent his arm during a time when deliveries, underhand in those days, were supposed to be stiff-armed. The superbly talented and extremely popular Creighton was, however, hands down, baseball's first tragic hero. Playing in a late-season game in 1862, he hit a home run. John Chapman, the on-deck batter, heard something snap when Creighton connected. "My belt," Creighton assured him as he crossed the plate. Within a week, Creighton had died—probably of a ruptured spleen. He was twenty-one years old.

Another effect of the war—and it is easy to overstate this—pulled baseball backward in time toward the early days of social exclusivity, rather than forward into "open membership" on clubs. Generally, blue-collar workers were more likely to be fighting than their merchant-class or white-collar brothers—Union Civil War draft notices being, effectively, negotiable instruments. So, in contrast to the generally increasing baseball commercialism of the war years, some teams returned briefly to their more "gentlemanly," class-defined roots.

But this was a blip. As early as 1859, the *New York Clipper* pointed out, correctly, that the idea of "pure amateurism" had a "sniff of aristocratic odor" about it. With the return to relative societal normalcy after Appomattox, there was almost no chance of returning to "earlier standards of amateurism, ethnic and geographic homogeneity, and class stability" in the society of baseball.

Seven or eight first-line New York area clubs were estimated to have shared over $100,000 in gate receipts in 1868. One club alone, the Mutuals, had a reputed war chest of $15,000. The *New York Times* estimated there were over a thousand baseball clubs in America in 1869, and 40,000 people (reportedly) saw an intercity battle between the Brooklyn Atlantics and the Philadelphia Athletics in 1866. Even the sniffy Knickerbockers, their influence dramatically faded, began holding promotions, including, in 1867, a ladies' day.

With this postwar baseball explosion—there were many more available players, certainly, but there were also many more teams clamoring for players—the sport became a seller's market, with ballplayers the sellers. The postwar baseball situation—with its frantic, no-holds-barred scramble for players, the only brake on which was an ineffective NABBP—can be accurately likened to current big-time college athletics and its scramble for high school stars, with both situations vulnerable to the temptations of corner cutting: sinecures, phantom jobs, sundry perks, under-the-table money, and so on. In addition, most of the baseball players of the post–Civil War era—unlike current college athletes—didn't even bother paying lip service to any controlling organizational ethical guidelines. They felt they deserved pay for playing ball—just as a carpenter deserved pay for pounding nails—and said as much, boldly, bluntly, proudly, constantly.

Examples of amateur/professional melding abound during this era. Albert Spalding—who, ironically, would later spend much energy and money crushing players' rights as financial free agents, was, in 1867, at the beginning of his professional career, offered a sham grocery store job in Chicago. He received $40 a week—a handsome salary. His primary duty was playing for the Chicago Excelsiors. George Wright, who played briefly for the Washington Nationals, a team of government clerks, listed his office address as 238 Pennsylvania Avenue—the site of a public park. People received shoes, clothes, and food and lodging to play in games. Supposedly, Boss Tweed, whose team was the New York Mutuals, threw nearly $40,000 a year toward phantom jobs for his players. Play-for-pay had become widespread enough in the five years after the war that scholars have created an economic index for the profession. The estimated "average" amateur ballplayer in 1869 earned anywhere between $600 and $2,500 a year. Though the last figure is almost certainly too high, even the lower figure is higher than the annual wage of an unskilled or semiskilled worker of the time: about $400.

Another common practice of the period was a sort of moonlighting: players lent their services to as many teams as the respective schedules permitted. George Wright, ostensibly a Philadelphia Olympic in 1865, played at least one game for the New York Gothams under the name of Cohen. Cap Anson, probably the best-known player of the nineteenth century, and, along with Spalding, one of John Ward's most effective adversaries, once dyed his hair and darkened his skin in order to play for a second team—this in an obscure league in Iowa.

The drive to win occasionally stepped far beyond all bounds of propriety. Though the most famous incident of "hippodroming," or the throwing of games, was the Chicago White Sox scandal of 1919, the practice is documented as early as 1865, in a game between the Eckfords and the Mutuals. The most dramatic example of dishonest play in the nineteenth century occurred during the 1877 National League season. Louisville, with the pennant seemingly theirs for the taking, suddenly began to lose games with disturbing regularity. Four players, including George Hall, the Louisville captain and the League's home run leader, were found to have thrown games. The League president banned the players for life. The disgraced players' ringleader, Jim Devlin, a twenty-eight-year-old pitcher, repeatedly pleaded for mercy. He wrote to his friend and former fellow ballplayer Harry Wright:

> I Can assure you Harry that I was not Treated right and if Ever I
> can see you to tell you the Case you will say I am not to blame I
> am living from hand to mouth all winter I have not got a Stich of
> Clothing or has my wife and Child. . . . the Louisville People
> have made me what I am to day a Begger.

Devlin, a handsome, bush-mustached, slightly bug- and cross-eyed Philadelphian, finally found employment as a policeman in his home town. He died, leaving his family impoverished still, in 1883, at age thirty-four.

By 1868, though the NABBP had grown rapidly—there were well over two hundred clubs at that year's convention, representing nearly twenty states and the District of Columbia—its powers were waning. There was, simply, no way to stop the spreading contagion of professionalism. Many amateur teams, against their wishes but in order to pay expenses (as well as maintain their competitive self-respect), often had to schedule games, and split the gate, against the very teams that most blatantly thumbed their noses at the genteel amateurism expounded by the NABBP.

But one last nail had yet to be driven into the coffin of baseball amateurism. Although professionalism—shadow or otherwise—was widespread, there was still strong local and regional pride. Players hired themselves out, certainly, and moved from team to team, but for the most part, they did so locally—or at least regionally. In 1869, however, a group of Cincinnati enthusiasts, mainly wealthy businessmen, threw all pretense to the winds and hired themselves a professional team, the best that money could buy, no matter where its players hailed from. Only one player was a Cincinnati boy and only one other was not from the East. These Red Stockings were paid well—the salaries guaranteed by contract (another first) ranged from $800 to $1,400, with Richard Hurley, a substitute, receiving $600—and practiced regularly under the strict discipline of captain Harry Wright. In mid-March, the team embarked on a sixty-game barnstorming tour that lasted eight months and took them from Cincinnati to New York to San Francisco. The team played before mostly large and enthusiastic crowds. Although profits barely outpaced expenses, an audacious step toward unapologetic professionalism had been taken. When the team returned to Cincinnati—a day ahead of schedule—it did so to throngs of wildly cheering citizens.

Finally, at the 1870 NABBP convention, its amateur member clubs, numbering in the hundreds but dominated by a score of overtly professional clubs, "adjourned *sine die*." The following year, ten professional clubs formed a new organization: the National Association of Professional Base Ball Players. The amateur organization, sickly from birth, was mortally wounded. The professional group—soon known simply as the National Association (NA)—though plagued by severe organizational problems of its own, and lasting only five years before it fell victim in a financial coup, holds honors as America's first professional sports league.

During its half-decade of life, the unwieldy NA consisted of twenty-six teams representing seventeen cities. In addition to clubs representing true metropolises, such as the New York Mutuals, the Philadelphia Athletics, the Boston Red Stockings, and the Chicago White Stockings, there were teams from smaller cities, like the Middletown (Connecticut) Mansfields, the Elizabeth (New Jersey) Resolutes, the Troy (New York) Haymakers, the Fort Wayne (Indiana) Kekiongas, and the Keokuk (Iowa) Westerns. Of the twenty-six teams, only three—Philadelphia, Boston, and the New York Mutuals—played every year of the NA's existence. Eleven clubs failed to survive a single season. In 1875 the Westerns disbanded—one of six teams (out of thirteen) to do so that season—after winning only one of the thirteen games it played. (Boston, the same year, played eighty-two games.) In 1872, two teams from Washington, D.C., the Nationals and the Olympics, played only twenty games between them before disbanding. Things had become so unraveled that in 1874, Boston and Philadelphia, looking for some real money, packed up and left for a twenty-one-game barnstorming tour of England.

The NA's problems were several and severe. Primarily, there was an immense financial disparity between teams, which manifested itself in wildly disparate win–loss records, uninteresting championship races, and an ensuing lack of fan interest. Boston, for example, won four of the Association's five pennant races. In 1875, it finished nearly twenty games ahead of second-place Hartford. Boston's record that year was 71–8, while down in the dark, dark cellar—and only counting teams that played at least half the season—the Brooklyn Atlantics won only two of its forty-four games.

This disparity in funds and talent was a function of the NA's primary flaw: a misguided populism. The cost of joining the Association was minimal—ten dollars. Many teams that came up with the initial membership fee could not meet their running expenses, notably wages and travel, so, to minimize their losses, they simply dropped out of sight.

The NA was a rapidly sinking ship, and it is unlikely it would have remained afloat for more than another season or two if left to its own devices. Its formal demise, however, was hastened by William Hulbert, a Chicago coal dealer and stockbroker as well as fervent White Stocking fan (and stockholder). Hulbert, embarrassed by and weary of the middle-of-the-pack finishes of his NA team, set about buying a pennant winner. By playing on the hometown strings of Albert Spalding, he persuaded the star Boston pitcher to switch to Chicago at the end of the 1875 season.

Hulbert signed, as well, three other Boston players—Ross Barnes, Cal McVey, and Deacon White—and Cap Anson, a young and talented infielder playing for Philadelphia. The signings were covert affairs—they violated Association by-laws about mid-season contract signings with different teams—but soon became public. (Spalding and his teammates, to their credit, played their hearts out for their lame duck team. Spalding pitched in 55 of Boston's 71 wins.)

Though the NA was basically toothless, Hulbert's signings were so blatantly transgressive that the organization could not ignore them and threatened to suspend the five players for the 1876 season. Hulbert did not even deign to swat away the NA fly. Instead, he decided to organize a new league.

The other National Association team owners, sensing not only Hulbert's power and resolve, but the astuteness of his proposed business plan, fell in line almost immediately. (Legend has it that Hulbert called a January meeting of NA team backers and, once the magnates were in the conference room, locked the door "to prevent intrusions from without . . . [and] make it impossible for any . . . to leave until I have finished what I have to say.")

Hulbert's creation was the National League of Professional Base Ball Clubs. The shift from "Players" to "Clubs" is significant. Hulbert's new organization would not "depend on a flabby federation of players." Instead, it would be first and foremost a business, run by businessmen, for businessmen, with all the expertise and perspicacity that only businessmen, they felt, could offer.

Hulbert, an excellent businessman himself, ardently (and correctly) believed that his league was viable. As well, he correctly recognized that the basic problems of the NA had stemmed from a lack of muscle, of actual and centralized power.

His innovations were immediate and sound: each franchise would be granted exclusive territorial rights (following this, no League team could play a non-League team, even in an exhibition game, in another League city); only cities with populations of 75,000 or more would be eligible for franchises; League dues were $100 a year (ten times that of the Association); each team would play each of the others five times at home and five times away; the fielding of ineligible players—ringers and moonlighters—would cause a team to forfeit a game; visiting teams would earn 30 percent of gate receipts; each team was responsible for police protection at its home field; minimum admission, per gentlemen's agreement, was fifty cents (comparable to public lecture and theater ticket prices); and alcohol and gambling were prohibited in the stands. Applications for League membership would be voted on by other members, and two "nays" would be sufficient to turn an application down. (The voting procedure, as specified in the constitution, required the use of actual black and white balls.) Players couldn't sit in the stands and socialize during games. No games would be played on Sunday. The best team at the end of the season—to be determined by the highest winning percentage—would receive a pennant, worth not less than $100, which would be inscribed with the team name, the year, and the motto "Champion Base Ball Club of the United States."

Despite these rules and their mostly strict enforcement, the League's first few years would prove rocky ones. Halfway through the 1876 season, Philadelphia and New York (which played in Brooklyn)—the League's two biggest markets—decided, in NA fashion, not to make scheduled western road trips in order to save expenses. Hulbert—who had installed a figurehead president—caused them to be bounced from the League. (Neither city would return to the League fold until 1883.)

The next year saw the Louisville hippodroming scandal. Two of the four dishonest players were legitimate stars and popular with fans: the hapless Devlin, who was the six-team League's second best pitcher; and George Hall, a slick-fielding outfielder, team captain, and 1876 League home run king (with five). Nevertheless, Hulbert banned them for life and thus stamped League authority indelibly in the minds of the players and the public.

Nine

We Trust He Will Pause and Reconsider

AS CLEVER AS William Hulbert's business plan was, as convincing as his shows of authority, as clear his new organization's superiority to the NA, the National League of 1877 was still a wobbly affair, beset with start-up problems. The Cincinnati club was in such financial straits that it folded for half a week in mid-season. Cincinnati was not the only perishable franchise. Before the 1878 season began, three of the League's original teams—Hartford, St. Louis, and Louisville—folded. They were replaced by Providence, Indianapolis, and Milwaukee. The viability of big-city professional baseball was anything but assured.

Nor, far away in Williamsport, was that of John Ward, who, with the collapse of the Williamsport team, was faced with another major career decision: should he settle down, perhaps in Williamsport, and earn college tuition money in some traditional way or should he try to find another Williamsport, give professional baseball one more try?

All the evidence made baseball seem the riskier choice. As he noted years later, his early experiences with the sport had been "particularly unfortunate. . . . During my first ten weeks of professional play . . . I received only ten dollars." But to the seventeen-year-old with several small notches of athletic success—nicks really—on his belt, all the evidence was, compared with the beguiling song of possibility, little more than the drone of dreary lecturers on a fine spring afternoon. Ward, with little hesitation, decided to shy his castor into a much larger baseball ring. He boarded a train for Philadelphia to try out for the Athletics, a nine that, unlike any he had yet played for, was "composed entirely of professionals."

Ward's recollections of his pre-Philadelphia ballplaying, especially his first few weeks of "professional play" in Renovo and Williamsport, were not only disingenuously rueful—it had been, after all, Ward's decision alone to leave Renovo for the potentially greener fields of Williamsport—but, as well, not entirely truthful. During the summer of 1876, when he was playing for Lock Haven, neither he nor his team could fairly be described as amateur. The intense rivalries between towns, in the form of the success of their baseball teams, had led to very blurry lines between amateurism and professionalism (the very sort of behavior that had, ultimately, spelled the doom of the avowedly amateur NABBP, the culmination of what a baseball historian called the sport's "twilight era").

Town-team boosters—usually local businessmen—searched high and low for players that might improve their local nine's fortunes. These ringers were furiously recruited. Sometimes they were offered suspiciously high-paying jobs—as was the case with Albert Spalding—or out-and-out pay-for-play deals, like those Ward accepted in Renovo and Williamsport. (The motive for subterfuge, as in the case of the ghost-jobs, was that there was still enormous currency placed on "localism." A wage earner could be considered a home-grown or settled product.)

Lock Haven, in 1876, was no exception to the recruiting game—nor was it very interested in disguising the fact. The local paper, the *Clinton (County) Democrat*, was sprinkled with items about newly arrived players who clearly were overt professionals:

O. A. Brown, the new catcher . . . arrived. Last year he played for the Atlantics, a professional club.

Mr. Weston, the new pitcher . . . arrived last Monday. He formerly played with the Mohawks and Etnas of New York.

Many small-town teams would schedule games with teams from larger towns, teams that were avowedly professional. The two teams would, most often, come to some financial arrangement: either a guaranteed fee for the visitors or, as was becoming more popular, a split of the gate. (Sometimes the "gate" was acquired not at the ballpark entrance but by passing the hat.) Lock Haven, for example, not only played teams from neighboring towns such as Renovo, Williamsport, Sunbury, and Danville, but also teams from farther-away Chester, Altoona, and Harrisburg, Pennsylvania, and the Wilmington (Delaware) Quicksteps, which billed itself as the "Champion Amateur Club of the United States." (This and other titles were, in most instances, almost entirely unofficial, less earned designations than advertisements.)

For his part, Ward, the student, probably received some remuneration while playing in Lock Haven, at the very least, train fare, meal money, and pocket change. If Ward and Lock Haven were amphibious—playing partly for the fun and competition and partly for remuneration—local newspapers were as loath to admit their team's hypocrisy as they were eager to point out professionalism's cancerous presence in other "local" nines.

For example, when one "Bond," the Wilmington Quicksteps' catcher, signed with Lock Haven after the Quicksteps disbanded—a common occurrence for traveling professional teams—the Williamsport papers immediately decried Lock Haven as a team full of ringers. Not so fast, the *Clinton Democrat* replied. Williamsport was whining only because Bond had earlier spurned *its* offer of employment: "How is this for 'importing players for special games'?" cried the petulant *Democrat* from its perch atop the moral high ground.

In the end, however, Lock Haven was hoist with its own petard. In September 1876 Bond moved on to a Louisville team, which the *Democrat*—shocked, *shocked*—called a "professional outfit." "With all his good qualities," the paper went on, "[Bond] treated our boys with considerable disrespect . . . as there was an agreement between the two parties, which can be shown."

Ward's decision to try to climb the ladder of professional baseball was not, then, entirely frivolous. He had been brushing shoulders with professionals such as Bond for at least two seasons, and having more than incidental success in the process. He had, no doubt, listened to plenty of war stories told by these itinerant ballplayers and found his head spinning with visions of large, appreciative crowds, fat paychecks (or fatter than he had seen) and exotic city life. As well, even if he hadn't played and held his own against these men, he was not, in his athletic self-assessment, burdened with modesty: he had been, for several years, a star athlete, a local hero: the best or one of the best baseball players in central Pennsylvania.

Ward's reputation may well have preceded his appearance at college. By 1875, when he and his chums organized the Penn State baseball club and prepared the campus diamond—their inaugural game was a 28–20 loss to Milesburg—Ward was a pitcher, the most important and, arguably, difficult position on a baseball team.

As a pitcher, Ward holds a singular place in the school's annals: he became, in 1875, the first person in Penn State history to throw a curveball. In those days the curveball—"an inshoot with a perpendicular twist"—was a wondrous new invention, one whose origins are misty as a bayou dawn. There are nearly as many claims made about who threw history's first curve as there are convenience stores in South Carolina. There are, as well, scores of stories about demonstrations of the curve. The stories—as they appear in many local newspapers between the end of the Civil War and the early 1890s—are so similar they take on the aura of folk tales. Ward's version is no different.

There is a boastful man—he is always young—on one side, and a disbeliever (of some authority) on the other. The disbeliever challenges the boaster. Plans are made for a demonstration of the boaster's skill. In Ward's case the demonstration took place near Old Main and the prime disbeliever was one Professor Buckhout (who later would serve as secretary at the faculty meeting in which Ward was dismissed from school). The hurler places three stakes in the ground in a long straight line. He then stands at one end of the stakes while a catcher awaits at the other. The hurler—throwing underhand, as was the custom in those days— releases the ball, which winds its way from the first stake to the near side of the second stake, to the far side of the third stake before the catcher snags the ball. The crowd gasps, the boaster is cheered, the disbeliever eats crow, and nothing is ever the same on God's good earth.

Ward said he learned the curve from James Kelly, a catcher for Lock Haven, one summer when Ward was vacationing and playing ball at Lock Haven with his brother Charles. Ward recalls the year as 1876, but it may have been 1875. He evidently learned well. Kelly hailed from Brooklyn and had caught a few games for a curve pitcher at Princeton. That pitcher might have been Frank Henry, or it might have been Ed Davis, or it might have been J. M. "Mac" Mann, or it might have been J. W. Hageman. If it was Mann, he said he learned the curve from "Candy" Cummings, who in turn attributed his discovery to watching the flight of clam shells he would throw into the wind on long afternoons on the beach near his Brooklyn home.

Kelly could not curve the ball himself, but explained how it was done. Ward practiced and mastered the technique. One day, Tom Poorman, Lock Haven's regular pitcher, who would later play three years in the major leagues, was being bombed by the opposing team. Ward, who had been playing third base, stepped in as the "change" pitcher, what we today call a reliever. Poorman took Ward's place at third. With nothing to lose, Ward "started to try" his curve. It proved such a "startling success that thereafter my services were in demand."

When the Bellefonte *Democratic-Watchman* caught wind of Ward's account, which appeared in newspapers in 1897, three years after he retired from baseball, it could not let a mere firsthand account stand without contradiction. The paper, citing former members of a local team, the High Boys, reported that Ward had learned the curve not from Kelly, but another Lock Haven player, Frank Hutter. Hutter, the paper went on, learned it from a state senator named Wood, who had learned it from Mann.

The *Democratic-Watchman*'s revisionism is highly suspect, not only because of its reliance on twenty-year-old secondhand accounts, but because the paper, during Ward's teenage years, and for a good part of a decade beyond, willfully ignored baseball on every level—disdained it even, preferring to fill its local section with items like these from the edition of August 18, 1876:

> There was a Dunkard meeting last Sunday somewhere near Bellefonte. . . . We believe these peculiar people and the Mennonites are the same or nearly the same.

> Ephraim Caton, a venerable negro, died, week before last.

> There were several extensive drunks in town on Tuesday, but no special damage was done to anybody but the drinkers.

As charming as these notices are, Lock Haven's paper was generally much more lyrical in its reporting: "WARM" was the lead one late summer day in 1877:

> NIGHTS—cool.
> Berries are scarce.
> School began Monday morning.
> Trout fishing one week yet.
> Crops look well in this township.
> J. J. Cummings left for Cleveland, Ohio,
>   Monday, to be gone three or four weeks.

To the *Watchman*, baseball was frivolous, a novelty. Though it did occasionally print game reports at length, generally it could not care less:

> We lit upon a base ball match last Saturday afternoon about
> halfway between town and the farm of Gen. Beaver. The clubs
> were a Bellefonte nine and one from Valentine's works. We did
> not stay to see the game out and do not know which club won.
> (April 18, 1874)

Readers, evidently, expressed their anger at the lack of coverage. The paper, finally, made its policy official:

> To Base Ball Players:
> We have received reports of no less than ten games of base ball
> played in different parts of the county during the past week. To
> publish them all would be to give more space to such matters
> than any live newspaper can afford. To publish some and exclude
> the others would be favoritism, so we have concluded to publish
> none at all. (September 18, 1874)

Perhaps the most extraordinary example of the *Watchman's* noncoverage of baseball came county fair week in the autumn of 1876. The game in question was hardly some minor occasion—one of the teams was the college nine, with at least two local boys on it. As Ward recalled it:

We played . . . on the fair grounds . . . in the middle of the [race track oval]. . . . In those days the catcher had no protection in the way of gloves, mask, chest protector or shin guards, and in the first four or five innings [Ellis Orvis, the catcher,] was battered by foul tips to the limit of human endurance, after which many balls got by him; and as there was no back stop, he ran many miles chasing pass balls and wild pitches. No bird dog ever spent a busier afternoon.

But the *Watchman*, which covered the fair in great detail, beginning weeks in advance of the occasion, was concerned about everything *but* the game. Especially interesting to the paper was the promised balloon ascension by "Miss Lizzie Ihling, Queen of the Aeronauts." Miss Ihling, niece of the "celebrated Professor Wise," would ascend in her balloon, named *The Republic*, dressed as the Goddess of Liberty. Miss Ihling was not only well educated, but "quite handsome," so much so that

Mr. J. W. Gephart, whose duty it will be to show the young lady around, already begins to feel his heart palpitating more rapidly than usual. We predict that after "Wes" witnesses the fair young "Goddess of Liberty" go up, he will be "gone up" too.

The launch, as it turned out, was something of a letdown. Instead of *The Republic*, Miss Ihling, who turned out to be merely "very pleasant looking," ascended in *The Amazon*. For such a brave and wondrous event, Miss Ihling's departing words were disappointingly mundane: "Good-by Uncle! Good-by All." She began her ascent at two o'clock in the afternoon, waving a little flag as she rose.

The trouble with balloon flights as drama, of course, is that a balloon, soon after launching, disappears from sight. Alas, the last *Watchman* balloon dispatch fairly sags with anticlimax:

[Miss Ihling] alighted on Sheriff Kline's farm, a short distance below town [after reaching] a point centrally over the town.

Unable to contain its disappointment, the paper's coverage turns distinctly sour.

We are sorry to say that the Fair now in progress is not a success, the display being a very poor one and the weather wet and disagreeable. . . . We saw elegant potatoes, corn, beets, pumpkins, apples, grapes and that sort of thing, but everything was in small quantities and the shelves were miserably empty and forlorn-looking. . . . We noticed several beautiful and very fine sketches in India ink by Miss Woodward, entitled respectively "The Return of the Swallows," "The Crown of Thorns," and "Heavenly Light 'Mid Earthly Shadows." . . . We saw some fine poultry, a family of rabbits. . . . we noticed a couple of parlor organs, some stoves, sewing machines, Swartz's washing machines and various other implements.

If only the paper, instead of examining Miss Woodward's sketches, had watched the game. The fairgrounds were down by the glass plant—call it a mile from the courthouse, west across Spring Creek, north across the tracks of the Bellefonte & SnowShoe, and the narrow waters of Buffalo Run, then west again—in the area called Sunnyside. There, on a temporary diamond—surrounded not by the phaetons, five-glassed landaus, barouches, and Victorias that would, in a short time, line the outfield boundaries of America's largest cities to watch John Ward spin his magic, but workaday buckboards and drays—country people, in from Axemann, Pleasant Gap, Centre Hall, Potters Mills, Howard, and Boalsburg, avidly watched a game of base ball.

They had clopped along the dirt roads—their field work for the year all but finished—their rigs full of squirming, impatient children and poles and tent canvas and blankets and pots and pans and utensils and food, for many of them would spend a night or two away from home. They wanted to watch Miss Ihling, certainly, but . . . the game was the thing. Just ask the men, with their pipes and chaws and clandestine jugs of tangle-foot—this was something else entirely.

What a grand occasion for that small town in central Pennsylvania, just before things snapped shut for the winter! And what a thrill for the players! For John Ward it was his first bona fide showcase game—the first of many in his career. It may well have been the last he played with his college chums. It was, almost certainly, the last game he would play in his home town, for love or money or any reason, for more than fourteen years.

When he did return to play, in 1890, he would be the captain of one of America's best professional teams, and he would be one of the most admired men in all the country.

Not a peep, however, from the *Watchman* that autumn day in 1876. A few years later, as Ward's star rose over the nation, the paper would cheer Ward to the echo, calling him "intelligent, well educated, a great reader, and a close observer of men and things, of nature and of art," and

> straight and muscular and as active as a kitten, [he] often aston-
> ishes his friends by his athletic feats. He is courteous and
> pleasant . . . a good conversationalist. . . . After a few more sea-
> sons at base ball, we believe his intention is to devote himself to
> the study of law. Altogether he is an excellent and promising
> young man, and has a flattering future before him. (December 24,
> 1880)

Hindsight is a glorious thing. The paper's attitude was markedly different when, the summer of 1877, it found out that Ward had traveled to Philadelphia to try out his skills:

> Monte Ward, youngest son of the late lamented James and Ruth
> Ward, of this place, a young man of talent and whom we had
> hoped to see a scholar and statesman, perhaps, has become a
> hired base-ball pitcher. There is no reason why a base-ball
> pitcher should not eventually become a great man, but the
> chances, for Monte's sake, we are sorry to say, are against it. . . .
> we trust he will pause and reconsider. . . . Monte, quit it, and go
> to your books again. (July 13, 1877)

Ten

His Pitching Is Simply Immense

Of ward's possible motives for deciding to continue playing baseball—a love of the game, dreams of travel and adventure, and the need to prove himself a success (not only to himself, but also to the editor of the *Democratic-Watchman* and other prescribers of Ward's future)—the strongest was surely money. He was hardly starry-eyed about the chance for reward, however. Not only did he admit to "little confidence in my ability to succeed among such players [as he would face in Philadelphia]" but as well, he toed a deep line in the sand: "I had seen that baseball was lucrative only to players in the first class, and I concluded that if I could not get into that I would quit altogether."

Ward's recollection of his journey to Philadelphia, in "Notes of a Base-Ballist," is a well-crafted affair. About the time of the Williamsport nine's demise, he writes, he received a telegram from the Athletics offering him a tryout. Ward "could scarcely believe its genuineness. To be a member of such a club was a professional height to which [he] had never even aspired."

He borrowed train fare and arrived in Philadelphia hungry, exhausted, and beside himself with self-doubt, only to find that his debut would be immediate. The Athletics were scheduled to play an exhibition game that very afternoon with Hartford—a middle-of-the-pack team in the fledgling National League—at the Union Grounds in Brooklyn. (The Connecticut franchise was financially weak and felt they might attract larger crowds if they played their "home" games that year in populous Brooklyn.)

Hartford was a team whose players—or at least their reputations—were as familiar to Ward as the story of George Washington and his "little hatchet." Though he had never seen any of them, "the very mention of their names filled [him] with awe." After another train ride and a ferry hop, Ward took his place on the field to pitch against Hartford. If he did well, he realized, he would be "admitted to the brotherhood," but if he failed, he would go home again, "relegated," he wrote, "to the army of exploded 'phenomenons.' "

Ward neglects to relate the game's outcome—he lost 5–0 in front of 200 fans—concentrating instead on his own struggle. In the first inning, a batter hit a high pop-up. Ward stood under the cloudless sky, growing "light-hearted and faint" as the ball came "zigzagging down in such a way that at one moment there seemed to be a half-dozen of them and the next moment I couldn't see any of them." Despite the high sky and the heckling of some fans, he caught the ball, gained his confidence, and "played a fairly good game."

Ward's version of events is an engaging one. It is, however, contradicted by an account in the *Philadelphia Times*.

> Ward came to [Philadelphia and] fairly begged to be given a trial and the Athletic managers allowed him to come. They were to pay his expenses until August 1, for until then his powers as a pitcher could not be fairly tested, as no important games were to be played. For two weeks he bothered the amateur clubs [he pitched against] immensely, and began to have a very exalted opinion of himself. He then wanted to sign with the Athletic, and was offered $20 a week. . . . He pitched in but one important game—that with the Hartford . . . and was then knocked all over the park. His success so far has been with amateur clubs.

Ward was undoubtedly scared and broke on his arrival in Philadelphia. His assignment against Hartford was indeed a trial by fire. And he was, in fact, "knocked all over the park." (It could have been worse. The game was "one-sided and uninteresting as the Hartfords, after the 3rd inning, made no effort to add to their score.")

But Ward's pitching loss was hardly the disgrace the *Times* suggests. The Hartfords were a seasoned bunch and the game was not only Ward's first at that exalted level, it was against players whose batting strengths and weaknesses he knew nothing about.

The biggest discrepancy between the two accounts concerns the original contact between Ward and the Athletics. Did he arrive in town on his own and badger the team for a tryout or did they send him an unsolicited telegram?

Ward's version, as it continues, makes no mention of his against-amateurs-only success; nor does it mention any other Philadelphia team except the Athletics. He merely says that after a time in Philadelphia he traveled to Janesville, Wisconsin, to play with the local club there, the Mutuals. The *Times* story—corroborated by some game accounts and statistics—points to a messier, more self-serving Philadelphia tenure and exit.

> No sooner was the offer made [by the Athletics] than he hunted up the Philadelphia club manager and told them what had been tendered him, and the "Phillies" agreed to give him an extra $5 a week. He joined the nine, but his first week's salary was all that was paid, as the team was not in a very flush condition. Then he went around to the Athletics again and made several propositions, which were accepted. A time was appointed for him to sign and he agreed to be there. His verbal promise was given to play with the boys in gray. [However, the manager] being out of the city and unable to attach his name to the contract, Ward took advantage of it and agreed to play with Milwaukee.

Ward's Philadelphia career lasted nine games, six of them with the Athletics (they played 97 games that year, winning 66 of them) and three for the disorganized, short-lived Philadelphias. He played well: he pitched a three-hitter for the Athletics against the Philadelphias, highlighted by his "wonderful curve-pitching"; a fifteen-strikeout shutout of Germantown; a 10–4 win against Defiance; and, as a "Phillie," a 5–2 victory and a 3–0 loss against the Wilmington Quicksteps. His cumulative record was 7–2.

Though, as the *Times* noted, the victories came at the expense of "amateur" teams, word of Ward's ability and potential was evidently good enough to persuade the Milwaukee club—a high-flying member of a league called the International Association—to offer Ward a $75 advance and $20 a week. The Milwaukee offer, generous as it was, had been matched, or even bettered, by the Athletics. So why did Ward head west? All things being equal, Ward's wanderlust got the better of him: if travel was his dream, it was preferable to travel as a baseball player than as an itinerant strawberry salesman. But all things were not equal. Milwaukee was a solid club, both athletically (they would become part of the National League in 1878) and financially. The same was not true for the Athletics: as late as February 1878, there was no indication that the Athletics would be able to field a team for the season (they eventually did).

Ward never played for Milwaukee. Instead, he began playing with the Janesville, Wisconsin, Mutuals. While the Mutes were not of the same caliber as Milwaukee—most of their games were against other state teams for the Wisconsin championship—they were hardly slouches. Four members of their starting lineup eventually played major league baseball. Two of them, Ward and Doc Bushong, became fixtures in the National League, while the other two, John Shoupe and Frank Bliss, would accumulate only sixty-three at-bats between them. Ward had a .500 record pitching for the Mutes, 7–7. Two of his victories, though, were noteworthy: he pitched a five-hitter to beat Milwaukee 4–3 and, as well, stung the National League Chicago White Stockings.

The reason why Ward hooked up with Janesville and not Milwaukee is unclear. The latter may have felt Ward still needed seasoning, and made some kind of "loan" arrangement with Janesville. Milwaukee may have had second thoughts about disrupting a successful formula—they played .600 ball that summer of 1877—and instead of playing Ward, allowed him to go to Janesville. Another possibility is that Milwaukee wanted Ward on their bench as insurance, an arrangement Ward found unacceptable and rejected. There is one last possibility, that there never was an agreement with Milwaukee: either the *Times* misreported Ward's destination or Ward himself misled the paper.

Ward's Wisconsin baseball career lasted less than two months. Toward the end of September, the independent Buffalo Niagaras telegrammed Ward, offering him a position with the newly formed team—one so strong that it would join the National League in 1879. Ward replied, collect, with canny enthusiasm: "Been absent telegramme received on return today send fare and will [de]part immediately." William Barnie, the Buffalo business manager, quickly agreed to the bold youngster's terms, and on September 27 Ward wired Barnie his confirmation: "Can leave on next train three p.m."

Buffalo baseball supporters were trying hard to rekindle the city's enthusiasm for a professional team, a "predominant" team that would "represent the city in matches against the nines of other cities." The city, like most of America, was baseball mad—as early as 1867 more than one hundred teams, representing all levels of ability, played on local diamonds. But the glory days of Buffalo's top-line team—the Niagaras—were long past. The Niagaras had been formed in 1857 and for years had played competitively against other high-caliber teams. In 1868 it beat the generally acclaimed national champion Atlantic Club of Brooklyn, 19–5. But by 1871, things had changed. The *Buffalo Express* declared that

> The national game is not thriving [here]. The Queen City will
> have to go without a nine, or form a stock company and hire one.
> Meanwhile, the lawns are being rolled for croquet.

Though it took six years, a "stock company" was indeed formed and the newborn Buffalo team played its inaugural game on August 3, 1877, against Rochester. The game ended in a tie after ten innings, called on account of train time.

Ward played his first game with Buffalo—as an outfielder—on September 29. The club, and Ward, played nine more games before ending the season against Rochester on October 16. Ward pitched that game, losing 3–0. His Buffalo statistics were poor. He was 0–3 as a pitcher and batted a microscopic .192.

Ward returned to Janesville for the winter, where he worked for room and board as a boiler tender. It was a meager winter for the young man, who found himself broke at the end of the season, having "not yet learned the lesson of economy . . . [and squandering his money on] peanuts and gingerbread." He also spent the winter sending his résumé to various baseball teams—a common practice at the time (both teams and players advertised in local papers and the national sporting weeklies). His search was successful. The following spring, when the 1878 *Spalding's Official Base Ball Guide* came out, Ward was listed as the starting pitcher for one of the best-known and most financially successful teams outside of the National League: the Binghamton (New York) Crickets of the International Association.

The Crickets, or Chirpers, played three sorts of games: exhibitions, against any sort of team they could schedule, including National League teams; contests against other New York teams for the informal "state championship"; and games against other International Association teams. How many games they played—anywhere from 70 to over 100—depended on their business manager's cleverness. He was not, as it would turn out, very clever, for the Crickets folded within two months of opening day.

They began their season in late April with a long road trip: Auburn (New York), Syracuse, Utica, and Pittsfield. The Syracuse Stars bombed Ward, winning 11–1. They got twenty-two hits and "sent Ward's balls whizzing all over the field." He lost his second and third games, as well, before he notched a win. He pitched thirty games for the Crickets that summer, and though his win–loss record of 14–16 is, on first glance, hardly notable, it must be said that he was playing with a team that had had, over the winter, a big personnel turnover. If the 1878 players fielded badly, which they did, it was generally attributed to the fact that they were not, as yet, "accustomed to each other's play."

Though the people of Binghamton generally supported the team, greeting the players *en masse* whenever they returned from a road trip, local sportswriters did not share this enthusiasm. On June 3, after being defeated by the Tecumsehs, of London, Ontario, the Crickets were greeted by this story, in the *Binghamton Daily Democrat*, certainly one of the most metaphorically eclectic bits of sportswriting in history:

A WATERLOO FOR THE CRICKETS

It has come, and with more than expected violence, sweeping everything in its path. We refer to the tidal wave which the "Tecumsehs" sent sweeping over the weak little "Crickets" yesterday afternoon. The steady Warriors from Canada swooped down on them with all their might, and nine scalps hang dangling from their belts, and the whole nest of Crickets is a house of mourning. Nine times did the "Red Indians" give the war whoop as they passed over the plate, while not even the faintest sign of a cricket chirp was heard.

Clearly the reporter loved his work. Three days later he filed the following:

> There was but a fair attendance on the baseball grounds yesterday to witness the game between the Crickets and Buffalos, and those that the cold and windy weather kept away may be thankful that they were thereby saved the seeing of a game, which the Crickets could and should have won several times over. . . . [The Crickets got twelve hits to the Buffalos' six.] The Crickets' errors were unexcusable and disgraceful, and discreditable, [showing] a great lack of judgment and discretion or a lack of discipline. . . . They should not be allowed to disgust the patrons of the game by such exhibitions of carelessness. . . . The Crickets need discipline. . . . Ward's pitching is simply immense, but he cannot win games unless properly supported, and he deserves it and it should be given him.

In general, Ward's individual star rose as that of the Crickets plummeted. The *Binghamton Republican and Morning Times*, reporting a 14–6 Crickets loss to Rochester on June 8, excuses Ward completely, saying that Ward was "hit hard because he had to pitch slow to favor the beatup catchers." On June 13 Utica beat the Crickets 2–1, despite Ward's "very effective" pitching.

The next day, the "unreliable Crickets" were beaten again by Utica, 8–2, in front of the largest crowd of the season. The *Republican* was, once again, beside itself.

> [The crowd] saw as disgusting an attempt to play ball as can be well imagined. Such a fine exhibition of ball playing as was given by the ex-Crickets [playing for Utica] we should think would make their successors to the name hang their heads with shame, by contrast, and cause them to realize how perfectly unworthy

they are to pretend to uphold and sustain the prestige of the name. In using these strong terms of disapprobation, which we think is deserved, we claim, however, that there is strong individual ability in the club, but we think it is not utilized or worked to the best advantage. They have a pitcher, who, in our opinion, has few if any equals, but he is not supported as he must be to win.

By late June, the Association was beginning to fray. The Auburn (New York) team was rumored to be in financial straits. The Allegheny club disbanded, taking with it the money that had been advanced for guarantees. (The custom of the time was for clubs to require this "earnest money" of visiting teams to minimize the number of no-shows. Most teams were created when local residents created a "baseball company" and issued stock. Tickets were $.25. If attendance was insufficient to pay the bills, the stockholders reassessed themselves, or issued more stock. The Crickets' monthly expenses were about $800.)

The financial straits of the Association continued to worsen. In a scheduling mix-up, the Pittsfield club came to town to play the Crickets, who were in Syracuse playing the Stars. A fight broke out between the two teams' business managers over whose fault the mis-scheduling was, as the guilty party was responsible for the $50 guarantee.

The Crickets went on a road trip about this time, but something strange was going on. The *Republican,* whose reporter seemed to have been suffering from the same prose malady that infected the *Daily Democrat's* reporter, wrote the following:

Les Enfans Perdus!!

Strange rumors were rife throughout our streets last night. Consultations were held in low whispers which at times changed into angry denunciations. The question was—where are the Crickets? Are they in fact "Lost Children"? They left here a week ago in charge of a very strong and able bodied, and it was supposed, able minded manager. They have been heard from several times since with evidence of doing good work. But [for four days] not a word has come to us from them notwithstanding the party in charge was instructed to advise the managers here of their every movement. Is it possible that the "Red Indians" of Canada drove them into Lake Erie . . . or did the storm of Saturday wash them from off the face of the earth? Shall we never hear the chirp of the Crickets again—never witness again attempts to steal impossible bases—never see fair chances of victory fooled away for want of discretion? O answer us—let us not burst in ignorance—or disgust. We love the Crickets for the surprises they afford us, but that they should become like the lost tribes, is too great a surprise.

The mystery was never explained. The Crickets finally returned, and on June 28 they beat the "Red Indians" of Tecumseh before a tiny crowd, which the *Republican* blamed on poor play during the road trip and a general "feeling of indifference" among the citizens of Binghamton. Ward pitched a one-hitter, and again was "simply immense," striking out eight and hitting a "beautiful straight" (line drive) over second base.

The next day, June 29, the Crickets returned to their disappointing ways. Against Buffalo, on a sizzling afternoon, the home team bobbled the ball every chance it got.

> The hot weather seemed to weaken . . . the Crickets, while per contra it caused the Buffalos to tear up the ground fiercely and run over anything like a Cricket that stood in their way.
>
> What a pleasure to the friends of the game it would be to see Ward properly supported once.

Mercifully, the misery of the Binghamton faithful would be cut short, for on July 10 the *Morning Republican* printed the Crickets' obituary.

> The Cricket base ball club has gone the way of three or four other International Association teams. . . . Yesterday morning the nine was broken up and the players granted their releases, which they were very ready to accept. . . . The reason given is lack of support. [Home game attendance] was not paying, as a rule, neither were the receipts on trips. . . .
>
> Several of the nine are secured for their pay, while others have from one to five weeks' wages due. . . . The latter offer to release

the [IA from all salary claims] if it will pay their bills about
town. . . . Most of the players can secure engagements elsewhere.
Ward will probably go to Syracuse or Rochester.

In fact, Ward's next engagement would be with neither Syracuse nor
Rochester. Instead he was engaged by the Providence Grays of the
National League.

Part II

All one day they played, that they might not miss their food.

—Herodotus,
History of the Persian Wars, i, 94.

Eleven

A Genuine
Muffing Exhibition

THE MOST INTERESTING and eclectic American newspaper being published in 1878—the year John Ward pitched his first game for a National League team against a National League team—was the *New York Clipper*, a sports and entertainment weekly published by Frank Queen. Though other sporting weeklies existed, only the *Clipper* served both actors and athletes. If a member of either profession needed news of his peculiarly swirling and itinerant world, the *Clipper* was the place to turn for news. The *Clipper* was nowhere nearly as lurid as the *National Police Gazette*, which also covered theater and sports, but whose primary enthusiasms were reserved for true crime and titillation. The *Clipper* was, however, much more informal and saucy than, say, *Harper's Weekly* or *Lippincott's* or *Cosmopolitan* or the daily papers—even the tabloids—which endlessly covered senatorial debates, political party shenanigans, and ongoing crises in such remote spots as Macedonia and Samoa. This is not to say that the *Clipper* turned its back entirely on non-sporting and nontheatrical news. Should a faithful reader feel it necessary to inform himself about a recent assassination or invasion or maritime disaster, he could always turn to the paper's brief "News of the Week Boiled Down," a section that, on a busy news week, sometimes took up half a column.

The *Clipper's* front page was dominated by a lithograph of a notable in the arts—Jenny Lind, say, or actress Helen Dauvray, or George C. Dobson—a "teacher of Banjo and Guitar"—or a famous soubrette or a leading man of opera bouffe. Often the lithograph would be accompanied by poetry or a serialized novel, the majority of them bad, and a good number of them epically so. For example, a front-page poem called "The Trage-dian's Soliloquy," written "expressly" for the paper by Edward E. Kidder, began like this:

> The audience had scattered far,
> Extinguished were the lights
> The actor in his dressing-room
> Sat peeling off his tights . . .

On the second page, members of the *Clipper* staff would answer general questions from readers, usually about show business. For brevity's sake the paper printed only answers:

1) H. H. Richmond—Apply to Brown & Barnes, dramatic agents, 854 Broadway, this city. Edward James, 90 Centre Street can supply the instruction books you desire.
2) Fire eating is a professional secret.
3) R. L. Jones—Yes.
4) J. P. Snead—He is traveling in the West.

The second page also included a list of people—usually actors and other theater folk, but also athletes—whose careers forced them to travel a lot and who had letters waiting at the newspaper's offices. The paper served as a maildrop. If someone was touring with a troupe through the Midwest, say, he could send a self-addressed stamped envelope to the *Clip-per;* the newspaper would forward the mail. The lists were divided into two categories: Ladies and Gentlemen.

The paper was thick with ads; the majority announced either the availability of performers or searches by theater managers and agents for performers.

Miss Nellie St. John, the Handsome and Dashing Balladist, advertised. So did Abdallah Ben Said's Celebrated Arab Troupe, and Mlle Adele, Mme. Bradbury, Mlle Azella, Mlle Lehman, and Mme De Corby, the Celebrated Equestriennes of the New Parisian Hippodrome.

Whallen's Buckingham Museum in Louisville, Kentucky, was looking for "Natural Freaks." Petrie and Fish, "The Original and Only Kranky Koons," let readers know they were "Home Again" after five years in Europe. The Alvin Joslin Comedy Company promised 180 laughs in 180 minutes, and The Imperial Russian Hussars were anxious to perform in your home town so you could experience a "marvel of Beauty," the two hundred yards of gold lace on each Hussar's uniform. John Robinson, impresario of John Robinson's Great Show, needed help: "I would like to hear," his ad read, "from Wild Australian Children, Wild Men of Borneo, Aztec Children and all other DESIRABLE CURIOSITIES."

A reader could buy sheet music, costumes, makeup, a Champion banjo—"the best . . . in the world," the necessary equipment to run faro games, billiard tables, billiard room noise subduers, and lots of lots of patent medicines—many of them offering cures for the "abuses of youth" and many more of them alcohol- or opiate-based. One ad, for "Tequila! Nature's Own Tonic," explained that the product would cure and prevent dyspepsia, indigestion, low spirits, general debility, muscular weakness, nervous exhaustion, loss of muscular power, tremulousness, sleeplessness, neuralgia, dizziness, and malarial poison. If one took these medicines too enthusiastically, however, other firms offered cures for "Opium and Morphine Habits—No pay till Cured." If, after being cured, a reader, flush with newfound energy, wished to embark on a new career, he could answer the ad offering a telegraph operator's instruction book for a dime.

If the actress Minnie Maddern's whereabouts were of concern, the astute reader could ascertain—from the *Clipper*'s formidably detailed itineraries—that she was scheduled to be in Fort Wayne, Indiana, from September 11 through the 15th and following that, in Huntington, Wabash, Logansport, Indianapolis, Grand Rapids, and Cincinnati. The curious would discover that Dion Boucicault had played in *The Shaughraun* and *The Colleen Bawn* the week before in Cleveland and that Seguin, Texas— population 1,800—had built a new opera house with a seating capacity of 400, a perfect place to go see The Human Fly: La Petite Aimee, Gymnast Extraordinaire! If it was the answer to why *Uncle Tom's Cabin* played to half-empty houses in Wichita one was looking for, one needed look no further than the *Clipper*: it was not because the production was flawed, or because Kansans were proslavery bigots, but because a fearfully sudden and violent snowstorm had paralyzed the city for most of a week.

Obituaries came under the regular heading "Death's Doings."

The sports pages included something for enthusiasts of all stripes: aquatics, cricket, shooting, billiards, chess, checkers, athletics (track and field), the turf, and especially baseball. In the aquatics section, one could find the results of the amateur rowing regatta that took place at Little Rock, Arkansas, on October 14, 1883. In the massive baseball section one could read—besides major league scores, game capsules, and gossipy tidbits—the outcome of games—amateur, collegiate, and professional—played anywhere in the country. Did Bozeman beat Helena, Montana, the week before? The Oscar Wildes the Excelsiors? The Eclipse the Stoutmen? Yale the New York Metropolitans? In the "Athletics" column, the news might be that at the Lawrence, Massachusetts, Caledonian games, William McLennan won the broadsword dance, James Flyn the hitch-and-kick, and William Robertson the sack race.

People were always cooking up challenges and announcing them in the *Clipper*. Daniel O'Leary, the famous pedestrian—yes, the same O'Leary who had a long-standing bet he could walk fifty miles in eight hours and who once conceded ten miles to the other walkers in a twenty-four-hour race—challenged all comers, for $1,000 each, to see who could walk one hundred miles the fastest.

About the same time, Wallace Ross, the "stalwart and skillful sculler of New Brunswick," let it be known that he would row against "any man in America" (with the exception of mighty Edward Hanlan) in shell-boats, over the distance of four or five miles, for the sum of $500 or $1,000.

The third week of July 1878, the week of John Ward's National League debut, was a busy one in America. The high surf at Coney Island did not daunt throngs of "surf-bathers," probably because it was so hot and humid in New York, with temperatures barely dipping below the 70-degree mark.

When people placed ads in the "Situations Wanted" section, they might describe themselves as single, young, respectable, and Protestant.

Out west, there had been an Indian uprising in Umatilla, Oregon. Near Bismarck, Dakota Territory, twelve Indians attacked one Cain, a mail-driver.

George Custer had been dead for only twenty-five months, and news-papers regularly referred to Indians as "savages."

The big news in the *Clipper* appeared in the "Trigger" section. Dr. W. F. Carver, the expert rifle marksman, had successfully broken 5,500 glass balls within 500 minutes. The good doctor had made his mark with nearly 42 minutes to spare, but "had his eyesight remained good . . . the number of missed balls (722) would have been undoubtedly much smaller."

The problem, it seems, was that the balls, one at a time, had been thrown aloft only twelve feet from Carver's weapon.

> . . . fragments of fine glass were constantly striking him in the face, and particles getting into his eyes, which from frequent rubbings became very much inflamed, and during the last three or four hours he suffered much from their condition. . . . As soon as the contest was concluded he was conveyed to his room in the hotel, and proper attention was given to his eyes, the inflamed state of which caused him loss of sleep during the night and acute suffering the following day.

Much of Illinois, Ohio, Indiana, Kentucky, and Tennessee was jellied with heat. *Coup de Soleil*, the headlines ran.

THE SUN'S DEATH-DEALING RAYS
*Fatal to Man and Beast in the Field,
the Workshop, and Street*

St. Louis was especially hard hit, reporting over fifty deaths from sun-stroke on July 15 alone—a toll that rose by the dozen daily for the best part of a week. In both Terre Haute and Vincennes, Indiana, it was 102 degrees in the shade, while in Indianapolis, "a perspiring citizen hung his instrument in the full glare of the sun and it marked 130 with ease." Mules and horses fell dead in the streets despite the best efforts of their owners to keep them cool—one popular treatment was to place water-soaked cab-bage leaves on their brows.

Cincinnati did not suffer as badly from the deadly heat as did St. Louis, but still, on July 15 it was dangerously hot: 90 degrees, equatorially humid, and still as a locked closet: "Now is the summer of our discontent," the *Cincinnati Enquirer* mused, "made glorious winter with crushed ice, mint, straws to show which way the wind blows, and a palm-leaf fan."

Under such conditions—as well as the fact that the two teams involved were generally unexciting middle-of-the-pack outfits—it is not at all surprising that only 517 people attended the 3 p.m. League game at the Avenue Grounds between Providence and Cincinnati. Still, the *Enquirer* pointed out, the game was of "unusual interest" because of the twin debuts of Cincinnati's Buttercup Dickerson in left field and "Providence's new pitcher, Ward."

Skinny, nervous John Ward—Wood, as the *Clipper* reported his name—was four months past his eighteenth birthday. For two hours and thirty minutes, he labored. Imagine the task! Shadeless, under the baking sun, hurling ball after ball toward hitters, racing down ground balls, backing up infielders' throws, all the while encased in long-sleeve cheviot.

Despite his best efforts in the noodling heat, Cincinnati tagged him for eleven hits. He threw three wild pitches and lost by four runs, 13–9. It was an ugly game, one of those games in which defensive sloppiness spreads like a contagion. Providence made 28 errors, Cincinnati 14. Lew Brown, the Providence catcher, accounted for 12 errors; Ward for another 7. (Brown's errors can, perhaps, be excused, as he was playing with no small amount of pain, having been hit in the nose by an early foul tip— "busted in the snoot chug" was how the *Cincinnati Enquirer* described the mishap.) The *Clipper* called the game a "genuine muffing exhibition." The *Providence Journal* agreed, calling the afternoon a "trial of the two clubs to exceed the other in the amount of errors" each could make. The *Enquirer* was more caustic, calling the contest "funny" and less a game than an "amusement." The crowd, the paper said, "cheered a good play whenever they could sift one out and identify it." Of the two debutantes, Dickerson "did very well." Ward's pitching was "pretty effective but too wild to be valuable," but his batting and baserunning were "very pretty."

Providence traveled 108 miles to Indianapolis after the game—either on the 6:40 p.m. Indianapolis, Cincinnati, and Lafayette local or the 7:00 express. Before 227 fans, Ward—still Wood in the *Clipper* box score— pitched again on July 16, hit a double, and began a successful double play. Providence won 4–2. Two days later, Ward shut out the Hoosiers 3–0. The *Providence Evening Press* declared that Ward "proved himself a puzzler [to

Indianapolis, who] declare him the best (or worst for them) pitcher they have faced this year." On the 20th, Ward again shut out the Hoosiers, this time 4–0, before fewer than 100 people.

On July 23, after nearly five weeks on the road, the Grays returned to Rhode Island and beat Milwaukee, 6–4, under clear, "delightful" skies and before an enthusiastic hometown crowd of 1,100 fans. Ward, said the *Journal*, "attracted marked attention, and after the first inning of the visitors, he could have counted numerous admirers among the spectators."

The *Evening Press* praised Ward's character: "One good thing about the lad is that he is not demoralized by a few safe hits."

Had there been such an award in 1878, Ward would certainly have been named Rookie of the Year. His final record was 22–13. His earned run average and his opponents' batting average were the lowest in the League for full-time pitchers. No pitcher allowed fewer hits per game than Ward. His winning percentage was the League's second highest. When Ward joined the Grays, they had been floundering in next-to-last place. By season's end they had climbed to third, eight games behind pennant winner Boston. But of all his first-year statistics, the most telling is this: Ward pitched six shutouts, only three fewer—in twenty-four fewer games—than Tommy Bond of Boston, the League leader.

In 1878 Providence was a first-year team, chosen by the National League to replace barely viable Hartford. The Grays had been quickly cobbled together. Their second baseman, Charlie Sweasy, who had played with the 1869 Red Stockings, was in his last year in the League, while the rest of the infield would see only four more years of League service—all of them undistinguished—among them.

Providence had pinned its faint 1878 pennant hopes on its pitchers: Tricky Nichols, who had won eighteen games the year before for St. Louis, and a promising rookie, Fred Corey. But Corey fell victim to an unspecified illness (he would eventually recover, but could only manage to win a couple of dozen games during the next seven seasons) and Nichols's arm dropped doornail dead soon into the season. Teams in those days carried only one primary pitcher, and perhaps a pair of understudies, who would either start a game in case of the primary's illness or injury or occasionally give the primary a day of rest. The understudies would also come in as relievers or "change" pitchers if the starting pitcher was ineffectual. Losing Nichols was a huge setback for Providence; losing both Nichols and Corey was an unmitigated disaster, since a team's third pitcher was often some position player competent only to mop up in lopsided games. While there is little doubt that Ward—who had already been mentioned as a curve-pitching "phenomenon" in the 1878 *Spalding's Official Base Ball Guide*—was a top-notch player, it was Providence's misfortune, and Binghamton's disbandment, that brought him to the National League one or perhaps two years earlier than might have been expected.

The next year, 1879, Providence won the League pennant thanks to three acquisitions—veterans Joe Start (first base), George Wright (shortstop), and Jim O'Rourke (outfield)—and Ward's League-dominating performance: he led all regular pitchers in wins (forty-seven), winning percentage (.712), strikeouts, and fewest hits allowed per game.

In September, the *Clipper* paid Ward high homage by printing his portrait alongside a short biography, which called him one of the "youngest and most promising players in the country," one who ranked "second to none at his position."

Moreover, Ward was immensely popular in Providence. The Grays' last game of the regular season came at home, against Boston, whom they pummelled 14–3. At one point, Colonel Henry B. Winship, the Grays' club secretary, halted the game and marched to the pitcher's box, where, with great fanfare, he presented Ward with a large "baseball" made of white blossoms. Then Winship turned to the crowd and announced that the floral arrangement came from "Ward's lady friends." Ward was speechless. He kept the beribboned flowers for years, not for sentiment's sake, but as a reminder, he told sportswriters, that "pride goeth before a fall."

It was a prophetic statement. The Grays, favored by many to repeat their championship play, instead finished second the next three seasons (the team itself dissolved forever after three more). Ward's pitching career would, after one more spectacular season, begin a four-year descent—gentle at first, steep at the end.

During the winter of 1879–1880, Ward and a few other ballplayers formed a picked nine to play exhibition games in the South over the winter—including a game in New Orleans against a Negro nine. The *Clipper* noted that the black players were a "little nervous," as no "colored team" had ever played in New Orleans against "their white brethren."

On his way back to Providence, Ward stopped by the *Clipper*'s Manhattan offices. It was the first instance of Ward's career-long courtship of the press. Ward's news was casual: he praised New Orleans for its hospitality and waxed optimistic about the Grays' chances to repeat the 1879 season's pennant run. The *Clipper* noted that Ward "looked in fine trim [and] splendid form and [was] going to make it troublesome for the opponents to earn runs from him."

The prediction was sound. In 1880, Ward pitched in 70 of Providence's 87 regular-season games. He won 39 of them and led all regular hurlers in both shutouts and earned run average. But the Providence bats developed holes. The team's collective batting average dropped 48 points from 1879, its slugging average 68. It finished a dismal fifteen games behind powerful Chicago.

There occurred, however, in the midst of the long, disappointing 1880 season, one extraordinary moment. On Thursday, June 17, owing to a time conflict with a popular local regatta, Providence moved up the starting time of its game with Buffalo from 3:30 p.m. to 11 a.m. Ward, who had beaten Buffalo 5–2 the day before, would pitch.

The Grays were expected to win, as Buffalo was a weak-hitting team—almost the worst in the League. Further, their leading hitter, Mike Moynahan, had been replaced at shortstop by Dennis Mack, whose batting average was 130 points below Moynahan's. On the other hand, the Grays could not just mail the victory in. The Buffalo pitcher was sophomore Pud Galvin—later John Ward's neighbor in the Hall of Fame—who had won thirty-seven games in 1879. The matchup was such that a large crowd—1,800—attended.

The wild card in this game was the starting time. Messer Field had been laid out for afternoon games. By virtue of the early start, batters would be staring into the morning summer sun.

Providence scored one run in the second inning, one in the fourth, and one each in the seventh, eighth, and ninth. Buffalo did not score any runs. John Ward had pitched a shutout.

Providence hit one double and three triples. Buffalo hit only five balls out of the infield.

Providence totaled thirteen hits. Buffalo had none. John Ward had pitched a no-hit game. No Buffalo runners reached first base. John Ward had retired twenty-seven Buffalo batters in a row.

According to the *Daily Journal:*

[The] admirers of the national sport . . . pronounced the fielding and the batting exhibition of the champions excellent in every respect, as not one of the players of the visiting club were able to secure a safe hit off of Ward's delivery, and not even [one man reached] the first bag without being put out.

The term "perfect game" had yet to be invented. It was, in fact, only the second such game in League history—oddly, the first had been pitched only five days earlier, by another young college boy, Worchester's J. Lee Richmond. There have been 169,565 regular-season major league games since opening day, 1871 through 1998. Only fourteen have been perfect: a frequency of one for every 12,111 games played.

After Ward's performance that morning in Providence, twenty-four years would pass before the next major league perfect game—pitched by Cy Young, for Boston of the American League—and *eighty-four* years before the next National League perfect game—pitched by Jim Bunning of Philadelphia on June 21, 1964.

Twelve

The Highland Fling

BASEBALL LORE comes to us like the ramblings of a charming, loquacious, insistent uncle. He rocks on the porch and tells stories that are, in turn, inspiring, bawdy, hearty, sad, sentimental, heroic, appalling, reassuring, alarming, and hilarious. Occasionally, they are even accurate.

The stories, however disparate, however truth-tussled, are underscored by a single assumption: that baseball, of all our sports, perhaps of all American institutions, is the one most impervious to change, a shining, exemplary constant in a compulsively shifting world. Transport an 1878 fan to today's Yankee Stadium and, within a couple of innings, after he finished blowing his mind at the size of the place, the price of beer and grub, the lights, the manicured field, and a thousand other mere details, he'd settle down, start keeping score, and root root root for the home team, recognizing its every move. So goes the Story of Baseball.

And Peter Minuit would recognize modern Battery Park, Orville and Wilbur Wright a Boeing 747, Henry Ford an Indy Car, or you your high school chemistry lab partner at the fiftieth class reunion.

Once, a fan was a "crank."

An inning was an "innings."

An innings was a hand.

A player was a hand.

A batter was a batsman.

A batter was a striker.

Once, games were won by the first team to reach twenty-one runs after an equal number of innings—be that number five, ten, or thirty.

Until 1863 it was not a written rule that a runner had to actually touch the bases.

For a very short time at the beginning of the 1882 season, players' uniforms indicated their position, not their team: everyone wore white pants and ties, but catchers wore scarlet shirts and caps, shortstops maroon, third basemen gray and white, and so forth. This agreement led to much on-field confusion, naturally, and remains the most addled-brained on-the-field experiment in the sport's history.

Once, any hit ball caught on a single bounce was an out. By 1878, Ward's first year in the National League, while fair balls had to be caught on the fly, foul balls caught after one bounce were still outs.

In 1887, a base on balls counted as a hit.

From 1878 through 1886, National League teams flipped a coin to decide who batted first.

Beginning in 1887, the home team got to choose whether to bat or to be in the field first. (Balls were so crude, and remained in play for so long, that it behooved a team to bat first, to get their initial licks on a "hard" ball, one that traveled well, before it became mushy. Gradually balls became better, and home teams invariably chose to bat last. Not until 1950, however, did the "home team bats last" custom become a rule.)

Before 1884 in the American Association (then a major league) and 1887 in the National League, if a pitch hit a batter, the ball was dead—the batter was not awarded first base.

For almost all of the nineteenth century, with the exception of one league and for one season—the Players' League in 1890—only rarely was there more than one umpire on the field per game. (Two-umpire games didn't become commonplace until 1909 or so.) Until the mid-1880s, an umpire stood, for the entire game, in foul territory in the vicinity of home plate, or behind the pitcher. By the late 1880s, following the lead of John Gaffney, umpires moved from one of those spots to another, depending on the game situation.

Until 1881, if an umpire felt like it, he could ask players and spectators their thoughts about a close play, and make his judgment accordingly.

A modern home plate is a five-sided slab of rubber. The side facing the pitcher is straight, the sides away from the pitcher come to a point: essentially the plate looks like a short pencil barrel tapering to its point. Until 1869, home plate was a circle. From 1869 through 1899 it was a twelve-inch square. Until the mid-1880s home plate was made of marble or stone, dangerous material into which to slide.

In 1871, "high-low" batting zones were introduced and were in effect through the 1886 season. During those years a batter told the pitcher in which of two zones he wanted pitches delivered. Essentially, he declared his own strike zone: "high" or "low." The high zone extended from the shoulders to above the belt (or waist, until 1877). The low zone extended from the belt (or waist) to above the knees.

If a pitcher didn't deliver a requested "high ball" in the high ball zone, or a requested "low ball" in the low ball zone, and the batter didn't swing, the pitch was declared an "Unfair ball." "Unfair balls" are known today simply as "balls."

In 1878, John Ward's rookie year, a batsman "walked" after receiving nine balls.

In 1880, a batsman walked after receiving eight balls.

In 1881 a batsman walked after receiving seven balls.

In 1884, a batsman walked after receiving six balls in the National League and seven in the American Association and the Union Association.

In 1886, a batsman walked after receiving seven balls in the National League and six in the American Association.

In 1887, a batsman walked after receiving five balls.

In 1889 and thereafter, a batsman walked after receiving four balls.

From 1876 through 1880—Ward's third year as a pitcher—if a batter had two strikes on him, and didn't swing at the next "fair" pitch, the umpire did not call him out. Instead, he gave him a "freebie," merely calling out a warning: "good ball." If, however, the batter swung and missed at the third "strike" or failed to swing at the "good ball" subsequent to the warning, he was called out on strikes. So it was one, two, three, or one, two, three, four strikes and you're out.

In 1881, the umpires' "good ball" warning was dropped.

In 1887, and in 1887 only, a strikeout required four strikes.

And on.

From the days of the Knickerbockers through the 1880 season—Ward's third—a pitcher could stand no closer than forty-five feet from home plate when he released the ball.

From the 1881 through 1884 season—John Ward's last as a pitcher—he was allowed to stand no closer than fifty feet from home plate when he released the ball.

Since 1893, pitchers have stood sixty feet six inches from home plate.

Since about that same year—no one knows for sure—pitchers have worked from atop a mound. The modern mound is ten inches high. Mounds did not exist during John Ward's day.

Modern pitchers work from a slab called the rubber. It is two feet wide and six inches deep. When a pitcher releases the ball, one of his feet must be touching the rubber. There was no rubber during John Ward's day. Instead, he had to deliver his pitches from within a "box," designated by four small wood or iron plates or chalk markings.

From 1869 through the 1878 season, the box was six feet square.

For the rest of Ward's pitching career, the box was four feet wide and six feet deep. Though there hasn't been a proper pitcher's box for 106 years, baseball terminology sometimes dies hard: if a pitcher is hit hard, he is "knocked out of the box."

But nineteenth-century pitching's most profound change concerned the act of pitching itself.

In 1878, Ward's rookie year, he had to stay in the box and, when pitching, keep his throwing hand below his waist.

In 1883, he had to stay in the box and, when pitching, keep his throwing hand below his shoulder.

In 1884, Ward's last as a pitcher, he had to stay in the box, but he could throw the ball any way he liked. The modern overhand throw had become legal.

In 1887, three years after Ward's last season as a pitcher, hurlers were restricted to taking only one step toward home when delivering a ball. But during Ward's pitching career, he and other hurlers had great leeway—twenty-four to thirty-six square feet of leeway—to accommodate whatever preliminaries to throwing the ball they felt most effective. Many observers thought these stylistics—run-ups and gyrations—excessive. The *Sporting News*, for one, thought the 1887 one-step rule a sound one, preventing pitchers from dancing the "Highland fling" with every throw.

Some men brought their arms back with a jerk before throwing; others were deceptively easy and graceful—economical. All in all, though, nineteenth-century pitching was something of a variety show. John Kirby, for example, faced his shortstop, spun on his left heel, and ran forward "with a grotesque sort of shuffle" before releasing the ball. Pete Conway faced third base (or first, or second, if those bases were occupied) and "executed his delivery while in the act of moving through the box." Dupee Shaw made "three or four preliminary flourishes with the arm, pumping the air industriously for a few seconds" before throwing. Moreover, between pitches, he indulged in a "great deal of scratching and pawing with both feet." Dan Casey, perhaps more than many other nineteenth-century pitchers, resembled a modern hurler. Casey, a southpaw, followed through on his "round-arm swing" with his body thrown "well forward" and his arm "extended at full length."

What about John Ward and his "remarkably puzzling" curve ball? What did he look like? Did he stand at the far rear right of the box and lope forward like a cricketer? Start at the back right and run diagonally to let the ball go at the front left corner? Start at the back line and run down the middle of the box, releasing the ball at the last second, like a ten-pin bowler at the fouling line? Did he "wind up" like some cartoon sandlot hero?

In fact, we know very little about Ward's pitching style. The most thorough extant description of his pitching style was written in 1928 by a Providence sportwriter three years after Ward's death and nearly forty-five years after Ward last pitched. His delivery was "peculiar. . . . He turned his back on the batter, faced second base, and, turning quickly, cut the ball loose toward the plate—at least when the bases were empty." Beginning with the 1879 season, pitchers, when delivering the ball, had to face the batter. The back-turning description of Ward refers to the 1878 season. Whether he continued his corkscrewing delivery thereafter is unknown. It is entirely possible he did, observing the letter, not the spirit of the face-the-batter rule, which did not specify how *long* a pitcher had to face the batter before delivery.

It also seems unlikely that Ward danced a highland fling—this maneuver was essentially a way of increasing velocity. Ward never, or rarely, relied on a fastball. He threw curves. If his delivery was "remarkably puzzling," his most effective pitch arrived with a "slow, gradually descending motion which completely mystifie[d] the batmen." He threw changes-of-pace. He was crafty, a thinker, a brain man, the professor. He noted strengths, weaknesses, and tendencies. He didn't (or couldn't) overpower batters, pitchers; he outwitted them.

In 1888, with his pitching career a half-decade behind him, Ward himself, in *Base-Ball: How to Become a Player*, shed some dim light on his pitching style and his attitude toward pitching. After a brief but adamant section in which he insists that a hurler's size is absolutely beside the point—"There are good pitchers of all sizes"—the grizzled twenty-eight-year-old veteran decries the current game, with its elimination of straight-arm pitching and newfangled allowances for such things as overhand pitching, which "place a premium on brute strength." Allowing that a pitcher must have some "speed" (and warning against the use of "too many different curves"), he sneers at

> so-called good professional players whose sole conception of
> [pitching] is to drive the ball through with all possible speed,
> while others whose skill and strategy have been proven by long
> service, are forced out of the position because they have not suffi-
> cient speed for the modern game.

More important, according to Ward, were endurance, "courage and self-control." A pitcher cannot let a fielding error or a lucky hit or any of the "little mishaps sure to occur in every game" divert his attention from the task at hand. Further, he must keep himself in excellent condition to withstand the withering effects of

> all day and all night rides from city to city, broken rest and hasty
> meals, bad cooking and changes of water and climate. . . . Only a
> good constitution, a vigorous digestion, the most careful habits,
> and lots of grit, will ever do it.

He then steps off his podium and discusses pitching in purely techni-cal terms: the importance of keeping the ball from the batter's sight until the last second; mixing up pitches; working out a signaling system with the catcher; keeping baserunners from taking long leads; noting batters' strengths and weaknesses through careful observation of stance, swing, and pitch preference; and being a good and alert fielder.

In conclusion, Ward returns to his central theme: that the best players are not necessarily brawny. Instead, they are possessed of wit, cleverness and psychic fortitude.

> There are some pitchers who are not hit hard and yet seldom win because they display such a lazy disposition, . . . that they put all the other players to sleep; and, again, there are others not so successful in the matter of base hits, who yet win more games, on account of the aggressive spirit they impart to their fellow-players. Let the pitcher be alive, then, and if he has any "heart" let him show it; let him keep up his spirits, have a reason for every ball pitched, and use his brain as well as his muscle, for it is only in this way that he can ever take a place in the front rank.

Thirteen

The Great Favorite

I F THE FANS in Providence loved Ward, so did the less easily impressed Boston and Providence sportswriters, who called him one of the "best general players in the country" and a "great favorite" of the baseball world. If Ward were to leave, said the *Sunday Star*, "no man of the nine, possibly except [outfielder Paul] Hines would be more missed by the Providence people." (There were, of course, exceptions to this adulation, such as an 1881 likening of Ward's fielding to a "kitten playing with Grandma's ball of yarn.")

But despite the praise of professional game watchers and the adoration of flower-bestowing fans, despite his stellar play during his first half-decade of National League baseball—including the breathtaking, if underrecognized, achievement of his perfect game, and the honor of being named team captain in June 1880—despite the headiness of the *Clipper's* kudos and his very healthy salary ($1,700 a year, more than five times that of an "average" American wage earner), and, finally, despite what must have been the rapidly lifting clouds of any guilt he might have felt about hastening his mother's death and being banished from Penn State, Ward's Providence years were not happy ones. In "Notes of a Base-Ballist" he all but dismisses his time there. "[In July 1878] I then went into the League with the Providence Club, where I remained till 1883" is the sum of his recollection of his Rhode Island years.

Four factors contributed to Ward's sourness—all of which had to do, ultimately, with the stunting of Ward's growing career and financial prospects. The least important reason for Ward's erasure of his Providence years was the memory of a brief, unsuccessful fling as an entrepreneur. Sometime in 1881, Ward purchased, from teammate Tom York, the Baseball Emporium, a sporting goods and tobacco shop located at 61 Dorrance Street, in central Providence. Ward moved the Emporium a few blocks to 75 Weybosset Street, but within a year, it had gone out of business.

Second, Ward had become convinced that he was surrounded by teammates who were bad apples, whose carousing and inattention to clean living kept the team—and Ward—from achieving anything approaching full potential. (This despite the Grays' 1879 pennant.) Ward's convictions in this regard were not entirely misplaced. The Providence team had quickly acquired a deserved reputation for excessive drinking, loutish behavior, and an informal attitude toward keeping in shape. (Ward was appointed team captain in June 1880. He was a disciplinarian, and his disgust with his charges' general flouting of his rules, and the general grousing his stern captaincy caused, likely led to his resignation from the position within a month.) In Ward's opinion, adherence to rigorous rules of fitness and sensible ones of moderation resulted in winning games. More than a few of his Providence teammates, however, felt differently. Two Providence players, Emil Gross and Lew Brown, were blacklisted for the 1882 season after charges of general dissipation and insubordination.

But the last straw occurred during an 1882 post-season exhibition series with Chicago. One night several Grays slipped out of their hotel rooms and caroused until dawn. Though the series went nine games, the Grays were badly outplayed, and many suspected that Chicago "relaxed" in order to stretch out the series and thereby increase each player's share of the gate. Ward, however, wanted to win, and had little desire to continue playing with unruly, shrugging, scofflaw teammates.

If Ward was at odds with the team personality, it was nothing compared to the growing anger he felt toward the Providence management. In "Notes of a Base-Ballist," Ward postulates that no player can, "with any credit to himself, play in the same club beyond a definite time. Three years is in most cases the limit."

Though Ward seems to be making a general rule here, it is difficult to believe him sincere. He had, by 1886, the year he wrote the *Lippincott's* article, seen scores and scores of exceptions to his three-year theory. A better interpretation is that he was speaking—with his usual indirection—specifically about his Providence experience.

The 1880 season was Ward's third in Providence. It was also the last in which he held center stage as a pitcher (for either the Grays or anyone else, as it would turn out) and also the last before he was, in his mind, thrown to the winds by Providence.

Despite Ward's wonderful 1880 performance—he was one of the three best pitchers in the League—Providence, stung by its distant second-place finish, decided to make drastic changes before the next season. Among these was a bold experiment: instead of relying on only one first-line pitcher, it would alternate between two.

Providence signed a relatively untried right-hander, Charles Radbourn, as Ward's pitching partner. Providence management's official thinking was this: two strong pitchers were better than one. If one man pitched every day, opponents would "become conversant" with his offerings; more importantly, an arm used half as much would be twice as fresh. Although the idea of expanded pitching staffs, rotations, and rested arms has been accepted baseball wisdom for a century, in 1881 it was novel, to say the least.

Ward must have been badly stung. He had, in 1880, won thirty-nine games—third most in the League—accounting for 75 percent of Providence's total victories. He ranked third among League pitchers in earned run average, winning percentage, complete games, fewest walks allowed per game, and lowest opponents' batting average. And as a show of thanks, he, a proven star, one of the brightest of the League's lights, was being asked to share the box with a rookie! Not just a rookie but one who also happened to be vain, profane, and immature. (Radbourn, in some team photos, not very slyly presents the photographer with an extended middle finger.) And where had this phenom gained his so-called reputation? Dubuque! Peoria! Indeed, in 1880, Radbourn had played a mere six League games, none of them as a pitcher, because of an injured shoulder!

"You're on next, John, after the dancing poodles."

Ward's bitterness, his sense of betrayal, increased over the years.

Although Radbourn did, in fact, become one of baseball's great pitchers, winning 309 games, including a record 59 one year, Providence's two-pitcher rationale proved temporary. In 1883, after Ward had left Providence, Radbourn pitched in seventy-six games—more than three-quarters of the Grays' total. In 1884, he pitched more than two-thirds of them. So much for rested arms.

But Ward had no choice, and share the pitching with Radbourn he did. In 1881, both Radbourn and Ward pitched more than 300 innings, but Radbourn's 25–11 record bettered Ward's of 18–18. (Ward, however, had a lower earned run average and more strikeouts than Radbourn.) Ward's future—at least his future with Providence—was clear, though: in 1881 he played more games as a position player—primarily in the outfield—than as a pitcher.

The following year, the pattern continued. Ward played 55 games in the outfield and pitched only 33, accumulating a 19–12 record. Radbourne, the same year, pitched in 55 games (going 33–20) and played the outfield in another 30 or so.

Ward never seemed to blame Radbourn personally for his displacement, and ironically, Radbourn was responsible for Ward's last record-book pitching triumph. On August 17, 1882, Radbourn, playing outfield behind Ward's pitching, hit a game-winning home run in the eighteenth inning against Detroit, breaking a 0–0 tie. The game remains the longest one-man shutout in history. Radbourn, by all accounts, despite a soaring opinion of himself, was a genial teammate and a fierce competitor—two assets Ward valued highly.

Ultimately, however, Radbourn's arrival worked in Ward's favor, for the furnace of his ambitions—regarding baseball and whatever post-baseball career he envisioned—was burning ever more brightly. After several seasons of mingling with other ballplayers on other teams, and traveling time and again to the various League cities—many of them more populous and exciting than Providence and many of them offering much greater professional opportunity—he had decided that not only did Providence the team not fit his personality and ambitions, but neither did Providence the city.

It wasn't that Providence was a "bad" baseball town. Providence then, as now, was in fact a good baseball town, filled with avid, knowledgeable fans. Providence was certainly large enough to support a National League team, and had a long baseball history. In addition to watching the Brown University nine—which had been playing as early as 1864—locals flocked to dozens of amateur and semiprofessional games of "town teams": the Providence Juniors, the Cranston Atlantics, industrial nines such as those sponsored by the Rhode Island Locomotive Works and the Providence Tool Company, and various others formed by militia units and ethnic social clubs.

So when Hartford's League team collapsed in 1877, boosters brought the franchise to Providence and set about building a 6,000-seat, state-of-the-art park—Messer Field, in Olneyville, a twenty-minute trolley ride from downtown. The trolley line connected prosperous suburbs with downtown, and, in a mutually profitable arrangement common in the nineteenth century, the company agreed to grade the field in exchange for rights to build a short spur directly to the park.

Management scheduled games to begin at 3:30, giving merchants and professionals an excuse to leave work early—3:30 was early, but not immorally so. There were special ten-cent bleacher seats. The Grays were heavily advertised and promoted, and newspapers covered the team enthusiastically, even posting telegraphically received scores of road games in their windows. As well, the Grays were certainly competitive, with one fourth-place finish, two thirds, and three seconds, in addition to pennants in 1879 and 1884. The team boasted stars such as Ward, Radbourn, and Paul Hines (in 1878 the League's first "triple-crown" winner—leader in batting average, home runs, and runs batted in). More importantly, there was a natural rivalry with Boston, which, Rhode Islanders believed, looked down its nose at Providence. All was in place for Providence's potential as a baseball showcase.

But Providence only fitfully supported the team. Games with Boston drew very well, and those fans who did attend games were avid, sometimes excessively so, but attendance figures over the life of the franchise—a very rough estimate would be 1,000–1,500 per game—rarely approached management expectations.

For example, on opening day of what would be a championship season, 1884, only 2,400 people were in the stands. In late August, against Chicago, a long-powerful team that fans loved to hate, fewer than 800 people attended. Toward the end of the same season, the *Providence Journal* predicted a crowd of 10,000 for a Saturday tilt against third-place Buffalo. (How they were going to fit into Messer was not discussed.) Fewer than one-third that number showed up.

Part of the reason for this lack of support was institutional: both the National League and local blue laws prohibited Sunday games. Since the average work week was five and one-half days long and many workers toiled six days a week, the sabbath ban effectively excluded Providence's large working class from attending games.

More importantly and less predictably, Providence's populace was slow to embrace the emerging concepts of urbanism and mercenary baseball. Providence had grown rapidly. It was a "city of strangers" who naturally gathered in smaller, more comprehensible, more familiar social units. Germans lived near Germans and considered themselves such, rather than Providencians. So did the Swedes, the Portuguese, the Cape Verdeans. Italians belonged to the Italian *Unione Benevolenza*, Germans to the turnverein athletic clubs. People lived not in "Providence" but on Federal Hill, or Smith Hill, or the East Side. They were carpenters, mill workers, union members.

These groups tended to support local teams—manned by their neighbors, their sons and fathers and uncles—instead of teams with players from San Francisco, Rochester, or Bellefonte, Pennsylvania. Town teams, at least the more important ones, regularly outdrew the Grays, and these "lesser" contests were a regular drain on the Grays' attendance. The best indicator of Providence's allegiances is this: frequently, the best-attended Grays games were exhibition contests against town teams.

This sputtering support, of course, led to the Grays' near-constant state of financial peril. The franchise rarely showed a profit. (After the championship 1879 season—one of its most financially successful—the team was $2,000 in the black, after receipts of $20,000. At least half the profit, however, was required to refurbish the field. Spin control is nothing new. Providence's press release to the *Clipper* said that the franchise had done so well that it could afford $1,000 in cosmetic improvements.)

At least once during Ward's days in Providence, stockholders were asked to subscribe money to make up season-end deficits. In 1880 the club released its players on October 11, after the season's end, but two weeks earlier than was customary. Teams generally played a series of exhibition games, either with natural rivals or against local teams or other League teams in non-League towns hungry to witness high-caliber ball. By releasing the players—which meant not paying them their last checks—the Grays bet, wisely, that they were not going to haul in any post-season profits. (It is not known if Ward, who was in the middle of a two-year contract, unusual in an era of single-season signings, demanded or received his last 1880 paycheck.)

This financial insecurity could not have amused Ward. Nor, as far as he could tell, did Providence's future look all that bright. In short, Ward began to feel he could do better elsewhere. He had played before huge crowds in Boston, Chicago, Philadelphia, and New York (a wild crowd of 5,000-plus saw the Grays play Chicago there in 1882). He was weary of being the big fish in Providence's small pond. Further, though not blinded by the bright lights of the major metropolises, he was very much attracted to them.

Bigger cities meant more fans. More fans meant more income for a baseball team. More income for a baseball team meant—presumably—higher individual salaries. Chats with players and, possibly, owners of other teams had convinced Ward that though Providence seemed to underappreciate him, other clubs would not.

Ward's restlessness was not a secret, and on October 9, 1882, he finally put to rest feverish speculation as to his whereabouts for the following season: he would not play for the New York Metropolitans, a powerful independent team that would soon join the upstart American Association; nor would he sign with Buffalo; nor the hated Bostons. It was understood he would not re-sign with the Grays.

Instead Ward signed with John Day's spanking new New York League team—the city had not had a National League franchise since 1876. John Ward, beginning with the 1883 season, would no longer be playing in the backwater of Rhode Island. Instead, he would be at center stage in America's largest city. Nor would he be paid a mere $1,700. His first-year New York salary was $3,100.

Fourteen

He Ran like a Deer

W
ARD'S 1883 NEW YORK team—they would not be known as "Giants" for several years—was, like 1878 Providence, an expansion team. It was cobbled together by the League in relative haste, in response to pressures exerted by the formation of a rival baseball league, the American Association.

This new organization had played its inaugural season in 1882. The Association, which would exist for ten seasons, was frisky—it halved the League's standard ticket price, to $.25, played Sunday ball, and, thanks in part to the influence of several beer baron owners, allowed alcohol to be sold in the stands, unlike the more temperance-minded League. The Association, lightly regarded by League magnates for the most part, had proved itself in its first year to be both popular and eminently viable, enough so, at least, to throw the fear of God into League officials and team owners.

The League reacted to the Association's threat—initially, at least—by creating an improved product and a streamlined organization. Among the most visible of the League's self-corrections was its decision to uproot its two weakest franchises—the small-market teams of Troy (New York) and Worcester (Massachusetts). The Worcester team moved, lock, stock, and barrel, to Philadelphia, the nation's second-largest market, while Troy was sold to two Manhattanites—John B. Day, a cigar manufacturer and Tammany politician, and Day's brother-in-law, Joseph Gordon. The two men already owned one team, the highly regarded independent New York Metropolitans. Day and Gordon took the bulk of the Troy team and distributed the players between their Manhattan holdings: the dimmer lights went to the Metropolitans, who would play in the Association in 1883, and the more established, proven, and promising players became part of the New York League team.

Four of the new New York players came from anemic Troy: catcher Buck Ewing, pitcher Mickey Welch, first baseman Roger Connor (whose lifetime home run record of 136 would be broken by Babe Ruth), and pitcher Tim Keefe. This quartet would, along with Ward, all eventually be inducted into the Hall of Fame. Unfortunately for New York, a baseball team consists of nine players, and the 1883 team would, after a promising start, finish sixth in the eight-team League.

Ward, though he had moved to an also-ran from a pennant contender, must have thought that he had died and gone to heaven, for, as he soon found out, whatever happened in New York (population about 2 million in 1880), including baseball, happened on a far grander scale than it did in homely Providence. Opening day of the 1883 season—May 1, twenty-three days before the formal opening of the Brooklyn Bridge—was no exception.

Day and Gordon had divided the area known as the Polo Grounds— then located at 110th Street between Fifth and Sixth Avenues, basically at the northeast corner of Central Park—into two fields divided by a low canvas fence, a temporary arrangement that allowed the Association Mets to play on the west half of the field and the League New Yorks on the east.

What a day May 1 was! The stands were filled with celebrities—Day and Gordon had sent out 1,000 invitations to "parties of note and influence"—among them the mayors of New York and Brooklyn, the aldermen of both cities, both the League and Association presidents, and the faculties of St. Johns, Manhattan College, Seton Hall, Columbia, Yale, Harvard, and Princeton. Further, the men had encouraged these luminaries to bring ladies with them. Ulysses S. Grant was in the grandstand, as was half of Wall Street and most of Tammany Hall. The Seventh Regiment Band—New York's favorite—entertained the crowd for a good hour before the game. The grandstand was packed with people, and hundreds of chairs had been placed out along the third- and first-base lines to accommodate the overflow. And way out there—beyond the far boundary of the outfield, roped off to keep the mad swarms from interfering with play—were banks of handsome private carriages and utilitarian four-in-hands filled with college students.

Is everyone in the city going to the game? No, of course not (certainly not those who couldn't manage to take Tuesday afternoon off), but it certainly seems that way. The Second, Third, and Sixth Avenue els are bursting—no matter the many extra sections ordered for the day. So are the omnibuses. A cab?—you might as well look for a stray giraffe as an empty hack! The chaos! It would be bad enough, but May 1 is also "relocation day"—the day that leases all over the city end. Dreaded warrants, with their two-hour warning of imminent eviction, fly like losing tickets at the race track. Everywhere are moving vans and chattel scattered in pitiful jackstraw ricks. The misery! The shrieks of the dispossessed—who knew there were so many languages on earth?—would melt Satan's heart, tax Milton's pen.

The traffic! Wagons wagons wagons wagons—unloading beer and halves of beef, vegetables, furniture, lumber, and coal. Casks, tanks, hampers, crates, cartons, bolts, bales. The screaming teamsters—Are they *all* drunk?—park where they like, for as long as they like. They drive up the boulevards' downside and down the boulevards' upside. Stay clear of them or be damned!

Dead horses lie in the streets. Dying horses snicker their last. Starving, hydrophobic dogs and crippled cats are everywhere. Steaming piles of horse shit, glistening, nostril-scorching fountains of horse piss. Livery stables—one every other block. Egg shells and coffee grounds. Mosquitos. Flies. Piles of ashes, piles of offal. Ponds of waste water. Thank God it isn't winter—then there'd be dunes of snow to add to the clutter. Beggars, con men, fruit and vegetable carts by the score. Is this New York or the Tangiers bazaar, for the love of Mike! Peddlers, rag men, tamale vendors, tinkers, newsboys, blade sharpeners blowing their horns; postmen blowing their whistles. Buskers, hucksters, beggars, addicts, cutpurses. The shivery scrape of iron wheels. There is no respite. Not even above. Damn Edison and his new generating plant. Damn the telegraph and the telephone: do they own the sky? The power poles are everywhere and their crossbars thick as tree branches: ten, a dozen, two dozen and more on a single pole!

Keep your eyes ahead—don't mind the belching, flatulent drunks staggering down the sidewalk. Don't be tempted by lottery notices, racing pools, or free lunches—the liquor or beer might come with knockout drops, also free of charge! Don't talk to that girl selling flowers: one syllable and she screams bloody murder that you made an indecent proposition—with her father and brother nearby. How convenient!

The baseball grounds are forever far, in another land altogether—but luckily upwind of the park's farms and shanty towns, the Irish squatters, the stink of the cows, goats, pigs.

At 3:30—the skies are partly cloudy, the temperature is 58 degrees—Boston takes the field for its fifteen-minute warm-up. Now they're gone and here come Our Boys! How dashing their uniforms—white pants and magenta blouses! They will show the world—they've beaten the Metropolitans eight games to one already—don't tell me those games don't count for something because they were only exhibitions!

There's S. M. Decker, the umpire. There's Buck Ewing and Burdock, the Boston captain. Burdock wins the toss and Boston takes the field. Buck Ewing strikes out. Big Roger Connor hits a triple to right. Here's handsome Johnny Ward, new from Providence, with his golden hair and trim mustache—doesn't he look the gentleman? He cracks a hard grounder to Sam Wise at short, who muffs it. Johnny has life and Connor scores. Hoorah! hoorah! The First Run in Franchise History!

Pat Gillespie gets a hit. Ward and Gillespie score on right fielder Mike Dorgan's single. Three to nothing and Boston hasn't even batted!

New York wins, 7–5. The pennant race is on.

Ward pitched the next day—don't tell *us* his arm is dead!—holding the beaneating bums to five hits. But that isn't the least of it, not by a long shot!

After eight and a half innings, the score was still 2–2. Connor hit a pop foul with one out, but Hines, the catcher, gave him life with an error. Then big Roger powdered the ball to deep center. Ohhh, they threw him out at home. Lord of mercy, Lord of sorrows. Two down. Things looked bad, boyo, terrible bad. Then Ward came to the plate. A foul pop-up. But Hines dropped it! Ward had life. Then he smacked one to left, over the fielder's head. Ward rounded first without thinking of stopping. There he went, around second, around third toward home. There was the throw. SAFE! A game-winning home run! In the bottom of the ninth! With two outs! The First Home Run in the History of the New York League team and the Polo Grounds Base Ball Field! He beat that throw by a whisker! He can fly! Oh that boy can fly!

The next afternoon, Ward came in from the field in the third inning to pitch for Welch, who was off his feed. And New York won again! Three in a row! Two in a row for Ward! He put Boston away like bugs in a bottle. He won his own game, again! In the bottom of the ninth. He got to first when the Boston pitcher, Whitney, dropped a pop fly. Then, with Connor on second, Gillespie hit a grounder. Boston forced Connor out at third, but clever Ward beat the throw to second. Then John Clapp—he won't last the season but his bat talked that day—hit one toward Radford in short right field. There went Ward, running like there was no tomorrow— that blue-eyed handsome man. He didn't even think of stopping at third! No—he kept flying toward home. GO JOHNNY! GO! Radford's throw home arrived late. New York 10, Boston 9! My heart can't take this!

Did you see the write-up in the *Clipper*? "Ward ran home like a deer— the ladies in the gallery said 'like a dear.' " Ha! That's rich! Like a deer? No, like a dear! There's a corker.

After New York's first victory, the crowd cheered and the regimental band struck up a modest number: "See the Conquering Heroes Come." Eventually, the "New York men retired to their quarters among the leaders in the championship race."

They held this position for much of a week. Unfortunately, the 1883 season was 106 games long and by October, New York had walked down the stairs toward the League cellar. (Even their sixth-place finish was something of a gift. New York fattened its 46–50 record by beating last-place Philadelphia 12 times in 14 games. The 1883 Philadelphias remain one of the worst teams ever to play major league baseball—they won only 17 games and lost 81.)

The 1883 season would prove to be Ward's last—essentially—as a pitcher. Although his record was a decent 16–12, he was, by even the most generous sort of statistical ranking, in the bottom quarter of the League's pitchers. In 1884, he would pitch in only nine games. He had become a position player.

Baseball annals are replete with players who start their careers at one position and move to another, or who, over the course of a career, help a team out in a variety of positions. Much less commonly a pitcher becomes a position player, or a position player becomes a pitcher, and almost never does it happen after the player has reached the major league level. Besides Ward and his teammate Tip O'Neil, the most famous exception is pitcher-outfielder Babe Ruth.

Ward saw his transition from pitcher to position player not as something to be proud of so much as something to rationalize. In a 1909 letter Ward indicated that his demise as a pitcher came as the result of a dramatic injury: "In 1884, I injured my shoulder so badly in sliding in Cleveland, Ohio, that I was never able to do much pitching afterwards, and it is painful to this day."

He was referring to New York's first series with Cleveland, the last week of June. The sliding injury makes for a tidy tale of hustle and self-sacrifice. Indeed, it has the well-turned sense of closure worthy of fiction. Ward might well have injured his arm in Cleveland, but well before 1884 it was generally known that his arm was in trouble. There was circumstantial evidence of it in Providence, and at least one report of chronic fatigue (or injury) during the 1883 season. *Sporting Life,* in April 1884, two months before the Cleveland incident, reported that "Ward's arm, which troubled him greatly last season, has already gone back on him."

Ward was a very careful man. He was careful with his money, he was careful about his physical condition, and he was careful, fastidious even, about his reputation. His sliding injury tale should be seen in the same light as his fabricated white lies about his exodus from college. Both tales are self-enhancing—leaving campus to play the game he loved is a more glorious infraction than stealing a chicken. Likewise, an arm going bad slowly through overuse, or more shamefully, an arm that could not adjust to changing pitching rules, makes not nearly the story a headlong baserunning dash does. Heroes throw coins across wide rivers. Heroes say "Damn the torpedoes; full speed ahead." Heroes rise to greatness from humble beginnings. Heroes are given a tryout in Philadelphia and their natural greatness is recognized; heroes do not whine and beg for tryouts and make nuisances of themselves.

Still, this particular lie—or self-delusion—about the "loss" of his arm is an odd choice, because the actual story of Ward's recovery and subsequent success is far more remarkable. Oddly, Ward treats the tale almost as an afterthought. After the sliding injury, he writes in *Base-Ball: How to Become a Player,* he began to play center field, where he learned to "throw left-handed." Then, after his arm had improved somewhat, thanks to inactivity, Ward moved to the infield and began throwing again with his right arm. Just like that.

Fifteen

Our Players

THE NATIONAL LEAGUE, for a good part of its first twenty-five years, was an entity beset by rival organizations—the American Association, the Union Association, and the Players' League—that threatened its hegemony. Further, it was characterized by plastic membership—a function, for the most part, of the wobbly, erratic financial status of individual franchises.

League membership varied from six teams to twelve. Twenty-one different cities, at one time or another, were League members. Hulbert expelled Philadelphia and New York—potentially the League's most lucrative and high-profile markets—after the 1876 season. Hartford and Louisville left. Cincinnati was, for years, on financial life support before it collapsed. Indianapolis, Milwaukee, and Providence joined the League. Milwaukee left, then Indianapolis. Buffalo, Syracuse, Cleveland, and Troy signed on in 1879. Syracuse dropped out before that season was over. Worcester came on board in 1880. Troy quit in 1882. So did Worcester. Cleveland vanished two years later. Buffalo and Providence disappeared the year after that. St. Louis dropped out, then returned. Indianapolis returned. Kansas City lasted one season. Washington played for four seasons, left for two, and returned for seven more. New York and Philadelphia returned to the fold in 1883, for good. Indianapolis disappeared again. Cincinnati reappeared.

For the better part of its first decade, the National League was a touch-and-go operation. In 1876, seven of the eight teams certainly lost money—front-runner Chicago being the exception. The 1877 season was to prove equally dismal: five of six teams finished in the red, led by St. Louis, which lost an estimated $8,000 on total expenditures of about $25,000.

Slowly things began to change. In 1881, Detroit, with $35,000 in gross receipts, managed a $7,000 profit. In 1882, Ward's last year with the club, Providence finally climbed into the black, with after-expense profits of nearly $7,000 on gross receipts just shy of $50,000.

Despite these success stories, it was not until the 1883 season that the League began to show real signs of general fiscal robustness. That year, all but two clubs showed a profit, with the exceptions, Detroit and Cleveland, losing only a couple of grand between them. Boston that same year raked in an astonishing $48,000 in profits. The next year, 1884, was, generally, even better—Philadelphia showed an end-of-year balance of $6,000, one that would nearly double the following year. The League described 1886 as "very profitable," and by the end of the decade, it trumpeted that its teams, between 1885 and 1889, had made a collective profit of nearly three-quarters of a million dollars. This was not necessarily a wise proclamation, because, as it would turn out, the players were listening closely. However, the League went on, its teams' profits were anything but excessive, as "eighty percent" of the sum was poured back into the business.

There were any number of reasons for the League's wobbly beginnings. Like other businesses, the various franchises had large start-up costs, not the least of which was building and improving their parks. Many teams' early investors were hobbyists, or merely opportunists. After throwing money into this strange, unpredictable enterprise, many of them got cold feet quickly. Shareholders got impatient—there were plenty of other opportunities to make money in the volatile but generally robust postbellum economy: manufacturing, steel, coal, shipping, insurance, dry goods, or lumber, for example. But baseball? What sort of animal was this?

Another contributing factor was the fact that the public, baseball crazy as it was, had to be wooed and educated to love professional baseball—at least that sort played by the League, whose rosters were filled by nonlocal mercenaries. People were accustomed to playing the game themselves, or—as in Providence's case—supporting local players. The idea of adopting a team of strangers, and indeed, the whole concept of a vertical talent structure—a "major league" whose level of play surpassed all others—had not been universally accepted.

Further, League magnates had embarked on a deliberate course to woo the "respectable" middle class—most notably by instituting the $.50 grandstand fee, refusing to play Sunday games (more specifically, they refused to campaign against blue laws prohibiting Sunday games in many cities), and banning alcohol sales. The League, then—by effectively excluding much of the working class—severely circumscribed the potential size of its daily gate.

Baseball owners and League officials, like good merchants anywhere, rolled up their sleeves and set to putting their business houses in order and improving their product. Many early rule changes, it can be argued, were attempts to calibrate pitching and hitting performance; fans lose interest quickly when one of these noticeably dominates over the course of a season.

Owners also began to reduce on overhead. Beginning with the 1878 season, they charged players $.50 a day for board on road trips and $30 a season for uniforms. Players were, as well, responsible for their own uniform laundering, replacement, and repair and for lost or damaged equipment. Arthur Soden, of Boston, was, by consensus, the most notoriously flinty-skinned of the owners. In the course of five years, Soden managed to cut his clubhouse maintenance by two-thirds: from $1,600 a year to $550. He also cut travel expenses by a similar percentage (probably by eschewing sleeping cars and better hotels).

The magnates didn't stop there. If we think of the owners as mayors of small towns, we can see another of their revenue-building schemes as the equivalent of setting up speed traps for their own citizens.

Owners began requiring players to take physical exams, on demand. The exams, performed by a team doctor, would determine a player's "fitness" for play. The players paid for these exams, but that was hardly the worst of it. Since players were not paid for injury- or sickness-caused inactivity, and since it was up to the team doctor, a team employee, to declare a player's fitness, the practice was ripe for abuse, especially if a team was not battling for a pennant or was facing a series with a team that was a poor draw.

This fledgling system quickly grew. Owner "concern" over players grew to include their minds and souls as well. Players—whose average salary in 1879 was about $1,400—began to be fined anywhere from $5 to $20 for such offenses as profanity. By the beginning of play in 1880 the League made the imposition of fines—heretofore the concern of individual clubs—official. The news appeared in that year's *Spalding's Official Base Ball Guide*—an annual compilation of rules, rule changes, League business meeting summaries, statistics, and standings. The Spalding sporting goods company, presided over by Albert Spalding, owner of the Chicago White Stockings, paid the League a fee in exchange for exclusive publishing rights.

"The League has no desire to cut down salaries," the *Guide* reported, in a section devoted to the proceedings of the League's annual meetings. "The highest interests of the game will be served rather by an increase than a reduction of salary expenses." But the League's intent was soon made clear. It had designed new rules so that each club could, without interference from the League, "exact from its players a more satisfactory equivalent for their salaries than has been the practice heretofore."

The rules themselves were announced in an "Address to Players" a few pages further on in the *Guide*. The "Address," ostensibly written by League president Hulbert, was most likely a Spalding/Hulbert collaboration. After hundreds of words reminding players that their individual behavior reflected directly upon the sport and the League as a whole, Hulbert explained the amended League constitution. Among other things, the new rules stated that a player could be suspended not only for the season during which a violation occurred, but for the "whole of the ensuing season, during which [he] is as absolutely shelved, disabled, annihilated . . . as though he had lost an arm or a leg."

Among the violations triggering such suspensions were "drunkenness, insubordination, or any dishonorable or disreputable conduct." Since these unilateral terms seemed vague even to the League, the Address annotated them, explaining that a player would be suspended from play "and from pay" when deemed by the club unable to play with the requisite skill by reason of illness, injury, insubordination, or misconduct of any kind; or, whenever he shall, by the Captain or Manager of the nine, be considered as *lacking in the zeal, willingness or physical condition necessary.* (italics added)

President Hulbert assured players they need not be concerned. They need only obey the code of conduct. Players soon enough found out that his assurance held true only as long as they didn't get sick or injured or even make an error (which reflected badly on their conduct). If they did happen to experience a lapse of judgment—throw to the wrong base, God forbid, or go 0 for 4 or walk in a winning run or muff a hard grounder between first and second—management had the right to simply blame the player for being out boozing the night before, or being out too late *not* boozing, and fine or suspend him. Fred Pfeffer, of Chicago, for example, was fined $100 in 1887 for a single misplay at first base. Another story, perhaps apocryphal, told of a player finishing the last five innings of a game with a broken wrist rather than forfeit his pay.

One of the more outrageous abuses of the "dishonorable conduct" clause came in 1889 when the Louisville owner, John Davidson, fined six of his players after a loss for playing poorly—and therefore exhibiting, evidently, a "lack of zeal" or "willingness." Davidson also threatened to fine them again if they lost the next afternoon. The team went on a brief wildcat strike. It was eventually revealed that Davidson, who had imposed something like $7,500 in fines that year, was in deep financial straits. The League ordered the players' fines rescinded.

But even the Louisville case pales beside the story of Ned Williamson, one of nineteenth-century baseball's most popular and well-liked players. In 1888, Albert Spalding organized a five-month barnstorming trip around the world—from November through March 1889. On the trip were two teams, the Spalding-owned Chicago White Stockings and a "picked nine," captained by Ward, the All-Americas.

In the beginning of March, the teams arrived in France. During the second inning of a game in Paris, played in cold and miserable conditions, Williamson drew a walk. While attempting to steal second, he tripped on the crude sand-and-gravel basebath and badly injured his knee.

Ned Williamson's given name was Edward Nagle. Born in Philadelphia in 1857, the husky infielder signed with Spalding's Chicagos in 1879 after playing for one year with Indianapolis and a couple of years in the Pennsylvania bush. He had lacquered hair, a pug nose, and bright, puckish eyes. Although hardly dissolute, he greatly enjoyed the company of cards and beer and like-minded teammates. He could not have been anything approaching dissolute, actually, because one of Spalding's requirements for his hand-picked tourists was that they be men of "clean habits and attractive personality, men who would reflect credit upon the country and the game." Williamson, by all accounts, was bright, affable, generous, and fun-loving. Although known as a fielder and not a terribly effective batter, he did swat 27 homers in 1884 (albeit over a very short right field fence), a mark that remained the major league season record until Babe Ruth hit 29 in 1919.

Almost everything about Williamson's life was charming and attractive. He had met his wife, Nettie, in New Orleans, where the White Stockings were playing off-season exhibition games in the early 1880s. Nettie, sitting with the wife of Ned's teammate, Silver Flint, saw Williamson come up to the plate. She vowed to throw flowers to him if he got a hit and won the game. He did and she did. The gallant, crowd-pleasing Ned picked the flowers up and doffed his cap to her. That night at dinner, he and Nettie were formally introduced. Though Nettie's mother disapproved of her daughter marrying a ballplayer, Nettie, an independent woman, felt otherwise and married Ned in June 1882.

Nettie, as it happened, was one of only a few wives to accompany the players on the world tour. When Ned fell writhing to the ground in Paris—it is impossible now to diagnose his injury exactly—she rushed him to the hospital, where, it was declared, a few days' rest would restore him. The prognosis proved wrong. He did manage to play one last game, in London—a game in which Spalding, whose memoirs never mention the original injury, praises Williamson's baserunning. Spalding recounts that after a Williamson dash, he, Spalding, turned to Edward, Prince of Wales, and asked, "What do you think of that!"

Williamson remained bedridden, in great pain, in a London hospital as the tourists played a final few games in Great Britain. He returned to America and began a long recovery. His knee finally healed sufficiently for him to take the field in August 1889. By that time, unsurprisingly, Williamson had lost several steps in his game (not to mention his "zeal") and it was clear that his light, if not extinguished, had dimmed considerably. He managed to play in only one-third of Chicago's games that year, batting a meager .237. He played one more year, retiring, at age thirty-one, after the 1890 season and buying into a saloon. Three years later, while visiting an Arkansas hot springs, he died of dropsy. (In the nineteenth century, dropsy was thought a disease. The term is obsolete today, and "dropsy" is understood to have been merely a symptom—excessive fluid retention in the tissues. Williamson probably died of kidney or liver disease.)

Spalding, on hearing of his death, wrote,

> I am sorry to hear of Williamson's death. He was a magnificent ball-player—the best, probably, all departments of the game considered, who ever lived. He was also a bright fellow and good-hearted. I have seen it stated that Williamson and I were "at outs"; so far as I was concerned that report was not correct.

It was probably fortunate for Spalding that Williamson was not alive to discuss their relationship publicly, because chances are excellent he would have disagreed quite strenuously.

Spalding, after Williamson's injury, not only deducted close to two-thirds ($800) of Williamson's 1889 salary—because he was not able to play—but charged him another $500 for Nettie's accrued world tour expenses. Ned and Nettie were responsible for medical expenses as well.

At the end of the tour, Spalding praised his own magnanimity by pointing out in bold letters that the tour cost him somewhere in the vicinity of $50,000. He added, somewhat more quietly, that gate receipts not only covered expenses, but turned a pretty profit. Perhaps the $1,300 he kept from the Williamsons helped.

Today Williamson is a footnote to the footnote that is nineteenth-century baseball, and Spalding's treatment of him a footnote to that footnote. If there was any lining to this cloud, it is that Williamson's treatment at the hands of Spalding served as tinder when the players turned their backs on the National League in 1890.

The ostensible reason for the Spalding/Hulbert crusade against carousing, slacking players—"a day's pay for a day's work"—was their assertion that drunkenness, gambling, and other evil behavior, by players and by fans, had played a large part in bringing the League's predecessor, the National Association, to ruin. Their insistence on player decorum and rectitude, on a rigid work code, would grow ever louder, eventually mutating into a code that centered on economic domination. Owners, Spalding and Hulbert felt, knew better than players, and if the players did not listen to their elders, they would have their allowances taken away.

The Spalding guidebooks, year after year, included a brief history of baseball and used boilerplate language to remind readers how corrupt and disreputable baseball had become before the National League had taken action—especially with regard to unruly players. The *Guides* credited the League and, to a lesser extent, team owners, with raising the game to a "higher degree of perfection," and included phrases such as "purification of the professional system" and "war upon crooks and knaves."

Spalding claimed that a sober player was worth two times the salary of a drinker. His Chicago team took a formal pledge to remain "bone-dry" during the season. When some of the White Stocking players fell from what one writer described as, for them, "dizzy summits of morality," Spalding hired a detective to birddog them. Other teams also hired detectives. Mike "King" Kelly, an outfielder/catcher for Cincinnati, Chicago, and Boston, was, in terms of fan popularity and general larger-than-life *bonhomie*, the nineteenth-century equivalent of Babe Ruth. When one of Spalding's operatives reported on yet another of Kelly's regular all-night binges, he included in his report the fact that Kelly had been spotted at 3 a.m.—long past curfew—drinking lemonade in a Chicago bar. Kelly, called on the line, was mightily offended at what he considered a damned lie. It was straight whiskey he'd been drinking, he told Spalding. "I never drank a lemonade at that hour in my life."

Though the Spalding *Guides*' lofty version of baseball history has to be considered overstatement, gambling (by players and fans) and dissolution (by players and fans) had indeed played a part in the systemic misadventure that had been the National Association. According to Spalding and Hulbert, the public—or at least the respectable middle-class public that the National League was trying to attract—would have little truck with paying good money to watch teams filled with drunken louts whose own interest in the outcome of the game might be mightily conflicted.

So, while the two men had a point, and it would be rash to discredit entirely the sincerity of their ceaseless moral crusade, one cannot discount financial motives behind their drumbeating.

Hulbert and Spalding were businessmen—modern businessmen for the times—and quick to realize, despite their pronouncements, that the National Association's "sinful" personality, its weakness for tolerating gambling and drinking, was only a symptom, not the cause, of its decline. What was needed, they felt—and what they created with the League— was an asylum run by vested authorities, not the inmates. Spalding had been a player himself, and many of his best friends were players. He prefaced his thoughts on the matter by saying that his opinion "carried with it no reflection whatever upon the business acumen or executive ability of ball players as individuals." He nonetheless believed, categorically, that "[no ballplayer] ever made a success of any other business while he was building up his reputation as an artist on the diamond." That is, players should play, and others would handle details such as salaries and working conditions.

What Spalding and Hulbert envisioned was nothing more or less than an industry built on the industrial model that was sweeping the country at the time. The new theory would be popularized after the turn of the century by Frederick Winslow Taylor in his *Principles of Scientific Management* (1914). Taylor had been obsessed with developing and perfecting a more efficient economic canon for decades before his book came out. His smug, beguiling book—reading Taylor is not unlike listening to a late-night infomercial, the sort whose soothing panacean confidence erases any niggling doubts—is best appreciated not as blueprint but as a summary of American industry during the last three decades of the nineteenth century.

At the time of the National League's formation in 1876, there was still in many industries a blurred line between management and labor, in part because most enterprises were small, the atmosphere informal, the workers (artisans) independent, the tasks—the making of a shoe or the joining of a cabinet—more or less the domain of the individual. Until the Civil War, a factory—except in certain industries, notably metal and textiles—was run more along the lines of what we would consider a small shop today.

Taylor—who prefaces his thoughts with the rosy prediction that all boats rise with the incoming tide—called for a formal separation of management and labor, of brain and brawn. Management would do "all work for which they are better fitted than the workmen, while in the past almost all of the work and the greater part of the responsibility were thrown upon the men." Management, Taylor shouted, not individual craftsmen, would decide work hours; management, and management's handmaidens, scientists, would decide the formula for cooking a batch of ore. Gone would be the crusty alchemist who threw a shovelful of this or that into a molten mixture. Management would keep records, including payrolls; management would designate specific tasks; devise new production techniques; create detailed work plans and quotas and delineate the quickest, surest way to perform even the least skilled task—unloading a boxcar, say, or shoveling slag.

The tasks themselves would become mere steps in a mechanized process, thanks to time-saving, labor-saving, money-saving machines and ever more precise division of tasks, all created by management's foresight and inventiveness. The examples of this transformation were evident everywhere. Philip Armour, of meatpacking fame, entered the business when the butchering process, beginning with live cattle on the hoof and ending with hanging halves at the corner meat market, was more or less an intimate, one workman–one steer affair. Armour transformed the industry, thanks to ranks of riflemen, hide-stripping machines, and mechanized overhead hook conveyors. In contrast to the glacial process of even a few years earlier, a mid-1880s gang of five at a model Armour plant could dress eighty cattle an hour. A decade later, the gang would be reduced to four, whose output was 160 dressed cattle an hour.

Southward, in late-1870s tobacco country, a skilled cigarette roller could produce 3,000 units daily. Within five years, a single rolling machine producing 70,000 cigarettes daily was the norm.

Accompanying this galloping modernization (and of course it was mechanization, not just adherence to Taylor's theories, that was responsible) was, in workers' eyes, dehumanization of labor. The transformation cut across nearly all existing craft and manual labor lines. Micro became macro, local became regional, and regional—with the help of railroads, whose track mileage would increase sixfold between 1870 and 1890— became national. The average American shop size, about six at the beginning of the Civil War, jumped to twenty in thirty years, with seventy-hand factories common in many industries—not including steel and textile plants, whose workers numbered in the several hundreds.

How this sea change must have excited Spalding, who instituted massive labor efficiencies in his rapidly expanding sporting goods factories. And how frustrated he must have become as he saw how resistant, how utterly defiant, professional baseball was to "Taylorism." Compared to other industries, the task of controlling baseball labor, of manipulating it, must have seemed to Spalding and team owners as difficult as pitchforking feathers.

Baseball's "product" is transitory, ephemeral, abstract. Baseball players' individual skills are certainly improvable, and the performance of individual players can be bettered, but the players' basic operations— throwing, catching, batting, running—can never be standardized or supplanted by new technology. They are, in their own way, as timeless as those of a farrier.

Further, in baseball, unlike, say, the steelmaking industry or the railroad-car manufacturing industry or the coalmining industry, labor cannot be easily manipulated. There can be no production lines, no production speedups; there is no threat of mechanization; there is no unlimited labor force waiting to replace quitting or striking workers (at least no labor force that will prove attractive to fans for very long). Baseball teams are, essentially, *al fresco* fifteen-to-thirty-man shops whose profitability not only depends on, but *is*, those men. Baseball's market niche (place in the standings) is absolutely dependent on, compared with the assembly line, unteachable, even atavistic skills.

But Spalding and the League could make headway in one area: micromanaging their workers' lives (both on and away from the "workplace") via the opening and closing of financial spigots. Baseball players were not, finally, immune to at least one ancillary effect of industrialization: a change from relative equality and independence among the workers to a system of strict workplace hierarchy.

What Spalding and Hulbert envisioned, à la Taylor, was to "separate the control of the executive management from the players and the playing of the game," an idea, Spalding said, that though "old as the hills" had never been tried inside the foul lines. To bolster this plan, Spalding continually pointed to the demise of the National Association as evidence "of the inability of ball players . . . to manage both ends of the Base Ball enterprise at the same time."

Baseball, Spalding went on, was "like every other form of business enterprise [and depends] on two interdependent divisions, the one to have absolute control and direction of the system, and the other to engage—always under the executive branch—the actual work of production."

If absolute control of the National League system was what Spalding wanted, absolute control—effectively—was what he got. The League constitution—from the beginning, and increasingly so with every year—was a despotic document, a jumbled mix of high-minded phraseology whose spectrum reached from paternalism to downright oppression.

The League was formed to "encourage, foster and elevate" the game of baseball; to make the playing of the game "respectable and honorable" and to "protect and promote the mutual interest of base ball clubs" as well as "professional base ball players." The chosen order of protectees is telling. In withdrawing from the National Association, the signatories noted that they hoped, with the formation of the League, to promote "harmony and good-fellowship *among ourselves* . . . and [protect] the interest of *our* players" (italics added).

The League was governed by a five-man board chosen by the owners (or their representatives) of member clubs. This same board—free of any sort of player representative or advocate—would hear all complaints, including those of players against their clubs. It would be the "sole tribunal" for any player "dismissed, expelled, or otherwise disciplined" by his team. The board's decisions would be "final and forever binding on both club and player."

Further, each club was empowered to "establish its own rules, and to discipline and punish its own players" as long as the rules and punishments did not contradict the constitution—which, handily, remained otherwise silent on the matter of constitutional violations, except for matters such as intercity games and roster raiding. In short, the document spelled out the powers and rights of owners and ignored those of players.

Players signed contracts with individual teams. If a player "jumped" his contract and played with another team, both the player and the signing team were blacklisted.

If a club decided to "release" a player from contract, which it could do with impunity, all it needed to do was notify the League secretary and testify in writing that the player had *not* been in some manner disreputable. However, if the club happened, by chance, not to so notify the League office, the League would have no choice but to assume the player had been "dismissed, discharged, or expelled." He would therefore be ineligible to play ever again in the League unless the board—the "sole tribunal" mentioned above—set aside his expulsion. Needless to say, this was a very effective way to get rid of troublemakers and, in good scientific managerial fashion, to keep the payroll lean.

Even if a player happened to be released "without imputation"—and was therefore eligible to play with another League club—he had to wait twenty days before signing another contract. Twenty days, of course, was more than enough time for clubs to collude, that is, settle among themselves not only which club might sign the player but also the player's worth, if any, to the signing club.

It was clearly a cozy situation for team owners, who had set up a virtual monopoly and exercised nearly complete control over their players.

Almost immediately after the League's formation, however, there appeared the first of what would be an ongoing series of outside threats to League control. The International Association (IA) was a group of non-League clubs, including three in Canada, that formed a thirteen-team league and began play in 1877. League and non-League players were wooed by the IA and a bidding war ensued between the two organizations. Officially, League salaries jumped by about 15 percent, clearly due to IA competition. Unofficially, players—no matter their suitors—reaped the benefit of "bonus money" and "winter advances," and a clever player could play off suitor teams against each other.

Unfortunately for the players, the IA, though initially viable, was badly governed and geographically splayed. It existed for only three seasons and was a threat to the League for only one. By 1878, League salaries had returned to their pre-IA levels (a development no doubt noted by 1878 League rookie John Ward). The League, to recoup its losses, began instituting fist-tightening policies. By the end of the 1879 season, Hulbert issued a forthright "State of the League" address:

> The season financially has been a little better than that of 1878
> but the expenses of many of the clubs have far exceeded their
> receipts.

The cost-cutting system expanded. Owners began to modify the "winter bonus" system that had become widespread during its brief skirmish with the International Association. Bonuses became advances and, in some cases, loans—offered at rates of 6–8 percent.

The League's financial state, according to Hulbert, stemmed from high salaries:

> The . . . results of the past season prove that salaries must come down. We believe that players in insisting upon exorbitant prices are injuring their own interests by forcing out of existence clubs which cannot be run and pay large salaries except at a large personal loss.

If salaries were a large expense—and they were—Hulbert was being disingenuous about their escalation. Salaries were not, in fact, growing. On average, they continued to drop for the next five years after 1877 to about 75 percent of even the pre-IA level—from about $1,700 to $1,300. They would not rise dramatically until the next League competitor, the American Association, began braying in the barnyard.

In reality—with the exception of the IA competition—the clubs' fiscal enemy came not from without, but from within; not from the players, but from the owners themselves. If players were reaping the benefits of bidding wars, these wars were internecine. Owners—then as now—fought each other for the services of star players and were in fact their own worst enemies. Moreover, this intra-League off-the-field, under-the-table competition was a seemingly incurable virus. Other leagues could be defeated, through wars of attrition or frontal assault, but owners found it impossible to tamp down their own ambitions.

Soon enough, however, the owners did discover what they felt was a cure: something called the reserve clause. But the clause would be merely a palliative, and one that caused century-long side effects, side effects that would alter the baseball industry forever.

Sixteen

The Aim of the League

ON SEPTEMBER 29, 1879, as the regular season drew to a close, the League's board of directors—that is, the team owners—met in extraordinary session at Pierce's Hotel in Buffalo, hoping to devise measures that would "work beneficially to the persons who risk their capital in the support of the sport."

The men came up with a system of player reservation—one that soon came to be known as the reserve clause. The clause—the central plank of the League's fiscal reform platform and likely the primary purpose of the meeting—was a profound, breathtaking bit of business, one, the owners suspected, so likely to anger players that its details were not immediately made public. Instead, Hulbert only referred to "measures [that had] been taken . . . to remedy the evil [of payroll excesses] to some extent for 1880."

The prototype reserve clause read as follows:

The undersigned . . . members of the National League . . . do hereby each with the other agree that in contracting with players for 1880 the players named below shall be assigned as follows:

Boston— Snyder, Bond, Burdock, O'Rourke, Sutton
Buffalo— Galvin, Clapp, Richardson, Crowley, Walker
Chicago— Williamson, Quest, Anson, Flint, Hankinson

Cleveland— McCormick, Kennedy, Glasscock, Richmond,
              Shaffer
Providence—Wright, Start, Hines, Ward, McGeary
Troy—   Evans, Caskins, Cassidy, Ferguson, Goldsmith

The said named players assigned above are to be considered and treated as members of their respective Clubs, meaning and intending here by that the men above as assigned shall be treated in all respects as players engaged and under regular contracts for the season of 1880, to the Clubs to whom they are assigned as above.

In other words, the thirty men named—generally those each team felt most valuable—suddenly were bound, for the upcoming season, to their current team, with no say as to their next year's employer. In essence the clause said that even if a player had signed only a one-year contract—for the 1879 season, say—those terms had been unilaterally changed. The League rolled over that 1879 contract to the following season.

The original clause applied to roughly one-third of each team's roster. But the owners recognized its enormous potential, and through the years expanded its perimeters. In 1883, the number of reserved players per team rose from five to eleven. In 1886, the number rose, per team, to an even dozen, and the following year, to fourteen—effectively an entire roster, since, on average, only sixteen men per team might play in more than ten games a season.

This contractual, unilateral labor lock, however, became even more wide-reaching and powerful. On its face, the clause seemed to apply for only a single subsequent season: should a player sit out that season—a bold and expensive move—he would then be free of the clause's reach and would be eligible to sign with another team desiring his services. That is, once again a "free agent," he could entertain bids from all teams and accept the most attractive.

This would not, however, turn out to be the case. Instead, the one-year rollover became perpetual and self-renewing. In 1887, eight years after the institution of the clause, for example, pitcher Jim McCormick—one of the original 1879 reservees—suffered a subpar season with Pittsburgh. Pittsburgh's offer to McCormick for the 1888 season included a pay cut. Insulted, McCormick chose to sit out the entire season, assuming he would then be able to sign on with a new team as a free agent. Pittsburgh, however, merely kept him on their reserve list. As Pittsburgh "property," he was effectively off limits to other teams. (It is likely McCormick was a victim of owner collusion; that is, they, as a group, "agreed" that Pittsburgh did indeed have a right to roll over his reserve status and they would not bid for his services. Other players, they guessed, would see the futility of actions like McCormick's. The stubborn McCormick, though only thirty-two in 1888, never played major league baseball again.)

In 1884, another player, Thomas Deasley, tried to sidestep the clause by signing a contract that included a reservation-exempt stipulation. The League held the stipulation invalid.

Even if a team "dropped" a player, he was not released from the clause. If, within ten days of the "drop," another club decided it wanted the player, the player was forced—if he wanted to play in the major leagues—to sign with that club.

In 1885, Michael Hines, a catcher for Providence, objected to being reserved. Providence, however, stuck to its reservation rights. Hines refused to recognize Providence's claim and sat out two entire seasons. In 1888 he finally relented, but managed to hang on with a new team, Boston, for only four days before he was cut from the roster. What makes the Hines case notable is the fact that Providence had gone out of business after the 1885 season. Hines, however, remained Providence's "property"—a salable asset of a nonexistent team.

The reserve clause, as the decades rolled on, spread to lower leagues. If, say, a player was toiling in the minor leagues, he was not—almost never, anyway—the property of that minor league team, but instead the property of the major league team that held his contract. (Sometimes the major league club owned and operated the minor league club as well.) This particular expansion of the reserve clause was extraordinarily unfair. Say a pitcher—a good major league prospect—was the property of a major league club that, though pitching-rich, wanted to keep the young player down in the high minors in case of an emergency, such as a roster-depleting injury on the major league club. The talented minor leaguer had two prospects, neither of which was in his power to bring about: he could be "sold" to another major league team that would use him; or he could remain in thrall to his original club, in minor league limbo. There remained a third course—the only one the player himself could choose: he could quit baseball.

During World War II, players who entered the service remained the property of their pre-military teams. The only exceptions to this took place if, say, while the player was otherwise busy machine-gunning Germans at the Bulge or recovering from wounds in a Solomon Islands field hospital, his original team sold or traded him elsewhere. Then, of course, he would become the "reserved" property of the new team.

Effectively, reserved players, beginning with the 1880 season, became tangible, absolutely secured assets, and their contracts became commodities, negotiable instruments on the baseball stock market. The reserve clause became—in the eyes of players, owners, and most fans—as inviolable as gravity, driving on the right side of the road, or measuring things in feet, pounds, and gallons.

The 1879 *Buffalo Commercial Advertiser* was upbeat about the new clause, saying it would "prevent unhealthy competition [among the clubs] and at the same time give each club a majority of its players for next season." Moreover, the paper went on, despite the seeming restrictions inherent in the new rule, nothing about it made signing a new contract compulsory. A player was free, it suggested, to sign with another team—a non-League team. This reasoning conveniently ignored one fact: League salaries were far higher than those offered by any other organization then in existence. It was the equivalent of telling an American steelworker—should he feel aggrieved with his labor contract—that he was free to go work in Mexico.

This notion of looking for well-paying baseball work outside the League was all but moot anyway, the *Commercial Advertiser* continued, as it had "not the slightest doubt that every sensible player who has the opportunity will remain where he receives fair recompense for his services and square treatment."

And square treatment was exactly, the paper said, what players would receive.

> Players need not imagine that [they] will be abused. They will be rated according to their value and reasonable salaries will be paid. The aim of the League is to reduce expenses so that clubs can live.

Other papers agreed with the clause's necessity. Salaries had clearly gotten out of hand. The *Cleveland Plain Dealer,* for example, pointed out that a player receiving $1,000 for an eighty-three-game season was getting $12 per game—roughly $6 an hour.

There was implicit in the *Plain Dealer*'s reasoning two curious, widely held assumptions concerning professional athletics. First is the idea that an athlete, unlike any other professional on earth, can demand an arbitrarily high salary and have that demand met, as if a player were a sort of mesmerist. The second notion—one born, perhaps, of envy—is that professional athletes do not, when all is said and done, hold working jobs. Instead, the shortstop, the pitcher, or the outfielder *plays.* Moreover, he only plays for a brief part of each day during a portion of a year. By all rights—goes the thinking of the teamster, the coalminer, the harried lawyer, the ad representative, the carpenter—a player should be willing to hit the field each afternoon for free, barefoot and grateful. Hell, goes the thinking, I'd *pay* to play major league baseball.

These attitudes—that ballplayers have the power to cloud owners' minds and that professional players do not perform "real work"—quickly took root in America and remain flowering, healthy plants to this day.

The following opinion appeared in *Sporting Life* in 1885.

> The base ball season has closed and about 200 professional ball tossers became gentlemen of leisure for the next six months. The professional ballist has a hard time. He rises every morning at 10 o'clock, takes a snug breakfast in the cafe, reads the Metropolitan newspapers, strolls out in the corridors and smokes a Regina Victoria, takes a nap before dinner, dines at 2 o'clock, takes a little exercise for a couple of hours, returns for supper, smokes again, and goes to the theatre in the evening with his girl and, of course, draws his salary. . . .
>
> Yes, the professional ballist has a tough time. Two hours a day for twenty-four days in a month and five months in the year this elegant creature has to play ball—something everybody knows is a great deal harder than ploughing or shoveling coal. . . .

If there is, or was, any rationale behind the reserve clause, it is that the economic underpinnings of a professional sports league are markedly different from those of other industries. The league's individual units simultaneously compete with each other—for players, for the pennant, for fan loyalty—and cooperate with each other, their goal being the presentation of an attractive total "product." Professional teams are linked as surely as a line of paper dolls. If a league falls into financial imbalance, then soon enough, the argument goes, it falls into competitive imbalance, the haves become the winners, the have-nots become the losers. Instead of tight pennant races and ballparks thick with hopeful fans, races are decided by mid-August or sooner, individual games by the third or fourth inning. Ballparks become lonely places, frequented only by die-hard fans. No one wants to watch the Dodgers play Central High.

The National League held that the reserve clause—primarily by allowing each team to protect its core assets, and thereby fostering at least some performance and financial predictability by preventing player-led frontier capitalism—would avoid this problem, one that had plagued its predecessor, the National Association. But the owners were in a state of fiscal denial: any society, even one purposefully designed to prevent it—and certainly one as weirdly artificial as a professional sports league—will eventually, somehow, achieve a state of financial (and competitive) inequality. Some members of a society—assuming that society allows for such movement—will find ways to become, and remain, rich. Others will never rise up from their relative poverty, or will do so only briefly. Still others may begin well off, but soon begin to decline. Economic parity—or, in an athletic league's case, performance parity—is, ultimately, a chimera.

The reserve clause, which in reality was designed specifically to save owners money through salary suppression, was promoted instead as a great social experiment: an equalizer, a competitive stabilizer. As such it was deeply flawed. It did not prevent, say, financially desperate Team A from selling players to Team B for cash. Instead, it merely prevented *Player A* on Team A from improving his situation by cutting a deal with Team B. Nor did it address cleverness: it did nothing to prevent a far-seeing or well-heeled club from offering promising non-League players—semi-pros, high schoolers—attractive contracts, thereby effectively cornering the baseball futures market. It did, however, prevent those young players, once signed, from seeking their true market value.

In fact, both of these scenarios developed into reality over the years. Valuable players have been sold for cold cash—most notably Babe Ruth by Boston to New York after the 1919 season. As well, clever teams have developed elaborate and effective "farm systems"—a sort of endlessly replenishing junior varsity.

By 1881, the National League had not only beaten back the competitive threat of the International Association but flicked away two other briefly pesky upstart annoyances—the Northwestern League and something called the Eastern Championship Association. As well, it was beginning to recognize the enormous economic potential of the reserve clause. These successes, coupled with slowly but steadily improving finances, seemed to bode well for the organization. But the League's aroma of success set entrepreneurial nostrils twitching. For the next decade-plus, the League would find itself engaged in a series of firefights with rival leagues.

The first of these was with the American Association, which began play in 1882 with teams in six cities: Cincinnati, Philadelphia, Louisville, Pittsburgh, St. Louis, and Baltimore. The Association was formed and mainstayed by magnates who had been unsuccessful in attempts to buy or establish National League franchises.

Initially, the National League found the Association an amusing organization, and League and Association clubs played exhibition games against each other. This period of civility, however, was brief. By May 1882, the Association had canceled all future interleague games, including a planned autumn "battle of the champions." This animosity came about in part because of a contractual dispute.

Two Detroit League players, Sam Wise and Dasher Troy, had, over the 1881–1882 winter, been induced to "jump" and sign Association contracts. They then decided to jump back to their League team. (The League had put intense pressure on the men to do so, claiming the men had no right to sign with the Association because they were "club property.") The Association—a nonsignatory to the League constitution—in turn offered a place for all "expelled, suspended or blacklisted" League players. As well, League players—expelled or not—saw a huge hole in the reserve clause fabric and began playing one organization off against the other. A trade war was on.

During this war, the reserve clause was almost overturned. Charlie Bennett of Detroit signed an option contract with Pittsburgh of the Association. In return for a $100 bonus, he promised to play with Pittsburgh the next year, 1883, for $1,700. Bennett, however, then changed his mind and decided to return to Detroit. Pittsburgh sued for breach of contract. Pittsburgh lost. A Pennsylvania circuit court found the Pittsburgh contract invalid, as it was so lacking in equity: according to the contract's terms, the judge argued, Bennett would have been bound for life to Pittsburgh, while Pittsburgh, on the other hand, was free to release him at any time.

The primary inequity in the Pittsburgh contract was its reserve clause, which was, for all purposes, identical to the League's reserve clause. Pittsburgh—and the Association—had two choices: force the issue by somehow having the courts declare that, if its own reserve clause was inequitable, then so was that of the League's; or let the sleeping dog lie. They wisely took the latter course, realizing that if they pursued matters to the logical conclusion—had the League's reserve clause overturned—a contractual free-for-all between the two organizations would ensue and the richer, stronger, better-established League would take the day in short order. Why no reserved and unhappy League player pursued matters is curious and unanswered.

Both the League and the Association left the courts and returned to the fields of play. Over the course of the summer, things turned out oddly. After the season's dust had cleared, the Association, with happy, alcohol-fortified fans and Sunday games—as well as its roster of baseball-starved cities whose combined population was nearly 500,000 more than those of the League—was a smashing success. One account suggested that five of the Association's six teams outdrew Chicago, the League's most popular team.

The subdued League cleaned house: it dropped weak sisters Troy and Worcester, added New York and Philadelphia to its rolls, and retreated from the moral high ground—allowing reinstatement of all previously blacklisted players (except game throwers).

These adjustments, however, proved inadequate. Some League franchises were making it clear they were thinking of defecting to the Association. The League quietly suggested a meeting with the Association to see if the two could, perhaps, agree to discuss, tentatively, a possible peace agreement, or at least a less mutually destructive arrangement of some sort.

The Association—which possibly had had a similar idea in mind from the start—concurred. At a February 1883 "Harmony Conference" the two organizations (and a third, the Northwestern League) came to terms, signing what became known as the National Agreement or Tripartite Pact and forming, basically, a cartel.

The agreement was a complicated one, but its basic purpose was the instituting of a hands-off policy. The parties reinstated blacklists, expanded the reserve lists from five to eleven, and, most importantly, vowed to forbear from tampering—the groups would honor each other's contracts, reserve lists, and blacklists.

With the signing of the Tripartite Pact, all was again well in the kingdom—at least the boardroom section of the kingdom. Nearly all Association and League teams made money during 1883, which the 1884 Spalding *Guide* called "beyond question the most successful one known." The *Guide* did, however, point out smugly that the League had won 27 of 31 1882 interleague games.

Even before the 1883 season ended, however, a group of capitalists, headed by Henry Van Noye Lucas of St. Louis, formed yet another league: the Union Association. The UA, philosophically at least, burned brightly; but soon, battered by the real world's fierce winds, it guttered into darkness.

Lucas, the millionaire scion of a railroad and real estate fortune and a transportation magnate in his own right, loved baseball dearly, playing third base on a self-sponsored semipro team and building a private diamond on the grounds of "Normandy," his estate. He was hungry for a local professional franchise, but St. Louis already had an Association team, the Browns, and the League's $.50 admission and ban on Sunday games would have doomed a League team to financial failure. Lucas, therefore, organized his own league.

Lucas—no known photo of him exists—remains an enigmatic and ultimately sad figure. Though a capitalist of the first tier, he seems to have had the heart of a player. His league would have no truck with a reserve clause, which he called "the most arbitrary and unjust rule ever suggested."

This stance is controversial. Lucas was evidently something of a clubhouse Johnny who enjoyed fraternizing with and buying post-game beers for players, during which occasions, one story goes, he became convinced of the wrongness of the reserve rule. On the other hand, he may have come to this conviction—attractive to players—pragmatically, after the League and the American Association rejected his offer to become a signatory to the Tripartite Pact—complete with reserve clause—and be recognized by the other organizations.

The UA constitution, though basically a carbon copy of those of the League and Association, differed dramatically in one way. "[W]e cannot recognize," the document read, "any agreement whereby any number of ballplayers may be reserved for any club for any time beyond the terms of their contract for such club."

Although established baseball men likely viewed Lucas as a sky castle–building hobbyist at best, they had been burned once, and were twice cautious. Abraham G. Mills, the League president, proposed blacklisting any player who jumped to the UA and then tried to return. (As one writer points out, the only people the League trusted less than baseball men in other leagues were baseball men in its own. While players who jumped might well be lured back to the League, it would only be through increased salary offers. Mills knew only too well the sort of temptation of which he spoke. When Sure Shot Dunlap of Cleveland jumped to the UA, Mills himself urged Cleveland to lure Dunlap back. When Dunlap asked for a raise of over 200 percent, however, Mills changed his mind.)

The American Association, for its part, expanded to twelve teams, hoping to secure both players and cities possibly interested in hooking up with the UA. The UA planned teams in many major league cities, including Baltimore, Boston, and Chicago, so the Association prohibited any of its teams from playing a team from "another association" that had invaded a National Agreement city. The League and the Association also allowed the Eastern League to be part of the National Agreement. Players for these clubs would thereby be unable to jump to the UA without being blacklisted, effectively blocking off any hopes the UA might have had of joining forces with the Eastern League, a popular minor circuit.

Nonetheless, players began jumping to the UA. Mills was furious—not so much at the ethics involved as the money. The UA's advances were often in excess of what, only recently, had been "regarded as a high *salary*" for a League player.

Some players had second thoughts, too, and returned to the League or the Association after initial jumps to the UA. The UA threatened lawsuits. The League retaliated boldly: re-jumpers were no longer welcome.

Underfinanced, informally run, and clearly of lower quality than either the League or the Association, the UA began taking on water quickly. Altoona dropped out before the end of May. The Philadelphia Keystones were gone by mid-August. Chicago moved to Pittsburgh, but collapsed in September. By the end of its 128-game season, only a couple of UA teams remained even remotely viable.

The UA disbanded in January 1885 after a single season. Ironically, Lucas soon managed to secure a National League franchise. He purchased the Cleveland League team and moved it to St. Louis in 1885, figuring that any losses he accrued going against the town's Association team were better than not being in the baseball business at all. After the UA's disbanding, the League, over Mills's apoplectic objections, reinstated jumpers. The Association followed suit.

Henry Lucas left organized baseball in 1886. Soon after, his golden touch disappeared. He lost a fleet of barges to a fierce storm, took some heavy real estate hits, and, in one last entrepreneurial burst, built an ill-fated velodrome. He died of blood poisoning in 1910. For his last three years he had been working as a city inspector in St. Louis for $75 a week.

Once again, the League and the Association were in command of the baseball fleet. To compensate for losses incurred during the UA war, the cartel instituted a $2,000 salary cap on individual players in 1885. Though owners violated the cap regularly, the idea sat badly with the players. They had not failed to notice—could not fail to notice—that whenever a second league appeared on the scene, salaries rose. During the Association's openly competitive first season and the UA's brief life, salaries had risen about 25 percent, from about $1,500 to $2,000 during the former and from $2,000 to $2,500 during the latter. Additionally, these pots had been regularly sweetened with bonuses and multiyear contracts. Team owners didn't have a monopoly on business acumen.

Seventeen

A Vampire
Keen for His Prey

OHN WARD'S SOPHOMORE year in New York, 1884, was disappointing
for both him and the franchise. Though the New Yorks improved on
1883's sub-.500, sixth-place season, tying Chicago for fourth place in
the eight-team National League with a 62–50 record, they finished a
distant twenty-two games behind pennant-winning Providence.

Ward struggled at the plate and in the field. He batted only six points
above the League average, and had trouble adjusting to the role of a full-
time position player (he pitched only sixty innings that year). He played
poorly in the outfield: his fielding average, for his fifty-nine games there,
was in the lowest third of the League. In the infield his fielding average for
forty-three games was eighth of fifteen second basemen.

These numbers, however, tell an incomplete tale. Ward's job was to
get on base. Once there, he was a master at unnerving the defense—as
shown by his debut series in New York. In 1884 Ward managed to get on
base regularly, often without being credited with a hit. He put the ball in
play—no small beer in those gloveless, error-filled days—and relied on his
speed to arrive safely at first. There his work had just begun. He scored
ninety-eight runs—only seven men scored more—so once on base, he
clearly managed to move around them with alacrity. As a baserunner he
was a skillful distracter. He worried pitchers with his speed, always threat-

ening to steal. Unfortunately, stolen bases weren't recorded statistically until 1886, but to score as many runs as he did, he had to have stolen many bases over the season.

He also let his temper get the better of him. In late September, New York made a quick western swing to play Cleveland and Buffalo. Sometime during the evening of Wednesday the 23d, after a one-run New York loss, Ward and umpire John Gaffney had a "little misunderstanding" in the rotunda of Buffalo's Genesee House hotel. Though he worked the next day's game, Gaffney reopened a facial wound "said to have been caused by Ward's ring" in the process. Ward, for unknown reasons, was neither fined nor suspended by the League for his actions.

Despite the looming end of his pitching career, what must have been an uncomfortable adjustment to position player, his unremarkable performances at bat and in the field, and his team's mediocrity, Ward does not seem to have been distressed. He attended the theater regularly, and finally embarked on the completion of his college education: sometime during the winter of 1883 he had enrolled at Columbia College.

Perhaps the most telling evidence of his contentment was that he did not, apparently, seriously consider jumping to the Union Association. Certainly he must have been courted—a player of Ward's stature would have been a bright feather in the UA's cap. He would not, however, have come cheaply. His official 1884 salary of $3,000—which probably did not include extra pay for being captain (which he was, briefly, during the season) or any bonuses offered to counterbalance extravagant UA offers—placed him among the three or four highest-paid players in the National League. Interestingly, many other highly paid players in the League that year would see their salaries rise incrementally, for the rest of the decade. Ward's, however, remained steady at $3,000 from 1883 until 1888, when it rose by $1,000—strongly suggesting New York had signed him in 1883 to an unusual multiyear contract to counter the UA's threat.

The following season, 1885, New York acquired "Move Up" Joe Gerhardt from Louisville to play second, and shifted Ward to shortstop, the most difficult and demanding infield position.

In *Base-Ball: How to Become a Player*, Ward is the tactful diplomat: no position is unimportant, no position does not require "consummate skill."

But it is the position of shortstop for which Ward reserved his greatest respect.

It has a "prominent place," on the diamond, Ward wrote.

> A short-stop should be a player of more than ordinary suppleness and activity. He has a large amount of ground to cover. . . . In chances for skillful plays and the employment of judgment, short-stop is second to no other position on the in-field. He is tied to no base, but is at liberty to go anywhere he may be most needed. . . . [The shortstop] must be possessed of some intelligence and a wit quick enough to see the point [of an unfolding play] and act before the opportunity has passed.

Ward was absolutely on point. New York likely understood that the clever, quick, supple Ward's "natural" position was shortstop. But 1884 was the year he had hurt his arm in Cleveland. By playing outfield he could rest his arm—by throwing lefty. Second base was also an easier position—easier certainly than shortstop, which requires longer throws—on his recovering arm: on many plays he could lob the ball to first or to the shortstop covering second.

Ward was not immediately pleased with New York's decision to play him at shortstop. In February 1885 he told *Sporting Life* that his pitching days were over, as his muscles bothered him when he attempted to throw a curveball, and that he was "anxious to make second base his home position."

The demands of the new position took their toll. Ward's hitting suffered badly. His average dropped twenty-seven points to an embarrassing .226. On defense, however, Ward shined: his 1885 fielding average was only fourteen percentage points behind Jack Glasscock of St. Louis, the League's slickest shortstop. *Sporting Life* singled him out for praise in mid-season, saying he was "as great at short field as he used to be in the pitcher's box. Ball playing comes as natural to him as eating does to other men." The *Clipper* agreed. "Ward's fielding," it reported,

> has been in a great majority of the games a model exhibition, his backing up, his remarkable activity and his skill in playing all the points of the position being especially noteworthy.

The New Yorks improved dramatically. Led by pitchers Mickey Welch and Tim Keefe, who between them won 76 games, the team won 85 games, finishing only two games behind pennant-winner Chicago.

Off the field, the dominant concern in 1885 was the fate of "reserve jumpers" and "contract breakers"—those players who had gone to play with the UA or had done so only to return to their former League or Association team. A further concern was the matter of now-teamless former UA players—neither jumpers nor contract breakers. How were they going to be assigned equitably to the League or Association teams that wanted them?

In February 1885, Ward weighed in with a long article in the *Clipper*, which introduced the piece as the work of "one admirably qualified by intelligence and experience to speak as the representative of the professional fraternity."

Ward had been mentioned in an earlier article as being in favor of the reinstatement of reserve jumpers, but not contract breakers. The February piece was Ward's reply. His prose, as always, was concise, forceful, and slyly self-effacing.

> What I do or do not favor may not make any difference at all,
> and I would not presume to give public expression to my opinion;
> but, since I have been quoted publicly, will . . . state my views
> more definitely, and, at the same time, more deliberately.

He favored the unconditional reinstatement of reserve jumpers and the conditional reinstatement of contract breakers. The gist of the article was that baseball justice needed to be tempered by mercy—that expulsion via blacklisting should be reserved for the sport's only "capital crime," crooked play.

Ward allowed that contract breaking was a grave offense, and that those men should be fined, but that "to err is human." Further, he pointed out, the League pot should be extremely wary of calling players black. The League had vigorously tried to lure contract breakers back—effectively tempting them to break a second contract. Why then, Ward asked, are the League and the Association now refusing to accept those men?

His words were occasionally barbed. Since the League had taken the "wise and simple" solution of allowing Henry Lucas, the energy behind the UA, to buy into the League's new St. Louis club, should it not accept those players formerly under Lucas's charge? "If there is going to be a love-feast," he wrote, "a general hand-shaking all around, let it include everybody."

He also used the occasion to sound off on the reserve clause. His opinions on this subject were extremely caustic. The clause, he said, was an *ex post facto* law, adopted by the League and the Association "for their mutual protection," and one that entailed "no moral obligation upon the players." Reserve jumpers were only "honest, hard-working players" punished for breaking a rule to which creation "they were not parties."

Later that winter, the Union Association conflicts were generally resolved. All the jumpers and breakers were reinstated, though the latter were fined—in some cases as much as $1,000. In addition, the League and the Association managed to patch together a complicated plan for the assignment of previously uncontracted "outlaw players," a plan that did not prevent cutthroat competition among teams searching for new players.

In retrospect—but in retrospect only—Ward's article was a shot across the bow in what would erupt, within five years, as a full-scale war between the players and owners. While he was at times sarcastic, and generally blunt, he was hardly inflammatory. He acknowledged the reserve rule was, in fact, a "protective measure," and stood firmly on the side of the inviolability of contracts, saying that owners, "who invest in baseball, must have some assurance of its protection, or there will not be men willing to go into the business at all." Additionally, he praised the League and the Association for doing "wonders for baseball" via generally "wise and careful" legislation, before calling on them to be reasonable in so "small a matter" as the jumpers and breakers.

In another light, however, the fact that a baseball player had gone public at all with his thoughts, even in such an evenhanded, arguably conciliatory way as Ward did, was notable. If baseball players did appear in print—and they did occasionally pen short dispatches—their thoughts were so completely reworked by editors that they were effectively ghost-written—which was not the case with Ward's article. To have a ballplayer succeed in writing his own piece, an essay to boot, was a singular occurrence.

Baseball management—team owners—generally thought of players as slightly addle-brained, half-formed beings, children really. As such, they had best be seen but not heard.

Spalding's 1884 *Guide* scolded players for "kicking" at umpire's decisions, calling the practice a "nuisance" and "discreditable." This was followed by a tongue-lashing on the evils of drunkenness and the damage that a "weak brother" (each team, it suggested, had at least one) could inflict on his fellow players. Chronic drunks, it reminded everyone, ran the risk being blacklisted.

Then the *Guide*, like a parent pointing first to unfinished meals and then to starving children in China, launched into an extended lecture about the "salary question." Players had become spoiled brats, their expectations passing "beyond the bounds of reasonable remuneration." Hardworking men such as streetcar drivers, conductors, porters, and laborers earned far less for a full year's work than did players, who were paid a year's salary for less than six months of "two or three hours of easy work" a day.

The lecture ended with a sternly avuncular, Aesopian admonition.

> One of the weaknesses of professional players is their aptitude to "grasp at the shadow while losing the substance." . . . [The] sensible player will prefer the home position with a sure salary, even if it is not very large, to a mere stopping place for a temporary period at fancy figures.

In this context, League and Association officials, though surprised at Ward's candor, probably thought it best to let him have his say. Ward was, after all, a paragon, what management wanted all ballplayers to be, or at least wanted the public to believe them to be: industrious, talented, educated, sober. If Ward was, as well, precocious, showing off with garden-variety scraps of Latin and the like, so be it. It was just a phase the young man was going through. Best to let him blow off a little steam.

In August 1885, nearly a full season after the UA scare, the League and Association, meeting in Saratoga, New York, revised the National Agreement. They did not announce the new document's terms until October, when the season was over and most of the players were scattered to their home towns for the winter.

The reserve clause was expanded to cover twelve, not eleven, players per club. Further, it became perpetual, simply rolling over year after year. The owners, by then, were enthralled with the practice of selling each other players. (The player, in most instances, realized no windfall from these sales, no matter what his worth was deemed by team owners. This practice could be doubly frustrating for a player. Say his salary with his original team was $2,000. He might be sold to another team for $4,000. The second team would then offer him a $2,000 salary. Open market values did not, evidently, include the players.)

The most important addition to the National Agreement, however, was the establishing of a $2,000 salary limit. They softened the blow by simultaneously setting a $1,000 minimum salary. *Sporting Life* thought the upper limit a capital idea. It pointed out that, after all, only three dozen players or so—a shade over 10 percent of rostered major leaguers in 1884—would be affected; the cap would foster better teamwork, since the salary differential between stars and journeymen would be lessened. And, echoing newspaper attitudes toward the original reserve clause, *Sporting Life* reminded all to look at the big picture: if clubs are financially healthy (thanks to the cap), they will live to pay their players for another season and another and another.

Finally, the paper opined, if players think they are being so badly served, they can find work elsewhere, though it doubted they would: "There's no one missed for long. Where people go, people come; the places get filled up."

Asked about the salary cap, Ward answered,

It [was] rather tough on the part of the late Convention in fixing the maximum. . . . Making $1,000 the minimum does not make it any better. I think base-ball is the game, but still the boys want the money for playing it. Some of the boys under this new arrangement will probably drop out.

If Ward's thoughts seemed innocuous, resigned, and even uncaring, they were also cleverly disingenuous.

Three days before the salary cap's announcement, nine New York players—Tim Keefe, Mickey Welch, "Move Up" Gerhardt, Mike Dorgan, Jim O'Rourke, Daniel Richardson, Roger Connor, Buck Ewing, and

Ward—had met and formed an organization they called the Brotherhood of Professional Base Ball Players. The Brothers—in the best tradition of fraternal organizations—swore

> To strive to promote the objects and aims of this Brotherhood, in accordance with the Constitution and By-Laws;
>
> Never to take advantage of a brother in good standing;
>
> Never to permit an unjust injury to be done to, or continued against, a brother in good standing, while it is in my power to prevent the same;
>
> To assist a brother in distress;
>
> To render faithful obedience to the will of the Brotherhood, as expressed by the decree of the council, or vote of my chapter.

The Brotherhood constitution's preamble was vague, formal, and high-minded—that is, in form and substance it differed hardly a whit from that of the National League. "[R]ecognizing the importance of united effort and impressed with its necessity in our behalf," the Brotherhood's purpose was

> To protect and benefit ourselves collectively and individually.
>
> To promote a high standard of professional conduct.
>
> To foster and encourage the interests of the game of Base Ball.

Two facts, however, suggest that the players were fully aware that the Brotherhood had the potential to be much more than merely another benevolent and protective fraternity. First is the timing of the meeting—clearly they had somehow learned the thrust if not all the details of the new National Agreement, which would be made public within the week. Second is their concern with secrecy—the Brotherhood's existence would not be made public for over a year.

There are several possible reasons for this initial secrecy: the men feared an overreaction on the League's part; the men had guilty consciences—as unthreatening as their goals might seem on paper, the men knew that, if push came to shove, the Brotherhood's real intent was to present a united front, a physical one if need be, to the League; they feared failure and ridicule (earlier that year, a Philadelphia sportswriter, William Voltz, never gaining the players' trust, had tried but failed to form a "beneficial society"); the men were united at the time in general sentiment only and had not as yet devised a specific platform or strategy. Lastly, they may well have realized that the Brotherhood's potential strength depended on its numbers—which, as yet, it lacked. For any or all of these reasons, the Brotherhood cat was kept more or less in the bag for over a year, and allowed to emerge only when it had developed a louder, more purposeful meow.

Ward was elected president of the Brotherhood—unsurprisingly, as he almost certainly conceived of the organization, called the formation meeting in the first place, and composed the group's guiding documents. As their first order of business, the members, with the onset of the 1886 season, began quietly recruiting players and organizing additional chapters. Within a year Brotherhood chapters existed in all eight League cities and counted a membership of about one hundred members—nearly 90 percent of rostered League players.

The ease with which recruiting proceeded is telling. It is entirely possible that the Brotherhood's original members obscured the organization's real purposes during the membership drive. Certainly they were good politicians. For example, the fingerprints of the fledgling Brotherhood—or at least John Ward—are everywhere on a small notice that appeared in the *Clipper* at the end of January 1886, discussing, hypothetically, the need for a beneficial association of professional ballplayers. The item mentioned three well-known players who, fallen on hard times, were in need of assistance. At a February benefit for one of them, Curry Foley, the organizer made a large point of announcing that the first out-of-town subscription for the former Boston and Buffalo outfielder/pitcher had come from none other than John Ward of New York. It would not be Ward's last act of generosity toward unfortunate fellow ballplayers, and there is no reason to believe that his donation to the Foley estate was born entirely of ulterior motives; but certainly the gesture did not escape players' attention.

But isolated good works go only so far. The success of the Brotherhood's membership drive pointed to three things: widespread anger, wariness, and cynicism of the players toward their employers; dissatisfaction with baseball working conditions generally; and, to a lesser extent, nineteenth-century player demographics.

The professional baseball community, even today, is a small one. In 1885 it was positively tiny—only 115 men played in fifteen or more League games that year. These 115 men, season after season, spent an inordinate amount of time together—both as teammates and as opponents. Baseball lends itself to long periods of relative idleness: for half of each game, most of a team is sitting next to each other, watching, commenting, gossiping. In addition, teammates spend much of the rest of their time—at least on road trips—riding from one city to another and, once arrived in a new town, sitting around hotel lobbies, eating, drinking, shooting the breeze, chasing women. In the relatively compact nineteenth-century cities, ballplayers no doubt ran into their opponents during the evening, at eateries, taverns, and the theater. Additionally, baseball, of all team sports, is easily the least purely combative—at least physically—and has never lent itself, despite rules against player fraternization, to isolation. In short, like sailors on a long voyage or soldiers posted to a distant frontier, ballplayers get to know each other very well.

Additionally, nineteenth-century baseball was an excellent host for the breeding of like-mindedness. From 1885 through 1890, approximately 36 percent of League rookies were of Irish descent, 31 percent were of non-Irish British Isles descent, and 24 percent were of German descent. Though it would be foolish to think of these three groups as being arm-in-arm buddies, when push came to shove, they formed a relatively homogeneous labor force. (Players were, whatever their differences, united on one front. With very few exceptions—John Ward being one—they wanted no part of mixed-race leagues.)

The owners inadvertently aided the players' cause. Through their relentless efforts to elevate the status of the sport and gain a more upscale, respectable, better-behaved and influential fan base, they also made the profession more attractive to the growing ranks of college players. These men, in turn, while lending a veneer of respectability to the game, also brought with them, if not more awareness of their rights as working men, certainly higher economic expectations and—at least in the case of John

Ward—a greater articulateness about these things. As well, these college men, with their increased number of economic opportunities, were less vulnerable to the vagaries and impositions of a single employer and potentially more independent than many of their teammates.

John Ward, certainly, is a case in point. Because his political philosophy comes to us more or less fully mature—with his newspaper and magazine articles—and because his upbringing was one, more or less, of middle-class comfort, the origins of his populist leanings—as we will call them for now—must remain a matter of speculation.

Certainly he had gained his fill of authoritative, unilateral power structures during his time at college. And certainly he did not forget the lessons of his early bush league teams—which either never quite found it within their means to pay him for his services or, as in the case in Binghamton, pulled the rug out from under him and his teammates without warning. We don't know what his thoughts were about the vicious railroad strikes and the executions of the Molly Maguires in the summer of 1877, but it is not unlikely the sympathies of his teammates—many of them from working-class Pennsylvania families—were with the strikers.

In 1879, in Providence, Ward's career coincided with those of three influential, older veterans: shortstop George Wright; outfielder Jim O'Rourke; and first baseman Joe Start. Ward would play alongside Start for four years, Wright for two, and O'Rourke for one. All three men, besides being heroes and on-the-field mentors of Ward, were outspoken and disgruntled men.

Start had escaped from the puritanical and penurious Spalding-dominated Chicago team before coming to Providence. Wright and O'Rourke, after contributing greatly to Boston's 1878 pennant (and the team's healthy championship season profits), had had the audacity to ask for raises from Boston's miserly owner, Arthur Soden—raises Soden denied. Doubtless the young Ward listened long and hard to these men.

Providence supplied several other finishing touches to Ward's baseball economics lesson. Not only did he arrive just a little late for the minor wage-bumping in the League during the short-lived presence of the International Association—something his teammates likely taunted him with, but he chafed at the audacity of Providence's shorting the team their last paycheck of the 1880 season.

Ward always took the long view regarding his future. He understood that banking on a career in professional baseball was to take the short view, at best, and a bet against ridiculously long odds, certainly. As he put it in "Notes of a Base-Ballist,"

> Our occupation is at best an uncertain one. A broken limb to-morrow may be the end of it for me. Besides, a player's reputation lies with the public: he leans on popular favor, and that he may find at any time to be but a broken reed.

Ward's long view coalesced into a master plan: he would, somehow, complete his college education. Later this plan would become more specific: he would become a lawyer.

Only fourteen months after his expulsion, he wrote to James Calder, Penn State's president, asking him for a "certificate of dismissal," which would help him gain entrance to another school. He would go back to college, he promised Calder, as soon as he had enough money "laid by" to do so. During the next couple of years, Ward evidently shopped around for a suitable campus. He was an unofficial and unpaid coach of the 1879 Dartmouth baseball team, rooming with the team captain and leading the team through workouts during the winter and early spring of that year. At least one obituary had him, as well, coaching the Princeton nine during the winter preceding the 1884 season.

Ward ultimately enrolled at Columbia College, which in the 1880s occupied buildings between 49th and 50th Streets and Madison and Fourth Avenues in Manhattan. This raises a chicken-and-egg question as to whether Ward's choice was a result of his moving from the Providence Grays to New York, or vice versa. One thing is certain, however: his sharp-eyed perception about the vagaries of a baseball career and his wide-scoped ambition worked to his great favor in 1882, his last year with Providence. In short, Ward made himself master of his own destiny.

Though he had been reserved by the Grays each year since the end of the 1879 season, Providence oddly left him off the 1882 list. The club probably knew it would do them no good to reserve him, and made the best of a bad situation by vacating Ward's slot for another player. First of all, Ward had no doubt suggested—either truthfully or strategically—to all concerned that he had already "laid by" enough money to quit baseball and return to school and that he was of half a mind to do just that. Secondly, he was in great demand: rumors flew that both Boston and Buffalo were hungry for him, and he could always "jump" to the American Association if Providence or any other League team didn't meet his price (assuming he decided to play instead of study). If, though, Providence wanted to keep him, *they* would have to meet his price, something the financially hamstrung club couldn't hope to do. So Ward, unbeholden to anyone, was relatively free to sign with New York, the Association, or Columbia University. It is entirely possible that Ward's later labor philosophy, as it applied to baseball, can be traced to the convergence of opportunity that year: he happened to be in the right place in the right time, with a goodly amount of leverage. If, in Ward's eyes, this opportunity of movement was only just and fitting, why shouldn't his fellow players, his colleagues, enjoy the same?

It did not take Ward long, after his arrival in New York, to set about securing his non-baseball future. He matriculated at the Columbia College Law School in the fall term of 1883. Though New York's regular season had ended on Saturday, September 29, Ward played with the New Yorks in an exhibition game against a Brooklyn minor league team on Monday, October 1, thereby missing the first afternoon of law classes.

The pursuit of the law was a popular one among many young American men at the time. During the last half of the nineteenth century the legal profession was expanding exponentially. In 1850, there were about 24,000 lawyers in the country, a number that nearly doubled by 1870 and rose to 64,000 a decade later, far outstripping the country's population growth rate. The lawyer boom was fueled primarily by the country's economic explosion and the rise of large corporations, which required, in turn, larger legal forces.

The formal study of law was, in general, going through a long, formative period of self-examination and reorganization during the last half of the nineteenth century. Should a law course be two, three, or four years? Should law students be trained by classroom work or by a combination of classroom work and old-fashioned clerkships? Should the study of law be exclusive or should it be part of a more general liberal arts education? Should law students be required to first have an undergraduate degree? Should the law be taught via general lectures or through the emerging "case" method? Should a law school be considered part of a college or should it be entirely separate from the college?

In general, as one scholar wrote, a law school's

> role [typically] was much closer to the Lawrence Scientific
> School of Harvard, or the Sheffield Scientific School of Yale,
> that is, to a technical school serving undergraduates and usually
> with a second-class status.

At Columbia, however, by the time Ward entered, the line between law school and the university as a whole was much more blurred. There, advocates of curriculum integration had, generally, long held sway; over the years, an entire subsection of classes (more accurately, lectures) had grown up, covering matters such as medical jurisprudence, political philosophy, ethics, and the history of constitutional law. Beginning in 1881, Columbia had established, in addition to the law school, another school, "designed to prepare young men for the duties of Public Life, to be entitled a School of Political Science."

There were many courses common to the two schools and, while a student could study law exclusively or political science exclusively, he could also study both. This is what John Ward did, becoming a Bachelor of Laws in the summer of 1885 and a Bachelor of Philosophy—effectively the undergraduate degree he had forsaken at Penn State, though a more advanced degree than the political science school's Bachelor of Arts—the following year.

Even if more traditional academics could not decide whether law students walked on land or swam in water during Ward's second college career, one thing was sure: the study of law had become extremely formal and the school's entrance requirements and course of study were extremely rigorous.

Since Ward was not a graduate of a "literary college," he had to pass an examination to matriculate. It is possible that Ward was considered a special case, and was required only to pass the Regents Examination—a sort of basic knowledge test on subjects such as English, history, arithmetic, geography, and composition. (Or he could have entered the school more tentatively—as a nondegree candidate—and bypassed exams altogether.)

But the ambitious Ward, anxious to show the world that his Penn State years had not been entirely frivolous, likely declared his intention to travel the difficult route of acquiring two degrees. Therefore he was required to take the "regular" law school entrance exam, covering Greek, Roman, American, and English history; English composition, grammar, and rhetoric; and Caesar, Virgil, Cicero, or "other Latin authors deemed by the examiner to be equivalent to the above."

Once in school, as one of 365 enrollees, he studied municipal law, constitutional history, political science, and international and constitutional law, and took part in moot courts. He read Blackstone's *Commentaries*, Perry on trusts, Washburn on real property, Fisher on mortgages, Stephen on pleading, Ortolan's Roman law, Wietersheim's *Geschichte der Volkerwanderung*, Maten's *Recueil des Traités de la Paix*, Calvo's *Droit International,* and many others, including, possibly, Ordronaux's *Judicial Aspects of Insanity.* The students labored, by the way, in a most ergonomic atmosphere: "Experts," the Law School catalogue noted, "having decided that the incandescent electric was the most perfect artificial light known, it has been ordered and will be in operation [beginning in 1884]."

After graduating, Ward was required—if he had not done so yet—to clerk in an established law office for at least one year. Then he could take the New York Bar exam. If he passed, he could practice as an attorney.

While he studied, Ward was spreading the word and influence of the Brotherhood and playing major league baseball. He played against Buffalo on May 27, 1885, the afternoon of his law school graduation ceremony, which took place in the evening. New York beat Buffalo 24–0. Ward had three hits, scored three times, and assisted in one of New York's two double plays. Luckily for Ward, the regular baseball season ended around the first week of October, about the same time as classes began. Unluckily for Ward, the baseball season began in April, while the academic year did not end until May 30. We can only assume he made special arrangements with his professors.

It is not surprising, given Ward's dual life during the years 1883–1886, that he was not especially active in campus life. He does not seem to have been a member of any of Columbia's literary societies, athletic clubs, or associations, not even the "Knights of the Cue." He was an active member of the Academy of Political Science, however.

His 1885 law degree was *cum laude*, by virtue of both his simultaneous study of political science and the fact that he had received an award: second prize (and $50) for "distinction" in constitutional history and constitutional law.

During his Columbia years, he lived, conveniently and, we can assume, comfortably, about three blocks from campus, at 139 East 48th Street. Little else is known, except for an epigraph in the *Columbiad*, the 1886 yearbook. Under a section humorously entitled "Grinds" appears the name W*RD (the students' names were all so encrypted):

> He carries but a doubtful Trace
> Of Angel visits on his hungry face.

But Brotherhood or no Brotherhood, political science lectures or no political science lectures, Ward and his New York teammates were still ballplayers, and the 1886 season was upon them. There were 120 games to play and a pennant to win.

On Saturday, April 29, the New Yorks opened against Boston at the Polo Grounds. As was becoming customary, the Seventh Regiment Band marched in from center field twice before the game, escorting first the Boston Club and then the New York Club. Boston wore gray jackets and trousers and red stockings and belts; the New Yorks white jackets and trousers and maroon stockings and belts. Scores of flags "snapping in the breeze" festooned the park. There were 16,000 people at the game, an "ocean of faces," wrote the *Herald*, "a bewildering stretch and height of humanity." The bleaching boards were "black with anxious thousands" while the grandstand held "thousands more." Behind the far outfield boundaries stood "hundreds" of carriages. Telegraph poles and trees were thick with young boys who had shinnied skyward to beat the price of admission. This was no "ordinary assemblage," whatever its size.

> There were young ladies, hundreds of them, sweet of face and wearing their new and beautiful Easter costumes. . . . And there were old ladies, hundreds of them, white of hair and of kindly expression . . . in hats of many shapes and gorgeous trimmings, with [a] wealth of beautiful corsage bouquets. [There were] clergymen, weary with parish duties and sermon writing; police justices and prominent lawyers, Stock Exchange members in their

own box, politicians in power and some who wished they had never been in office, Columbia College boys, amateur athletes of days gone by. [Altogether they] made a picture creditable to the city, even as it was complimentary to the occasion and the great American game.

The teams were tied after two innings. Bouquets were thrown to various players by maidens of "pink cheek" and a messenger delivered a floral horseshoe—from an unknown sender—to Buck Ewing, Brotherhood man and New York catcher. The game remained tied after nine innings, then ten.

In the bottom of the eleventh, however, Ward, shortstop and president of the Brotherhood, who had already hit safely twice and stolen two bases, got a single off Charlie Radbourn, Ward's old Providence teammate and future Brotherhood member. Joe Gerhardt, second baseman and Brotherhood member, hit a double. Ward pulled up at third. Jim O'Rourke, Ward's old Providence mentor and current center fielder and Brotherhood member, hit a fly to Rick Johnson, Boston center fielder and future Brotherhood member. Ward waited for the ball to land in Johnson's hands, then tagged up and raced toward home.

The ball was following him with the speed of a bullet. Within ten yards of the goal and victory he threw himself upon his face and with outstretched hand touched the bag.

"Saved!" shouted ten thousand or more New Yorkers. "Splendid!" cried the ladies. . . . "Bully!" whooped the Stock Exchange gentlemen. . . . The field in an instant was black with people and Gerhardt and Ward were taken upon willing shoulders and carried triumphantly to their quarters.

All Con Daily, Boston catcher and future Brotherhood member, could do was walk off the field in helpless disgust.

On May 11, eleven members of the Detroit team joined the Brotherhood. On May 15, three members of the Chicago team joined the Brotherhood. Two more joined later that season. On May 19, ten members of the Kansas City team joined the Brotherhood.

On May 29, nine members of the St. Louis team joined the Brotherhood; later that season, four more followed. Three of the original nine, most notably Jack Glasscock and former Ward teammate and friend Jerry Denny, later turned their backs on the Brotherhood. In that organization the two men were thereafter branded "star deserters of the world."

On May 31, New York was in third place, close behind Detroit and Chicago.

On June 9, John Ward and twenty-three other students received their diplomas from Columbia College's School of Political Science. Part of the ceremony consisted of the salutatory poem, delivered by Oscar Joseph Cohen in Greek, a poem that, the *Times* reported, "every one except the ladies listened to and pretended to understand and to be interested in." It was, the paper went on, the "sort of thing" that became "rather tiresome when they had to try and appreciate [as well] a Latin poem which Mortimer Lamson Earle shot over their heads." Ward was one of only four to become Bachelors of Philosophy.

On June 12, the Brotherhood signed up sixteen members of the Boston team. On June 30, New York was in third place, four games behind Detroit. On July 12, the Brotherhood signed up eight members of the Philadelphia team. Later, another eight Philadelphias joined. On July 15, the Brotherhood signed up three members of the Washington, D.C., team. By fall, thirteen more joined them. By August 2, New York, though still in third, had fallen a distant eight games behind first-place Detroit.

On October 9, the season ended. New York—whose manager, James Mutrie, had the previous October predicted that a pennant was a "dead certainty"—finished third, ten games behind Detroit and twelve and one-half behind Chicago. The team, as far as its fans were concerned, had been a major disappointment: a talented, highly paid group that was doing little but failing to live up to its potential.

In August, Ward's "Notes of a Base-Ballist" appeared in the popular *Lippincott's* magazine. It is an odd bit of work—by turns grumpy, cynical, hilarious, self-serving, and politically bold—especially in the context of inspirational success stories that follow it in the magazine. After a brief autobiographical account (minor leagues, nervous tryout in Philadelphia, Providence), he discusses "modern ball." He felt that rule changes, including the freedom to throw overhand, had tipped the game too far in the pitchers' favor. On a more abstract level, he opines that fans sometimes expected too much of ballplayers. They might be model citizens, but they might not be. He reminds his readers that ballplayers, generally, do one thing well, and one thing only: play baseball.

> [They] are selected not so much with reference to their social
> habits or intellectual attainment [as to their athletic skills]. Base-
> ball problems are not solved by logarithms, and I know some
> excellent players who speak French quite indifferently.

He then launches into an extended, loopy fulmination on the harsh reality of a ballplayer's life. While admitting that ballplayers enjoy unusual benefits and higher-than-average salaries, and that baseball's seasonal nature "offers fine opportunities to a young man of large ambition and limited means" (such as his own winter trips to New Orleans and San Francisco), he says that the greatest of a ballplayer's joys occurs "on the 1st and 15th of each month, when he draws his pay."

But what, he goes on, about the line that he hears daily: "How pleasant to travel over the country as you players do!"?

> It is anything but pleasant to travel as we do. We play every day,
> with just time enough between dates to reach the next city. The
> ride is usually made by night; and, what with the loss of sleep and
> the fatigue of the games, we lose all appreciation of the interest-
> ing and the beautiful. I am often so worn out in body and mind
> that my sensibilities are dulled. . . . I have long since given up all
> idea of doing any reading or studying during the playing season. I
> am satisfied to sit down in a chair in the evening, and feel fortu-
> nate only to be left alone.

But solitude is rarely to be his.

> Picture, now, if you can, the agony of a man in this condition
> when pounced upon by that bane of the ball-player's life, the
> base-ball "fiend."

The "fiend" is little more than a "vampire . . . keen for his prey. You *feel* him coming down upon you, and every nerve tingles at his approach."

The fiend asks about yesterday's game and today's game and the game tomorrow.

> You make your replies as brief as possible, hoping that he may see that you don't want to be disturbed. But nothing can discourage him. . . . The consideration that should teach him that a man in any employment will grow weary of being forever and eternally quizzed about that and nothing else, that consideration seems to be a moral quality foreign to his organism. A long pause or a particularly brief response may drive him off for a moment, but, like a Jersey mosquito, he comes buzzing back, and the only way to get rid of him is to kill him.

Eventually, the ballplayer loses his patience, and after yet another question from the fiend,

> If there is a spark of life left in you, this will bring you to your feet. Bursting with indignation . . . you give vent to your feelings in language which is forcible, if not elegant. After it is all over, you are half ashamed of yourself for having lost your temper. You turn to walk away, feeling that you have needlessly made an enemy. To your surprise, he inquires if you are going down the street. Answer yes, and he will coolly say, "I'm going that way, and I'll walk with you."

On a far more sincerely angry note, Ward expands his previous views on the state of the League and the reserve rule. The rule, he writes, is an unjust one and must be modified. He suggests it be tempered with an escape clause (which in fact is what exists today) whereby a player, after serving under the reserve rule for a few years, then becomes in some manner a free agent.

The rule, he continues, whatever its original purpose, has mutated into something that has turned the players into little more than objects of capitalist speculation, objects that, incidentally, receive no benefits from their sale—either in the form of increased salary or in the form of a percentage of the sale price.

Ward then steps back briefly to praise League executives for their general campaign against the evils of gambling and drunkenness, both in the stands and on the fields. But, he points out, if baseball has freed itself from "unhealthy surroundings," likewise the "character and deportment of players have improved and the game has grown steadily in popular favor."

In a final salvo, he abandons the legalese he used in his *Clipper* piece, instead opting for stinging analogy. One ancillary effect of the reserve rule—the selling of players without their consent or compensation—he first likens to a "live-stock transaction" before upping the metaphorical ante:

> In the old days an able-bodied slave sold for from twelve hundred
> to twenty-five hundred dollars, while the highest price I have yet
> heard of as being paid for a ball-player was one thousand dollars.

This figure would quickly become laughably low—in 1887 Chicago would sell Mike Kelly to Boston for an astonishing $10,000. Ward himself, in 1889, would find his theoretical market value hovering around $15,000. But Ward's hatred of the principles involved would grow ever stronger, and his two images—the player as livestock and the reserve rule as a form of slavery—would, before his war with the League ended, be repeated often.

On November 11, a month after the conclusion of the 1886 season, the Brotherhood made its existence official by holding its first general meeting in New York. The agenda was modest. The wider membership formalized the election of Ward as president; Detroit's Dan Brouthers, the League home run king, was elected vice-president; and Tim Keefe of New York was named secretary-treasurer.

The members authorized Ward to attend the League meetings later that fall. Ostensibly his mission was to give players at least some voice at the playing-rule committee sessions, but more importantly, his presence was designed to serve notice that the Brotherhood would be an activist organization.

As far as Ward, at least, was concerned, the playing rules part of his mission at the League meeting was a success. Ward, and many others, felt that the ever-elusive "balance" between pitching and offense had tilted too far toward the former. This the League remedied: four strikes, not three, would be needed to strike a batter out (this rule lasted only one year); a walk would be issued after five, not seven, balls; and most dramatically, pitchers would have to have at least one foot on the rubber when delivering, thereby eliminating the "highland fling"—and greater speed. (As a nod to pitchers, batters could no longer demand "high" or "low" pitches.)

(One other rule—it too only lasted a year—made 1887 an anomaly: walks counted in the scorebook as hits, which made for some almighty averages. Until modern statisticians adjusted his mark, Tip O'Neil of the St. Louis Association team was credited with a .492 batting average—the baseball equivalent of a three-minute mile. O'Neil's revised mark stands at .435.)

So much for Ward's initial influence on baseball's ruling board. In other business the reserve rule was revised again: clubs could now reserve fourteen, not twelve, members of a squad.

The *Clipper*, a week or so after this revision was announced, printed the thoughts of an anonymous correspondent. The *Clipper*, like other papers of the time, played fast and loose with the definition of "correspondents," and in all likelihood the correspondent was Ward himself. The article called the reserve rule an "outrage," "worse than slavery," and called upon the "so-called Brotherhood of Professional Players" to "abolish this abuse of power."

New York fans wanted a pennant in 1887, but they weren't going to get it. The team began poorly. By the end of May it was barely playing .500 ball. It coughed to life briefly over the summer, then settled back into mediocrity, finishing in fourth place, ten and one-half games behind Detroit.

The team's problem was pitching. Though the roster included two of the League's most feared pitchers—Tim Keefe and Mickey Welch—the rest of the staff, to put it kindly, was a pack of mutts. Also, New York persisted in a two-man rotation while the three teams that finished ahead of New York in the standings—used three- and four-man turns.

Local fans and baseball writers, however, preferred to lay the blame more abstractly. They felt the team suffered from a collective ailment: management was guilty of "lukewarmness" (whatever that was); the players of "indifference and laziness." They were spoiled and "flattered and petted"; these "high salaried and fortunate individuals," one writer complained, "imagine that they owned all Manhattan Island. Conceit and big head[s] are unwholesome but nonetheless common vices of the successful baseball player of today."

These criticisms were lightly veiled jabs at the New York captain—the field boss, Ward, who set the lineups, told the fielders where to shift, told players when to bunt and when to steal, benched players for lack of effort, and was effectively the team tactician, the man we today call a manager. Although the *Clipper*, speaking modestly for the entire city of Manhattan on the eve of the 1887 season, had written that there was "a strong feeling in this city" that if Ward were given his head—as filled with baseball gray matter as it was—the New Yorks would win the pennant, New York ownership felt differently. On July 12, Buck Ewing replaced Ward as captain.

This change generated much public speculation, the sort of tempest in a teapot that baseball fans delight in and that causes nonfans to excuse themselves from the room.

Had Ward resigned or been fired? *Sporting Life* suggested resignation, and likened Ward to a tyrannical sea captain who "ruled his men with a rod of iron, and sympathy he knew not of." When, however, the captain gave orders to give chase to a French frigate, the men stood on principle, refused the order, and were mowed down. The captain, "seeing all was lost, jumped overboard and was drowned."

In another article, two officials, one of them John Day, president of the New York club, said there was a "hostile feeling" toward Ward among the team and that at least three of the starting nine refused to talk to him.

Ward and his manager, James Mutrie, disagreed. (Managers as yet did not direct on-field traffic as they do today. Then, generally, "managers" were business managers, though Ward and Mutrie likely consulted on general strategy throughout the season.) Mutrie said there was no ill will and that Ward had resigned. The hostility business, Mutrie said, "has a fiction twang." Ward himself said he had resigned and had no enemies on the team, "certainly . . . none who could not command my friendly services at any time."

Whatever Ward's status with his teammates, he remained a fan favorite. On July 13, his first post-captaincy game, the Polo Grounds crowd of 1,500, "very sorry that the brainy little fellow had found it necessary to drop the reins . . . applauded him to the echo" every time he came to bat. Day himself, when asked about a rumored $5,000 offer from Pittsburgh for Ward, said he wouldn't sell Ward "for $50,000."

Despite these distractions, Ward in general was having the time of his life. Freed from whatever obligations he had felt as a student, he played in all of New York's 129 games, led the League in stolen bases, was second in total hits, and tied for third in batting average. Additionally, he was the League's best-fielding shortstop. And he had for several months been seeing a very popular (though sometimes critically maligned) actress: Helen Dauvray.

In August 1887 *Lippincott's* ran another article of Ward's—this his most scathing and volatile denunciation of baseball labor practices to date. Even the 4,000-word article's title—"Is the Base-Ball Player a Chattel?"—was inflammatory and pugnacious. Ward briefly outlines the reserve clause's history, pointing out, as he had in earlier writings, that the rule had been effected unilaterally and in already-existing contracts and was, therefore, an *ex post facto* rule. Then he spears Spalding and former League president Hulbert, accusing them of masterminding a pernicious spin-control operation in which all blame was laid at the feet of the players.

> According to them, the player who accepted a proffered increase
> of salary was a disorganizer and a dangerous character, from
> whom protection was necessary, while the club official who
> offered it was but a poor weak instrument in his hands. . . . I do
> not hesitate to say that I believe base-ball has more to fear from
> the reckless and improvident methods of some of its managers
> than from all the faults of the players.

He describes the League and the Association as a dual monopoly—one that, octopus-like, surrounds any new league that organizes. "There is now no escape for the player" from the "great good judgment and the remarkable instinct for self-preservation which has always characterized" the League.

He then launches into a tirade:

> Like a fugitive-slave law, the reserve-rule denies [the player] a
> harbor or a livelihood, and carries him back, bound and shack-

led, to the club from which he attempted to escape. We have, then, the curious result of a contract, which on its face is for seven months, being binding for life, and when the player's name is once attached thereto his professional liberty is gone forever. . . . [The result is] serfdom which gave one set of men a life-estate in the labor of another. . . . Its justification, if any, lay only in its expediency. . . .

Instead of an institution for good, it has become one for evil; instead of a measure of protection, it has been used as a handle for the manipulation of a traffic in players, a sort of speculation in live stock, by which they are bought, sold, and transferred like so many sheep. . . .

Encouraged by the apparent inactivity of the players, the clubs have gone on from one usurpation to another until in the eye of the base-ball "magnate" the player has become a mere chattel. He goes where he is sent, takes what is given him, and thanks the Lord for life.

After a year of quiet base building and several months of relative inactivity, the Brotherhood had thrown down a gauntlet—one that would quickly be taken up by the League.

On August 28, within a fortnight of the magazine's appearance (and its subsequent excerpting in several newspapers, including the *New York Herald* and *New York Times*), the Brotherhood held a long-planned meeting at a New York hotel. The group held their cards close to the vest—saying only that they hoped to "consult together in regard to the inauguration of certain reforms in the method of making contracts for the season of 1888" and to initiate negotiations with the League so that the latter would formally recognize the Brotherhood as a "permanent organization" and include it in its annual convention.

In a third bit of business, the Brotherhood continued its public relations campaign by adopting a resolution to "break up dissipation" among its members, instituting a series of heavy fines for drunkenness. The *Clipper* felt this resolution showed, above all, the true and infinite goodness of the Brotherhood, an organization that "has the best interests of the game at heart and . . . recognizes that those interests are also mutual."

League president Nicholas Young, with Spalding whispering in his ear, declined to recognize the Brotherhood, though he allowed as how he would be willing to receive an informal committee of League players to discuss contract issues.

Ward, highly insulted, threw statesmanship to the winds. If Young persisted in his refusal to recognize the fledgling organization, he promised that no Brotherhood man would sign a contract for the 1888 season. Furthermore, he suggested, there were plenty of capitalists with money to burn who would like nothing more than to form an entirely new league.

Ward had overstepped, or he had stepped too quickly, and he knew it. Ward quickly retracted his statement about a syndicate of capitalists, but it was too late. The League reacted angrily. An unnamed New York daily, according to the *Clipper,* had warned the Brotherhood to watch its step, as the League does not "take bluffs" lightly. The paper pointed out how Lucas and the Union Association had been crushed like bugs. The *Clipper,* in turn, said that one man's crushing is another's pillow plumping: Lucas got everything he ever wanted—a National League franchise.

By late September Ward was, briefly, in full, chaotic retreat. He issued another retraction of a badly stated opinion about some of the contract reforms the Brotherhood might seek from the League at the annual meetings.

> I expressed the opinion *individually* that there was no good reason
> why contracts, instead of for one year, might not be made for
> two, three or even five years, and I meant of course *if agreeable to*
> *both club and player.* But as for making this condition obligatory, I
> never entertained any such absurd idea. [italics added]

Then he seems to remove the widest plank from the Brotherhood's platform. "What the Brotherhood wants now is an equitable contract. It concedes to the clubs the privilege of reservation. [To] the reserve-rule . . . we have no objection." But, in the same breath, Ward refers to "tyrannical" contract abuses—without naming them—reiterating that until they were removed, no Brotherhood members would sign 1888 contracts. Either Ward was learning the political ropes the hard way or he was, by speaking on both sides of an issue, already accomplished in the profession.

Young replied patly that reforms would be dealt with by "the old and usual means" at the League meeting.

Ward hit the roof.

"The old and usual means?" What old and usual means? Has it been customary for the players to be represented at the meetings of the League? Or has the League shown any recent disposition to legislate for the interests of the players? The "buying and selling" of players was unheard of three years ago. . . . [The] means of which the players of a [disbanding] club are peddled around at so much per man and without regard to the player's wishes, is a growth of the past year. It is from these same old and usual methods that we seek to escape.

Young seemed unconcerned.

Mr. Ward's last letter is in some respects a remarkable one, and may or may not be construed as a declaration of war upon the League. . . . I suppose contracts will be prepared as usual and submitted to the players for signature. This test of the sincerity of the men will be a crucial one and will serve in a measure to indicate how much in earnest they are in this movement.

Ward would leave on a barnstorming trip to the South before heading to California to rejoin his "picked nine" on their tour. He would do so, however, as a married man.

Eighteen

Her Tiny Hands Beat Each Other Rapturously

HELEN DAUVRAY WAS BORN either Nellie Gibson or Helen Gibson in either Cincinnati or San Francisco in either 1857 or 1861. Foremost among her many qualities, good and bad, was a profoundly developed sense of the dramatic. The woman had flair. For example, when asked about those attributes she most admired in her husband, Helen replied that he was not only charming and well bred, he was "informed" and "cultured." In fact, he spoke "five or six languages fluently," a statement accepted on its face and repeated by many writers down through the years. In fact, unless one counts English and any smatterings of classical Greek and Latin that Ward picked up during his years at Penn State and Columbia, Ward was no more a polyglot than a badger is a bear. (It is entirely possible, of course, that Ward himself was the original source of the story, for he was an occasional fabulist. He once told his second wife—so convincingly that she, in turn, repeated the story as gospel—that New York's Polo Grounds had been named after a certain Polo, one of Ward's hunting dogs.)

Helen was well known in theatrical circles for her "exceedingly nervous constitution," her swoonings, her self-dramatizations. She made sure the world never forgot how assiduously she worked at her craft. Why, her company would rehearse a play once daily *except* for the day preceding an opening, when they would run through the play twice! "That," she told American reporters, "is a French idea." And it may well have been. She regularly worked herself into such a state during performances that she needed to be carried, after the final curtain, from the stage to her dressing room, where the prostrate actress would be administered smelling salts.

She was tiny—the word is Helen's Homeric epithet—buxom, oval-faced, ambitious, wealthy, intelligent, energetic, talented, and litigious. Her eyes were black, "brilliant and alert," and, while not large, were "set far enough apart to suit an artist." Her hair was deep brown—for all purposes black. Young, she looked sweet, with a petite nose and delicate features; during her early career she was often cast as a pert, saucy heroine. She could pass for a small-town Methodist minister's high-spirited daughter—the one who didn't give a fig what people said about her! As she aged, though, her bright round face began setting up. Her nose became broader, more low-slung, her eyes hard: they broached no nonsense. Don't try to fool Helen Dauvray! they shouted. Helen Dauvray, who looked like the iron-fisted owner of the most popular saloon in town; Helen Dauvray, who, had she posed for photographers not in a swirling yards-of-white-cloth gown and a huge, confectionary hat but in austere black, might have played a Mediterranean widow, aging and grim and forbidding.

Her father died soon after Helen's birth. Her mother remarried a man named Williams and the family moved to Virginia City, Nevada. At five, Helen made her stage debut as Eva in *Uncle Tom's Cabin* at Maguire's Opera House. (During a good part of the nineteenth century, many entertainment halls called themselves opera houses or lyceums or museums. This lent them an instant aura of grandeur, allowing them to sidestep the still somewhat disreputable term "theater.")

"The little Gibson girl," with her "bright and precocious" ways, was an immediate success. She moved from the mining towns to San Francisco and expanded her repertoire. Besides Eva, she played the Duke of York in *Richard III* and Pearl in *The Scarlet Letter*. By 1869, her star rising, she toured the country in now-forgotten popular plays such as *Fidelia*, *No Name*, and *Katie Did*.

Helen arrived in New York and made her debut at Wood's Museum on June 20, 1870, in a month-long run of *Popsey Wopsey*. This twice-a-day revue called on her to play, in turn, a young girl in a song-and-dance, an Irish boy, a Dutch girl who danced in wooden shoes, and a boy who drummed and played the banjo. Her stage name was "Little Nell, the California Diamond."

Audiences were struck by Helen's "youth, sincerity of purpose and . . . crude talent." Critics reacted "kindly." After *Popsey Wopsey* closed, she performed briefly in another play and resumed her national tour, eventually returning to California. Little Nell next embarked on a long tour of Australia. By the time she returned, a year or so later, she had a healthy bank balance that, on the advice of friends, she invested in cheap stocks, at least one of which—Comstock Mines—became flabbergastingly valuable.

Now rich as well as ambitious, and eager to complete the education she had missed while touring, teenaged Helen set off for Europe: first to Milan, where she took piano and voice lessons, and then to Paris, to study French.

"I knew hardly a word of the French language," she later told the *New York Times*,

> and I began by engaging a preceptress . . . with whom I devoted five hours daily to solid study. My early training as an actress no doubt assisted in the rapidity of my progress and in a few months I spoke French tolerably well.

The former Little Nell decided she wanted to act again, this time, however, on the French stage. She managed to gain an audience with M. Ludovic Halevy, a renowned French dramatist, and told him of her plans.

> He could not restrain himself from telling me the idea was simply insane. He said the French public had no interest whatever in Americans, and that even if they had there were more native actresses there than could find employment. . . .

Helen returned to her apartment and cried for half an hour. Then she dried her tears, called her preceptress, and added two hours a day to her French lessons. A year later, she began making the rounds of Paris to secure a manager. Until she encountered M. Gautier of the *Folies Dramatiques*, however, she met with nothing but derision. Gautier, it turned out, was in love with America and everything American, and after listening to Helen's French, assured her he would cast her in a small part immediately.

Helen refused. She wanted to star in her own play, written expressly for her. She offered to pay for the play if Gautier would supply the theater. Gautier agreed and introduced her to a playwright, Paul Ferrier. On September 1, 1884, Mlle. Helene Dauvray debuted in *Miss Maggie*, Ferrier's adaptation of *Nan the Good-for-nothing*.

According to Helen—and as much as we like her, we must remind ourselves to take almost anything she says with a grain or two of salt—she first drew applause barely minutes into the performance. By the end of the play she was being heralded from the rafters by the audience, by Gautier, by his comanagers, by playwright Ferrier—who, fearful of the play's reception, had kept his name from the playbill—and by the severest critics.

Miss Maggie ran for nine weeks before Helen, "completely shattered" by the nervous strain of her work, collapsed. Following doctor's orders, she returned to the United States, but only after a farewell breakfast in France attended by "the most brilliant men and women of Paris."

She must have anticipated that the voyage would prove a tonic, for her arrival in New York was preceded by an avalanche of publicity stating that Mlle. Helene Dauvray of the French stage would soon be gracing the stages of America.

Helen—or Helene, as she was referred to upon her arrival—was a whirlwind. By year's end she had commissioned a play for herself and booked the Star Theatre, bought a luxurious "double mansion" at 49 Park Avenue, near 37th Street, in the fashionable Murray Hill district, and begun courting the press with enviable success. Both the *Times* and the *Dramatic Mirror* printed extensive pre-opening interviews with her, and in both, Helen made a point of mentioning her success in Paris and her enthusiasm for the upcoming production. The *Times* whetted readers' appetites by pointing out the sumptuousness of Helen's living quarters—complete with stables that cost $70,000, one of the "most elegant affairs of its kind in New York," "stocked with valuable horseflesh."

But her lifestyle was of secondary importance, serving only as evidence that her claims of a dazzling array of costumes for her upcoming play were not to be "regarded with suspicion by the general public for the reason that some rather extraordinary exaggerations have been made known in this direction." Her stage diamonds alone cost more than $60,000, Helen informed the world.

While the *Times* only hinted at Helen's high spirits and sprightly temperament, the *Dramatic Mirror* preferred the show-don't-tell school of expository prose.

"I only play here four weeks," she began, "and then I am to return to Paris. I am, as you perhaps know, still a member of the *Folies Dramatiques*, and am only here on a leave of absence. . . . One remains a member of the *Folies*, you know, until they send in their resignation. . . . Oh, you want to know something about my play? Do you want the plot? Oh, no, you have seen that already. Well, then, it is going to be beautifully mounted, and I have an excellent supporting company. [I am playing] a high comedy part. Don't say it's *soubrette* or you'll drive me wild. . . . I forgot to tell you [in addition to my Swiss mountain dance] I sing two French *chansonettes* in the course of the play. They will not display my voice to much advantage, but I think they will please the audience."

Mona opened on April 27, very late in the 1884–1885 season. (The theatrical season, before the advent of air conditioning, generally opened in early fall and ended in late May or mid-June.) By all accounts, Helen's wooing of the press was a wise move. Generally, the critics hated the play passionately, but were very kind toward Helen. They commented, almost in unison, on her great stage presence and potential and remarked that they could not wait for her next vehicle, in which, they hoped, she would not repeat her mistake of choosing a *Mona*.

The *Times* called the play "dull" and "a mass of stupid talk." The *Herald* called the play tedious and "lacking in incident" and began its review with a well-honed barb: "A new play, a new star and a good company combined last night to give as little entertainment as could be found at any theatre in the city." The *Clipper* scratched its head at the fact that Helen's title character, in the novel an Irish girl, had become an American with an English accent who spoke broken English, sang in French, and performed a Tyrolean dance.

However, the *Times* spoke of Helen's "fresh and engaging manner, her absolute self-possession and the earnest and sympathetic labor she bestowed upon unpromising material." The *Clipper*, like the *Times*, noted her engaging manner, her "ease of carriage" and the "airiness" of her performance. The *Dramatic Mirror* spoke of Helen's "bright, intellectual face, magnetic presence, graceful carriage and thorough knowledge of stage technique."

All in all, *Mona* was a tepid success—it ended its two-and-one-half-week run on May 16, two weeks prematurely.

Helen engaged Bronson Howard—one of the country's most popular playwrights—to create a vehicle for her. Howard was a meticulous worker. Over a thirty-six-year career he wrote twenty-seven plays, only one of which, *Shenandoah,* is even slightly remembered today. His trademark was his unabashed celebration of the American feminine spirit. Time and again his work pitted a free, guileless, honest, spirited, intelligent American woman against a hypocritical, hidebound, plum-in-mouth European aristocracy. While it is dangerous to hoist the saddle of century-old popular sensibilities on a present-day horse, we are probably safe imagining a typical Howard heroine as a sort of Doris Day character plunked down in a laughably rigid and tedious Boston or London.

Helen knew her playwright. *One of Our Girls* opened November 10, 1885, at the Lyceum, and ran to packed houses for six and one-half months. Kate Shipley became Helen's signature role.

Kate Shipley is a lively American woman who falls in love with an Englishman in Paris. Her energies there are directed toward preventing the arranged marriage of a French girl with a villainous, dissipated rake.

Critical reaction was mixed. The *New York Tribune* said that as Kate, Helen was nearly perfect. Though she lacked, perhaps, the range to deal with Kate's "private depth" of feeling (a sentiment echoed by others), her "affluence of animal spirits and of rich apparel was seen with pleasure, in a performance replete with delightful buoyancy and frolic." Helen "quite captivated the audience."

Other reviews were more measured—though something about Helen made most critics reluctant to cut her at the knees.

The *Dramatic Mirror* however, cruelly predicted the stern, unwelcoming visage of the older Helen:

> Miss Dauvray should restrain an inclination she has to make
> ludicrous mugs. They may feel funny inside, but they look like
> paroxysms of toothache outside. [She] should immediately
> change her style of hair-dressing. The flat, smooth bands of black,

and the four hair fish-hooks on her forehead, give a cast-iron expression to her otherwise pleasant face.

After taking the summer off, Helen gathered up most of the original cast of *Girls* and opened the 1886–1887 season with an exhausting road trip: a week in Boston, a week in Philadelphia, and a week in Washington, D.C., in October, followed by November performances in Baltimore, Chicago, Louisville, and Cincinnati. Back in New York, the players immediately began rehearsing two plays simultaneously, a minor work called *A Scrap of Paper* and another Bronson Howard work, *Met By Chance.*

A Scrap of Paper—a revival of a quarter-century-old French play, *The Fly Trap*—fluttered across the stage for a fortnight, playing to enthusiastic, well-heeled crowds (which the reviewers spent an inordinate amount of time discussing) before closing on January 8. A small flap ensued when the *Mirror* discovered that the audacious Helen had asked Lester Wallack of Wallack's Theatre for his prompt books of the play. " 'Egad!' he exclaimed. 'Somebody will be asking me to put my hands in my pockets and hand over my watch and pocketbook next.' " The *Mirror* sternly scolded Helen, saying that to ask for a manager's stock in trade—his prompt books—was "too much to expect even of so obliging and gallant a man as the manager of Wallack's."

By all accounts, Helen was, oddly, ill-suited to the role of a witty, sophisticated French woman, but once again the critics could not bring themselves to lash out. The *Dramatic Mirror:* "she has neither the presence nor the manner requisite to the representation of [her character,] there was however *finesse* in some of her work." Tne *Herald:* [Dauvray] gave a "spirited, refined and highly effective performance." The *Tribune:* "[Though] scarcely possessed of the rich, warm, woman-like nature . . . and the complete command of nimble raillery [necessary to her character,] Miss Dauvray was brisk and vivacious."

As it turned out, 1887 would prove to be one of the most intense, exhausting, disturbing, exciting, and high-profile years of Helen's life. The long-anticipated new Howard/Dauvray production, *Met By Chance,* opened on January 11, 1887, at the Lyceum and was roundly dismissed as hopeless: badly written and badly acted. The *Dramatic Mirror* called it overstaged:

In style, tone and treatment it is far beneath any work that Mr.
Howard has submitted. [It is] talky, stupid, uninteresting. . . .
The stage, like Miss Dauvray, was overdressed. . . . Her
dresses . . . must be seen to be appreciated. They baffle the
descriptive power of the masculine sex.

The critics' pounding aside, *Met By Chance* was, for Helen, a mixture
of good and bad news. The good news was that the Lyceum crowds, such
as they were, were of the most fashionable and appreciative sort. The bad
news was that Helen, confident of the play's success, had rented the theater—with no return clause in the contract—until May, and had effectively guaranteed her company work for that period. With *Met By Chance*
closing before the end of January, even Helen's abundant bankroll would
be strained.

Helen managed to open *Peg Woffington*, another comedy, by January
31, and with it struck silver. It played to enthusiastic audiences for five
weeks, and most likely would have been able to continue to pack the
house, had not Helen, fearful of fresh competition in the form of "second
season" openings in March, presented two new plays.

The critics were noticing large seams in Helen's acting.

Helen *is* one of our girls. She is a thoroughly cool, clever, plucky
American woman, with lots of taste, and a faculty and stage
knowledge which are palpable . . . [and in many scenes she is]
clever, saucy and bright [However, Peg is also] high-colored, exuberant and emotional, and this Miss Dauvray is not.

Peg Woffington was a demanding role—one critic likened it to that
of Hamlet—and Helen was clearly in over her head. Nonetheless,
the "interesting, if not brilliant" production of the play pleased the public, as did Helen, who met with nightly curtain calls and thunderous
applause.

Helen's company finished the season with *Walda Lamarr* and *The Love
Chase*, two critical failures that audiences loved.

Helen was the darling of the town, which the *Dramatic Mirror* had to
acknowledge:

Whatever else may be said of Miss Dauvray's work, it is at least considered of so much interest that her premieres draw possibly the most select and refined gatherings to be found under the roof of a metropolitan theatre . . . and in that exalted patronage she finds encouragement and applause beyond her individual deserts as an actress.

After *Walda* closed in early April, the exhausted Dauvray troupe filled the last three weeks of the season with a revival of a Sheridan Knowles comedy, *The Love Chase*.

On May Day, the season—and Helen's obligation to the Lyceum— was over. Helen announced she would summer and recover at The West End, in Long Branch, on the New Jersey shore.

As if the difficult season were not enough to send a body off for a quiet, recuperative summer, Helen had had to deal with a stalker.

Around the middle of February, during the run of *Peg Woffington*, Helen had begun receiving mash notes from a Chicago salesman, Joseph Golding. Golding had first seen her on stage in the Midwest. He followed her to New York, where he had taken rooms near Washington Square. The letters were bold. "My adored Helen," "My dearest darling," they began. "You are my guiding star, my light, my beacon. I adore you. I have found out that you are not married. If I am mistaken, God pardon me and pardon you."

In one letter, he suggested they meet downtown, near the corner of Bowery and Canal Streets, for ice cream and oyster stew. He told her he had been born on Pike's Peak, that he had given up a $3,000-a-year job to be near her. He sent his card to her after performances. He stood outside her house after she returned home, gazing forlornly at the "rays of gaslight that came from her window." He followed her "like a dog." He knocked on her door and asked to be granted an interview. He signed his letters "Yours distractedly."

At about 2:30 in the morning of Tuesday, March 7, Helen and her sister, Clara, noticed Golding once again standing across from Helen's window, gazing upward in a "most ridiculously dejected manner," as the *Times* reported. There came a loud knocking at the door. On the steps stood a policeman, holding Golding by his collar.

When the officer asked why he was bothering the woman, Golding replied, "I couldn't control myself. I had to. . . . I am perfectly sane. . . . When I see the light in her window, I think I see her. I watch it every night until it goes out."

Golding, a "fine-looking young fellow, with dark hair and eyes, and well-dressed," appeared before a judge, who asked him if he did, in fact, love Miss Dauvray.

"As God is my judge, I love her," Golding replied. "I can't eat; I can't sleep; I can't work; I must follow her. I have fought against it. It is stronger than I."

The judge decided that Golding would have to serve some months in jail or furnish $300 in bail—to be forfeited if he was found to be bothering Helen during the next three months.

Reporters refused to take the affair seriously. The *Times* dispatch ended thus:

> Mrs. Helm [Helen's sister] said "I am quite sure he is insane, poor man," and became nearly lachrymose as she thought again of her would-be brother-in-law's melancholy fate.

Golding's arrest, however, may have been timely. The entire contents of his pockets were a single dollar and a six-inch knife. Golding's fate is unknown, but there is no record that his and Helen's paths ever crossed again.

In late May 1887, three weeks after the closing of *The Love Chase*, Helen's personal life again made headlines. The story ran under the banner "Love's Loans," and was an account of testimony before a judge and jury in a lower New York City court.

Several years earlier, it seemed, a young woman, Eva Heaton, had taken up with Leonard F. Tracy, a handsome, dark-haired, mustachioed Lothario. The two had met in Philadelphia, where they were both members of a well-respected dramatic association. Heaton, an aspiring actress, had been working as an electrician for the troupe. Thanks to those wages, as well as the income from some savvy investments in the stock market, she had a "snug" bank account. The unemployed Tracy paid Heaton "assiduous attentions" and asked her to marry him. She accepted and began supporting her fiancé for the best part of two years. One day, however, she received a letter from him calling the engagement off. Tracy had decided he could not have an actress for a wife: Eva Heaton had by then become Etelka Wardell, the leading lady in productions such as *White Slave* and *Wages of Sin*.

As it turned out, Tracy had hightailed it to Europe shortly after he wrote the letter. Many months later he returned, with a new bride—another actress, it would turn out—by the name of Helen Dauvray.

Heaton/Wardell then produced for the court a promissory note for $5,000 plus interest, signed by Tracy and dated mid-January 1882. Tracy, who at the time of the trial was working as a salesman for a Manhattan iron company, told the court that he had indeed signed the note, but only under duress. Heaton/Wardell had threatened him with blackmail, to "blast his reputation"—presumably with Helen—unless he complied with her wishes and signed the IOU.

The next day, an irate letter from Helen Dauvray appeared in the *Times* asking the paper to allow her "space in your columns to correct some mistakes" concerning the Tracy affair. Helen had, indeed, married Tracy in 1881, but the marriage had been a failure—the two were separated and divorced within a few months. Since she had already divorced in January 1882—the time of the promissory note's signing—Tracy's affairs were no concern of hers, nor did he have any claim on her fortune. Therefore, since she could not be blackmailed, Tracy's defense was a bald lie.

The judge, however, had already agreed with Heaton/Wardell, and had ordered Tracy liable for the $5,400 he had borrowed.

Helen probably spent time that summer of 1887 at the shore as well as some time upstate, at Saratoga Springs. She also spent much time in stifling Manhattan, at her Park Avenue home, which she shared with her sister Clara and her brother, Adolph Gibson. There was the business of the upcoming theatrical season to attend to. Helen was well known for attending to all details, big and small, from the casting of the plays to the color of ink on the programs. The gossip columns reported that Helen had acquired another interest as well. She was a regular attendee at the Polo Grounds, watching baseball games.

She was usually accompanied by Clara and Adolph, and had a grand-stand seat along the first-base line. She was an avid enough fan not only to keep score, but to keep it conscientiously. If she was unsure about a play, she would turn to the nearest reporter (her seat was near the press box) for help. Her attitude toward the game itself, moreover, was one of high seriousness. She did not appreciate the high jinks of George Gore, for example, a boisterous and often drunk New York outfielder. Gore delighted in diverting opponents' attention from matters at hand. He would "dance" on the base paths and play the clown by turning his cap brim backward (an early instance of this current fashion statement). Helen, well shaded and busy with her notations, was heard to mutter, "Is that man crazy? Why don't he behave himself?"

Helen's enthusiasm for the game transcended mere attendance, however. In June, she persuaded Nicholas Young, the National League president, to donate a prize to the victor of the post-season playoffs between the League and Association pennant winners. The prize, a handsome cup, was made of sterling silver and reportedly cost $500. The design on its front showed a batter waiting at the plate, a catcher's mask above him, and pennants and a pair of baseballs on either side. Crossed bats formed the handles. The Cup's inscription read:

THE DAUVRAY CUP
presented by
MISS HELEN DAUVRAY
to the players winning the
WORLD'S CHAMPIONSHIP

But, as would always be the case with Helen, nothing was done quietly or without fanfare. One newspaper—and it is difficult not to see the extravagant hand of Helen in this "leak"—reported that the cup came from Tiffany's. This may have been the case, but the Tiffany Company, which maintains a meticulous archive of orders and designs, has no record of such a cup being ordered.

As well, Helen's best intentions were considered ill conceived. League president Young, in a rare nod to populist sentiment, had some reservations about the fact that the cup would be held by the winning club's president. (The cup was to be awarded each year. If a team won the cup for three consecutive years, the cup would become that team's permanent trophy.) Young preferred that the victorious players, not the team executive, be honored. Helen, miffed, withdrew her offer entirely.

In short order she reconsidered her withdrawal and graciously conceded Young's point. She adjusted her offer: in addition to the cup, each player on the first winning team would receive a handsome gold badge depicting a batter, a diamond-shaped field, and two crossed bats.

Helen's generosity was not universally acknowledged. The popular *National Police Gazette*, for one, called the whole business an "advertising play."

> What is wrong with Helen Dauvray? Is she not of sufficient importance in the theatrical world, that she is seeking notoriety and cheap advertising in baseball circles by offering a costly "loving cup" as a trophy?

Then, in early September, Helen fell ill. Her worried family attributed the illness—which they described as a "spasm"—to overwork. Her agent, however, dismissed concerns that the illness was severe and, forgetting that the Gibson family was of solid Ohio/California stock, suggested that the episode was "much exaggerated by her family, who have the veritable temperament of the French." The agent assured all that the upcoming season was not in jeopardy.

Three days later, however, the "spasm" had become "nervous prostration," from which Helen had been suffering "for weeks." Further, a team of doctors advised Helen, as soon as she was able, to "seek rest and recuperation" in the country. Until her recovery was complete, the doctors continued, she would be forced to abandon her theatrical preparations.

Two days after that, on September 9, came the official announcement that Helen had disbanded her company for the upcoming season—throwing more than a score of people out of work. (This was especially bad news for the troupers, coming as it did late in the summer, when most companies were already in place.)

A small furor erupted. The *Times* reported that Helen's condition was an excuse "not accepted generally among the members of the profession as altogether genuine." They felt Helen's real motive was financial, that after losing so much money the previous spring—an estimated $35,000— she had asked her sister for a loan and been refused.

Snapping like a cornered animal, William Hayden, Helen's manager, called the *Times* report inaccurate and beneath contempt. Should Helen embark on a new season, it would be at life's risk. Further, Hayden implied—somewhat ambiguously—the whole notion of a family contretemps was so much bilge.

> I am wholly in ignorance with reference to any such expenditures, or with regard to any such loss having entailed itself upon Miss Dauvray or her connections, due to her engagement under my management.

(Several weeks later, the *New York Tribune*, in what seems an authoritative article, tends to split the difference between the two schools of thought. Of the previous season's plays, all but *Met By Chance*—which lost $11,000—covered expenses.)

Hayden then read a statement from one of Helen's doctors:

> I hereby certify that for the last two years Miss Helen Dauvray has been under my professional care . . . that during this time she has repeatedly suffered from attacks of nervous prostration and from excessive exertion and prolonged nervous strain; that during the past Summer, as she informs me, this has been worse than ever, and attended by convulsive attacks which were thought epileptic in form. . . . in my judgment, it has become absolutely necessary for her to suspend professional work of all kinds for two or three months to avert the entire loss of her health.

While that seemed to put the matter to rest for the nonce, there was at least one person in greater New York, and a very influential person it was, who refused to buy a single syllable of these denials and amplifications. That person was the *Dramatic Mirror's* widely read columnist, "Giddy Gusher." "I remember reading a pathetic article about Miss Dauvray's almost hopeless condition in the morning paper," Gusher wrote,

> [yet] finding her on the soft side of a pine plank at a ball game that afternoon. The day following the tearful type told me she was twined in a sheet . . . and the next day she sat in the sun on

the Polo Ground three hours with the thermometer at 120 degrees in the shade. Miss Dauvray combined fatal illness with baseball in a truly wonderful manner. I might have known that something more than the wild delight of witnessing the national game brought that lady off a death bed so often.

Gusher's withering observations appeared in the *Mirror*'s October 22 edition, a reaction to the stunning news that on October 12, only six weeks after Helen's initial collapse, Helen Dauvray had married John Montgomery Ward in Philadelphia.

The *New York Times* had scooped its many rivals by twenty-four hours. On Wednesday, October 12, the morning of the actual ceremony, the paper announced the marriage. This was page one news, running between reports of the expected resignation of Robert Garrett, president of the Baltimore and Ohio Railroad, and a terrible rail disaster in Indiana, in which ten people, and possibly double that number, had been "burned to a crisp beyond means of identification."

The marriage, the *Times* went on, explained in part Helen's well-known devotion to baseball.

> [She] aggressively and enthusiastically championed the home team. Her tiny hands beat each other rapturously at every victory of the Giants and her dark eyes were bedewed at every defeat. But the thousands of spectators who observed Miss Dauvray's emotions little suspected that one of the Giants had any precedence over the others. . . . It was noticed that she always applauded Ward when he made his appearance [and was] especially happy whenever he made a brilliant play. But she was so loyal to all the team that no importance was attached to this shadowy preference.

The next day, the other papers caught up with the *Times* and played the marriage under banner headlines: WARD—DAUVRAY; BASEBALL—DRAMA UNITED; ART WEDDED TO ATHLETICS; ACTRESS AND SHORT STOP; A DIAMOND ROMANCE. Additionally, within the articles' texts writers indulged in a feast of wordplay: Ward had signed "a contract for life" (the *Tribune*); the marriage was a "double play," Helen a "handsome catch," and the marriage's secrecy another example of Ward's crafty "base-stealing" (the *Clipper*).

The *Herald*, however, outrhapsodized all others:

> Baseball and drama joined hands yesterday and linked fortunes in the persons of Mr. John Montgomery Ward and Miss Helen Dauvray.
>
> And the gods applauded, while mortals, being less favored, waited until the news came around their way.
>
> It was meet enough that manly prowess and brain should be wedded to womanly beauty and art. So said everybody who heard of it. It was as if a hero of the Olympian games had stepped out of the arena and up to the portico of the Temple and had espoused a young devotee of Minerva.

The *Times* took credit for precipitating the sudden marriage. Sometime on the evening of Tuesday, the 11th, according to Helen's older brother, Adolph Gibson, a reporter came to the door of Helen's house on Park Avenue and asked Helen to verify rumors of an upcoming marriage.

Aghast that word had leaked out, the family consulted hastily. They all agreed—Helen; Ward; Adolph; Helen's sister, Clara; Walter Hudson, Helen's private secretary; and Ward's good friend and attorney, J. F. C. Blackhurst—it would be best for John and Helen to marry as quickly as possible, thereby avoiding tedious and persistent hounding by the press. According to Adolph, the lovers had been engaged since the previous spring. Originally they had planned to wait two years to marry—a period of time that would allow Helen to enjoy a final pair of stage seasons and Ward a final pair of baseball seasons. Adolph, however, had urged them to reconsider, if for no other reason than that they weren't children any longer. This advice seemed to make more sense after Helen's illness, Adolph told the *Times* reporter. Though the tentative date seemed to change almost daily, by October 11 the ceremony was more or less set to take place in early or mid-November.

But since the *Times*'s hunch had proven correct, Adolph continued, the publicity that would follow the public's learning about their marriage "struck terror" in Helen's heart. Adolph advised his younger sister and Ward that they were "public persons, and the reporters will be on your trail for three weeks. So much notoriety before your marriage will be dis-agreeable. . . . Marry to-morrow morning and avoid it."

It was agreed. Ward enlisted Blackhurst to visit the newspapers and formally announce the wedding, while feigning ignorance as to its loca-tion. According to Adolph, a decision had not been made until 3 a.m. of the 12th.

After a hasty breakfast of rolls and coffee, served at 7:30 the same morning, John, Helen, and Helen's sister and mother took a closed car-riage to the Desbrosses Street Ferry (three blocks south of today's Holland Tunnel). They crossed to Jersey City where they caught the nine o'clock Philadelphia express.

At Philadelphia's Lafayette Hotel, another of Helen's sisters joined them. Ward went to the clerk of the Orphan's Court, took out marriage license number 13,960, returned to the hotel, and, with Helen's family, drove to the Arch Street Presbyterian Church. A Reverend Chapman performed the ceremony.

The couple spent the afternoon driving through Philadelphia parks, then attended the theater. The remainder of the evening and part of the next day were spent "receiving" well-wishers, including the former gover-nor of Pennsylvania and fellow Bellefontian, George Curtin. John and Helen then traveled to Washington and Bellefonte and returned to New York City ten days later. After a brief stay in New York, where Ward attended the annual National League meetings, the newlyweds caught up with most of the New York team in St. Louis and traveled with them on a post-season barnstorming tour of the South and West.

Two days after their elopement, the pair were thrust sideways back into the news when Helen's brother, Adolph, was arrested for assault—a nineteenth-century euphemism for rape—at Helen's home at 49 Park Avenue.

The charges were brought by Annie Allen, a young Scottish servant in Helen's employ. Allen, twenty-two, had been working in the house as a domestic for a couple of months. She had two children, who were staying with her husband and his family in Nova Scotia, where he worked. Allen said that Adolph, thirty-two, had initially taken "liberties" with her some time earlier, not long after he had returned from South America to New York to stay with his sister.

On Tuesday the 11th Adolph again "insulted" Allen on the stairway. She resisted him "so forcibly that his eyeglasses were broken."

Three days later, Adolph, alone in the large house except for the servants, evidently entered Allen's room at 4 a.m., gagged Allen with her sheets and "nearly smothered her." Although the gallant Allen struggled "successfully" with her assailant for the nearly half an hour, she finally succumbed, her "body and limbs a mass of bruises and her strength nearly or quite exhausted."

Clara put up Adolph's $5,000 bail, offering the Park Avenue property as security. Upon his release from the Yorkville jail, Adolph was indignant:

> I don't know anything about what this woman is talking about. I am perfectly innocent of the charges. . . . When she was paid off and went away she said to [Clara] "I want $5,000 to settle this thing."

Allen's lawyer, Elias G. Levy, demanded that Adolph be interrogated, which he was ten days later. During the interrogation, Annie Allen broke down at least twice, bursting into fits of weeping. Five months later, on March 21, Allen withdrew her suit.

The Ward-Dauvray marriage stirred a small tempest: Would he retire? Would she give up the stage? What did the marriage mean for the New York team? How, if Ward did not retire, would marriage affect his playing? The answers were not long in coming. Helen, honoring her new husband's wishes, would give up the stage. Ward, in turn, had no plans to retire immediately. He and Helen had talked about this at length, and, despite their comfortable financial situation—Helen's fortune was well known, and Ward was reported to be making $8,000–$10,000 a year (the figures were inflated)—and Ward's long-held ambition to quit the diamond and practice law, he did not plan to do so for at least a few years.

Had Helen's "sickness" of the late summer and the disbanding of her company been her convoluted and dramatic method of relinquishing a stage career in accordance with her future husband's demand? That was the likeliest explanation for symptoms that took her off the stage but allowed her to convalesce at baseball games and watering holes during September. However, Helen's and John's motives and actions that late summer of 1887 were much more complex and mysterious.

As it turned out, at the time of their elopement to Philadelphia, they had already been married for nearly six weeks, after a brief civil ceremony in New Haven, Connecticut, on August 31. New York was playing the last game of a short series with Indianapolis that Wednesday, but Ward—who had played the day before—was not in the lineup. The following day, against Detroit, Ward did play. New York lost 5–1. Ward went hitless and was scolded by sportswriters for his fielding.

How did such a high-profile and immediately recognizable couple keep their actual marriage—the one in New Haven—a secret from both the public and the press? The likeliest answer is that they bribed city officials to keep mum. It is also possible that the ceremony was performed by a friend of Ward's or a friend of his friend Blackhurst, with the actions entered quietly in City Hall records.

Larger questions loom, however: Why did John and Helen marry, midway through the baseball season, in what seems to have been some haste? Why did they not announce it with all the appropriate fanfare? And why did they marry *again*, rather than simply springing the news that they had been husband and wife for six weeks?

The most plausible scenario is that Helen was pregnant when they were secretly married on August 31. That would explain her September bouts of sickness, her inability to go on stage the next season, and the disbanding of her acting company.

Then, she had either a miscarriage or an abortion, negating the necessity of ever mentioning the secret marriage. (An odd detail of her September indispositions was a report that Helen had undergone "thermocautery," a newfangled electrical procedure sometimes used to stanch bleeding.) When the *Times* reporter came knocking, with questions about the upcoming nuptials, the couple had one of three choices: confess to the August 31 secret marriage, raising a storm of questions and gossip; keep the press wondering, again subjecting themselves to continued bird-dogging; or, do the deed again, and be done with it.

Nineteen

What in Thunder
Cross-Eyed Men Were Made For

THE 1887 POST-SEASON barnstorming tour was to be a fun-for-profit time for the ballplayers. And though the players and those wives who accompanied the team did enjoy themselves—Helen and other "team ladies" hosted a gala reception in New Orleans's St. Charles Hotel for local dignitaries, for example—the tour did not quite live up to its billing. Besides a cool fan reception in California, there was in the air a continuing, escalating battle of wits and ever more barbed exchanges—reported in the sporting press—between Ward and the Brotherhood and the League and Association, prefatory to the annual winter meetings. As well, reports began drifting north of the New Yorks' general misbehavior, lackadaisical play, and heavy drinking.

(In larger incidents of public unrest, there was a horse stampede along Main Street in Los Angeles as well as the gathering of a mob of Negroes in Pattersonville, Louisiana. The Negroes were angered by what they felt were excessive house searches after the murder of a white man. One newspaper's coverage of the Pattersonville incident ran under the headline BAD COONS.)

Ward, nominally in charge of the New York "picked nine," quickly telegraphed papers and refuted reports of bad behavior as "false and purely sensational." In fact, he said, what had happened was that a fight had broken out in the stands. Mike "King" Kelly of Boston, who knew one of the combatants, jumped into the crowd and calmed the situation. It was true,

215

Ward continued, that Kelly then enjoyed a beer with the fans, but he was their hero, and his actions further calmed troubled waters.

As for the games that the team had supposedly canceled due to inebriation, those reports, Ward wrote, were false as well. The cancellations were merely a contractual misunderstanding. Ward's team had discovered that the local team, from New Orleans, was receiving $5 a man per game, while the visitors, playing for a share of the gate, only got $3.

Ward left the team to return north for the mid-November League meetings in New York. There, Ward and other Brotherhood members—Dan Brouthers, Ned Hanlon, and John Morrill—set up headquarters in the Barrett House, near Madison Square Garden's Fifth Avenue Hotel, where the League was meeting. From Barrett House, they sent formal notification of their wish to discuss concerns. The League, acting "puerile in the extreme," very quickly decided Brotherhood matters would be taken up last, thereby forcing the four men to hang fire for the best part of two days.

An agreement was, finally, worked out between the two groups, but the work of Ward and Company hardly seemed to deserve the accolades it received. *The Sporting News* dubbed Ward the "St. George of baseball, for he has slain the dragon of opppression," while the slightly more restrained *Clipper* called the agreement a "triumph" for the "plucky and determined" Ward.

The League did, in fact, officially recognize the Brotherhood—though the act was largely symbolic. Beyond that act, however, it is difficult to see, from the Brotherhood's view, much heat or light generated by the meeting, especially after the mountains of smoke that preceded it.

Much of the twenty-section agreement the League approved preserved the status quo or dealt with petty disciplinary matters such as fines for drunkenness and the obligation of a player to obey his captain "cheerfully and promptly." The reserve clause was left intact, and one of the Brotherhood committee's primary demands—that contracts include actual salary figures—was rebuffed in short order.

Ward, however, seemed pleased with matters in general. In an informal interview with *Sporting Life*'s Harry Clay Palmer in Chicago, as Ward and Helen headed west to rejoin the barnstormers in California, Ward, "well-dressed" and "prosperous looking," waxed generous about the previous few months' bickering.

He seemed to avoid answering Palmer's most pertinent suggestion—that, had the Brotherhood merely published a "model" contract, similar to the one finally approved in New York, wouldn't all the fussing and fighting and bitter words have been avoided? Further, wouldn't the public have then had a better view of the Brotherhood, as opposed to the one Palmer said it now had, that of a quarrelsome, secretive lodge of spoiled brats?

Ward patronized Palmer, calling him "my boy." He then blamed the press for distorting matters in the first place. The Brotherhood was not purely a "labor and capital"–minded organization. Rather, it was one interested primarily in protecting players' rights and evening the balance of power.

Moreover, Ward went on, the importance of this preliminary round of negotiations was twofold. First, the Brotherhood existed formally, recognized now and forever by the League. Second, explained the recent graduate of Columbia Law School, by spelling out in the contract such things as the reserve clause (previously, the contract referred to the League constitution, which included the clause) and having the contract approved by two parties, matters had been whisked from the shadows of "baseball law" and thrown into the bright light of statutary and common law.

Ward's idea was, roughly, this: until the November meetings, it was as if the League had erected a large and fancy dwelling on a busy street and called it a tent, thereby avoiding cumbersome, expensive zoning laws, safety regulations, and property taxes. What Ward and the players had managed to do—by demanding and receiving a more explicit contract—was get that tent properly redefined as a skyscraper.

Ward and Helen returned from California in the first week of January 1888. The West Coast leg of the tour had neither drawn large crowds nor engendered much excitement among the press, and the Wards had lost interest in the enterprise. While they had been gone, Frank Richter, editor of the influential weekly *Sporting Life*, had proposed a revolutionary "Millennium Plan." Richter envisioned organizing all League and Association clubs into a revenue-sharing cooperative, one that would, among other things, pay players according to a mandated salary schedule. Further, the reservation system would expand to include all minor league teams—though major league teams could draft for themselves a small number of minor league players each year. The most radical aspect of the plan was that the two major leagues, and not the individual teams, would hold reservation rights to players—all but one player per team. The rest of the players would be distributed via an annual draft.

Richter's plan was only one more variation—a bold one, to be sure—on a theme that many baseball men, including Spalding, had been batting around for a while. The problem these plans addressed was a thorny one: reserve clause or no reserve clause, salaries still had not fallen to a level satisfactory to owners. In fact, the average League salary had increased modestly—a little more than $150—between 1887 and 1888. Some players—Ward among them—saw their salaries increase dramatically. Ward earned $3,000 in 1887, the last year of his multiyear contract, $4,000 in 1888, and $4,250 in 1889. Tim Keefe, Buck Ewing, and Roger Conner—all, coincidentally, Brotherhood members and teammates of Ward—received $500 raises. Big Dan Brouthers, one of the Brotherhood committee of four at the 1887 League meetings, saw a $700 raise between 1887 and 1888.

The causes of this salary inflation are debatable. Was the increase in fact general, and a function of improved 1887 offensive statistics—derived from rule changes? Was the increase not in fact general, but a mirage caused by a few skyrocketing salaries? Or was it the old conundrum—individual owners unable to resist paying top dollar to retain proven talent and acquire potential talent? (In all likelihood it was a little of each. Certainly the League had one eye on offensive statistics—from the 1888 season on, walks were no longer considered hits as they had been in 1887, and three strikes were an out.)

What does matter is that the League, despite the tentative cooperation promised at those fall 1887 meetings, would continue on course, and cinch its belt tighter as far as the players were concerned. It wavered in its promise to "look into" having salaries written directly into contracts. (The Brotherhood wanted that to expose the fiction of the salary limitation rule.) More drastically, the League reneged on its promise never to sign a reserved player to a contract for a salary lower than the previous year.

Ward turned his attention to baseball. The 1888 season began rancorously for the New Yorks, who were, increasingly, being referred to in the press as the Giants, a moniker supposedly bestowed on the team by their manager, Jim Mutrie, after an 1885 pre-season game. New York fans, who badly wanted a pennant, were in a generally foul, nearly mutinous mood from past-season disappointments. This mood was hardly improved by the fact that two of their favorites—Ward and pitcher Tim Keefe—had demanded significant raises: from $3,000 to $5,000. When the club balked, the players held out, that is, they refused to play until their demands were met. High-stakes poker, this business of holding out. The club risks the loss of a player's services. The player risks his salary, a deterioration of his skills, and fan loyalty. (Holding out is, in some ways, very close to a no-win situation for the player. Even if he does receive his desired salary, the pressure on him to justify that salary is enormous. Boobirds flock when a well-paid player stumbles.)

Ward, signing on opening day, finally settled for $4,000. Keefe held out a week longer before also settling for $4,000. Ward, it would turn out, had a miserable year both at the plate—batting only .251—and in the field, where his fielding average was next to lowest for all League shortstops.

Keefe, however, proved worthy of his new salary. He led the league in wins, strikeouts, earned run average, and winning percentage. Keefe was overpowering—opposing teams hit a paltry .196 against him. During one stretch he won nineteen consecutive games. Though New York stumbled badly out of the gate, they had climbed to first place by the end of July. To the delight of their fans, they won the pennant by nine games.

Just before they moved into first place, the team acquired a mascot, a "freckle-faced street urchin" named Fred Boldt. Fred had hooked up with the team in Chicago, and to the players it seemed that when he was around, the team won. The players—Ward was a notable exception—doted on the boy, feeding him well and buying him new outfit after new outfit.

Team mascots were popular in the nineteenth century. They were part of a widespread belief, by both ballplayers and fans, in "supernatural intervention." Whether athletes are more superstitious than nonathletes is arguable, but certainly the extreme vicissitudes of sport would foster behavioral tics among its participants: I struck out last time, this time I took a drink from the cooler and hit a triple. I shall, therefore, always take a drink from the cooler before heading to the on-deck circle.

The *Chicago Tribune*, in 1890, made a more sociological argument for the prevalence of superstitious practices among ballplayers, suggesting that many of them came from the "lower-class, poorly educated" segments of society, those more prone to harmless irrationalities. Mascots, the paper went on, were usually "chosen for some hideous peculiarity, such as a dwarfed figure, hump-back or crossed eyes." Skin color, evidently, fit under the category of "hideous peculiarity," for, the paper went on,

> If a little [n]egro, black as the ace of spades, dwarfed in every limb, and with crossed eyes could have been secured the ideal mascot would have been presented to the gaze of the base-ball world.

In the nineteenth century, visiting teams dressed in their hotels and traveled to the ballpark as a group, on a streetcar, omnibus, or hired carriages. Local cranks would line the route to the park, jeering the visitors, or, in many instances, "throwing a hoodoo" on the players—maybe by chasing a black cat in front of the team bus or having a cross-eyed man—a popular symbol of misfortune—stare the team down. The visitors' mascot's job, therefore, was to negate the bad magic with his own hoodoo. Once at the park, the mascot, in between serving as a batboy and leading fans in cheers and generally entertaining them with looniness (not unlike today's Phillie Phanatic), would stay busy counteracting fan hoodoo and throwing out hoodoos of his own.

Ward's lack of enthusiasm for Fred Boldt was based on either personal enmity, an idea that the mascot's antics were a distraction, or a specific disbelief in the powers of mascots. Whatever his objections, it was not because he was not superstitious. The previous fall, Ernest Thayer, a reporter for the *San Francisco Daily Examiner* who also dabbled in poetry, had interviewed some of the New York players during their barnstorming tour and written a piece about their various tics.

Roger Connor, the heavy-hitting first baseman, found barrels standing on end a good omen. Buck Ewing had developed an elaborate talismanic system involving "colored" women: it was lucky to be brushed by the skirt of one, even luckier to walk between two "Negresses." Moreover, the darker the lady, the better the luck.

Ward's superstitions, if more socially adroit, were equally esoteric: supposedly, before a game, he read a single chapter of the penal code of the state in which he found himself. Additionally, when Ward served as captain, he required his players to wear their "road uniforms" on the last game of a home stand, believing the uniforms needed to "become accustomed" to the experience before them.

Ward's most powerful superstition, which he shared with Keefe and New York manager Jim Mutrie, was a common one for the times: the sighting of a cross-eyed man forebode terrible luck.

Once, toward the end of his career, Ward's team was playing a three-game series in Philadelphia. The players, already in uniform, were waiting in the lobby of the Continental Hotel for their omnibus to the ballpark. The bus arrived and Ward asked Frank Richter, the *Sporting Life* editor, for a favor.

"I wish you would step out and see if any cross-eyed men are about. They are about the only things I am afraid of."

Richter did so, and called back that the coast was clear. Captain Ward ordered his team on the bus. Moments later a "cross-eyed Negro" jumped on the rear step of the bus. Ward's catcher, Con Daily, sitting in the last seat, called forward to Ward.

"Don't look, John. Shut your eyes, Johnny."

Daily threw the "startled darkey" off the bus.

Four blocks along, a "shock-headed urchin" whose eyes "were bent attentively on each side of his nose" jumped on the bus. Again Daily warned Ward, and again he threw the would-be hitchhiker from the bus. Before the bus arrived at the ballpark, four more cross-eyed boys, including a "poor hollow-cheeked consumptive," tried to catch the bus and were, in turn, unceremoniously ejected by the vigilant Daily.

Ward was beside himself. He thanked Daily but told him he had no choice but to sit him out and play Paul Cook instead.

"Con, I don't feel right about all those cross-eyed kids . . . You were the one who saw them, you know."

At the last minute Ward changed his mind. In the fourth or fifth inning, Daily sprained his ankle sliding into second. Not only did Ward's team lose badly, but Daily was out of action for nearly two weeks. On the day of his return, the hapless Daily ran across yet another cross-eyed boy.

This time he kept the news from Ward. Sure enough, during the game, Daily was seriously injured. He told Ward about the pre-game sighting.

Ward threw up his hands, wondering "what in thunder cross-eyed men were made for, and what right they had to interfere with base ball!"

The rivalry between Chicago and New York was one of the most fierce in the League. In early June, Chicago had come to New York for the first time that season; with great energy, the Chicagoans lampooned New York's annual opening-day Seventh Regiment–led festivities in the Polo Grounds by marching across the entire field clad in ostentatious swallow-tailed coats, led by their baton-twirling "colored mascot," Clarence Duval. Not to be outdone, the next day all eighteen New York players marched from the center field locker room to home plate wearing swallow-tailed linen dusters and white top hats. Though the fans loved the general mockery, the *Clipper* did not, reminding readers that though the "farce will long be remembered [it] should never again be repeated. The dignity of the national game should be upheld at all times."

By mid-August 1888, with the New Yorks enjoying their first-place standing, DeWolf Hopper, one of the era's most loved comic actors as well as a baseball fan and a friend of Helen, suggested to his boss at the McCaull Opera Company that the troupe spend the afternoon at the Polo Grounds being entertained by the team. That evening they would return the favor by hosting the New Yorks and their opponents, Chicago, at Wallack's Theatre.

The opera company scrambled to organize the entertainment. Hopper, the evening's main attraction, was at a loss to come up with something special for the gala. Then he remembered a poem he had seen in a newspaper and clipped, one written two months earlier by Ernest Thayer, the *San Francisco Daily Examiner* reporter who had discussed ballplayer superstitions the year before.

The house was packed to the doors, and when the two clubs came in they were given an ovation.

Just before the opera began Gen. Sherman, who is as fond of baseball as he used to be of forced marches, walked down the aisle [and was] instantly recognized by the ball-players in the boxes, as well as by the majority of the audience. Some one of

Chicago's team began to applaud, and everybody took up the cue and the old General bowed quietly to the impromptu reception.

As might be expected, Hopper let himself loose on the subject of baseball, and the men laughed heartily at the bits that the comedian threw at them. . . . In honor of the occasion he recited with brilliant effect . . . "Casey's [sic] at the Bat." The audience literally went wild with enthusiasm; men got up on their seats and cheered, while old Gen. Sherman laughed until the tears ran down his cheeks. It was one of the wildest scenes ever seen in a theatre, and showed the popularity of Hopper and baseball.

Three days after Hopper's public debut recital of "Casey at the Bat"—which he would recite over 10,000 times before his death in 1935—*Sporting Life* reported that the Washington League team was keenly interested in obtaining Ward. They would either buy him outright from New York or offer two players, Barney Gilligan and Dupee Shaw, in trade. A trade wasn't likely—Gilligan was a weak-hitting catcher and Shaw a dead-armed pitcher. Ward reacted coolly. He let the world know that, no, in fact, he would not object to moving to Washington—for there he could make use of the nation's "great law library." There was, of course, one problem: as a Brotherhood member he objected categorically to being sold.

The possible transaction was big news in baseball circles. *Sporting Life* reported that besides his value to baseball owners—rumors would eventually place his sale price at $12,000 to $15,000—he was "talked of more than President Cleveland."

After the regular season, the New Yorks met the St. Louis Browns, winners of the Association pennant, in a championship exhibition series. Although most baseball books mark the start of what we know as the World Series as the year 1903, in fact there were post-season championships nearly annually beginning in 1882.

These proto–World Series were a mixed lot. Three times they were not played at all, due to bickering. Some of them featured the first-place team playing the second-place team; one of them featured two split-season League champions only; one series lasted only two games, another, in 1887, fifteen. The 1890 series ended in a tie: 3–3–1.

The New Yorks dominated the 1888 series. They won their deciding sixth victory after eight games. The problem was, the series had been pre-determined to last ten games. The last two games drew a total of only 1,123 fans.

By the time of the last out, however, John Ward was well on his way toward Oxford, Nebraska, where he hooked up with a pair of barnstorming teams that were on the first leg of a several-months-long trip around the world.

Twenty

Vedi Napoli e Poi Mori

BY OPENING DAY of the 1888 baseball season, Albert Goodwill Spalding was a wealthy man—president of the Chicago League team and the dominant figure in the burgeoning, highly profitable, and high-profile sporting goods industry. In 1876, Albert and his brother, Walter, with an $800 stake advanced them by their mother, had opened a small athletic equipment store on Randolph Street in Chicago. At the time, Walter was a bank clerk and Albert, who had returned to his home state with William Hulbert, founder of the National League, was pitching for Chicago.

Spalding was an extraordinary athlete. He had led the National Association in wins in every one of its five years, and did the same in the National League in 1876, effectively his last year as a professional player. In six seasons, he had won 247 games. (He pitched only eleven innings in 1877.) The major league record for career wins, Cy Young's 511, is surely as untouchable a mark as baseball has. However, if we extrapolate Spalding's brief career to Young's lengthy one—twenty-two years—Spalding would have left the game with 889 victories.

By 1879 the Spaldings had opened a separate bat factory, and over the next decade they bought out several competitors—who continued selling sporting goods under their original brand names. By 1887, the Spaldings were reportedly turning a million bats a year. By 1896 they employed more than 3,500 workers, had plants scattered across the eastern half of the United States, headed a huge mail-order business, and listed "depots," carrying a complete line of Spalding goods, in sixty-five cities, including Honolulu; Helena, Montana; Sydney, Adelaide, and Melbourne, Australia; and Auckland, New Zealand.

The A. G. Spalding and Brothers Company, by the turn of the century, sold and manufactured croquet, golf, and tennis equipment, roller and ice skates, bicycles and bicycle shoes, footballs, football uniforms and shoes, hunting and fishing goods of all kinds, and, of course, baseball equipment—bats, bat bags, score books, ball-and-strike indicators, pitching toe-plates, bases, shoes, jerseys, pants, caps, stockings, cleats, gloves, and catcher's mitts, masks, and chest protectors. The Spalding ball was the official National League ball. *Spalding's Official Base Ball Guide*, which sold 50,000 copies a year, was the League's official publication. The *Guide* was a highly effective publicity tool for baseball. It included individual and team statistics for both the League and the Association and various intercollegiate associations, a day-by-day record of all League and Association games played the year before, a schedule for the upcoming season's games, and the game's official rules. It also served as a soapbox for League/team owner policies by printing an annual history of the game—as much editorial as factual—and, most years, a state-of-the-sport report that reminded one and all, players and fans alike, that baseball's continued success depended on the wisdom of League officials and team owners. It also included dozens of pages of advertisements, most of them for Spalding sporting equipment.

Spalding was an excellent, aggressive, and energetic businessman. He was also a spirited nationalist who could not imagine any greater good to be bestowed upon the world than the game of baseball. His first venture overseas came in 1874, when the Boston and Philadelphia National Association teams toured Britain in mid-season, playing exhibition baseball as well as cricket.

In 1888, Spalding once again turned his thoughts across the ocean, though in the opposite direction. His 1911 work of autobiography and history, *America's National Game*, says that since baseball had become so popular in America, he felt "the time had come when this great pastime should be introduced wherever upon the globe conditions were favorable to our peculiar form of outdoor sport." He neglected to mention that if baseball became universally popular, Spalding baseball equipment might well become so too.

Baseball was already popular in Hawaii, and, according to Spalding, the British colonists of the South Pacific islands, New Zealand, and Australia had "a racial love for outdoor games." He therefore dispatched his secretary, Leigh S. Lynch, in February 1888 to make arrangements for a tour of "the Antipodes."

On October 20, 1888, most of the trip's logistics had been worked out, and the tourists, as they were called, left Chicago for San Francisco by special train. Aboard were two squads of ballplayers—most of Spalding's Chicago League team and a picked nine, the All-Americas—consisting of "men of clean habits and attractive personality, men who would reflect credit upon the country and the game." John Ward was the All-Americas' captain and shortstop. In addition the entourage included several players' and executives' wives, a few of Spalding's friends, and three journalists, Harry Clay Palmer of the *New York Herald*, Newton Macmillan of the *New York Sun*, and "Mr. Goodfriend" of the *Chicago Inter-Ocean*.

Ward was not on the banner-decked Chicago, Burlington & Quincy train that pulled out of Union Station that night. He was instead in St. Louis, resting up after the fifth game of the post-season series between the New York League team and the St. Louis Association team, winners of their respective pennants. After the eighth and deciding game of October 25, which New York won 11–3, Ward, Helen, and pitcher Ed Crane hopped a westbound train and met the tourists' party at Oxford, Nebraska.

The teams played in Denver on October 27 before 7,500 fans. The game was a poorly played affair. The following day, however, the game—the teams' ninth in eight days—was more artful, thanks in no small part to Ward, who played shortstop in a "masterly fashion," to the delight of the crowd of 6,000 who basked in warm, Indian summer weather.

The teams then left for San Francisco, their embarcation point, with stops at Colorado Springs and Salt Lake City. The teams' arrivals were opportunities for civic festivities: parades, sightseeing, and lengthy, multi-course banquets. Between the hospitality and actual ball games, the tourists rarely had a moment of free time. Nonetheless, on their first day in Denver, the Wards bought some property—three lots, near Cimarron and 18th Streets. They had likely made preliminary arrangements the year before, when they had stopped in Denver on their honeymoon. The price was a lofty $25,000. The *Rocky Mountain News* welcomed Ward to the local tax base and singled him out for praise for acknowledging the cheers of the audience at the Saturday night opera.

The tourists, in California a fortnight, stayed in the Bay Area except for a two-day, two-game trip to Los Angeles. Though their schedules were crammed with banquets, tours of local attractions such as the Cliff House Hotel and Chinatown, and gala stage entertainments, they did manage to play some ball.

They did so, for the most part, badly. Besides sloppy exhibition games against Chicago, Ward's team managed to lose to Oakland, the California League cellar-dwellers, 12–2, and to the Pioneers, 9–4. They also lost both of their Los Angeles games.

To make matters worse, Ward and Ned Hanlon, who were to play in a Chicago–All-America game at San Francisco's Haight Street grounds on Sunday, November 11, sauntered "leisurely" onto the field, out of uniform and nearly an hour late. Ward, according to the *San Francisco Daily Examiner*, had merely "performed his old trick of keeping the crowd waiting." A week earlier, Ward had missed another game—to the fans' disappointment—because he had gone quail hunting.

In general, San Francisco was less than impressed with their eastern visitors.

> Spalding and his players have not done much for baseball on their visit to this city; the two clubs have played several games, and in but one have they put up the variety of ball they are capable of doing. Their games [demonstrate that] the clubs of the local league are capable of playing as good ball as any. . . .

> [Waiting for Ward and Hanlon] the audience sat in their seats and shivered and used language not usually heard on a Sabbath day. . . .

> Ball-players cannot train on late hours and alcohol and win . . . not against such players as the Oaklands. . . . Yesterday they played against nine picked men of the United States and

won with hands down. . . . Ward was the only one who did anything worthy of mention.

On November 18, the party sailed for Honolulu after a final banquet,
this at the Baldwin Hotel, featuring, in what would become a familiar
theme, a menu that celebrated players and destinations: green turtle à la
Kangaroo, *petite pâte* à la Spalding, stewed terrapin à la Ward, and Frisco
turkey à la Foul. The next day, the *Examiner* noted sarcastically that with
the departure of the stars, "San Francisco will have an opportunity of witnessing some good ball playing by the local leaguers."

Though the tour's purpose, ostensibly, was to promote both baseball
and good will, there was, among certain key members of the group, tension and simmering ill will. A few weeks before leaving for Hawaii, Ward
had taken shots at Spalding, the other League owners, and Cap Anson,
the captain of the tour "rivals," Chicago. Ward's volley took the form of a
long article in the October *Cosmopolitan*, "Our National Game." Much of
the piece is an extended summary of the nature of the game and the
"manly" attributes it requires, including "strength, courage and skill."

While much of the article is bland and forgettable, Ward singles out
Adrian "Cap" Anson—who had not joined the Brotherhood, and had
made clear that he had no intention of doing so—for stinging criticism.

> His reputation as a "kicker" is familiar not only to all attendants
> at the games but to many who have never even seen him. [Anson
> was, in fact, known as "Baby."] [Though] he is not one of your
> senseless kickers who finds fault merely because he is being
> beaten. . . . It is true, however, that he will go to the outside limit
> of the rule every time, and, while his claims may be legitimate so
> far as the rule is concerned, they are not always in accord with a
> sense of fair play [and] he will occasionally stoop to certain ques-
> tionable tricks upon the field and encourage these in his men.

Ward follows this candid assessment with his by-now familiar opinion
of "baseball law": the national agreement formalizes a "monopoly," a trust
"[a]s compact and effectual as the Standard oil, the sugar or any of the
other trusts. . . ." The reserve clause causes a player "[t]hough guilty of
no crime . . . [to become] a professional outlaw." Owners see players as

"goods" and "able-bodied slaves." Player-selling is as "vile" as prostitution, and a practice that brings "dishonor" to the sport. Baseball is governed by a "reckless law unto itself" and its destiny is in the hands of "numskulls."

Ward also wrote a short piece for the *San Francisco Daily Examiner* that appeared on the eve of the tourists' departure. It is generally sour, one long moan about overbearing fans, withering heat, numbing cold, sore muscles, and the constant fear of injury.

Even Helen got into the writing business that winter, though Ward likely had a hand in her efforts. In the *New York Herald* under her byline, she wrote "Baseball and the Ladies," a bit of fluff that champions baseball as the perfect sport for distaff viewers: "I have always believed that what was good and honest and manly enough for our brothers to practice was pure enough for us to witness." She chastises American women for lagging "far behind" their English counterparts when it comes to sports appreciation, and suggests that learning about baseball is not unlike learning to appreciate classical music: first the theme must be recognized, then its embellishments and variations.

After restating her belief that though women have played "ball" of some sort or another since classical times (an idea she almost certainly got from Ward), Helen registers a few objections to the "modern game," including conversations between players and spectators, loud arguments, loud coaching, and dirty grandstands: "A lady is often obliged to dust with her handkerchief the wooden seat or bench to which she is assigned." Finally, Helen takes managers to task for their most unpardonable act of omission:

> If the managers knew how the picturesque beauty of the scene
> was enhanced by neat, clean uniforms, they would never allow
> for the sake of a paltry sum their players to appear in such untidy
> costumes as are sometimes seen. Surely the laundry expense of
> the season would not be a serious tax on the club's exchequer.

As well, Ward had been commissioned to write dispatches by the *Chicago Tribune*. Generally these are lighthearted, facile bits of work, suggesting strongly the general mood of adventure and opportunity and less-than-fanatic competition—at least at the tour's outset—among the travelers. For example, Ward unwittingly corroborated the *Examiner*'s suspicions about the reasons behind the tourists' poor play in San Francisco. From Ogden, Utah, Ward wrote of the ballplayers' "Order of the Howling Wolves"—led by, Ward puns, various "untamed spirits."

> The sole object of the order, so far as discernible to an outsider, seems to be to howl, and this they do upon the slightest provocation and in a manner that resembles as nearly as possible the wailing of a moonstruck dog.

If their behavior continues, however, Ward goes on, he

> may have occasion soon to record the death of one or more of the members [as] mutterings of vengeance are growing louder . . . and the probabilities are that these bright young men who imagine the soul of wit to be in making life miserable for the rest of the world will be given genuine cause to howl.

Ward then has fun with Utah.

> One of the curiosities of Salt Lake is a Mormon convert who, though sane on all other subjects, has gone daft on one. The tenth article of the Mormon profession of the faith declares that "Zion will be built upon this continent."

Taking this literally, Ward continues, the man has

> caused to be built a most fantastic-looking structure, and he has decorated the exterior walls with bands and streamers of red cambrie, making it look for all the world like a Chinese "Joss House." . . . At night the building is illuminated by three large lamps placed in each window, so that if the Lord should come in the darkness he cannot mistake the house. If this monomaniac had sufficient intelligence and force of character who knows but that he might be the founder of a new religious sect.

Ward, aware of the San Francisco crowds' disappointment and cynicism, assured readers the games between the touring teams were as hotly contested as any League championship game, and that any charges of hippodroming were false. Evidently he was nearly alone in his opinion, because Spalding, who previously had offered $1,000 to the squad that won the most games on the tour, refined his offer, handing over $55 to the winning team immediately after each game "as a more immediate inducement"—and possibly as a way of circumventing the players' arranging for a final fifty-fifty pot split. Ward protested that "no inducement at all was necessary." (The inducements, in fact, ended completely—evidently for financial reasons—after the tour was extended beyond Australia.)

Ward also reassured one and all that the tourists were not playing poorly because of dissipation—an opinion that contradicted his earlier description of railroad high jinks. To bolster his argument, he pointed out that Ed Crane, one of the men thought by "'Friscans" to be playing while under the influence, had never taken a drink in his life. The accusation against his teammate and fellow Brotherhood member, he felt, was another "striking instance of the injustice that is so often done ballplayers." He justified his own absence while bird hunting by saying that the trip—to the sloughs near Watsonville, where game was "thick as crickets"—was one of a lifetime. Of Chinatown, he said that anyone who had visited that ghetto would surely favor exclusion of the Chinese from America.

Ward's reports were, generally, buoyant and energetic. Occasionally they approached the lyrical. He described the San Francisco fog as the "next thing to a rain, and comes rolling down over the hills like drifting snow." Occasionally he was downright humorous. Of a baseball park in Los Angeles, he said of its location five or six miles outside the city that it must have been conceived of by "some maniac."

Just before the *Alameda* sailed, Ward reported, Spalding had floated a trial balloon among the players: that the tour, instead of retracing its steps from Australia, might continue instead westward, through the Mideast and Europe and then to New York. This found a most positive reaction.

One evidently unanticipated result of the tentative change of plans was that Helen, who had planned to travel with the group, decided to abandon the tour. Instead, she and her sister, Clara, would travel to Europe, Helen under the alias "Mrs. Howard," and rejoin the tourists in Malta.

The Americans' stay in Hawaii was brief and exhausting. The tourists arrived a day later than expected, on a Sunday morning. The island, at the time, was as much a theocracy as Utah, and Sabbath baseball was illegal, much to the disappointment of the thousands who met the ship dockside and who later got up a futile petition to make an exception to the law. After breakfast on the morning of docking, the party toured greater Honolulu, swam, and visited the homes of wealthy planters and businessmen.

That evening, King Kalakaua hosted a banquet—for some reason not forbidden under the Territory's blue laws. To Ward, fascinated by the "score or more of Kanaka girls in bewitching 'holuku' attire," the most curious aspect of the evening was poi, which "gray-colored paste" he described as "in appearance and consistency not unlike that used by a billposter. If eaten without condiment, as is the practice with . . . the natives, it is also not unlike it in taste."

The ship left that same night, barely twelve hours after its arrival. After a mail stop in Pago Pago and a two-day, one-game layover in Auckland, it arrived in Sydney, Australia, on December 14. Greeted by steamers "laden with gentlemen and ladies," the *Alameda* tied up at a dock crowded with bands and cheering well-wishers.

The ballplayers stayed in Australia the best part of a month, playing exhibition games of baseball and cricket at Sydney, Melbourne, Adelaide, and the gold fields of Ballarat, as well as touring the countryside and attending official luncheons, banquets, and gala theater performances on a nearly daily basis. There was one mishap in Australia. One of the tour members was "Professor Bartholomew," a daredevil whose business was to ascend in a balloon and then return to earth before a game. In Ballarat, Bartholomew crashed into a cornice, badly injuring himself.

The reports the accompanying American journalists filed from Australia, "Her Majesty's Colony," were generally glowing, filled with references to "immense throngs" and regular crowds of "several" thousand. The *San Francisco Daily Record*, however, told a different story, calling the Australian leg a "flat failure." Australians, it went on, found baseball not what "it was cracked up to be" and the crowds, initially in the low thousands, soon dwindled to the low hundreds. The *Clipper* disregarded such reports, saying that though the *Record* called itself a "newspaper of stature," it was "alone in its perception."

There was also an embarrassing moment when a game threatened to end in a fight. The argument—over the legality of Ward's pitching delivery—was between Ward and Anson. Spalding, who had tried to present his players as genial sportsmen, colleagues whilst opponents, threw "oil on troubled waters" by offering to umpire the rest of the contest, Ward said.

The ballplayers left Melbourne on January 8, stopped briefly in Adelaide, and then began the long voyage to Ceylon. Their ship, the *Salier*, carried a cargo of wool and, according to Cap Anson in his autobiography *A Ballplayer's Career*, a "mixed lot of emigrants . . . Chinamen, Hindoos, Turks, Cingalese, Italians and Germans." This polyglot population, as well as the international crew of waiters, being unfamiliar with American ways, according to Anson, decided that the Chicago team's mascot, Clarence Duval, was an Indian prince. (Anson may have meant Indian chief.) Anson does not say how much this misrepresentation was encouraged by the players.

Duval was no more Indian, East, West, or American, than was John Ward. Spalding, who at best merely tolerated Duval, quickly informed the crew of his true origins, and the hapless Duval was "set to work during the meal hours pulling the punka rope . . . an occupation that he seemed to regard as being beneath his dignity, though his protests fell on deaf ears."

Duval was, in fact, a diminutive adult African-American. He sang, danced, and twirled a mean baton. Anson, the Chicago captain, had somehow met Duval years earlier, "togged him out in a suit of navy blue with brass buttons," and hired him to accompany the team during the season.

Duval, whom Anson refers to regularly as "the little coon" and "the little darkey" and "an ungrateful little rascal," had, without notice, left his mascot job and run off with a white actress, Mlle. Jarbeau, during the 1888 season, disappearing from sight until he somehow hooked up with the tourists east of Denver. Throughout the tour he dressed in what seems to have been some sort of circus ringmaster's outfit, and would entertain various assemblages with his dancing, twirling, and "mimicry."

The whole setup seems unimaginably degrading to modern sensibilities, and without suggesting a shred of an apology for the players' generally sorry treatment of Duval, it might best be seen within the era's context. America in 1888 was—with exceptions of course—a vicious, violent, and racist country. Americans who played baseball in those decades, were—with exceptions of course—likewise vicious, violent, and racist men. (One of the more chilling headlines of the age appeared in in the September 7, 1887, *New York Herald,* above a story concerning a pair of young Alabama black men accused of murder: TWO LYNCHINGS EXPECTED.)

Baseball tells the story of its whites-only early history this way: a few talented blacks were tolerated in the chaotic, or at least plastic, early days of professional baseball, and perhaps, somehow, God willing, there might one day have been a place on the field for the exceptionally talented and well-behaved Negro in certain cities for certain games.

But, the story continues, a single man, Cap Anson, stopped all that. In 1883, Toledo, of the Northwestern League, had signed a light-skinned, Oberlin- and University of Michigan–educated black man, Moses Fleetwood Walker, to catch for them. In August, Chicago came to town for an exhibition game, and the team's captain, Anson, refused to play against a team fielding a black man. Anson was one of the National League's brightest stars, as well known as any ballplayer of his day to the average fan. The Toledo manager, Charles Morton, no doubt with an eye on the turnstiles rather than the future of racial harmony, defied the powerful Anson, and just before game time wrote Walker into the lineup. Morton's hand was strong: if Anson kept his vow, Chicago, according to the contract between the two teams, would forfeit the gate receipts. Anson backed down but was quoted by the *Toledo Blade* as saying, "We'll play this here game, but won't play never no more with the nigger in." (Oddly, Anson's autobiography is a model of erudition and graceful English. Perhaps the book was ghostwritten, or perhaps the *Blade,* as was the custom then, took liberties quoting him.)

The next year Walker and his brother, Weldy Wilberforce Walker, were both playing for Toledo, this time for its American Association (major league) team. What a fun year that was for the Walker brothers, especially Moses (Weldy appeared in only five games). Toledo opened the season on the road, in Louisville. The *Louisville Commercial* (which regularly ran ads looking for "colored boys" as gofers) suggested that if other Association towns could accept a "brunette" ballplayer, then perhaps Louisville could as well. Unfortunately Walker played an error-filled game and the *Commercial* excoriated him.

When the Toledo team traveled to Richmond, there was a death threat against Walker. Later, an exhibition game against Chicago was canceled because of Anson's objections.

Walker spent the 1885 and 1886 seasons with Cleveland of the Western League and Waterbury of the Eastern League before moving up to Newark of the International League (IL), a well-run and well-established league whose players' abilities were only a few notches below those of the National League and the American Association. *The Sporting News*, noting that there were several talented blacks in the IL—Frank Grant of Buffalo was the league's leading hitter that year—wondered when it would be called the "Colored League." If the IL was a haven for black players, it was only a haven of sorts. The *Hamilton* (Ontario) *Spectator* wrote of a minor injury to Walker this way:

> Walker, the coon catcher of the Newarks, is laid off with a sore knee. It is insinuated by envious compeers that in early life he practiced on hen roosts until he got the art of foul catching down fine.

During the 1887 season, Walker and Anson would again collide. Anson, in Newark for an exhibition game, raised his usual objections against playing against a "brunette" and, as he had the last time he met Walker in Toledo, he prevailed and both Walker and George Stovey, another Newark black player, were dropped from the lineup. Stovey, a pitcher, and Walker were known as the "black battery." The next day, International League directors voted, six to four, to ban new contracts with black players. The six aye votes came from teams with no black players; the four nay votes came from teams with black players.

There was an outcry from both the press and IL fans at the directors' decision—loud enough to make the league modify its ruling: black players would not be banned, but no team would be allowed to keep more than one on its roster. Walker played the 1888 season with Buffalo—which, because of Walker's early signing, and its re-signing of an already rostered player, Robert Higgins, was allowed two blacks. When Chicago came to town for a September exhibition game, Anson's reaction was predictable. The game went on without Walker and Higgins. As David Zang, Walker's biographer, points out, "Anson's policy was now so widely accepted that the white press did not even report his slight with Walker."

If Ward and Anson stood on opposite sides of the labor-management gulf—Anson was, effectively, part of the Chicago management—they also faced off on the issue of race. Though documentation is sketchy, it seems that Ward, after his New Yorks played Newark in an April 1887 exhibition game, was so impressed with Walker—who threw Ward out attempting to steal—and George Stovey that he implored his club to offer contracts to the two men. The rumor created such a stir—fueled by Anson—that the supposed offer was rescinded.

But if Anson, a large, intimidating, forceful man and a vastly talented baseball player, was a virulent bigot—and we must assume that anyone who time and again refers to Clarence Duval as a "no account nigger" in his autobiography is a virulent bigot—he was hardly alone in his attitudes. According to David Zang, when the International League directors voted to ban blacks, they were not forcing their own views on the league so much as acting

> in behest of many of the best players, those who had to share the field with Fleet Walker and many of whom reportedly threatened to leave the league [had it not] decided to draw the color line.

The International League players were not alone in their segregationist views. For example, on the mediocre 1884 Toledo Association team was one Tony "the Count" Mullane, a hard-headed businessman (his constant contract battles are mind-boggling) who happened to be a wonderful pitcher and a dandy—he wore fine, flamboyant suits and had thickly curled hair and a deep-swoop, highly waxed mustache. In addition to being ambidextrous (he sometimes pitched from both the left and the right side to a single batter), he was one mean son of a bitch. He liked to throw at batters. *Sporting Life* called him a "man of the most sordid nature."

Note, however, that the newspaper was speaking of his attitude to hitters, not blacks, which was another aspect of the Ireland-born Mullane's "sordid nature." His racism was so deeply embedded that it extended to his battery mate, Fleetwood Walker. In 1919, Mullane wrote about the 1884 season.

> [Walker] was the best catcher I ever worked with, but I disliked a Negro and whenever I had to pitch to him I used to pitch anything I wanted without looking at his signals. One day he signalled me for a curve and I shot a fast ball at him. He caught it

and walked down to me. He said, "I'll catch you without signals, but I won't catch you if you are going to cross me. . . ." And all the rest of that season he caught me and caught anything I pitched without knowing what was coming.

Things had not changed much by 1888, at least not among the men on Spalding's world tour. The two-week sail to Ceylon was characterized by discomfort and torpor. Ward wrote that there were days when the "sun beat down so fiercely upon the deck that the boys lay in their bunks panting like lizards and cursing the weather by every saint in the baseball calendar." Pitcher Ed Crane suffered especially, and spent the voyage "dripping like a sponge . . . his face as red as a boiled lobster."

One day, a couple of the players noticed a "streak of light" near the boat, which the captain informed them was a man-eating shark of a sort so vicious that they had been known to "spring on the deck of a steamer, select a victim and make their escape before they could be thwarted."

The captain then ordered that the "sea wolf," which continued to follow the boat, be caught. A heavy line and a huge hook were prepared, and a debate of sorts about the appropriate bait broke out. According to Ward,

Anson offered to solve the question . . . by offering Clarence Duval, the little ebony-hued mascot . . . as a tidbit for the shark, but Clarence made such strenuous objections that the plan was abandoned. In lieu of the pickaninny . . . salt pork was fastened on the hook.

Later, according to Anson—Ward evidently found this part of the story distasteful and did not record it—the men presided over a mock trial at which a jury decided that the "chocolate-colored mascot" must take a bath. "A madder little coon" would have been difficult to find. So angry was Duval, in fact, that he grabbed a bat and swore to kill his tormentors, something, Anson says, he "might have done . . . had not a close watch been kept over him until his temper had burned itself out and he had become amenable to reason."

So, with much hilarity, the days passed on shipboard.

———

In Colombo, canoes of swimming and diving "Malays, Cingalese and Hindoos" speaking a "strange and incomprehensible gibberish" greeted the tourists. There followed a lightning tour of the city, a morning baseball game of no consequence, and the generally shared opinion, voiced by Ward, that Colombo was a "queer sort of a place inhabited by a queer sort of people."

Ceylon was truly terra incognita for the young Americans, and cause for head shaking at the alien culture that went far beyond garden-variety racism and cultural narcissism. Tommy Daly, the Chicago catcher, viewed the "hundreds of howling, chattering, grotesquely-arrayed natives" and declared that "if these cranks begin to kick at the umpire, he's a goner."

The company sailed through the Suez Canal and boarded a train for Cairo. At a small station about twenty miles from the capital, Chicago outfielder Pony Ryan entertained the tourists by dressing Duval in a drum major suit, putting a rope around the mascot's waist and a catcher's mask over his face. He then held onto the rope's other end and paraded Duval along the platform. In Anson's view,

> To the minds of the unsophisticated natives, the mascot appeared some gigantic ape that his keeper could with difficulty control, and both men and women fell over each other in their hurry to get out of his way.

After a day or so of touring Cairo, including its "gambling hells," cafés, and the Turkish, Moorish, Algerian, and Greek quarters, Ward's All-Americas mounted camels, and the Chicagos donkeys, and headed toward the Pyramids, which they reached at two in the afternoon. There they played a game—the All-Americas won 10–6—under difficult circumstances, as every time a ball went into the crowd, according to Anson, the "Arabs would pounce upon it and examine it as though it were one of the greatest of curiosities." Only after a "row" could the ball be retrieved.

(Years later, Ward waxed nostalgic about Egypt, saying that the contest played "under the shadow of the Pyramid on the very plain where Napoleon drew up his troops and told them that forty centuries were gazing at them" was the most extraordinary game of his career. He also said that the crowd, after watching the game attentively, squatting in "grave, oriental attitudes," ran to the players demanding baksheesh. "They thought they ought to be paid for watching us play.")

Ward's dispatches were becoming testy. Whether it was the rankling presence of Anson; the rankling absence of Helen, who had wired Ward that she would not meet the tourists in Malta or anywhere in Europe, or merely the accumulated weariness that accompanies extended travel, it seems clear his good spirits had begun to abandon him. In contradiction of his later, rosier memories, he described the Egyptian ball field, with the Pyramids as backstop, as a "diamond formed in the shifting sand." Ward reported the players unimpressed with Egypt, and agreed with second baseman Dandelion Pfeffer that the Arizona desert could give the Sahara article "cards and spades and beat it on general vacuity and flatness."

The players, including Ward, climbed the face of the Sphinx to pose for a photo. They attempted to throw balls at the Sphinx and over the Pyramids. "Every player took a shy at the right eye of the Sphinx . . . but only left fielder Jack Fogarty succeeded in giving the colossus a black eye." Ward's casual attitude toward these antics is curious, for even Spalding said that the "native worshippers of Cheops and the dead Pharaohs" were horrified.

But Spalding also dismissed Egypt, both as a country and as a potential market for his products.

> In a country where they use a stick for a plow, and hitch a donkey and a camel together to draw it . . . it is hardly reasonable to expect that the modern game of baseball will become one of its sports.

Ward, in turn, called Italy "the land of Macaroni" and opened his first European dispatch cynically.

> "*Vedi Napoli e poi mori*" is the Neapolitan way of saying that Naples is a beautiful city. The distinguished linguist, Mr. John Healy [in reality a Chicago pitcher] insists, however, that the expression is merely a play upon words, and he is borne out by the fact that we have seen Naples, yet still feel a desire to live.

Though Ward allowed that the city's setting, a natural amphitheater, was idyllic, and the presence of Mt. Vesuvius "unusually impressive," he could not get past the "narrow streets, insolent cabmen, professional beggars, and open presence along the principal streets of the disgusting 'latrines.'"

At one stop a player stole a trumpet by which stationmasters signaled engineers to proceed. The Italian authorities were less than pleased, and when the train arrived at Naples, Ward says, a "small division of the King's army" investigated the tourists, asking more questions "than would fill out a life insurance policy."

The ballplayers' single game in Naples, played on the Campo di Marte, ended badly when a young Italian boy was knocked out by a foul ball and spectators swarmed onto the field. Ward later revealed that the fans were only partly to blame for the fiasco. In the fifth inning of the scheduled seven-inning game, with the All-Americas ahead 8–2, Anson went into his "baby act." He wanted the game declared void because of the crowd situation. The umpire disagreed, so Anson and company took their equipment and returned to the hotel. Ward said that he and his teammates were the "maddest lot of players that ever left a field, and we violently swore we would not play another game on the trip." Although tempers cooled some, Spalding had to ride herd on both Anson and Ward, reminding them—not for the first time—that they were guests and "missionaries."

After an eight-hour train trip, the troupe arrived in Rome and were shocked when authorities denied them permission to play in the Colosseum. Since there were no other suitable enclosed grounds in the entire city, the Americans saw this refusal as a "gratuitous insult." Further, the Italians, the ballplayers thought, never stated their reason. Did they base their objections on the fact that a game in the Colosseum would be a desecration—even though it was the site where "mighty athletes of an olden day battled for mastery"—or was it simply that the tottering walls of the edifice were unsafe for spectators? Even an offer of $5,000 in payment did no good. Instead, and in something of a huff, the game was played at the Piazza de Sienna before the likes of King Humbert and an assortment of diplomats, princes, and princesses. Chicago won 3–2.

The plan to play in the Colosseum dramatically illustrates the tourists' imposing ignorance of the world beyond the American borders. In the first place the Colosseum floor was far too small and oddly shaped for any sort of proper baseball game. The oval proper measures about 270 feet long (a little more than double the distance between home plate and second base) and about 170 feet wide (less than half again the straight-line distance between first and third bases). In other words, the playing surface was shorter and narrower (at its widest) than an average-sized softball field.

Additionally, there was another, far less surmountable problem: there *was* no playing surface. The original surface—probably sand—rested on a an extensive platform of wood. This platform also served as a ceiling for an extensive underground network of dressing rooms, storage rooms, machine-rooms, and animal cages during the Colosseum's glory days. Over the centuries, the Colosseum was battered by at least four earthquakes that sent huge amounts of stone toward the center of the edifice. The floor supports rotted and collapsed and the gaping "basement" filled with debris.

For most of the nineteenth century archaeologists had been busy restoring the Colosseum. Part of the work involved *removal* of debris. By 1880 much of the substructure had been cleared, leaving the walls standing. Basically, the Colosseum's floor in 1889 did not resemble a playing field so much as a great ragged stonework maze.

After a final game, in Florence, the players left for France, stopping briefly in Monte Carlo, where Ward's ill temper erupted. Ward invited two teammates—Ned Hanlon and Jimmy Manning—to dinner at a hotel across from the Casino. When the bill came, Ward noticed that he had been charged $7.50 for three orders of asparagus. "Did he kick?" Ned Williamson told *The Sporting News*. "Well, rather."

Williamson wrote that Ward settled up, though ungraciously, only to find out that the waiter had misplaced the group's overcoats and umbrellas. The overcoats appeared in short order, but the waiter claimed that no umbrellas were in the claim room.

> John said, "You frog-eating fool! Do you mean to stand there and insinuate that I lie? When I entered this place it was raining torrents." At that moment Ed Hanlon whispered in John's ear

saying "John, feel in your pocket for the checks. I am sure we left the umbrellas at the Casino." John made his exit as soon as possible and afterward returned to extend an apology.

City officials refused the ballplayers permission to play in Nice, so the Americans' first French game was in Paris, on March 8, at the Parc Aristotique. The spectators included aristocracy, much of the American diplomatic corps, and many workmen who took time off from their labors building the Eiffel Tower.

France, evidently, didn't take to the game, though the players and their wives decidedly took to Paris. Spalding, especially, was disgusted by Gallic indifference, as was the *New York Herald*, which, echoing Spalding's customary breadth of vision, wrote:

> The Frenchman is as unlikely as the Italian to become interested in baseball. He is too impatient and impulsive to ever undertake that study of the game that is necessary.

How relieved the Americans must have felt landing in England after a rough Channel crossing. They played their first game before 8,000 fans, including Edward, Prince of Wales, at the Kensington cricket oval in a damp fog. Tours, theater, banquets, and two more London games followed—at the Lord's and Crystal Palace grounds. Then, after a brief trip to Bristol and another London game, the group left in a special, luxurious nine-car train—two dining/lounge cars, two baggage cars, and the rest sleepers, each emblazoned with THE AMERICAN BASEBALL CLUBS on the sides. They stopped at Birmingham, Sheffield, Bradford, Glasgow, Manchester, and Liverpool, playing cricket and baseball, going to banquet after banquet, and being besieged by curious crowds. Photographs of the ballplayers on the Sphinx and at the Colosseum were displayed in shop windows and offered for sale. Newspaper stories on the Americans took up entire pages. Brother Country! Mother Country!

John Ward, however, did not partake of the enthusiastic reception the tourists received in Great Britain. Shortly after the ballplayers' crossing of the Channel, he sailed for New York, arriving on March 23, a fortnight before the rest of the group, to banner headlines, such as the *Herald*'s

Johnny Is Home Again

The *Chicago Tribune*'s reporter described Ward as "a young man whose face is familiar to thousands of base-ball admirers all over the Union." Ward, the correspondent continued, "fashionably attired in garments of the latest London make," "tripped down the gang-plank of the North German Lloyd steamer *Saale* . . . with as much confidence as when he saunters to third base after a neat three-bagger." The ballplayer-lawyer cited "private business" concerns for his early return. These concerns were twofold.

First, his marriage was evidently in deep trouble. Helen had not only declined to go on the tour but she had also retreated on her early promise to meet the troupe in Europe. To add insult to injury, she did not even meet Ward's ship when it docked, or as was customary, when it entered New York Harbor. After a few expansive and innocuous remarks about the success of the trip and his pleasure at being on American soil and some vague remarks about the state of the Brotherhood and its complaints about the League, Ward begged weariness to reporters and went immediately to the Marlborough Hotel, on Broadway and 36th Street, which Helen had been calling home for several weeks.

His second concern was baseball and the Brotherhood. In retrospect, Ward's boilerplate remarks to reporters—along the lines that time will tell how League/Brotherhood affairs would pan out—were determinedly casual. If Ward had envisioned the tour as a once-in-a-lifetime opportunity to see the world, with his wife, and perhaps a chance to spend time with Spalding discussing baseball business, his hopes had been badly dented. The first blow fell in San Francisco, with Helen's change of plans, the second in Australia, when he found out that the League and Spalding had badly outfoxed the Brotherhood.

Only four days after the November departure of the *Alameda* from San Francisco, the League had, at its annual meeting, approved sweeping new legislation. This addition to "baseball law" would precipitate the players' war of 1890.

During the winter of 1888–89, Albert G. Spalding organized a world tour
of American baseball, featuring his Chicago White Stockings and a
"picked nine," the All-Americas, of which Ward was the captain. Here, the
baseball tourists visit the Sphinx. Ward is one of the two men standing
in the center of the Sphinx's chest. He is on the left, wearing a sweater.
(Baseball Hall of Fame Library, Cooperstown, N.Y.)

The announcement in *The Sporting News,* in the fall of 1889, of the Brotherhood's plan to form a rival baseball league. (*The Sporting News*)

SLAVERY DAYS AGAIN.
THE ANNUAL BASE BALL AUCTION—"GOING! GOING! GONE!! FOR $12,000."

A cartoon from the *New York Daily Graphic,* November 27, 1888, mocking Ward and his metaphoric linking of baseball players and slaves. The caption reads: "Slavery Days Again. The Annual Base-Ball Auction 'Going! Going! Gone! For $12,000.'" Twelve thousand dollars was the rumored price the Washington National League team was willing to pay New York for Ward's services. The figure represents approximately twenty-five years of wages for the "average" American worker at the time. (*Transcendental Graphics*)

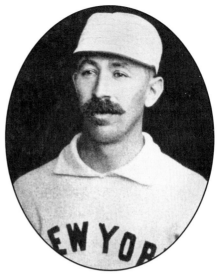

Top left: Albert G. Spalding, owner of the Chicago White Stockings and the Players' League's most powerful adversary. (*Transcendental Graphics*) *Top right:* William "Buck" Ewing, a Brotherhood member whose behind-the-scenes efforts to forge a compromise between the Players' League and the National League led him to be branded a traitor by his former teammates and friends. (*Transcendental Graphics*) *Bottom right:* Ned Williamson, one of the most popular baseball players of the nineteenth century. A Chicago White Stocking, Williamson was injured during the world tour of 1888-89. His subsequent mistreatment at the hands of Spalding became a rallying point for the rebellious players. (*Transcendental Graphics*)

Top left: A rare action shot, taken in 1892, of Ward when he was playing for the Brooklyn National League team. *(Transcendental Graphics)*
Bottom right: Ward in 1894, his seventeenth and final major league season. *(Transcendental Graphics)*

Ward at Fox Hills Country Club, ca. 1904. (*Spalding's Official Golf Guide for 1904*)

Katherine Waas, Ward's second wife, whom he married in 1903. (*Maria Sinn*)

Ward, now a successful Manhattan lawyer, ca. 1910.
(Baseball Hall of Fame Library, Cooperstown, N.Y.)

Top left: Ward on his Babylon,
Long Island, estate with
"Bob," his favorite hunting
dog, ca. 1920. (*Golf Illustrated,
January 1931*) *Bottom right:*
Ward a year or two before his
death at age sixty-five.
(*Corbis/Bettmann-UPI*)

JOHN MONTGOMERY WARD
1878 — 1894
PITCHING PIONEER WHO WON 158,
LOST 102 GAMES IN SEVEN YEARS.
PITCHED PERFECT GAME FOR PROVIDENCE
OF N. L. IN 1880.
TURNED TO SHORTSTOP AND MADE 2,151 HITS.
MANAGED NEW YORK AND BROOKLYN IN N. L.
PRESIDENT OF BOSTON, N. L. 1911-1912.
PLAYED IMPORTANT PART IN ESTABLISHING
MODERN ORGANIZED BASEBALL.

Ward's plaque in the Baseball Hall of Fame.
(Baseball Hall of Fame Library, Cooperstown, N.Y.)

Briefly, the League had instituted what quickly became known as the Brush Plan, named after its sponsor, John Brush, owner of the Indianapolis team. The Brush Plan, basically, grouped all players into five ironclad pay categories:

Class	Salary
A	$2,500
B	2,250
C	2,000
D	1,750
E	1,500

Not only was the new plan—formulated and passed without even pro forma consultation with the Brotherhood—a direct violation of the informal agreement the League and the Brotherhood had worked out the year before, but Ward could not help but see the timing of the plan's passage as a blatant act of treachery on Spalding's part. No League business was ever undertaken without the approval of Spalding, and it was none other than Spalding who had planned the world trip and who had enticed Ward to join it as the All-Americas' captain. Fred "Dandelion" Pfeffer, a Brotherhood member who played for Chicago in 1889, claimed that Spalding confessed to planning the tour, in part, to keep Ward out of the country during the League meetings of 1888. So, instead of attending the meetings and screaming bloody murder at the Brush Plan, Ward was lounging idly in a deck chair on a ship steaming toward Hawaii.

Ward most likely first heard of the plan only when he was halfway around the world in Sydney, which in yet another marvel of the modern age was in cable contact with America. A return cable would have traveled overland, to Port Darwin, and then, through a combination of land and sea legs, to Banjuwangi, Java, and on to Singapore, Penang, Madras, Bombay, Aden, and Alexandria. From there the

> operator at Alexandria starts the dispatches out into the sea and, traversing the bottom amid the wrecks of the navies of the Punic wars, the nineteenth century news of the base ball games in Australia throb through the cable from Alexandria to Malta and

from there to Gibralter, to Lisbon, to Port Curno, to London, to Waterville, Ireland, to Canso, Nova Scotia, then south to New York where it arrives at the Oriental Hotel at Manhattan Beach, crosses Sheepshead Bay, goes into Flatbush under ground, passes under Brooklyn streets, comes over the Brooklyn Bridge, runs under Water Street as far as Beaver, and then goes up Broad, where it comes up from the pavement and enters the office on the first floor of the Drexel building at Wall and Broad.

Assuming he knew about the plan, why did Ward continue on the tour—albeit in an ever fouler mood—in daily contact with the treasonous Spalding, instead of returning home?

In the first place, Ward knew full well that the baseball-following public was wildly enthusiastic about the tour. When Boston's Mike Kelly, a fan favorite, backed out of the tour at the last minute, he had been lacerated in the press. If Ward the traveler couldn't pass up a chance to see the world, Ward the politician knew that he had best not squander any public support the Brotherhood might need in the future. Second, there was nothing to be accomplished stateside. The meetings had concluded, the magnates and players scattered for the winter, the damage done. Third, Ward knew that the only magnate who really mattered was Spalding. Ward perhaps thought he and Spalding could come to some compromise, gentleman to gentleman, while they were removed from the daily pressures of the press and the public.

But it didn't happen.

The Americans, without Ward, left England, crossed the Irish Sea, and played in Belfast in the rain and in Dublin before large crowds. In Dublin, many of the fans were "handsomely and fashionably dressed ladies, and their bright colored costumes blended beautifully with the surrounding scenery." But however enthusiastic the ballplayers' reception in the British Isles, it paled against the one they met upon their return to America on April 7, 1889. A crowded steamer and an equally crowded tugboat of "warm hearted merrymakers" ran out to meet the tourists. The tourists' ship, the *Adriatic*, landed at the West 22d Street pier, and the parties checked into the Fifth Avenue Hotel. Spalding was "brown as a berry"; Clarence Duval looked like a "very lively little stick of licorice."

Before setting out for a long round of games—in Brooklyn, Philadelphia, Boston, Washington, D.C., Cleveland, Pittsburgh, Indianapolis, and finally Chicago—the players and their wives settled in for the first of an equally long round of banquets. This was held at Delmonico's, on Monday night, April 8, for the tourists and over two hundred of their closest admirers—none of them women. The invitations were as "carefully restricted as those to entertainments in honor of effete royalties in Europe." (Helen Dauvray appeared briefly, in the "balcony, beside the band," and "looked down upon the scene.") The guest list included the mayors of Brooklyn and Jersey City, prominent members of the New York Athletic Club, Bar, and Stock Exchange, newspaper publishers, the actors Digby Bell and DeWolf Hopper, and Mark Twain, who gave the keynote speech.

Though this banquet would prove to be the largest, most elaborate, and most star-studded of the many dozen the players had experienced since they left Chicago nearly six months earlier, it differed only in detail, not substance.

The diners sat at eight long tables that

> groaned under a fragrant burden of rose-banks, potted palms,
> callas and allegorical floral designs. Sugar models of base-ball
> favorites in approved Graeco-Roman attitudes were placed side
> by side with pink-shaded candles and succulent counterfeits of
> the calf-skin ball.

The walls were thick with tropical flora, American shields, banners, mounted bald eagles, and photographs of the players. An orchestra played American, Australian, and Hawaiian songs—these last a fitting tribute to King Kalakaua and other "well-meaning potentates."

The menu came bound in colored ribbon. On its face was a globe afloat on a sea of clouds that were themselves surrounded by illustrated scenes from the tour. This was the fare:

Oysters
Sauterne

Broth Ceylon
Cream of asparagus

Radishes, celery, olives
Patties Columbia

Red snapper, Royal sauce
Potatoes with parsley
Sauterne

Filet of beef with mushrooms
Spinach
Champagne

Braised Capons American style
French peas
Claret
Sweetbread Italian style
Mixed string beans
Roman Punch

Plovers
Lettuce salad
Burgundy

Pudding, Schiller sauce
Fancy ice cream
Pyramids

Fruits, cakes, coffee
Cheese
Liquors

The speeches and toasts—there was a separate toast card—did not begin until ten o'clock. After a lengthy list of "regrets" were read, Mayor Chapin of Brooklyn spoke, Mayor Cleveland of Jersey City spoke, Spalding spoke. Anson, introduced as "the greatest general of the ball field," spoke briefly and with self-deprecating humor: "They say I have pretty good qualities for kicking, and, if I could kick out of making any remarks here I would do so." He went on to say this was the proudest moment of his life. He thanked all present for their "patronage" and regretted that Ned Williamson, "whom everybody loves," was still abroad.

Ward, introduced as a "skillful ballplayer, an accomplished writer, and a man who has added dignity to the profession," followed Anson, briefly and blandly.

> We are about to complete a delightful trip and a delightful experience and I assure you we have seen it in first class style . . . but Fire Island lighthouse was the most impressive thing we saw.

Eventually, Mark Twain rose and "bore with characteristic equanimity the cheers which greeted his rising and delivered himself of one of his characteristicaly droll speeches." He had been introduced as a Hawaiian native, which he denied, to loud laughter. But he admitted that he had, in fact, visited the "Sandwich Islands," which he described as

> that peaceful land, that beautiful land, that far-off home of profound repose, and soft indolence and dreamy solitude, where life is one long slumberous Sabbath and the good that die experience no change, for they but fall asleep in one heaven to wake up in another.

This last remark also met with laughter. The gist of his short speech was an elaborate trope about Hawaii's singular nature. The Islands, he said, were "incongruous."

> In baseball you've got to do everything just right, or you don't get there; in the Islands you've got to do everything just wrong, or you can't stay there. You do it wrong to get it right, for if you do it right you get it wrong. . . . Think of it, [in Hawaii] the ten takes the ace! . . . Well, the missionaries are always going to fix that, but they put it off and put it off . . . and so [Hawaii] is going to keep on going down and down, and down, till some day you will see a pair of jacks beat a straight flush.

There were more speakers. Chauncey DePew imagined the influence of baseball if John Ward were to play for Washington (such rumors were in the air): "the Senate adjourns [and] the President dismisses the crowds of office-seekers and goes on a vacation." There were several calls for both Anson and Ward to stand. Finally, around midnight, DeWolf Hopper and Digby Bell took the stage.

> The remarks of both speakers were so funny that the company seemed transformed for the time into automatons who had been set laughing and could not stop [and] the number of aching sides in the room was just double the number of those there.

On into the night, until

> the most expert ball player in the company could not have judged a "fly" ball tossed through the tobacco smoke that rolled in a heavy blue mass up against the draperies along the walls, over against the balcony, and which hung from window to window like a gauze screen.

The next day, Chicago met the All-Americas in Brooklyn for a game. The contest was described as "rather uninteresting." And Ward, the *Clipper* noted, was for some reason "particularly off" in his fielding.

Twenty-One

A Look of Expectancy on His Face

T HE 1889 SEASON would prove to be one of baseball's most ran-corous. But for Jeff Dolan, the year meant little. Dolan died in California's State Insane Asylum in Stockton on November 9. He had played catcher for the Knicks of San Francisco as well as other Bay Area teams over the years. A few seasons earlier, he had been struck on the head by a foul tip, the injury resulting "in insanity." From the moment the ball hit Dolan,

> His memory seemed to have stopped . . . and he has been waiting ever since to catch that ball. He would stand for hours in the asylum yard in the attitude of a catcher, with hands reaching out for a ball and a look of expectancy on his face.

We have no way of knowing how 1889 began for Edgar S. Howard. We do know it ended terribly. Howard—he is described only as a "young boy"—was returning from his day's chores when he joined a sandlot game already in progress. What had he been doing that day? We don't know, exactly, but likely attending to some field clearing or the destruction of a beaver dam. He dug in at the plate, waiting for the pitch. The pitch came in wild and hit him near the hip.

An explosion followed, and the whole fleshy portion of his right arm was blown away. He also received other injuries, which were more serious. The boy had been given a dynamite cap, and he put it into his pocket and forgot all about it when he began playing ball. He was carried to his father's house, but was not expected to survive long.

Albert Goodwill Spalding would begin 1889 the blithest of spirits. Hadn't he, personally, been responsible for the single most glorious episode in the history of baseball?

Hadn't the cream of the crop of American manhood recently returned from a trip around the world, showing heathens and Mother England and her colonist sons and daughters alike the meaning of spunk, of clearheaded vision and invention? My God, man, if cricket was a game, then baseball was a better game! If some close-minded wops couldn't see their way to opening a door from the musty past and letting the Olympians of the present play in their rickety, crumbling, oh-so-precious little Colosseum, then that was their problem! What a shining example of manifest destiny that trip was: as great a symbol as the transcontinental railroad! The telephone! The electric light! The Brooklyn Bridge! The subduing of the savage red man!

Just gaze on the photograph—available everywhere—of the tourists standing proud and tall and ramrod straight, in their blindingly alabaster uniforms, on the brow and nose and cheeks of that ridiculous old Sphinx. Had any Egyptian ever thrown a ball over the Great Pyramid? Had they even tried? Had they even thought of it?

Hadn't kings and princes and ambassadors the world over watched the boys at play? Hadn't the lovely Irish ladies been unable to conceal their blushing admiration of the boys when they took the field in Belfast and Dublin? As *Spalding's Official Base Ball Guide* put it,

> The greatest historical event recorded in the annals of the
> national game was undoubtedly the journey. . . . The pluck,
> energy and business enterprise which characterized the
> unequaled event reflected the highest credit on Mr. Albert G.
> Spalding, as the representative spirit of Western business
> men . . .

And that was not just Spalding blowing his own horn, not by a long shot! Look at the *Melbourne* (Australia) *Argus*—and though the *Argus* may be only a newspaper read upside-down by antipodal ex-convicts 10,000 miles away, no truer witness to Spalding's achievement was ever penned:

> Right worthy of welcome did those visitors appear—stalwarts
> every man, lumps of muscle showing beneath their tight fitting
> jersey garments, and a springiness in every movement which
> denoted grand animal vigor and the perfection of condition. We
> could not pick eighteen such men from the ranks of all our crick-
> eters.

And hadn't DeWolf Hopper added a verse to one of the songs in his act? And a grand new verse it was:

> Our twenty American athletes who roamed
> In climes that are foreign have now returned home.
> They've played the world over before crowns and courts;
> They've shown effete Europe the noblest of sports,
> They've shown the old foreigners how to have fun
> With the mystical curve and the lively home run,
> And now let us greet them with our main and might.

Of course some White Stocking fans were not quite as giddy as Spalding and Hopper. "Ardent Admirer" wrote this for the *Chicago Tribune*:

> Welcome, boys, welcome, from over the seas,
> Once again bare your brows to the cooling lake breeze,
> Wear proudly your jewels, plug hats and high collars
> You are each worth to Spalding some $10,000

"Anonymous," as well, felt compelled to write about the players' "high capacious brows," their "manly forms," "sun-browned skin," and "hands that Wales himself pumped up and down." But, Anonymous con-cluded, the fact remained that, over the course of the tour, the Chicagos had lost more games against the All-Americas than they had won. Perhaps Spalding would find it helpful to take the boys down to Arkansas to unbind their charley horses and boil out the "foreign grub."

Fans are fickle beings—Chicago's second-place finish in 1888 was fine only if one was satisfied with second place. All they asked for was what New York had: a pennant flying from the grandstand and a World Championship under their belts! And Chicago's work was cut out for them—New York's roster included some of the most talented players in the history of baseball.

It included six future Hall of Famers: shortstop Ward, left fielder Jim O'Rourke, first baseman Roger Connor, catcher Buck Ewing, and pitchers Tim Keefe and Mickey Welch. Between them, Keefe and Welch would win fifty-five games in 1889. (Cannonball Ed Crane would win another fourteen and even Ewing would win a pair.) In addition, the lineup included right fielder Silent Mike Tiernan, who would lead the League in runs scored and walks (Connor would take RBI and slugging average honors); solid, dependable second baseman Danny Richardson; and center fielder George Gore, a .300 hitter. The team's one weak spot was at third base, where Art Whitney, thirty years old and nearing the end of his career, would hit only .218 and field a modest .882.

But even in New York's seeming monolith cracks had appeared. Even before he left on the world tour, Ward had been the focus of weekly, even daily speculation that he was going to leave New York—for Boston, Washington, even Denver. Some rumors centered on money, others on intrateam friction: Ward was arrogant, intolerant of teammates' behavior, aloof. The *Chicago Tribune*, however, pointed out that owner Day and manager Mutrie would never let Ward go to rival Boston, since Ward would bring with him "many of the fine points studied out last season" in New York. But, the paper went on, there was indeed trouble in the clubhouse.

> Ward is not liked by the members of the champions. Ewing, O'Rourke, Keefe, and others never speak to him. Tim Keefe is a modest young man, but his opinion of Ward is anything but a pleasant one. It seems that the papers got hold of a story to the effect that Keefe and Ward's sister-in-law [Helen's sister, Clara]

were about to get married. Keefe took pains to have it contradicted in the Boston papers but when he got to New York the
next spring he found his old captain cool. Ward evidently didn't
like the idea of having Tim as a member of his family. . . . This
state of affairs is said to cause Ward many a sleepless night, and
they do say it has something to do with the return to the stage of
Mrs. Ward, who arrived home from Europe last Sunday [January
27, 1889] . . . and is already making preparations to start on the
road with her own combination.

There was speculation Ward wanted managerial powers. (Captains
were being replaced by nonplaying managers as field bosses—as was the
case in New York.) The *Clipper*, however, doubted New York would let
Ward go anywhere. He was too valuable—if not as a fielder, batter, and
baserunner, then in intangibles.

There is no doubt but that Ward thoroughly understands the
other men of the team as they do him. . . . therefore little is to be
gained by letting him go. . . . no other man can jump in and give
to the other players the same confidence that Ward does, or
that . . . can fill Ward's place in every particular.

The dollar figures bandied about were astonishing: Boston would pay
New York $12,000 for Ward's release. Ward, in turn, would get $5,000, a
25 percent raise from his 1888 New York salary, and a $1,000 bonus if the
Hub team won the pennant. Washington upped the buyout price to
$15,000. One report suggested Pittsburgh was interested. Even papers in
Denver—nothing approaching a major league city in those days—suggested that, since Ward and Helen had bought property in the Mile High
City, he bring his expertise to bear there. Mike Kelly, who had changed
his mind about going on tour at the last minute, was saying that Boston
had promised *him* the 1889 captaincy. Boston, however, replied that that
promise only held if the team was unable to sign Ward as captain.
    (Kelly, probably the most popular baseball player of his time, was a
man of Ruthian intemperance who had never managed to exhibit much
of a case for his being executive timber. In early March 1889, to cite only

one example, Kelly was scheduled to recite "Casey at the Bat" at a gala Boston Elks benefit dinner. Instead of Kelly, however, an emcee appeared on stage. "Mr. Kelly," he said, "is with us . . . but the fact is he can't speak above a whiskey—beg pardon, I mean a whisper—and finds it impossible to speak the lines.")

Ward himself was consistently coy about his plans, exasperatingly so, the press felt. One story referred to Ward as "President of the Base-Ball Players' Brotherhood, ex-Captain of the Giants, and manager-elect of the Washington Grays and the Bostons."

In fact, there was little chance that Ward would sign with anyone else but New York, if for no other reason than the Brotherhood's unconditional opposition to the sale of players.

In late March, with matters still up in the air, Ward misplayed his hand slightly. He and some other players visited New York president Day's office on Maiden Lane. There, Ward stated candidly that he would, in fact, rather not go to Washington. He was concerned that too much would be expected of him—Washington was a terrible team. Day, however, suggested that he might just accept a Washington offer and sell Ward. Further, Day encouraged Ward to soften his opposition to player sales and think of a move to Washington as an opportunity.

Whether Ward took this rebuff personally or recognized it for the bluff it was, he continued to dance undecided before the public and the League. Would he accept a sale to another team? Would he refuse a sale? Would he quit baseball entirely? He finally signed with New York—for $4,250—on April 24, opening day. Only a few days before Ward's signing, Tim Keefe—who would, in fact, marry Clara Helm on August 19 and become Ward's brother-in-law—had tried to put rumors of bad blood between them and between Ward and other New York players at rest, though his announcement was guarded and obscure at best. "Whatever differences there may be between Ward and the other players," Keefe told the *Clipper*, "there is not one of them but appreciates his magnificent work on the field."

Keefe signed shortly after Ward and the New Yorks were ready for the season. (There was the little matter, however, of where, exactly, the team was going to play. New York state and city turf battles about street rights-of-way would keep the team out of the old Polo Grounds for most of the season. Instead, they would play a pair of games at Jersey City, then move to tiny, swampy, mosquito-besieged St. George Park on Staten Island.)

But all of the above—signings, holdouts, trades, rumors of trades, and team dissension—are as much a part of baseball as hits, runs, and errors. Without this endless over-the-clothesline chatter, true fans would have little to live for during that dead season that falls between the last game of autumn and the first game of spring. In addition to speculation about Ward's 1889 home and New York clubhouse relations, of course, hot stove leaguers could fall back on discussing rookies, sore arms, and the endlessly shifting balance of power between pitchers and batters. With all this and the world tour to keep track of, the winter of 1888–1889 was a fan's slice of heaven.

Additionally, what had not been news most of that winter was, as far as fans were concerned, good news. The brewing battle between the owners and the Brotherhood seemed to have dropped from the face of the earth. This was not, in fact, the case, it just seemed that way: the primary combatants happened to be wintering on the other side of the globe.

Lastly, that winter the hot stove league could mull over more than the annual post-season summary, pre-season predictions and wealth of statistics included in Spalding's annual *Guide*. John Ward's book *Base-Ball: How to Become a Player* also appeared. Though the bulk of *Base-Ball* is devoted to position-by-position instructional chapters, it included, as well, a short section of baseball history and a brief discussion—with accompanying diagrams—on the physics of the curveball.

The book is, on the whole, an erudite and gracefully written document—one that, somewhat surprisingly, remains a useful primer for current students of the game. For the most part it illuminates and mirrors Ward's personality. It is thoughtful, rigorously researched, full of "inside information"—such as, for example, how a baserunner might get a jump on a pitcher, or how a pitcher might best overpower or outthink a batter. It is lucid, logical, formal, and scattered with prescriptive passages: "A shortstop must know when to expect a throw if he himself be covering second"; *"Keep away from saloons."* It is inspirational, but only by dint of its no-nonsense enthusiasm and love of the details of the game. It does not indulge in airy aphorisms and avuncular cajoling. It never puts its arm around the reader's shoulder to say "Well done" or cluck the reader under the chin and tell him he'll do better next time. It is not "just a game" to the author. While Ward must have assumed his readership was composed primarily of schoolboys and amateur ballplayers, he is a demanding tutor. I will give you this information, he is saying. Follow it to the letter and you will improve your game. If you don't, however, it is no fault of mine.

On several occasions the book is sarcastic:

> The theory of batting is simplicity itself. All that is necessary is to wait until the ball comes over the plate and then hit it on a line back into the field. From the grand stand, nothing could be easier. . . . It is amusing to sit in a base-ball crowd and hear the remarks. There are more good batters and umpires and all-round ball players . . . within one's hearing, than are to be found in both the contesting teams.

Occasionally, it is just plain mean. Discussing the necessity of team-work between infielders, he chides former Providence teammate George Wright, who once, years earlier, should have tossed a ball to his second baseman. Instead,

> George attempted to make the play alone. He touched second, but by the time he was ready to throw [to first, the baserunner] came against him, and the result was a wild throw . . . and both runners scored.

Ward, however, did not end his recollection there.

> We were beaten finally . . . and lost the championship. It should be added that the game would have been won again in the eighth inning but for the unpardonable stupidity of one of the Providence base-runners.

The one exception to the stern, businesslike, *removed* tone of the book, however—and one that also illuminates Ward, or at least Ward the flirtatious, Ward the suave—comes in the opening pages of the first chapter, entitled "Theory of the Game—A Chapter for the Ladies."

It is a clever bit of legerdemain. He manages, in the course of a couple of hundred words, through reassurances and gentle mocking, to placate both his male readers—who felt the game to be solely their domain—and his female readers—who in increasing numbers were attending and enjoying the game. This leads into a brief, inclusive summary of the game's rules and a final, lingering *oeillade* toward the ladies.

Baseball, Ward begins, was long supposed "Not a proper sport for the patronage of ladies. Gradually, however, this illusion has been dispelled." One game will pique the female "novice . . . who soon discovers that she knows all about it . . . she is surprised and flattered by the wonderful grasp of her own understanding . . . she likes it with all her might."

While the sport, he goes on, has no more "ardent admirers" than ladies, they have their weaknesses, and he implores men to take a "young lady" to her first ball game at "first opportunity." "Her remarks about plays, her opinions of different players . . . and the questions she will ask . . . are all too funny to be missed." She is a "violent partisan," and "if her favorite team fails to bat well she characterizes the opposing pitcher as a 'horrid creature.' " When the teams have finished the pregame practice, she will want to know "with charming ingenuousness, 'which won.' "

Ward then, turning to the ladies, allows that they can, in fact, and often do, become knowledgeable fans, but that transformation is not a given. "Unfortunately, some men are not able to intelligibly explain the theory of base-ball, while others are so engrossed with the game that they do not care to be disturbed." So, "for the benefit of those ladies whose escorts either cannot, or will not, answer their questions," Ward is only too willing, in his humble way, to attempt to do so.

Ward's book was well received and went into at least two printings. The *Clipper* called *Base-Ball* "the standard authority on the nation's game" and "by long odds the best book on base ball ever printed." It was also curiously sanguine when discussing, at the end of his historical introduction, "baseball law" and labor relations within the sport. Certainly the introduction was much more sanguine than was his *Cosmopolitan* article of the previous fall. In fact, Ward, for the most part, drops his firebrands so completely in *Base-Ball* that he stops just shy of sounding like an apologist for League policies.

After his lengthy preprofessional history, Ward writes of the formation of the National League, praising its founders for ridding the game of "baneful influences": gambling, freeloading spectators, and revolving among players—that is, players moving at will (even in mid-season) from team to team.

This last problem, he goes on, was solved by the creation of the reserve rule. In a short discussion of the rule, he seems to take, at least initially, management's line.

> To this rule, more than any other thing, does base-ball as a business owe its present substantial standing. By preserving intact the strength of a team from year to year, it places the business of base-ball on a permanent basis and thus offers security to the investment of capital.

This said, he suggests that the rule is hardly perfect and is, indeed, a "usurpation of the players' rights." *This* said, he posits that the rule is "perhaps, made necessary by the peculiar nature of the base-ball business," and despite the rule's unfairness, the player is "indirectly compensated by the improved standing of the game."

His language becoming stronger, he then puts the blame for the reserve rule's imperfections on the club owners, saying that its basic purpose is to protect them from their own greed, not that of the players.

> [Baseball's labor and financial problems are] directly traceable to those who controlled the clubs. Professional players have never sought the club manager; the club manager has invariably sought—and often tempted—the player. The reserve rule takes the club manager by the throat and compels him to keep his hands off his neighbor's enterprise.

He adds—after a reminder to all that "base-ball laws were not construed for [players'] protection"—that it was, perhaps, both wise and inevitable that players turned to "combination as a means of protection." The "combination" was the Brotherhood—of which he then gives a brief history, concluding that

> the time has not yet come to write of the effect of [the Brotherhood] in base-ball affairs. It is organized on a conservative plan,

and the spirit it has already shown has given nothing to fear to those who have the broad interests of the game at heart. That it has within it the capacity for great good, the writer has no manner of doubt.

Ward must have rued the day he wrote that generally appeasing "business" section. For by the spring of 1889, not only was he bone-tired physically (he had played in something like 200 baseball games during the previous calendar year, and was facing, without much more than a few weeks' break, 130 more games), but thanks to the Brush Plan, he had been outplayed by the League magnates, the "numskulls," as he had called them in *Cosmopolitan*. He was also personally embarrassed: Helen had announced that January that she was returning to the stage against Ward's wishes and tongues were wagging that the two were, effectively, estranged.

The Brush Plan was likely the main order of business among the Brotherhood members—Ward, Dan Brouthers, Charles Radbourn, Billy Nash, and Charlie Ganzel—who met at the Fifth Avenue Hotel, facing Madison Square, in late April, a few days before the opening of the 1889 season. The players discussed the plan generally, aired other grievances, assessed, informally, the level of player disgruntlement, and laid out possible strategies for the upcoming months. Ward leaked to the *Clipper* that the magnates had best prepare to deal with the Brotherhood. For the first time, the possibility of a player strike was made public. "Demands will be made upon the magnates during the championship season, when, if necessary, a strike could be made effective," reported the *Clipper*.

The players recognized that on its face, the classification scheme was, as a method of self-discipline, farcical—at least for the immediate future. They also realized that it was extremely troubling in the long run. No one expected the owners to stick to their scheme. Even though the plan seemed ironclad—its definition of salary included "bonuses, rewards, gifts, emoluments and every other form of compensation expressly or impliedly promised" a player during a contract's length—many players, especially "Class A" players, would still find extra money flowing to them. Tim Keefe pointed out another fraudulent aspect of the plan, calling the classification "rot." "The clubs," Keefe said, "send in the salaries [they wish to pay] and [League president Nick Young] puts [the players] in categories to correspond."

The plan was, the players realized, nothing if not a salary cap, one that would eventually come to roost. Though the plan's terms exempted players already under multiyear contracts, those contracts would eventually expire. Further, the owners, who likely knew the scope of the Brush Plan weeks or even months before the previous fall's meeting, had, during the traditional contract-offering period at the conclusion of the season, offered far fewer multiyear contracts. Also, though relatively few players were earning in excess of $2,500, the plan was a patient one. Eventually the older, established, better-paid players would retire (if their multiyear contracts did not end first). Incoming players would be paid according to the plan (or at least a majority of them would be). The plan seemed to allow for a two-tier system for a number of years, until, inevitably, the older, better-paid players had all but disappeared.

Another player concern was the fact that the classifications would not be determined solely quantitatively—via batting, fielding, baserunning, and pitching statistics—but qualitatively as well, factoring in such intangibles as "earnest team work, and exemplary conduct, both on and off the field." This "exemplary conduct" clause was nothing if not a further codification of the long-practiced and highly arbitrary "fine" system: if a player went into a slump, it could be attributed to his burning the candle at both ends, hardly "exemplary conduct." A player's classification would fall—at the drop of a fly ball—as surely as the sixth inning follows the fifth.

Last, the plan included a clause that, though generally unnoticed at the time, was extremely unfair. If the League decided that the classification system had been violated, both the team *and* the player would be punished: the club by a $2,000 fine—not exactly petty cash, but hardly a bank breaker—and the player by his unconditional release. While this clause could be justified as some sort of "equal justice under the law," the moon could also be seen as a wheel of green cheese. Theoretically, the released player was also an "unreserved" player, but in fact, he was not. The League could take the player and unilaterally assign him to another club. Except in the case of a very prominent player—whose "violation" would be unlikely ever to come to the fore in the first place—an unconditionally released player, essentially a relatively expendable player, would serve as an example of the price one paid for disobedience. The player might well find that for some reason, no team was interested in him. Effectively, via owner collusion, he would be blackballed.

A few weeks later, again at the Fifth Avenue Hotel, Ward held another board meeting, one at which "greatest secrecy was maintained." The Brotherhood officers were daily more angry at the League's continuing refusal to discuss general grievances, but, under the influence of the cautious Ward, did little but form a grievance committee. In June, the Brotherhood formally requested that League president Young toss out the classification system and end all selling of players.

The League stalled by forming its own committee to discuss the Brotherhood petition. The two sides were set to meet on June 25, but just before that day, Ward and Spalding met alone in Chicago during a four-game series with New York.

The meeting was discouraging. Spalding rebuffed Ward, saying that whatever concerns the players had, they hardly merited immediate attention. Spalding vaguely suggested that the annual November League meeting would be a better time for formal discussions, a position he reiterated a few days later.

Ward, while insisting the Brotherhood had no plans for any sort of concerted labor action, told the *Clipper* he thought any delaying tactics on the League's part were "unwise." Tim Keefe was less circumspect, saying that Spalding was going to "regret" his decision. It is impossible to say what Ward's deepest feelings were about any concerted, dramatic, radical action on the players' part at that time. He might well have known that nothing short of a hammer blow to the head would get the owners' attention. But he was also the players' elected leader and their chief, if unofficial, tactician. As such he felt that radical action, such as a strike, could have dire consequences in terms of both public support and the health of the Brotherhood.

A feeble, disorganized, premature labor action would ring a death knell for any sort of effective opposition or true alternative to League/Association control. He no doubt spent much of his time that early summer of 1889, as the New Yorks made road trips, cooling Brotherhood hotheads as best he could, reminding them, among other things, of the quick demise of the Union Association.

Additionally, Ward may well have thought there might be yet a chance to create some wiggle room. Baseball executives were hardly a united front. Ferdinand Abel, owner of the Brooklyn Association team, was opposed to the Brush Plan, as was John Day, the New York owner, with whom Ward was extremely close. Day told the *Clipper* in late June that, he was "utterly" opposed to the three features of the plan that the players found most objectionable: the salary limit, classification, and the sale of players.

> The salary limit law was made for the benefit of the [financially unstable] Louisville Club, and the wrecked condition of that organization shows of what little benefit the law has been. [Classification] was a wrong in the beginning, has been of no use whatever . . . To the sale of players, I have always been opposed, and, except in the case of Ward, have never offered a player for sale. . . . This sale of players is . . . the thing which the Brotherhood will ask to have rectified and I think the request would be a just one.

Ward, while continuing his work behind the scenes, kept up a steady barrage of publicity in the pages of the sporting press. He denounced classification, which he felt "in spirit a nullification of every benefit derived by the players," especially in that many players had been classified at lower salaries than they had received the previous year. He agreed with Day on the immediate reason behind classification, citing Brush's Indianapolis franchise specifically:

> The rule was passed . . . to allow several of the weaker cities to at least clear expenses. . . . Indianapolis has about as much right in the National League as Oshkosh. Yet, if the League admitted the latter city, would it be fair to ask Denny, Myers, Boyle, Glasscock, etc. to play there at figures which would allow Oshkosh to clear expenses?

Detroit, he continued, had earned $54,000 in profits in 1888. He estimated the aggregate annual profit of League teams at $200,000 to $300,000. He challenged the League to shore up its weaker sisters, or find stronger ones. Whatever the League chose to do, he continued, it should not be at players' expense.

Ward's campaign was, briefly, effective. On July 9, Spalding wrote to Nick Young, League president, with a wide-ranging proposal. (Spalding, Young, and others had, undoubtedly, already discussed and approved this "proposal.") Spalding's plan, at first blush, was arrogant and defiant, a pail of gasoline thrown on flames. He proposed to extend the classification scheme downward from the "major leagues" to all of professional baseball, classifying lesser leagues from A to D, with salaries descending from $200 a month for class-A leagues to $600 a year for the class-D leagues. He also suggested—clearly as a way of co-opting current minor leaguers—a $1,000 bonus to any class-A league player called up to the League or Association.

The plan, however, showed Spalding's concern about player unrest, for it included a pair of large olive branches.

Although the reserve system would remain intact, the classification system would be modified: those League or Association players with both three years' service and "exemplary" habits would be exempt from classification. Further, to discourage the sale of players, the "sale price" of a player would be divided: one-quarter to the player, one-quarter to the League or Association, and one-half to the selling club.

This was a well-thought-out proposal, crafted by a canny, concerned businessman, and one that, when all is said and done, answered the players' demands with a reasonable compromise. However, whether or not the proposal offered too little as far as the players were concerned, it certainly arrived too late, for by early July, neither Spalding nor Ward were able to rein in their respective runaway wagons.

Individual owners, Spalding included, were acting like bullies and, as far as the players were concerned, these schoolyard acts of aggression and niggardliness spoke much louder than reams of discussion about workplace freedom and dignity and even the far more concrete matters of wages and classification.

The players' tongues wagged. They talked of Handsome Henry Boyle. Boyle had been sick in 1888, and was docked for his nonplaying time by Indianapolis. Okay, okay. But Brush, the team's owner, fined him another $100 for "allowing" himself to become ill! (Players were hardly hypochondriacs; they played with broken fingers and badly bruised muscles and sprains. Charles Comiskey, owner of the American League Chicago team from 1901 to 1931, recalled that during his thirteen-year playing career, from 1882 to 1894, if a player varied his slide into a base, it was not so much a matter of strategy as survival: "We only [did so] as the bruises on our bodies dictated. It was much like broiling a steak. If rare on one side, turn it over.")

The players also talked about poor Ned Williamson, who had been forced to pay his own hospital bills in London after his Paris injury during the world tour, and, as late as midsummer, was still out of work. In early July, Williamson's friends organized a benefit for him. Two amateur teams played and raised $1,000. Williamson made clear that he felt betrayed by Spalding, who had promised that the "season will not be lost to you, play or no play," but who had neglected to "extend to me such an invitation."

The players also spoke of mistreatment in the Association. Yank Robinson had been publicly shamed by St. Louis owner Chris Von der Ahe during a game after Robinson had cursed Von der Ahe for fining him $25 for a dirty uniform. When Robinson refused to travel with the team to Kansas City, Von der Ahe suspended him. Robinson's teammates threatened a wildcat strike. Though they relented at the last minute and caught a late train, the powerful St. Louis team managed somehow to lose to the hapless Kansas City Cowboys, 16–3, 16–9, and 18–12. The St. Louis players "like Bre'r Fox said nothing" about charges they had deliberately thrown the games. Von der Ahe rescinded Robinson's fine and St. Louis beat Kansas City in the last game of the series, and then, with Robinson back on the field, managed to squeak by Columbus 21–0.

In Louisville, another Association franchise, players had been fined for profanity, for bad baserunning, for missing signs, for failing to slide, and, in the case of second baseman Dan Shannon, for missing a thrown ball.

But the highest-profile near-insurrection in 1889 was the case of Jack Rowe and Deacon White, two veteran Buffalo players who had been forced to move, with the entire Buffalo franchise, when it was sold to Detroit. Rowe and White, sobersided, intelligent men, had long pooled their savings and, intent on returning to Buffalo, had become part-owners of that city's International League team, for which they planned to play. Unfortunately, Detroit had sold the pair to Pittsburgh. Pittsburgh management, citing the National Agreement (to which the International League was a party), said the two would play in Pittsburgh or "get off the earth."

White replied, "No man can sell my carcass unless I get at least half." Players all over the League were ready to strike on Rowe and White's behalf. Ward, however, quietly, forcefully, urged patience. Sign one-year contracts with Pittsburgh and trust him, Ward told the men. The players did so.

Ward was playing well—he batted .299 for the 1889 season—and seemed to be, as usual, in excellent shape. Nonetheless, after the June 20 game in Cleveland, he declared his arm sore. He did not rejoin the team until July 8, fourteen games later. At the time, New York was trailing first-place Boston by a few games. It was hardly in the best interests of his club for Ward, who was almost certainly on Brotherhood business, to leave.

With his own masterful sense of drama, Ward returned to New York to play against Pittsburgh in front of 10,000 people for the first game played in the spectacular, expansive new ballpark that John Day had built: the New Polo Grounds, at 155th and Eighth Avenue. The park wasn't quite completed, and thousands of people took to watching the game from Coogan's Bluff, on the west, which quickly became known as "Dead Head Hill." It was a free and fine spot from which to watch a game—well shaded, and unlike the park itself, combed with refreshing west breezes.

On July 14, Brotherhood representatives from all League teams met at the Fifth Avenue Hotel, where Ward revealed his master plan. The evident symbolism of the date, Bastille Day, was not lost on the League. However, instead of a nod to an earlier set of revolutionaries, the day was merely convenient. The 14th was Sunday, an off-day for all players, and a day when all teams happened to be within a few hours' train journey from New York.

The plan approved at that meeting would not be formally announced for nearly four months—after a highly publicized Brotherhood meeting on November 4. But between the Bastille Day meeting and November 4, the group's intentions would be one of the most ill-kept secrets of the summer—probably by the players' own design. Brotherhood members, however, officially denied any knowledge of baseball matters except the state of the pennant race. In late September, with his team neck and neck with Boston for first place, John Day of New York spoke with his players about the Brotherhood's "alleged scheme." Day reported that

> each man has told me that he did not know anything about it, and that any attempt to form an organization by which two or more clubs are owned or governed by the same parties will lay these same clubs open to the most severe criticism.

The New York players—who genuinely liked Day, whom they felt was a fair man—were not exactly lying. They were commenting on some disinformation—likely provided by Ward—that had appeared thus far in various newspapers. In fact, there *was* no possibility of "syndicate baseball." That idea—that all profits and losses of individual clubs be pooled and shared by the League or several common owners—had been met coolly when Ward, during his "sick leave," had broached it with Brotherhood members. Ward's plan—the Brotherhood's plan—was far more breathtaking in scope than any mere recalibration of the status quo.

Twenty-Two

A Magnate Bee
in Their Bonnets

T HE BROTHERHOOD WAITED until after the end of the 1889 season—and any formal post-season play—to announce its plan of action. It was, as it turned out, a fortunate decision, because the pennant races—in both the National League and the American Association—were barn burners, walloping good contests that consumed the attentions of the several teams involved and riveted "cranks," as fans were then called. The post-season series, between Ward's New Yorks and the Association Brooklyn team—the first all–New York metropolitan area "world championship" series ever held—contained more than its share of controversy.

The League pennant race—between Boston and New York—was not decided until the final day of the season. Brooklyn—known informally as the Bridegrooms because of the number of eligible and recently eligible bachelors on the roster—won the Association championship by two games over St. Louis, climaxing a long uphill climb after losing seven of their first ten games.

The post-season championship, which New York fans were eagerly anticipating, and which was daily ballyhooed in both Brooklyn and New York newspapers, turned out to be a sour, unsatisfying affair, filled with unsportsmanlike conduct. Both teams were accused of delaying games, hoping to take advantage of onrushing darkness. There were also accusations of unfair umpiring. Fan interest quickly waned. An average of

10,000 people came to each of the first three games, while the final six averaged fewer than 3,000.

In the first game, played at the Polo Grounds, New York overcame a five-run deficit and led Brooklyn by two runs after seven innings. New York then argued that the game should be called on account of darkness. But the umpires, Brooklyn resident Bob Ferguson and erstwhile Ward nemesis John Gaffney, allowed the game to continue for one more inning. Brooklyn scored four runs—in part due to darkness-caused New York errors—and won.

New York easily took the second game, played on Saturday, October 19. On Sunday night, the New Yorks were honored at a gala benefit organized by DeWolf Hopper, Digby Bell, and James Barton Key, manager of the Broadway Theatre. The affair was both very profitable—each Giant garnered about $190 from ticket and souvenir sales—and extremely long.

Mr. E. E. Rice led the orchestra in the "Seven Ages" waltz. The Clipper Quartet sang. Mr. Harry Pepper sang "Dreaming." There was a recitation by Mr. John Kellerd, a piano solo by Mr. Gus Williams, another recitation by Mr. Charles Coote, an aria from *The Hermit's Bell*, a recitation of "Casey at the Bat," a song, another recitation, a story, a banjo duet by the Great Ruby Brooks and Mr. Denton, another "talk," a duet of Rossini's "Quis est Homo," another recitation, a recitation of "The Boy on the Left Field Fence" by DeWolf Hopper, a song by Miss Marian Manois, and a concertina solo. Finally, the pennant was presented, followed by short speeches by the players. Since Buck Ewing was too shy to give a talk, the last word from the stage was a "neat little speech" by Ward.

The benefit ended about midnight; luckily for the New Yorks, the game scheduled for Monday was rained out and rescheduled for Tuesday. The game, again umpired by Gaffney, this time in tandem with Tom Lynch, was initially exciting but finally preposterous. The umpires, who had been under pressure since the seventh inning to call the game, suddenly did so in the bottom of the ninth, with Brooklyn ahead by one run and New York threatening—with the bases loaded and only one out. Gaffney needed an escort to the umpires' dressing room.

The fourth game was patently unfair. Gaffney and Lynch called the game—again due to darkness—after only six innings, just, coincidentally, after Brooklyn had taken a 10–7 lead. After exchanging accusations of poor sportsmanship, John Day and Thomas Byrne, the Brooklyn team president, adjusted the series rules: games would begin earlier, only captains could "address" umpires, and games were not to be delayed for any reason. The New Yorks proceeded to win five games straight before crowds whose paltry numbers were due as much to fan disgust as to unseasonably cold, wet weather.

Ward's play in the sixth game of the series—if not one of those "turning points" commentators make so much of—certainly illustrates the value of the nonquantifiable coin with which he filled his team's coffers. Brooklyn had taken a 1–0 lead into the bottom of the ninth inning. Mike Tiernan flied out; Buck Ewing grounded out. Brooklyn was one out away from another victory and a 4–2 lead in the series. Then, as the *New York Times* described it,

> "Our John" Ward came to bat. He was stern and resolute and perhaps the coolest man in the inclosure. John is noted for doing the proper thing in close games and every eye was riveted on him. He hit the ball with all his might and it went past [first baseman] Foutz and [second baseman] Collins [and] Ward reached first base.

Roger Connor—the New York slugger who had hit a team-leading thirteen home runs that season—then came to bat.

> Visions of home runs, three baggers, doubles, and even beggarly singles arose before the gaze of all present [but] before he had a chance to strike Ward darted for second. He got there. Flushed with success, he never waited to get breath, but made a dash for third and reached that point in safety.

Connor hit a sharp grounder to the shortstop, who made an error, and Ward came home with the tying run.

> This was the signal for an outburst of enthusiasm. From the outset the New-York "cranks" were compelled to hold their peace and listen to the exultant remarks and shouts of the Brooklynites. Their corked-up enthusiasm knew no bounds and

they shouted as only metropolitan "cranks" can. Hats, canes, and umbrellas were thrown in the air; old men, young men, middle-aged men, and small boys slapping each other on the back, and a feeling of joy pervaded the atmosphere. During the excitement somebody shouted "Ward—Ward—Johnny—Ward!" It was taken up by the vast assemblage and nothing but the name of the favorite short stop could be heard for some minutes.

Then, with the score still tied in the bottom of the eleventh inning, Ward came to bat with two out and a man on second. He hit a slow "bounder" toward shortstop, driving in the winning run.

On Wednesday, October 30, the day after they clinched the series against Brooklyn, the New Yorks celebrated once again. Arthur "Hi Hi" Dixwell, a well-known and vociferous baseball crank, was so impressed with New York that, even though he was a Boston fan, he presented each Giant with a diamond scarfpin. Each player, additionally, earned a tidy post-season paycheck: a little under $600–$190 from the Broadway The-atre benefit and another $380 as his share of the championship series gate receipts. (The players, in turn, presented Polo Grounds superintendent Arthur Bell with an $80 overcoat and groundskeeper Pete Daily with a suit of clothes and an overcoat.)

After the clubhouse formalities, John Day invited the assembled to lunch at nearby Barier's Casino, where the food was "sumptuous," the music celebratory, and the toasts and wine abundant. But, as the *Clipper* reported, "There was a tinge of sadness . . . that cast a gloom over the lit-tle gathering." Everybody present—the victorious players, their genial and well-liked manager, Jim Mutrie, and even the owner John Day—well knew that they might never again join together as a group. There might never again be a League team in New York and, indeed, chances were excellent that before long there might not be a National League. For though the Brotherhood's master plan was still officially undisclosed, it had become, in the last several weeks, one of the country's worst-kept—though rumor-deformed—secrets. Would the Brotherhood found a syndi-cate—that is, a new league of jointly owned teams? Would the National League and the American Association merge, dropping their least viable teams, to better compete with such a new baseball organization? What did it mean that the Brotherhood had leased land in Manhattan at Eighth

Avenue and 157th Street for the following year? Would the Brotherhood players stick to their threat not to sign their 1890 contracts immediately after the 1889 season, as was the custom, but instead wait until after the November League meetings? Would Spalding make good on his threat that any Chicago players who refused to sign contracts would be served with an injunction? What would the verdict in the court of public opinion be if there were some sort of insurrection? *Sporting Life*, eventually a solid Brotherhood supporter, had already weighed in with an early opinion, that it was "un-American" for scores of individuals to be "manipulated" by one man—Ward. If, in whatever form, a new baseball league was formed, would the presidency be offered to New York club president Day? Or the sportswriter Henry Chadwick?

All that anyone knew for sure was that something huge was in the works. Day, for one, at the time of the clubhouse/casino celebration, had been whistling past the graveyard for at least a fortnight. As his team clinched the League pennant and rumors about the Brotherhood's plans for the 1890 season ran wild, Day told the *Clipper* that he hoped the inevitable—whatever it was—would not occur.

> The players may have some fault to find with the present rules,
> and, for my part, I think there can be one or two changes
> made. . . . We can do away with both the salary limit rule and
> sale of players. No man should be compelled to play with a team
> that he had any objections to joining. It is one of those evils that
> has crept into the rules that were never intended. I think there
> will be no trouble between the League and the Brotherhood this
> Fall.

But the die had been cast. At 1:20 p.m. on November 4, at the Fifth Avenue Hotel, the Brotherhood's chapter representatives met. After three hours of old business, a "dead silence" fell as John Ward stood to address the group.

"Brothers," he began, and gave a brief history of the League's unwillingness to meet throughout the summer. He ended with the following reminder: "Our organization still continues to be a protective one, endeavoring to promote and elevate our national game by every honorable means."

The group then adopted a "card"—which became known as the Brotherhood Manifesto and was almost certainly written by Ward—to be delivered to the public:

> At last the Brotherhood of Ball Players feels at liberty to make known its intentions and to defend itself against the aspersions and misrepresentations which for weeks it has been forced to suffer in silence. It is no longer a secret that [we] have determined to play next season under different management. . . .
>
> There was a time when the League stood for integrity and fair dealing; to-day it stands for dollars and cents. Once it looked to the elevation of the game and an honest exhibition of the sport; to-day its eyes are upon the turnstile. Men have come into the business for no other motive than to exploit it for every dollar in sight. Measures originally intended for the good of the game have been perverted into instruments of wrong [and are used] in the most arbitrary and mercenary way.
>
> Players have been bought, sold and exchanged as though they were sheep instead of American citizens, [told] either to submit or get out of the profession in which they had spent years in attaining proficiency. Even the disbandment and retirement of a club did not free the players from the octopus clutch, for they were then peddled around to the highest bidder.
>
> . . . [W]e began organizing for ourselves and are in shape to go ahead next year under new management and new auspices. We believe it is possible to conduct our national game upon lines which will not infringe upon individual or natural rights. We ask to be judged solely upon our work, and believing that the game can be played more fairly and its business conducted more intelligently under a plan which excludes everything arbitrary and un-American, we look forward with confidence to the support of the public and the future of the national game.

At seven o'clock that evening the press was given both the manifesto and a second document, which outlined in detail—sweeping away all rumors—the Brotherhood's master plan.

The men had organized an entirely new baseball league, one that would begin play in 1890 in direct competition with both the National League (NL) and the American Association. The new organization was called the Players' National League of Base Ball Clubs (PL). It would consist, initially, of eight teams: six in current NL cities—Boston, New York, Philadelphia, Pittsburgh, Cleveland, and Chicago—one in an Association town, Brooklyn, and one in Buffalo, where Jack Rowe and Deacon White would be among the owners. (Ownership was evidently the carrot Ward had dangled before the two angry veterans earlier.)

Each club was controlled by an eight-man board. Four members were elected by players and four by "contributors," as each team's financial backers were called. Foremost among these contributors was Albert Johnson of Cleveland, the brother of Tom Johnson, that city's reform mayor. Johnson was a successful businessman—he was a streetcar magnate—an avid baseball fan who regularly socialized with visiting players, and a fervent opponent of baseball's control over the players. He thought that the reserve clause, for example, was an affront to the free market, and that the NL's treatment of players in general was "unmanly." Johnson was not a blind idealist: he saw a new team and a new ballpark in his city as a way to expand his business.

> I have seen streetcars on the opposite road loaded down with
> people going to games and it occurred to me there was a chance
> for a good investment if I could get grounds on a streetcar line
> owned by my brother and myself.

Johnson had originally been contacted by Pittsburgh outfielder Ned Hanlon, in midsummer of 1889. Johnson, in turn, contacted other like-minded capitalists and introduced them to Brotherhood planners. Before long, these "angels" were in place. New York was backed, for example, by stockbroker Edward Talcott, tobacconist Colonel Edward McAlpin, and former state senator Cornelius Van Cott. Brooklyn's money was provided by E. F. Linton, a banker, and Wendell Goodwin, another streetcar executive.

The Players' League was to be governed by a sixteen-man senate—two representatives from each team, one picked by players, the other by contributors. The senate, in turn, would elect two of its own as league president and vice-president, and hire an "outsider" as secretary-treasurer. (Frank Brunell was the first secretary-treasurer. Though nominally an outsider, the former sports editor of the *Chicago Tribune* was a good friend of John Ward's.)

Teams shared all gate receipts equally. The home team kept all concession profits.

Each team managed its own fiscal affairs in a prescribed order: first covered were operating expenses, followed by players' salaries (guaranteed by the backers and supplemented, before the season began, by a $40,000 "insurance" fund). As well, each team was required to contribute $2,500 toward end-of-season prizes, to be awarded in descending order, beginning with $7,000 for the first-place finisher.

Any and all money left over was to be distributed among each club's backers and players according to the following formula: the first $10,000 to backers, the second $10,000 to players, and any profits beyond that split equally between the two groups.

The classification system was abolished. Any former National League or American Association player who had taken a pay cut in 1889 because of classification was to be paid at his 1888 salary.

The reserve system was abolished. Instead, players signed three-year contracts.

Players could not be released until the season had ended, and then only by a majority vote of a club's board—half of whom, of course, were the players' teammates.

Players could purchase stock in their teams, and were encouraged to do so.

Finally, the blacklist was abolished, but players found guilty of corruption or drunkenness would be punished.

Other details about the new league soon emerged, some of them curious considering the relatively populist bent of the master plan. Sunday ball games were forbidden—a fact many Players' League opponents pointed to as a "desertion" of the proletariat; as well, alcohol was banned in ballparks—another slap, some thought, at the working man the league was supposed to celebrate. Both of these rules were likely made reluctantly, with organizers knowing full well they were vulnerable to charges of hypocrisy. One possible explanation is that Ward and his brothers had to admit that, for better or worse, the National League had set the baseball standard for respectability, and had shown that closed gates on the lucrative Sabbath did not prevent handsome profits. A less high-minded possibility is that Players' League organizers, insecure about public reaction, felt they must dress themselves up—like ring announcers at prize fights.

In a pair of less controversial decisions, the new league planned to use two umpires per game—something players themselves had long desired—and to move the pitcher's line back eighteen inches. This last move, the new league's planners hoped, would foster a livelier offense, as would the adoption of a "lively" ball.

Tim Keefe, who had opened a sporting goods store with a former minor leaguer and Spalding employee, W. H. Becannon, on lower Broadway in Manhattan, was given the Official Players' League Ball contract. Charges of favoritism soon rose—every baseball aficionado knew Keefe was a prominent Brotherhood member and Ward's brother-in-law—but the Players' League refuted the charges, saying simply that Keefe & Becannon had offered the lowest bid. Keefe & Becannon, understandably, advertised heavily in the *Players' National League Official Guide*. One of their products was the Special Players' League Red Tip bat, which did, in fact, have a red tip, and was made from "selected second growth ash."

Sporting Life reported on the November 4 meeting with headlines usually reserved for Indian massacres:

IN HOSTILE ARRAY

*The Brotherhood Takes
the Great Plunge*

*All Relations With
the Parent Body
Severed*

*A New League
Temporarily Organized*

The report that followed was detailed, sobersided, and generally objective, consisting mostly of transcriptions of official documents. It did quote an unnamed backer as saying that the "capitalists" and players were in harmony and had the players been allowed to arrange all the details the capitalists would have received many more concessions than were made.

Other papers were less objective: "The action of Ward . . . compared with that of the man who slew the goose of golden egg fame, tends to make the latter appear as a man of keen judgment and foresight," went a *Detroit Free Press* editorial. "The Brotherhood contract is an excellent thing—for the capitalists," the *New York Herald* opined, adding that "capitalists are capitalists all the world over, as the players will find out." The *Cincinnati Enquirer* changed Ward's middle name to "Much-Advertised" and accused him of grandstanding.

Initially, the *New York Times* merely reported, in great detail, the proceedings of the November 4 meeting, though it did manage to round up some quotes and anecdotes other papers missed. Chicago second baseman Fred Pfeffer, the paper said, ran into Spalding as Pfeffer left for the Brotherhood meeting.

"You fellows don't know how to run a League," Spalding reportedly told Pfeffer. "It takes brains as well as money to run base-ball."

"That's so, Mr. Spalding," Pfeffer replied. "But the brains of your organization have always been among the players. When backwoodsmen and old fossils can make money in baseball, there is a bright prospect in store for us."

The unbridled enthusiasm of the players, however, was best exemplified in a *Times* note about the "King of the Diamond" Mike Kelly—who, it is easy to imagine, was piffilated at the time of the reported incident.

> When . . . Kelly walked into the Fifth-Avenue Hotel, he was at once made the centre of an admiring group. He wore a tight-fitting pair of imported trousers, a tall silk hat, a beaver overcoat, patent leather shoes with russet uppers, and he sported a bright-red boutonniere. He was radiant with smiles . . . when he caught sight of George Billings, a son of one of the leading stockholders of [Kelly's former National League club] Boston.
>
> "Well, sonny," he said to young Billings, "tell pop that I'm sorry for him. If he wants a job next season, I'll put him to work on one of my turnstiles. I'm one of the bosses now and [my for-

mer bosses] the understudies. . . . Next year . . . former Presidents will have to drive horse cars for a living and borrow rain checks to see a game."

The *Times* soon became one of the Brotherhood's most vocal and persistent critics. It repeatedly ridiculed the players' cries of ill-treatment. It called the notion of the "down-trodden baseball player" about the "queerest example extant of Labor crushed under the iron heel of Capital." It went on to call the players prima donnas, and mocked the "sprained thumb" that more often than not turned out to be as "illusory as the medical certificate with which the lyric artist resents the smallness of her dressing room." The average ballplayer, the paper went on, has "waxed fat and kicked." It then quoted Samuel Johnson: "Upon some men, providence has bestowed reason and judgment; upon others the art of playing the violin." The new league was doomed, the *Times* concluded:

> The outlook of an organization in which the performers are to represent Capital, Enterprise, and Labor, and to absorb the revenues in the forms of Interest, Profits, and Wages [does not] seem to us very brilliant.

Over the next year, Ward and the Players' League's best friends were the sporting weeklies: *The Sporting News, Sporting Life,* and the *Clipper.* The last, in an early and typical editorial, wrote that "the Brotherhood players withdrew . . . to better their condition [yet] are denounced as 'rebels' and 'wreckers.'" So constant and influential were these papers that the NL established a weekly of its own, the *Sporting Times,* a house organ the *Sporting News* regularly referred to as "Sporting Death" and "the Spitting Times."

One of the NL's first moves to counter the players was to hire the prestigious Manhattan law firm of Evarts, Choate & Beaman, which quickly began researching legal action against Ward and Buck Ewing for contract violations.

The *New York Herald* pointed out that NL players who sign PL contracts and Brotherhood members who sign NL contracts are both called "deserters. Isn't it funny?"

Spalding, at least initially, remained determinedly (and transparently) aloof:

> All I know about the Brotherhood is what I read in the newspapers. To tell you the truth I am not bothering my head about the Brotherhood. [The National League] will hold its meeting and begin play as usual next season [and] those players who will not be on deck will not be missed, as their places will be filled by other equally good men, and they may then retire, as there will be no opening for them elsewhere.

But Spalding soon realized he had vastly underestimated the strength of the Players' League, the extent of its organization and backing, and the seething anger many players felt toward their former employer. He fell into a state of prolonged apoplexy.

Within a fortnight of the manifesto's publication, the National League published a rebuttal, written by Spalding, John Day, and Boston League owner John Rogers. The language was as intemperate and hyperbolic as that of the manifesto. It asked the public to compare the facts about the NL with the "selfish and malicious accusations of its assailants." It called the Brotherhood's charges of "slavery" "meaningless and absurd," spoke of the Brotherhood "conspiracy" and "false promises" to its members, and questioned the need for any forthright organization to require a "secret pledge" to keep a "plot" quiet. The Brotherhood's new league, Spalding continued, was "an edifice built on falsehood." The Players' League had "no moral foundation" and was founded by "certain overpaid players to again control [baseball] for their own aggrandizement [and] to its ultimate dishonor and disintegration."

Where Spalding, Day, and Rogers left off, Spalding and Henry Chadwick took up in the 1890 *Spalding's Official Base Ball Guide*, of which Chadwick was the editor. The *Guide* pinpointed the genesis of the insurrection at the moment when some ambitious players got the "magnate bee in their bonnets." As well, these "conspirators" had dishonored Spalding's world tour hospitality by meeting during the tour in "secret council" to plan the uprising.

Remember, we are not talking about normal working men, Spalding/Chadwick wrote, but people who are "paid excessive salaries for their labor." One player especially, in whose veins ran fast the "desire for self-aggrandizement," became the "master mind of the whole revolutionary scheme." This man—clearly Ward—first organized players with the "ostensible" object of mutual aid and assistance to needy players. Soon enough, though, they had been

> influenced by special pleadings, false statements and a system of terrorism peculiar to revolutionary movements [which includes] treachery, mendacity and false pretenses.

Such was Spalding's anger that more than twenty years later, in his autobiographical summary of early baseball history, *America's National Game*, he can hardly restrain himself. By that time, the Players' League had become a distant memory; the National League and baseball had become as much a part of the culture as the Fourth of July and Uncle Sam, and Spalding himself a much-respected multimillionaire and theosophist living in luxury overlooking the Pacific near San Diego, California. In his book he calls the Brotherhood "unscrupulous mischief-makers" and "fakirs," although he does allow that the men were sincere "in motive."

> I did not believe [however] that their contentions were based upon safe or sane business theory. [Ward's early organization did little but] breed dissatisfaction; for its meeting afforded most excellent opportunities for the men to rehearse to one another their real or fancied grievances, and to plan and plot measures to secure relief.

The epithets that Spalding hurled the Brotherhood's way were common management-to-labor missiles in America during the 1880s. The decade—most ignominiously identified with the Haymarket bombing of 1886—was characterized by unprecedented accumulations of ever-larger amounts of capital in fewer and fewer hands, an unprecedented roiling on the part of labor—a roiling whose ferocity Gerald Grob describes as "difficult to exaggerate"—and an accompanying, rapidly increasing enmity between workers and owners.

Though the decade was never exactly a period of labor calm—between 1881 and 1885 there were about 2,500 strikes, involving roughly

620,000 workers—the last five years, the time between the Brotherhood's founding and its Manifesto, were positively deafening: from 1886 through 1889, the number of strikes had nearly doubled, to 4,849, and the number of workers involved approached one million. Further, these work actions were hardly localized: among the companies struck were the Wabash, Union Pacific, Reading, and Missouri, Kansas and Texas railroads and the Chicago stockyards. (Workers would strike against the huge New York Central railroad in 1890; disastrously, at the Homestead, Pennsylvania, steelworks in 1892, and against both Pullman and the Great Northern railroad in 1894.)

Spalding's outrage is understandable, but his accusations were wildly innacurate, for the Brotherhood was, in most ways, far removed from any sort of firebrand labor agitation. Perhaps the most accurate assessment of the 1890 baseball/management battle was a retrospective one. In 1900, during the midst of another baseball labor/management battle, Samuel Gompers of the American Federation of Labor, called the Brotherhood War "practically a fight of capital against capital."

Gompers and his A.F. of L. were one of two ideological and tactical models toward which the Brotherhood could look for inspiration. The other was the Knights of Labor, led by Terence Powderly, the former mayor of Scranton, Pennsylvania. If the A.F. of L. were fish and the Knights fowl, Ward and the Brotherhood were nothing if not a mixed grill.

Briefly, the Knights of Labor (whose influence was seriously waning by 1890) was a reform labor movement, while the A.F. of L., whose influence and power in 1890 were in ascendancy) was a model of trade unionism. Reformists, generally, were more idealistic: Powderly's group, in many ways, can be seen as one that looked forward by looking backward, toward a more humane, personalized time, a time of small-shop artisanship. It wanted to smooth jagged, ripping edges of the wage system by promoting cooperative models of production and trade. Powderly disdained and discouraged strikes (not always successfully), which he found "distruptive and dogmatic," preferring the art of negotiation. He also championed grand notions of land reform as part of the means toward a societal reshaping. Powderly's ethereal vision did not even allow him to support something as straight-forward as the eight-hour-day movement.

Gompers, on the other hand, was practical and impatient. He emphasized organizational strength and organizational financial security. Instead of Powderly's more national view, Gompers emphasized local and regional craft-line integrity—steel puddlers was such a group; carpenters another—because, in part, he felt that societal reform couldn't take place until strong, effective, cohesive organizations were in place to institute that reform. Following, the A.F. of L. of the 1880s had little truck with the unskilled: craft equaled power. Gompers concentrated on the here and now: better wages; increased benefits; better working conditions, shorter working days. He saw no point in trying to re-establish the master-workman world of artisans. Though a Marxist in his youth, he had come to believe that the march of capitalism was inevitable: he asked only that the workers' contribution be recognized and, more importantly, rewarded. If the capitalist refused to treat his workers with dignity, refused to share in the accumulation of wealth equitably, then the workers had every right to retaliate—via all-out labor actions, especially strikes—to achieve the desired end.

Probably the most telling difference between the two men came during first few months of the Players' League's first year, 1890. Gompers immediately endorsed the Players' League in their fight. In late January, 1890, he told *Sporting Life*:

Laboring men all over the country are in sympathy with the players in this fight . . . over six hundred thousand skilled working men in this country . . . want to see the players succeed in freeing themselves from League slavery.

Powderly was disdainful of Gompers and what he saw as his hollow grandstanding. "Lasting reforms," he wrote, "are never secured in a hurry." "Boycott the [National League] and save labor," he continued, sarcastically. "Thus runs the declarations of the Federation now."

And the Federation did support the Brotherhood. Gompers and various union officials met with Players' League representatives in strategy sessions; A.F. of L. local organizations passed resolutions supporting the new League as did iron and steel workers unions, cloth cutters, and locomotive firemen. The Clothing Cutters Assembly #2583 of Jersey City fined members who attended "non-union" baseball grounds. A musician's union prevented a local band from playing at the Pittsburgh National League team's opening day.

The new league's support extended even beyond organized labor. Yale and Princeton moved their annual baseball game from the National League grounds to Philadelphia's Brotherhood Park; the Benevolent and Protective Order of Elks passed a resolution supporting the new league.

Whether or not it would have made a telling difference in the end, the Brotherhood and the Players' League did not reciprocate this support. The no-Sunday-games, no-alcohol and $.50-admission decisions were direct insults to, and de facto exclusions of, the working classes. So was the ignoble business that took place during the last frantic days of construction of the Players' League park in Chicago. When local carpenters went on a city-wide strike, the team, racing against time, called in scabs to finish the job.

Ward held organized labor at arm's length. Certainly, he never publicly embraced the labor movement, or recognized their support publicly. But Ward's group incorporated aspects of both the Knights and the A.F. of L. during its short life. If the Knights were idealists who wished to return to the days of some labor/management equity and who preferred negotiation to disruption, so was the Brotherhood. Ward, during the two years preceding the formation of the Players' League, was time and again rebuffed by the National League. The League was reluctant to recognize the Brotherhood and when they did, did so only nominally. This was a direct insult to Ward's and the players' vision of themselves as the elite of the elite, the craft crème de la crème. (A modern equivalent might be a medical doctor's union.) The National League's rudeness, its disdain, finally forced the players to take action, no matter how reluctant they were (and there is no reason to believe that had the League been smart enough to "co-opt" Ward and the Brotherhood, there would have been any revolt) because the League, by its actions, had questioned their "manliness." The code of manliness, according to Bruce Laurie, dictated that one was a

> vigilant spirit unafraid of standing up to a boss or foreman. [Further] he was more effective in a group, a collective . . . faithful to an ethic of mutualism . . . [M]averick tradesmen earned the con-

tempt of fellow workers expressed with a rich vocabulary of epithets suggesting they were selfish or unmanly sycophants.

On the other hand, the Brotherhood, tactically, followed the lead of Gompers: though it never struck (shades of Powderly), it took dramatic, uncancelable action; it discarded ideology for practicality, theory for fact. The reformation of baseball society would follow immediate gain, be a function of strength.

There is one last twist to the Knights/A.F. of L. schizophrenia of the Brotherhood. Though its original vision was probably closer to Powderly's, and its confrontational plunge akin to the tactics of Gompers, the organization of the League itself was nothing if not a model of reform union cooperativeness. Even so, it was amphibious: a cooperative populated by closely bonded craftsmen.

Rhetoric aside, the National League had been rattled to the core by the Brotherhood's announcement. At their November meeting, NL magnates made several important amendments to "baseball law," changes that, not surprisingly, spoke directly to the Brotherhood's major grievances. (Meanwhile, the Players' League ignored these concessions, and went about its business, signing players, acquiring ballparks or leasing land or building parks on land that had been acquired earlier.)

Among the changes the NL made that November were these:

1) While a player would still have to gain the consent of his club to negotiate with another team, if that consent were given, negotiations could proceed. If a sale did take place, the player would be allowed a cut of the sale price, if both teams involved consented. (The Brotherhood laughed out loud at this change, pointing, correctly, to the powerful "if" clauses it contained.)

2) If a club disbanded, for whatever reason, a player was considered to have been released from both contract and reservation. While this seemed a huge concession, it was not in fact. Players understood that the NL, in general, and especially in the absence of the Players' League, had become essentially stable, and "disbandment" a rarer and rarer occasion. Further, no clear-thinking Brotherhood member doubted for a second that if an NL team was about to fail, it would quickly, in this period of war, be bailed

out somehow. Besides, though a player might be "released," approval of any negotiations with another NL team must come from the NL office itself.

3) The classification system was abolished.

More quietly, the NL began offering multiyear contracts, and also offered to pay expenses home for any player released while his team was on the road.

None of this meant much more than zero times six to the Brotherhood members. Their distrust and anger ran so deep that they were convinced these concessions were not only built on sand, they were insulting, as well—as insulting as a company paying greatly increased wages to attract strikebreakers. "If we are worth all that now," the players said to themselves and everyone who would listen, "then why weren't we worth it a few months ago?" More than anything, though, Brotherhood members were bolstered by the NL's actions: they were nothing if not a scream of self-admission, on the NL's part, that it was a rapidly listing ship, which indeed it was.

By the spring of 1890, with opening day looming, the NL had, in fact, been deprived of the services of the great majority of its players, as well as nearly all its "star" attractions—including Ward, Buck Ewing, Roger Connor, Mike Kelly, and Tim Keefe. Among the very few first-line players who chose to remain in the NL were Cap Anson, who, besides being a close friend of Spalding, was a Chicago stockholder; New York pitcher Mickey Welch; John Clarkson of Boston, the NL's best pitcher in 1889; and several Indianapolis players—Jack Glasscock, former Ward Providence teammate Jerry Denny, Amos Rusie, and Henry Boyle among them—who, originally Brotherhood members, had "jumped" back from the PL.

Ward was furious with these men.

The desertions . . . were inevitable. Denny sold his birthright for the $750 he was cut by the classification law last season. . . . Boyle sold himself for $42 docked pay and the return of a fine of $100 [money that the Brotherhood had tried earlier but failed to have the NL return to Boyle]. The precious pair were dear at that. . . . Glasscock was bought too. . . . [He] professed fidelity, and went around doing the National League's dirty work with an honest mask on his face. . . . Never will I or any loyal man play on any field with one of that sweet trio again.

The National League in 1889 consisted of approximately 130 players who had appeared in at least fifteen games. Only 38 of them—29 percent—remained on NL rosters in 1890. Another way of looking at the massive defection is this: of 124 Players' League men who participated in at least ten games in 1890, 81 were former NL players. Twenty-eight were from the Association and a dozen or so came from other leagues. The Pittsburgh NL team was particularly hard hit: only one of its 1889 rostered players took the field in 1890. To make matters even worse for the NL, in many cases their former players signed with Players' League teams in the same town where they had played the previous year—forcing the issue of fan loyalty.

Hundreds of thousands of words were printed on the Players' War over the winter of 1889–1890, in both the sporting weeklies and the daily press. The two sides traded accusations and misinformation. They screamed insults at each other. They threw buckets of mud. Hyperbole rose to new heights. Daily skirmishes were detailed in the crabbed columns of the press. Even the most ardent crank would have been hard-pressed to keep straight all the intrigue, the cries of betrayal, the shouts of loyalty, the rumors of subterfuge and bad sportsmanship. The atmosphere was supercharged and no one could pick out the rare truthful strands from the wide bolts of mendacious cloth the NL and the Brotherhood spun.

For better or worse, most of the sports-following nation was aware of every writhing nuance of the pre-season jostling of the two sides in the Players' War of 1890. Moreover, Americans formed strong opinions about the participants' guilt, innocence, and motives; concluded that justice or injustice had prevailed; and finally were worn down by the onslaught of verbiage and looked forward to the day when, at last, the fighting would end and baseball as they once knew it would resume.

Here are only a few of the typical baseball headlines from that long-ago winter:

Hoy Signs with Players' League in Buffalo

Ward says PL Deserters Have Ruined Their Reputation

People in West [i.e., Illinois, Indianapolis] Favor Players' League
8–1

Agents Signing Players to [National] League Have Telegrams
Stolen by Players' League Sympathizers and Sent to Ward

Mickey Welch Signs with League: "Simply a Matter of Business,"
Says Welch

A Few More Deserters

Players Signed

Buffalo News

Carroll—Pittsburgh Catcher—Heard From

A Lie Nailed

More Signings

Players' League Gaining In Strength With Each Day

Land for [Name Your City] Players' League Park Secured

Ward's Hot Shot: Some of His Critics Ably Answered

Mills to Ward: The Latter Handled Without Gloves,
Some Statements and Claims of the Players' Leader Reviewed

The League: Latest Movement of the Senior Body

Spalding Points Out Benefits of Reserve Rule

*Chicago [National] League Club Declares Dividend—And This
Club Was Said to Have Lost Money Last Season!*

As in all wars, there were incidents of "heroism" as well as those of
"treachery." It is difficult to tell how many of these so-I-sez-to-him-I-sez
stories occurred as reported, or were embellished by zealous reporters. For
example, when it was reported that slugging Roger Connor had been
approached to jump from the Players' League back to the NL, Connor
supposedly told the magnate involved, "There isn't money enough in
New York City to buy me to jump my contract."

Perhaps the only verifiable story along these lines is one concerning
Mike Kelly, the charming, dissolute, wildly popular star who managed the
Boston PL team in 1890. Evidently, no less a figure than Spalding himself,
Kelly's former owner in Chicago, asked him to drop by Spalding's hotel
one day in late June, when Kelly's new team was in Chicago for a four-
game series. After a brief, cordial conversation about nothing much at all,
Spalding offered Kelly a dram or three of whiskey.

"How are things going with the game, Mike?" Spalding asked.

"Oh, the game's gone to ———."

"What? You don't mean to say that the managers are getting discouraged?"

"Aw, ——— the managers!"

"Why, what's the matter?"

"Everything . . . ; everybody's disgusted; clubs all losing money; we
made a ——— foolish blunder when we went into it."

Spalding—whose re-created conversation this is—then quietly
placed a $10,000 check on the table.

"Mike, how would you like that check . . . payable to you?"

"Would Mike Kelly like $10,000? I should smile."

". . . that's not all, Mike. Here's a three-year contract, and I'm authorized to let you fill in the amount of salary yourself."

The highly flustered Kelly asked his former boss for time to think
about things. Before long, he returned, and Spalding noticed Kelly's "set
jaw" and the "bright sparkle to his eye that somehow seemed to augur ill
for the success of my mission."

"Well, Mike, where have you been?"

"I've been taking a walk. I went 'way up town and back."

"Have you decided what you're going to do?"

"I've decided not to accept."

"What? You don't want the $10,000!"

"Aw, I want the $10,000 bad enough; but I've thought the matter all over, and I can't go back on the boys."

In his autobiography Spalding, unsurprisingly, turned this incident into one of self-celebration.

> Involuntarily I reached out my hand in congratulation of the great ball player on his loyalty. We talked for a little while, and then he borrowed $500 of me. I think it was little enough to pay for the anguish of that hour and a half, when he was deciding to give up thousands of dollars on the altar of sentiment in behalf of the Brotherhood.

A sadder and shadier story concerns catcher/infielder/outfielder/sometime-pitcher Buck Ewing, a staple of the New York team since 1883, Ward's rival for the team captaincy, and a man whom the *Reach's Official Guide* of 1919 named, along with Ty Cobb and Honus Wagner, as one of the top three players of all time. As well, the 1989 edition of *Total Baseball* named Ewing "the greatest all-around player of the nineteenth century."

Ewing was a quiet, unassuming man, and hardly handsome—his chin was weak and his eyes always photographed squinty and narrow. Like many of his New York teammates, he was fond of owner John Day.

In early August, *Sporting Life* broke a story about some PL players who, it had been rumored and "verified," had been approached by NL magnates about jumping their contracts. John Day, the story went, had gone to Boston and asked to meet Mike Kelly. Kelly refused. Then Day and Spalding approached Ewing and asked him to attend a meeting, telling him that Kelly, and perhaps others, would be in attendance. This meeting may or may not have taken place—it was denied by all parties. Spalding, however, publicly sowed seeds of dissension among the Brotherhood—and seeds of doubt about Ewing's loyalties that would never, finally, wither away. Spalding said that he did not try to corrupt Ewing and didn't think that Ewing had "any thought" of leaving the Brotherhood. However, he went on,

Mr. Ewing is a sensible man, and he realizes that the base ball
situation is a serious one for the players, and he would naturally
like to devise some plan to settle the difficulties now in the way
of a prosperous continuance of professional base ball.

Ward, publicly at least, said he saw through Spalding's craftiness and
suggested Spalding would "give up a large sum of money to injure the new
league" with clandestine tactics such as had been reported. Ward went on
to say he had heard "considerable about the Ewing and Kelly story but
[didn't] believe either of them would think for a moment of deserting the
Brotherhood."

Privately, however, rumors persisted that Ewing was under the sway of
Spalding. In January 1891, after the Players' League had been folded into
history, the *Clipper* ran a story by an unnamed Chicago correspondent
that was remarkably detailed.

According to the report, there was, in fact, a fair amount of grumbling
about tactics and the movement's ultimate prospects by some of the
Brotherhood members. Among them was Kelly, who had had a candid
conversation with Anson—very likely in a saloon, or at least with Kelly
in a booze-fueled, expansive mood. Kelly told Anson to talk with Ewing if
Anson doubted his word. Anson did, and Ewing evidently agreed with
Kelly that some players were wavering in their support of Ward and the
Players' League.

Anson then went to Spalding, who was about to leave for Europe.
The two men, along with John Day, took a carriage ride uptown from the
Fifth Avenue Hotel. In the far north of Manhattan Island, the carriage,
which by this time was being followed by a second vehicle, stopped at a
"dimly lighted tobacconist's." The magnates and Anson were soon joined
inside by Ewing and Danny Richardson, shortstop on Ewing's New York
Players' League team.

Ewing repeated his doubts about the stability and resolve of the PL
participants. Richardson concurred, though hesitantly.

Spalding postponed his European trip and began a series of meetings
with Kelly. Eventually the idea of a counter-manifesto was proposed. The
document would explain the players' displeasure and make it clear that at
the end of the season, the signers—Ewing, Kelly, and probably Richard-

son among them—were set to return to the NL. The day the document was to be issued, however, at a sort of press conference in Youngstown, Ohio, Spalding and Day received a telegram reading, "Don't come; the bird has flown."

The ambivalent Ewing had evidently backed away. Without his presence, the other signers' feet grew cold as well. Spalding left for Europe.

The *New York World*, through anonymous sources, said that any such idea of a cabal was rot. Richardson and Ewing had, in fact, met with Spalding, Day, and Anson "to discuss the situation," but when Spalding stated that he was willing to deal with the players but not with the new league's capitalists, the players left. (The *World* also said it was Kelly, not Ewing, who backed out of the Youngstown conference.)

The story—and the many variations that must have raced through the ranks of players over the next few months and years—is important beyond its veracity or nonveracity. It, more than any other single incident, illuminates the cloak-and-dagger air of the times: secret meetings at obscure locations; carriage trips that meandered through the streets of Manhattan to throw off tailing hawkshaws; interrogation room tactics on both sides ("Ewing's going to be there. Kelly's already signed"; "If Ewing isn't there, I'm leaving"; "I'll sign if Kelly's signed"); and partisan press coverage.

It also suggests that accusations about the Brotherhood's "secret" nature and "ironclad" oaths had about them the ring of truth. (The Brotherhood had devised a system of code names for their telegraphic communications: NL magnates were animals—Spalding was "Fox"—and individual players were objects—chairs, tables, etc. It must have been thrilling, this subterfuge.)

While the Brotherhood's internal pressure for solidarity was hardly Stalinist, and its code of silence hardly *omertà*, the organization had a definite party line, and woe to the man who diverged from it. Even a popular, respected, and probably honorable man such as Buck Ewing was felt to have committed offenses—candor, doubt, and a desire for peace—that were, in the eyes of the Brotherhood, tantamount to treason.

If the accusations against Ewing were merely a plan to cause schisms via slander, they were effective, much more so than the silly ones accusing Ward of intemperate language. When speaking to a reporter, Ward evidently chose words that "if correct, would at once stamp him as being one of the lowest of blackguards." A *Sporting Life* reporter then wrote that this accusation was false, saying that Ward "seldom, if ever" used an oath, and no man with "such a sweet little woman for a wife" would act that way. The article ends with a call for truth to be the currency of both sides. (Evidently the *Sporting Life* writer excluded himself from this standard: Ward had an extremely salty tongue.)

The American Association was, effectively, ruined by the war between its old and new rivals, quickly becoming a leveled no-man's-land across which the other armies advanced and retreated. After the 1891 season, the Association—its teams sold, abandoned, or merged into an expanded National League—folded.

The Brotherhood's battle was with the National League, not with its weaker sister. Ward wanted to fight a single-front war and deal with the city-states of the Association later.

Ward could not dismiss the Association entirely, however. The Players' League knew the upcoming season would, despite their cheerful, incessantly confident statements, be a hard-fought one even on a single front. Ward wooed the Association, and in December floated a trial balloon, suggesting a Players' League/Association combine of some sort, pointing out the Brotherhood's strength and the disadvantage to the Association of being part of a three-way fight for fan support.

The Association rebuffed Ward. In hindsight the decision was disastrous and puzzling. It is possible it was merely a bad business decision, that is, the Association did not take the Players' League seriously. It is also possible the Association felt that its natural ally was the NL—its well-established rival, with whom it had gained some semblance of parity and enjoyed a civil, though hardly chummy, relationship. There is also the possibility that the NL had already approached the Association with some manner of olive branch—the NL not wanting a three-way war any more than the Association or the PL did.

Whatever the reason, the Association, by rejecting the PL's offer, shot itself in the foot. Not only did the PL begin raiding the Association rosters with waning reluctance—eventually picking up thirty or so of its players—but the NL dumped two of its own least viable franchises, Washington and Indianapolis, and successfully wooed two of the Association's most powerful franchises, Brooklyn and Cincinnati, to its camp. The clearly disheartened Association made the best of a bad situation (including the defection of its most popular player, Charles Comiskey of St. Louis, to the PL) and gathered up a hatful of embarrassing new franchises in second-tier cities such as Toledo, Rochester, and Syracuse.

Besides the public scramble for the hearts and minds of the fans and the generally *sub rosa* wheeling and dealing for the hearts and minds and wallets of the players themselves, the Brotherhood War was fought on a third front—that of the law.

Briefly, the New York NL team tried to enjoin Ward and Buck Ewing from playing with any new team, on grounds that they had violated their contracts, which included the reserve clause.

Law, to the layman, is a strange creature, as imposing as an elephant, as unreadable as a cat. To the initiate, on the other hand, the law is as clear as a mountain stream, as precise and economical and efficient as a box score. I am a layman. I will do my best.

In August 1882, Charlie Bennett, an excellent catcher who wielded a decent bat for sixteen years in the major leagues—mostly for the NL's Detroit Wolverines—signed a paper with the Allegheny (Pittsburgh) club of the American Association. This club, having not yet become a party to the National Agreement with the NL, was busy signing as many NL players as possible.

The paper Bennett signed seems straightforward enough. The catcher promised and bound himself—for an advance of $100—to sign "a regular contract" with Allegheny in October and play with them in 1883 for a salary of $1,700. Bennett changed his mind, however, deciding to stay with the Wolverines in 1883. Allegheny sued for breach of contract.

Bennett won. The court said, essentially, that the paper Bennett signed was too vague—even though it spelled out a salary—to be a "mutual" and "certain" contract; that it was essentially no more than a sort of "option" agreement, not a final one. As well, Allegheny's contention that they would be hurt financially because of the loss of Bennett's services was disallowed as premature: the 1883 season hadn't started yet.

The Bennett case is notable not so much because it speaks to the reserve clause—which the Allegheny contract was a form of—but because it was baseball's first instance of contract litigation. It is also an opportunity to tell a sad story. During a hunting trip after the 1893 season, Bennett, hoisting himself onto a chugging train in Wellsville, Kansas, fell onto the tracks and lost both his legs. He opened a tobacco/newspaper store in Detroit, where he was so popular that he was given a "day" at the ballpark, at which he was presented with a wheelbarrow full of silver dollars. He died in 1927.

The Association could have appealed the Bennett decision, on grounds that if *their* "contract" with Bennett was invalid, then so were all NL contracts, which were effectively similar documents. The Association chose not to pursue the matter, however. Any victory would have proved Pyrrhic: if the NL contracts—and their reserve clause language—had been found invalid, there would have been no barriers to an all-out bidding war for players, one the weaker Association would have lost.

On December 23, 1889, the New York NL club (formally the Metropolitan Exhibition Company) served papers on Ward. The club wanted a preliminary injunction to prevent Ward (and, by inference, every 1889 NL player) from playing for someone else in 1890.

The hearing took place on January 16, 1890, before Judge Morgan J. O'Brien of the New York Supreme Court. The New York club argued these points:

1) The term "reservation" in the contract was clear and unambiguous.
2) The contract was between Ward and the Giants.
3) Ward had "unique value," and the loss of his services to another club would be deeply harmful to the Giants.
4) Ward understood perfectly the terms of "reservation," because he himself had drawn up a supplementary contract that set reservation at certain terms—his 1890 contract would not be for less than his 1889 contract.

Ward's lawyer countered at some length.

1) "Reservation" might have meant one thing at one time, but, over the years, its meaning had been expanded unilaterally by the NL and its clubs, becoming a deformed and abusive instrument.

2) Ward wanted a final decision, not a temporary injunction. The uncertainty of anything temporary would cast a pall over the Players' League and have a chilling effect on its investors.
3) The "reserve clause" was not a matter between Ward and the Giants, but really a contract between clubs, an agreement not to sign each other's players.
4) The contract was unfair and one-sided.

On January 28, Judge O'Brien made his decision, refusing to grant the Giants' request for a temporary injunction. In fact, the decision was firmly in favor of Ward, even though some of his arguments were rejected.

1) The term "reservation" was, in fact, clear and unambiguous.
2) The contract was, in fact, between Ward and the Giants, and was *not*, as Ward contended, a contract between signatories of the National Agreement.
3) This was not the time for a final decision, and, in fact, was a perfect venue for a temporary injunction—were it deemed proper—to be issued.
4) The Giants *would* suffer great harm from the loss of Ward's unique services. "Between an actor of great histrionic ability and a professional base-ball player, of peculiar fitness and skill . . . no substantial distinction . . . can be made."

However, the judge found, the contract, and especially the reserve clause, was not "definite" and in fact was "indefinite and uncertain." (O'Brien listed a half-dozen hypothetical questions the contract left unanswered: "What does the defendant, Ward, agree to do? What salary is to be paid him? What are the terms and conditions of the alleged agreement for the season of 1890?") The contract was also neither fair nor mutual, "both as to the remedy and the obligation." O'Brien singled out the fact that a player was bound for a year (or indefinitely) and yet a club could release that player with only ten days' notice.

The NL was stunned by the decision—*Sporting Life* called it "mortifying" for the organization—which allowed Ward (and others) to play in the new league. Within a few weeks, however, it roused itself—though only to futilely unimaginative and repetitious action. The Metropolitan Exhibition Company filed a breach of contract suit against Buck Ewing. The only real difference between the Ward and Ewing cases was one of legal venue: the former was held in state court, the latter in the United States Circuit Court in New York.

The Ewing hearing began on March 14, only six weeks before 1890 opening day. The decision came twelve days later. It cited the Ward case (and also quoted Ward that the reserve rule "takes a manager by the throat and compels him to keep his hands off his neighbor's enterprise") and, although virtually unreadable (it was evidently against the law for judges to herd their written opinions into manageable paragraphs), came down strongly in favor of Ewing.

The judge, William P. Wallace, took his cue from O'Brien, and in the course of his decision asked many questions of the contract at issue. For example, "Does the contract embody the definite understanding of the parties to it in respect to their reciprocal rights and obligations after the season of 1889 shall have ended?" The answer was "No." The judge found there was no "definite or complete obligation upon [Ewing's] part to engage with the club; he also found the contract "coercive" and "wholly nugatory," at most a "contract to make a contract if the parties agree." He ended by saying that although Ewing, by refusing to negotiate with the Giants, had breached a contract, it was not "the breach of one which the plaintiff can enforce."

After one more run at the locked door—the Giants asked for a permanent injunction against Ward and were turned down—the legal battles ended and the 1890 season was set to begin.

It is difficult to overstate the implications of the Ward and Ewing victories. If Ward and the Brotherhood's long-term goal was the abolition of the reserve clause as it existed, then, after the state and federal court decisions, they stood at the gates of El Dorado. They knew this—or certainly Ward did—and the Brotherhood lawyers knew this. Certainly the NL knew—from the resounding dismissal the judges had given to its arguments—that, were the issue of the validity of the NL's contractual language to be tested in court, it would buckle like a cheap lawn chair. (The Ward and Ewing decisions did not set a precedent. They were merely denials of temporary injunctions. The issues of the case would have to be decided in trial and upheld on appeal.)

In fact, in September 1890, the NL, not only to woo Brotherhood members back but also in anticipation of further court action, *did* suspend, at least partially, the reserve clause. The new contract terms said that any NL team could sign a player—especially a Players' League player—to a contract without first getting permission from other NL teams. That is, New York no longer would have a special hold on Ward, and should he return to the NL, he could sign, without penalty, with Pittsburgh, Boston, or any team.

The partial suspension of the reserve rule, however, was a one-time introductory offer, made out of desperation. The "new" rule was rescinded as soon as the dust settled over the fields of the Players' War.

But a central question remains: Why—since the courts had clearly given Ward and Ewing the keys to El Dorado—did they not open its doors? Judge O'Brien, in fact, had invited Ward to do just that. He pointedly offered to judge the issues of the case and assist in all ways in "securing a speedy trial."

Clearly, the NL, certain it would lose in court, did not wish to accept O'Brien's offer. We can only surmise that Ward and company, confident of eventual victory, decided that there would be plenty of time for the court battle after the season ended. They wanted instead to fight the NL on the field. It was a decision—whether born of vanity or bullheadedness or after careful consideration—that was, in retrospect, shortsighted in the extreme. For the reserve clause, in various forms and in various professional sports, proved to have more lives than a sack of cats. In fact after being in a primal way responsible for strike after strike in professional sport leagues, and after making several trips to the Supreme Court of the United States, the reserve clause lives today—though greatly modified since Ward's day and its terms mutually agreed upon (by players and owners) in collective bargaining sessions.

A second question arises, however. Why did not Ward, after the collapse of the Players' League, pursue matters? He certainly had a motive, and plenty of opportunity—he played in the NL, and under the restraint of the very reserve clause he had battled against, for four seasons after 1890.

A final answer is elusive. Without overstating the matter, I think

Ward's heart—after the end of the Players' War—was, if not broken, in a state of severe disrepair and disillusionment. He simply could not (or, always a possibility, would not) gather either the strength or the will for further fight. Though his was a fiercely competitive nature—and this at first glance makes his subsequent lack of action more mysterious—perhaps even it had its limits. He had been defeated once, decisively, and could not contemplate another loss.

Twenty-Three

So Cheer Them
to the Echo, Lads

THE PLAYERS' LEAGUE announced its 1890 schedule in mid-March, as did the National League. While the PL's was hailed as a model of efficiency and economy, the NL's was widely ridiculed. *Sporting Life* called it "the most wonderful schedule ever, [one] which occupies the singular and unprecedented position of pleasing nobody." Among its deficiencies were fourteen off days per team and another nine days lost to "awkward" and expensive railroad trips to the likes of Indianapolis and annoyingly out-of-the-way Washington.

The NL quickly realized its misstep and took drastic action: by mid-April, it had dropped both Washington and Indianapolis—adding Cincinnati and Brooklyn—and revised its schedule. Not only was the new plan more efficient, but, defiantly, it had NL teams playing, as often as possible, in the same cities on the same days as Players' League teams.

Most observers expected the PL to adjust its schedule accordingly, in part to avoid the head-on competition for fans. It did not. *Sporting Life*, through whose pages one had to look long and hard for any criticism of the new league, sighed deeply and wrote that though the PL's "break not bend" policy was "manly," it lacked a lick of business sense.

Ward, meanwhile, had traveled to Cuba to try to interest local clubs in some exhibition games. The Cuban teams, in the middle of their own season, demurred. So instead, Ward's Brooklyns and the Philadelphias sailed to Savannah to train briefly before working their way south, then north—playing in St. Augustine, Jacksonville, Macon, Montgomery, Augusta, Mobile, and New Orleans—preparatory to the April 19 regular season opening. Ward sent regular dispatches to *Sporting Life*—entertaining mixtures of humor and vitriol, gossip and dogma. In one, he discusses the perils of sea travel, especially the "apprehensions of mal de mer," and the reasons the New Yorks played so badly against the Philadelphias in the southland:

> They have one great advantage over us at this time. Being all men of medium size they have not suffered so much from lack of "condition" as we have. With Orr at 215, [Art] Sunday 205, Daily 205 . . . we have a heavy handicap in superfluous avoirdupoise. . . . But a few more days' hard work will . . . enable some of the heavy-weights to take several more reefs in their belts.

Following this jocularity, however, Ward tees off on Henry Chadwick, the editor of the *Spalding's Official Base Ball Guide* and a harsh critic of the Players' League.

> Our *quondam* good friend [Chadwick], once upon a time the soul of accuracy and reliability [is these days] becoming positively sensational, going off half-cocked upon the slightest provocation. [Chadwick completely misunderstood a recent story] and took me to task for something which was said in a jocular spirit. . . . Mr. Chadwick ought to accept *cum grano salis* any personal story at this stage of the base ball fight.

Ward went on to call other critics "wishy-washy, milk-and-water characters who have not the courage of their convictions." He never, though, completely lost his humor. Walking along Broadway on March 27, he ran into his friend and former manager Jim Mutrie, who had stayed with the NL. Ward shouted out the first line of Mutrie's New York crowd-pleasing chant: "Who are the People?" Mutrie responded on cue: "We Are!" And the two men shared a laugh.

Ward's Brooklyns began their Players' League championship season with a four-game series at Boston followed by a four-game homestand against Philadelphia. But for most New York cranks, the 1890 season truly began on Wednesday, April 30, when Buck Ewing's New Yorks traveled across the East River to meet Brooklyn at Eastern Park, festooned with "flags and banners of all nations." Six thousand fans attended, including many ladies "attired in bright Spring costumes, lending an additional charm" to the gala occasion. First came a short concert by the Twenty-third Regiment band, then some political oratory, which the crowd greeted with animated impatience, heckling the speaker, a local politico, with shouts of "Now you're off!" and "Take your base!" Finally, after a ritual shaking of hands between the teams—a show of brotherhood—the game began at five minutes past four.

Perhaps one of the songs the band played was one recently published, in honor of the PL, by Boston's Chas. Blake and Co.:

> Hurrah for the gallant lads
> Who boldly struck for right!
> The dauntless souls, like knights of old
> Who fought and won the fight!
> Mammon's greed, Oppression's power
> They boldly now defy.
> So cheer them to the echo, lads,
> And fling your hats on high!
>
> CHORUS
>
> Cheer them to the echo, lads,
> Make a ringing noise,
> Hurrah, hurrah, hurrah, hurrah
> For the gallant Brotherhood boys

One of the two umpires was Ward's on-field antagonist, John Gaffney—sure enough, the game was interrupted five times with "kicks," one of them lasting twelve minutes. Ward got a single, stole a base and scored once. Brooklyn won going away, 10–5, in a game that was considered "slow" and "dragging" in that it took all of two hours and twenty minutes.

On the same day, 17,000 attended a Boston/Philadelphia PL game. Until 1890, attendance was rarely a notable part of game reports—commented on only if the crowds were especially huge or minuscule. All that changed during the three-league summer of the players' revolt. Players knew, owners knew, sportswriters knew, and fans knew that after all the shouting and posturing, the high-minded sloganeering and base mud-slinging, the predictions and speculation, attendance and attendance alone would make or break the leagues' fortunes. So attendance figures became a sports-page staple—one that, as it turned out, was completely untrustworthy.

The first indication of the new fascination with baseball's body count came quickly. A week or so after the season began, *Sporting Life* ran a table that must have chilled the hearts of NL magnates.

In the first homestand for both the NL and PL New York teams— played April 19, 21, 22, and 23 against the respective NL and PL Philadelphia teams—the PL outdrew the NL three to one. After sixteen games in each league—again, on identical dates, and for the most part in identical cities—the NL had drawn 29,000 and the PL 50,000.

The newspaper's reckonings were, for all purposes, the last accurate ones for the 1890 season. Attendance figures—in those days of almost literal head counting—were notoriously slippery, even in the most conscientious hands. And in 1890—a year that gave the term "ballpark figure" a bad name—there were few conscientious hands in either organization. Even Spalding, who went to great lengths to catch the PL number crunchers in lies—he hired undercover inspectors at various Brotherhood ballparks—said, many years later, that the truth was a rara avis that year.

In place of powder and shell, printers' ink and bluff formed the ammunition used by both sides.

If either party . . . ever furnished to the press one solitary truthful statement as to the progress of the war . . . a monument should be erected in his memory. I have no candidates to recommend for the distinction. As to my own case, I am sure that I can establish an alibi from the realms of truth.

During the season, he made much the same admission of mendacity on the NL's part. His only defense was that oldest of schoolyard retorts: the other guy started it. After raking the PL across the coals for alleged mendacity, he added, "We have done some lying ourselves, but nowhere near as strong as the other fellows."

The Players' League, besides charging the opposition with padding, pointed out—probably correctly—that NL ducats were being handed out like candy, at barbershops, tobacconists, barrooms, and newsstands in NL cities. A *Pittsburgh Press* report told of a postman who "confirmed the statement that almost the entire letter carrier force had tickets, not only for their own use, but for distribution" along their routes.

Another report, this by *Sporting Life*, which was careful to note that its figures were "not, however, guaranteed to be correct," showed that of the announced attendance of 2,853 on July 21, when the New York NL team played at Chicago, over 1,200 tickets had been "complimentary," while another 600 were either discounted for ladies or cheap bleacher seats.

Sporting Life estimated 1,800-per-game attendance as a break-even mark—for either league. We have only one set of figures that are not only contemporaneous but generated by a *somewhat* disinterested party— *Reach's Official Guide*, the Reach sporting goods company's guidebook of the American Association. The 1891 edition showed the PL drawing 981,000 fans and the NL 814,000, for a PL per-game average of 1,854 and an NL average of 1,510.

The posturing of the two leagues was unrelenting and finally wearisome to fans, who were not only numbed by what they perceived, rightly, as disinformation, but were beginning to suffer from a glut of what they began to realize was a hobbled version of their beloved sport. The faithful *Sporting Life*'s advocacy became, at times, downright embarrassing. With Boston leading Ward's Brooklyns by almost eight games with only fifteen left to play, the newspaper called the pennant race a "great battle" and "still as close, exciting and uncertain as ever."

Certainly, the National League had been gutted, and was presenting, at best, a shadow of major league baseball. But even the best teams in the Players' League were not, finally, "whole"—everywhere were glaring weak spots in lineups. The *New York Times* said that the diminished quality of baseball had caused "unfeigned apathy" among both cranks and the "baseball public" and predicted that, should the "absurd" war continue another season, the average baseball enthusiast would become "extinct as the dodo." While the *Times*'s anti-PL bias clearly informs its grumpiness, it was speaking some truth. All but the dimmest baseball follower could solve the season's simplest equation: if you steep your tea in one-third more water than usual, your morning drink will be one-third weaker than usual.

By mid-season, the two organizations were both showing signs of financial fatigue. The PL board, on July 17, issued a statement that its teams were "flourishing," something that must have taken the Cleveland and Buffalo owners by surprise, as their teams were drawing home-game averages of 942 and 871 fans, respectively. Indeed, at the same July 17 meeting, the PL assessed each club $2,500 for "campaign purposes." The Pittsburgh franchises, as well, in both leagues, were in sad shape. The PL club, evidently one of the "campaign purposes," needed an infusion of cash—which it got—for it to last through the season. To the Pittsburgh NL club must go honors as one of the most inept and certainly the loneliest teams of all time. It won only 23 games, losing 113, and drew average at-home crowds of 232. Additionally, the Pittsburgh NL club was the defendant in at least two suits alleging nonpayment for bats and balls.

For its part, the American Association had become such a non-player—in both the public's and the media's eye—that the *Clipper*, by September, had stopped running box scores of Association games, substituting instead line scores. Minor leagues—the other set of innocent civilians in this war—reportedly suffered great attendance losses as well.

The highest-profile casualty, however, was Ward's old NL team, the Giants, which had been among the teams hardest-hit by defections and would finish a miserable twenty-four games out of first place in 1890. They averaged, even by generous estimates, fewer than 1,000 fans per game in 1890. They drew 80,000 fewer fans in 1890 than the New York PL team and 140,000 fewer than the Giants of 1889. In July, against Chicago, long a reliable draw, a total of only 1,727 fans watched a three-game series.

At a secret conference in July, Giants president John Day swallowed his pride and begged his fellow owners for financial help. If he didn't get that help, he threatened, he might sell out, lock, stock, and barrel, to the PL. For a financially drowning man, Day was bargaining with his fellow owners from a position of strength: if the NL lost its flagship New York franchise, it might as well admit defeat. Immediately, Spalding and Arthur Soden of Boston each bought $25,000 worth of stock in the club. John Brush of Indianapolis, who had already sold several players to New York to help shore up the Giants, tore up the notes he held. Another six thousand dollars or so of stock each were purchased by sporting goods dealer Al Reach and F. A. Abel. Despite the thousands upon thousands of words that Spalding had written over the years trumpeting the evils of gambling, he overlooked the fact that Abel was a well-known professional gambler.

In early October, the NL took another body blow. Aaron Stern sold his majority share of the Cincinnati club to Al Johnson of the PL for $25,000. Stern's shrugging comment on his motives for the sale must have seemed, to the NL magnates, a deep and bitter draught of capitalism's most potent medicine:

> I want to say right here that I don't stand on sentiment in this
> matter. . . . When Al Johnson asked me what terms I would
> accept, I said "half down and half in a minute."

Everyone with half a mind knew that, in the absence of a complete surrender by either the PL or the NL, some sort of peace agreement was the only way out of baseball's red-ink lake. The notion of three—or rather, two and one-half—viable major leagues was evidently supremely fallacious.

Spalding, in statement after statement, bemoaned the fact that, as he saw it, professional baseball had somehow run its course and was no longer the people's choice, though he did not say what, exactly, had taken its place. He was, in all probability, crying crocodile tears. His strategy was this: if he—long baseball's most ardent and successful supporter—could convince the public that baseball, so popular in 1889, had become less popular in 1890, then the logical conclusion was that the blame lay directly at the feet of the new addition—the Players' League. Further, if he repeated himself enough, not only the fans but also the fledgling capitalists—fledgling in the business of baseball at least—of the PL would look at their emptying wallets and become believers. Spalding's disinformation campaign—more people watched major league baseball in 1890 than they had the previous year—was, as it would turn out, a canny one.

The season ended, finally, in the first week in October, plagued by a week or so of dismal weather and poor attendance. Brooklyn won the NL pennant, Boston the PL pennant, and Louisville the American Association pennant. Brooklyn met Louisville—vying, ironically, for the Dauvray Cup—in a post-season championship series unsullied by either drama or closure. The series ended prematurely because of lack of interest—the last two games drew fewer than 1,000 fans total—and bad weather, in a 3–3–1 tie.

With actual baseball finished for a while, the rumor mill began working overtime. Unlike the air of the pre-season and long summer—with its talk of defections, skulduggery, and all-purpose treachery—that of the post-season was thick with speculation about possible mergers, possible interleague signings, possible player shifts, possible franchise shifts, possible realignments and separate peaces, and possible conferences to discuss possible solutions to baseball's exhausting and evidently stalemated war.

The Association Athletics were broke.

There were liens on the Brotherhood Brooklyn park.

The Brooklyn NL and PL clubs would merge.

By a 5–1 margin, PL clubs wanted to play on Sundays and charge $.25 admission for 1891.

The PL buyout of the Cincinnati club was off.

The PL buyout of the Cincinnati club was on.

Ward would go to the Chicago Association club and manage it.

The Ward move to the Chicago Association club was a plan by Spalding to create a natural rivalry, line his pockets, and cripple the PL.

Spalding wanted Ward for his Chicago NL club.

Pittsburgh wanted Ward.

Boston wanted Ward.

Ward wanted to be a magnate in 1891, not work for one.

Ward would retire and become a street railway magnate.

Ward would play for New York's NL team.

Ward would go to Cincinnati.

Ward declared the PL a "permanent figure in the base ball world."

———

Shortly after the season ended, Ward and his Brooklyns made a short trip to Bellefonte. In Bellefonte the Brooklyns beat a picked nine, 5–3, before a large crowd that included students from Pennsylvania State College, who had been given a half-day holiday to watch the game. The next day the Brooklyns played against another local team, in Renovo, where, despite cold, rainy weather, another large crowd attended. That evening Renovo put on a band concert and dance. Between the game and the dance, the Brooklyn team presented Ward with a diamond ring.

Before he left for Pennsylvania, Ward, in an interview with the *Clipper*, sounded confident that the Players' League would continue and thrive—confident enough, certainly, to take the time to make an appearance in his home town with his new team and possibly do a little bird hunting, as well.

Ward told the *Clipper* he saw no reason why there could not be peace between the NL and the PL, and suggested a new national agreement, one that would keep interleague raiding to a minimum, create a uniform set of rules, and include a provision for interleague post-season play. As far as the reserve rule went, he felt that the PL philosophy of multiyear contracts satisfied both the owners' search for stability and the players' complaints that they had been held hostage.

Ward sounded like a confident man, and indeed he had every reason to feel that way. When he spoke to the paper he most likely had advance notice of the agenda at an upcoming joint National League/American Association meeting in New York. At that meeting, on October 10, Allen W. Thurman, owner of the Association Columbus team, made a long and impassioned appeal for a peace conference. He suggested that nine delegates—three from each league—meet for preliminary discussions.

Conveniently, there happened to be three representatives from the PL just down the street (they were monitoring the NL/Association meetings) who were ready, willing, and able to get the ball rolling. Thurman's peace initiative was not some spontaneous, wildcat affair. He had been busy for some time speaking with various PL capitalists—talks evidently brokered in part by Buck Ewing—about the need for just such a conference.

Thurman went on to suggest, as a way to begin the proposed conference, a consolidation of the three existing organizations into two new leagues:

League A	League B
Boston	Boston
Philadelphia	Philadelphia
Chicago	Chicago
New York	Baltimore
Brooklyn	Washington
Pittsburgh	Louisville
Cleveland	Columbus
Cincinnati	St. Louis

Although at first glance the proposed leagues were nothing if not an excuse for a dogfight—one league would have the New York stage all to itself, for example, an obviously unacceptable alignment financially—Thurman made it clear that his was only the merest preliminary platform, from which, if all parties were sincere, could grow a more suitable arrangement.

The informal conference that Thurman suggested actually got under way. Almost immediately, the PL representatives, feeling generous, made a major concession: they would not be averse, should other considerations be acceptable, to abandoning the Players' League name in the spirit of peace. The Association made a similar offer. Spalding, however, said the National League would never, *never* abandon its hallowed name. The PL spokesmen hardly expected the NL to do so—there was, after all, fifteen years of tradition to be considered. Spalding's adamancy, his lack of diplomacy, sat very badly with the others. They felt that Spalding had jumped on their initial offering as a sign of weakness. The peace conference, hardly begun, came near to breaking up over nomenclature. Eventually, however, Spalding and the NL agreed to adopt a new name *if* all other details of consolidation and amalgamation were acceptable.

After this exhausting business, the delegates adjourned, having made plans to reconvene on October 22. Before that meeting, the rival magnates planned to caucus informally, discussing various possibilities, and the advantages and drawbacks of each. *The Sporting News,* predicting that these "brainstorming" sessions foretold nothing but peace, wrote that "the greatest war in base ball history" was effectively over, and that the sun, on opening day of 1891, would shine on a bright, peaceful baseball world.

In another seeming peace initiative, the NL formally announced the changes in players' contracts it had promised a few weeks earlier. Among these was the much-ballyhooed dropping of the reserve clause. It would be replaced with an "option or right to renew" the contract on the club's part. Effectively, however, the change was cosmetic. Nothing in the new clause spoke to the question of what would happen should a player decide not to sign. The NL, however, was hoping the revised language might per-suade a judge or jury that the NL had removed the reserve clause's most objectionable aspects.

Whatever long and rocky road lay ahead for the delegates, John Ward must have left with his team for Bellefonte and Renovo with a light heart. The PL, though hardly unbruised, had survived what could only be imag-ined as the roughest year in what would be a long and glorious life. Its opponent, the NL, was a mess: effectively reduced to six teams—Cincinnati had been bought and Pittsburgh was insolvent—and its linch-pin, New York, alive only because of an extraordinary one-time financial bailout. Even if the future Players' League went by another name, and even if there were more contractual compromises, the PL, it seemed, had been triumphant.

However, while Ward visited his relatives in Bellefonte, danced and drank and talked about the old days with the good citizens of Renovo, and brushed the back trails in search of game birds, victory had, in all proba-bility, already been snatched from his hands.

Twenty-Four

A Sudden Tumble into a
Deep and Wide Pitfall

P ERHAPS THE PLAYERS' LEAGUE'S biggest post-season mistake was to agree to confer with the National League at all. For as clever as it had been in its original organization, its continued viability was, finally, contingent not on idealism but on the bankrolls of its backers. And those backers—at least the three representatives at the post-season peace conference—were, when compared to A. G. Spalding—the man responsible for the unfolding events that fall of 1890—hard-nosed businessmen of the second rank.

Or perhaps the PL's biggest mistake was the composition of the "peace committee." Wendell Goodwin, the Brooklyn streetcar magnate, Al Johnson, the Cleveland streetcar magnate, and Edward Talcott, the New York stockbroker, were businessmen first and baseball lovers second, while Spalding's twin obsessions—money and baseball—were intramolecular. Spalding took the players' revolt as a personal insult, while Goodwin, Talcott, and even the politically idealistic Johnson were without the fire of outrage in their bellies, or at least as hot and fierce a fire as in Spalding.

Perhaps, though, the true seeds of defeat had been sown a year and more earlier. There is no way of telling how rosy a financial picture Ward and his Brotherhood lieutenants, back during the summer of 1889, had painted for their wallet-holding partners. This is not to say that the Brotherhood's projections were deliberately false—though they may well have been. And this is not to say that the PL backers were children being offered candy by groups of beguiling schoolyard strangers. It is just to say that, possibly, the enthusiasms of both the players and the backers may have overrun their stone-cold calculations. So when the inaugural season proved less wildly successful, and more emotionally fraught, than anticipated, it would prove far too late to convince the backers that a second year would be different. Perhaps, those backers realized, surveying the clutter of the ballroom after the band had packed up, Spalding and the NL boys had not been lying when they spoke of the hard business of baseball ownership.

Or perhaps the reasons the PL failed were more mundane: flawed business management; a too-low initial stock offering; a too-low estimate of the league-wide "insurance pool"; the "manly" but foolhardy retention of a head-butting schedule; a too-generous first-year salary scale; the curiously sniffy decisions to forgo Sunday ball, to lower admission prices, and to ban the sale of alcohol. Perhaps it should not have held organized labor at the arm's-length distance it had.

Perhaps the new league should have been less civil, and fought an all-out war for those players who had chosen to remain in the NL—more of them than the Brotherhood originally estimated. Perhaps it should have marched like Sherman through the Association ranks—devoured that organization entirely, thereby establishing a strong second flank.

Ward himself, in one of his rare public utterances in which bile replaced wit, laid the blame for the PL collapse on "stupidity, avarice and treachery." Despite the artlessness and vague paranoia of his words, Ward's analysis was, finally, accurate in its all-encompassing sweep.

The Brotherhood, regardless of the impression it worked so diligently to present, was not a monolith. Instead it was a highly dedicated, one-issue political party.

Though it would be as unfair to blame Buck Ewing for the ultimate failing of the PL as it would be to blame Cap Anson for drawing baseball's color line, Ewing was certainly instrumental in its demise. Ward was certainly thinking of Ewing when he spoke of "treachery." But Ewing was not treacherous—except in the context of a closed-ranks, oath-bound organization—so much as foolhardy in his unilateral and naive dealings with the opposition, his misguided sense of timing, his bullheadedness, and his skepticism about the ultimate success of the new league. As well, it cannot be assumed for a second that Ewing was the only Brotherhood member to have serious doubts about the 1890 revolt.

Ewing had never agreed with the hands-off approach advocated by Ward and others. His early-season meetings with Spalding and Anson are evidence of this. Also, as manager of the New York PL team, he was—as field managers have always been in baseball—closer to his "owner," Edward Talcott (actually a managing partner), than were other players.

By the time the NL owners met in early October—and formed their "peace committee" with the PL threesome—Ewing had already swung into action, meeting with both Talcott and John Day, owner of the New York NL team. What Ewing had in mind—perhaps as a first step toward peace—was some sort of consolidation of the two teams.

A very likely by-product of these Ewing/Day/Talcott meetings—and we have to speculate here—might have been the sharing of financial privy information, in the interests of candor. Day told Talcott, perhaps, the extent of the beating he had taken—which was not news to anyone. Talcott then told Day, perhaps, that, truth be told, things had not gone so swimmingly over on his side of the ledger either. Day then told Talcott, perhaps, that in fact, even in the best of times, baseball was a precarious business. Talcott then told Day, perhaps, that none of the other PL franchises were exactly buckling under the strain of carrying money to the bank. Then Day might have laughed and said, "Tell me something I don't already know."

Or maybe Talcott spilled his thoughts to Ewing, who told them to Day, who sympathized and concurred. Then Ewing told Talcott of Day's sympathizing and concurring. Then Talcott spoke to his fellow magnates, and Day spoke to his fellow magnates and everybody knew everything about everybody else.

It is easy to make too much of these secret side meetings—after all, Goodwin, Johnson, and Talcott, the PL "peace committee," were meeting publicly with NL representatives. Also, the trio's eagerness for a settlement of some kind was clear—as shown by their willingness to abandon the PL name—and quickly apparent to the canny Spalding.

What happened?

The most widely accepted version of the initial meeting of the NL and PL (and Association) says that Spalding somehow cajoled the PL men—Goodwin and Johnson specifically—into spilling their guts about their desire for peace and the state of their and their colleagues' bank accounts. Spalding himself concurs, modestly, in his memoirs. The PL representatives arrived at the Fifth Avenue Hotel, he said, "bearing a flag of truce." Spalding, sensing the men's vulnerability, bluffed the men into thinking he (and the NL) would accept nothing but an "unconditional surrender." To his great surprise, he goes on, "the terms were greedily accepted."

We should take Spalding's account with a grain of salt. If the man fell into a puddle, he would try to convince the world his socks had needed washing. Although Goodwin, Johnson, and Talcott were no doubt weary, frightened, chastened, and impatient, they were also hardheaded businessmen, well versed in the game of bluff themselves. It is nearly unimaginable that they would collapse without some sort of fight. In fact, *Sporting Life* contradicts Spalding entirely, saying it was the NL that first opened its books to the PL men. Those men "looked for a gold mine and found only a nugget." (Of course, the NL might have presented "cooked" ledger sheets.)

Whatever took place, this was the result: a few days before the scheduled October 22 reconvening of the peace committee, Talcott and some of his fellow stockholders met with John Day in New York. After a few hours they emerged with a draft of a consolidation agreement. The two New York clubs, recapitalized at $250,000, would become one, with the PL shareholders having controlling interest.

This separate peace, which would seem to be a victory for the PL, was instead a death blow: the new club was to become a member of the National League. The Players' League was left without representation in its most profitable city. The rest of the PL backers, realizing the fallout of this consolidation, panicked, and began ingloriously shoving past each other to gain a seat on any available lifeboat.

Sporting Life sized up the situation immediately and pulled no punches in its October 18 edition:

PLAYERS' LEAGUE
A SUDDEN TUMBLE INTO A DEEP
AND WIDE PITFALL

*Present Unenviable Position of the New
League—Wrong to the Players
—The Proper Course For
the Capitalists*

Even though there might be ways out of the dilemma for the PL, the paper said, it cared "not to point them out; neither has it any advice to give, since that would probably be wasted, as in the past, and it may be that the Players' League capitalists are sick and really willing to be 'absorbed.' "

The paper went on, at some length, to say that while the capitalists could mend their broken fortunes in their own way, as they had in the past, by trying to "wipe each other out," the players themselves were being thrown on the ash heap. They had invested much more, proportionately, than the capitalists, and were soon to be left without even a livelihood. The paper assumed the players would be blacklisted by the NL.

Ward, just returned from Pennsylvania, was stunned, but collected himself quickly to whistle past the graveyard.

> I do not begin to believe all the things I have read. The clubs of the Players' League authorized the appointment of a committee to confer with a committee from the National League and report back to our central board. It had no power to decide anything without the ratification of the entire body of clubs.

Talcott, saving face, vowed that he would never accept the name "National League" (as if that mattered), and Al Johnson was gruffly insistent that nothing had changed. "The danger at present is that the National League, seeing our willingness to end all strife, may construe it as evidence of weakness." To which *Sporting Life* added, "His words were prophetic."

On October 21, the day before the three-league peace committee was to reconvene, the Brotherhood's eight-man central committee—Ward, James O'Rourke, James White, Arthur Irwin, Fred Pfeffer, George Wood, Ned Hanlon, and Tim Keefe—met at the St. James Hotel. Their distrust of Goodwin, Talcott, and Johnson as representatives was massive, and the Brotherhood petitioned to be included—as a three-man delegation—in the talks. They were initially rebuffed, one NL man saying that while he and the others "have the highest regard for Messrs. Ward, Hanlon and Irwin [the three potential additional delegates] as ballplayers and bright fellows . . . we can never allow . . . men who have knifed us in the back [to] enter into a secret conference with us."

Nonetheless, Ward persisted. He had as much right as anyone to be in the meeting, he said, as he had invested "all his money," some $3,800, in the New York club. He appealed directly to Spalding, asking him whether, as a former ballplayer himself, he felt mere ballplayers his inferiors now. Finally, using somewhat contradictory logic, he said that while each representative group consisted of three members, the Brotherhood men were, in fact, not individuals, but a unit—therefore it mattered not if the PL group had three or six or sixteen individual members. (It is not clear whether Talcott, Johnson, or Goodwin would be removed to make room for the Brotherhood bloc.) Alternatively, Ward pointed out that in actual fact the NL and the Association were acting in concert. Therefore, it was only fair that the other side, the PL, be represented by six men.

Unsurprisingly, the Brotherhood was excluded from the conference by a vote of six to three.

It is difficult to say whether Ward & Co.'s presence at the "peace conference" would have made any difference at all, and even more difficult to say if Ward actually believed he could make a difference or merely wanted to stare his new and old enemies in the face as they talked—with hopes of shaming Talcott and the others. In all likelihood, the Brotherhood could have sent three hundred men to the conference table without changing the result. What the October 22 conference was about, in reality, was paperwork, details. A separate peace was breaking out all over the baseball world. The Players' League, over the next two months, would become weekly more desiccated, and by January a husk.

On November 10 the Pittsburgh PL club merged with the city's NL club. After John Addison, the PL backer, sold his team he was asked if he was going to pay his players the money he owed them. "I'll see them hanged first," he said. "We took in $57,000 and paid the players $41,000. That's enough for 'em. I'm sick of 'em and the whole business."

On December 29, the Chicago PL club, after long negotiations, merged with the Chicago NL club.

Brooklyn was next, consolidating with the NL club in January, again after long negotiations.

The Association expelled its Philadelphia team, the Athletics, for reasons of unviability: the Philadelphia PL team took its place.

Al Johnson of Cleveland, the original PL capitalist, held out too long. By the time he accepted an NL cash offer, the NL realized he had nowhere to go with his Cleveland club. A lawsuit ensued. Cleveland's players were absorbed by other teams.

Buffalo was the PL wallflower. There were no teams left for it to merge with, in any shape, manner, or form. It disappeared from the face of the major leagues.

The details of these mergers, realignments, buyouts, stock transfers, and settlements gradually emerged over several months. Lawyers and accountants worked overtime. There was much wrangling and shouting and more charges and countercharges than there are dogs in a county. The sporting press reported every numbing detail faithfully, the accounts fascinating as actuarial tables.

Stupidity, avarice, treachery.

Human nature is what happened.

Tim Keefe announced he was going to sue the Players' League, as his contract for balls was supposed to run for three years. In May 1891, Keefe and Becannon dissolved their sporting goods partnership. The dissolution was not amicable. Tim Keefe's wife, Clara, who was a sculptor of some note, sailed for Europe with her nephew in July, on the *Etruria*. She planned to search the continent for ideas for a sculpture to be exhibited at the upcoming World's Fair. Ten days later, on July 21, the New Yorks released Keefe, who was struggling on the mound, with little fanfare. Philadelphia picked him up and he pitched decently for two more seasons.

Ned Williamson, Silver Flint, and a few other veteran players organized a novelty team called the Chicago Heavyweights. Their average weight was around 200 pounds.

Another popular player, first baseman Big Dave Orr—he hit .388 for Ward's 1890 Brooklyns—had been stricken with paralysis (he probably had a stroke) at Renovo, during Brooklyn's brief post-season swing through central Pennsylvania. The ensuing medical reports were, at least superficially, promising. Confined to his bed in Brooklyn, the "jolly" ballplayer remained in the "best of humor" though suffering considerable pain. His left side was completely paralyzed and his right arm swollen with rheumatism. He traveled to Hot Springs, Arkansas, returning forty pounds lighter (Big Dave was five feet ten and weighed 240 pounds). He could move his left arm and walk. He never played baseball again. He umpired in amateur leagues and in 1914 was a caretaker for the Brooklyn Federal League team. He died the next year.

Ward arranged for a $100 floral tribute for James G. Fogarty, a loyal Brotherhood outfielder, who had died of pneumonia.

Ward also arranged for $200 of remaining Brotherhood funds to help out Larry Corcoran, a once-promising pitcher for Chicago who was dying of Bright's disease.

Ward singled out Al Johnson, the prime capitalist mover of the PL, as a source of deep "personal regret." Although he surmised that Johnson felt he had been sold out by his fellow PL magnates, whose treatment of him was "shameful," Ward shrugged and quoted an old maxim: "When you're fightin' Injuns . . . fight 'em Injun style."

Nor would Danny Richardson or Roger Connor forgive Johnson. Those two and Ward, however, saved their deepest enmity for their former teammate Buck Ewing, who they said had been working all season in concert with the NL. Ewing, one of the men said, was

worse than any of the deserters. He claimed to be a friend of the new movement, while in reality he was its bitterest opponent. He was a cunning traitor, and the Brotherhood, to a man, blames him for the demise of the league.

The men also had their suspicions about Boston's Mike Kelly, but could verify nothing.

Ewing's self-defense was that he was merely helping the two sides explore peace. But in addition to his several meetings with the NL and his brokering of talks between Talcott and Day, he left himself open for criticism by suggesting that it was "wrong, entirely wrong" for players to own stock in their own teams. He cited a player who was so interested in the gate at every game—tabulating every "half dollar"—that his play suffered badly.

The *Herald* reported that some former PL capitalists said that had they met their NL counterparts earlier, they never would have gone into the baseball business. They had found that instead of "unmerciful and heartless" men, the NL magnates were quite the opposite.

Frank Brunell, the PL secretary, became a contributor to *Sporting Life* in the winter of 1890–1891, commenting on baseball's post–Players' War transition and writing an informal insider's history of the Brotherhood movement. One of his favorite topics was "treachery from within." He fully exonerated Danny Richardson and Mike Kelly from any duplicity. Ewing's actions, however, were an entirely different story.

The players' and Brunell's vitriol is understandable. Brunell had been made to look like a fool. Barely a fortnight before the wheels of the PL came off, he announced, quite loudly, that "we have won the fight. Our people and the public know it, and that's all we want. We will be stronger than ever and better able to make a fight next season."

As far as the players were concerned, Ewing's actions were indefensible. No ballplayer likes to lose, of course, especially in a close game. But forgiving a teammate for a mistake is one thing. Forgiving Ewing was impossible: he had, they felt, deliberately thrown a hanging curve and allowed a banjo hitter to belt one out of the park.

Ewing, for his part, never absolutely denied his culpability. He admitted despairing about the new league's finances and talking to Colonel E. A. McAlpin, the PL president, as well as Talcott, because he did not want to see them losing any more money. At that point, however, Ewing said, the two men "showed their hand" without his urging.

He was hardly repentant. The PL was failing, he believed. If it did fail, then the players would not get paid. "Everybody knows that a ball player only has eight or ten years to make his money on the field. . . . it is to the interest of every player to make all the money he can while he is playing ball."

Brunell did not excuse himself completely from blame. He said the two-umpire system was expensive and should have been tabled for a year or two. He also regretted what he felt was the too-large roster of each team. Altogether, the new league laid out $60,000 for "extra men" (though he did allow that because of wartime conditions, the extra men were deemed necessary), $9,000 in salaries and expenses for the extra umpires, $11,000 in extraordinary legal fees, and another $20,000 in miscellaneous expenses.

He estimated that only the Boston PL team made money, about $17,000 after expenses of $60,000. New York lost $10,000, Chicago less. He was vague about other teams' losses.

Shortly before noon on January 16, 1891, the Players' League, with the ratification by the old and newly created clubs of the NL and the Association of a new National Agreement, officially ceased to exist.

A small group from the former PL—Ward, Brunell, Al Johnson of Cleveland, and Frank Richter of *Sporting Life*—waited nearby for the news of the new agreement. Then they retired to Nick Engel's Home Plate Saloon at 16 West 27th Street, just off Broadway. (Engel, a friend of Ward's, a longtime baseball crank and supporter of the PL, billed himself as "Umpire.") The saloon had become an unofficial PL clubhouse the last many months.

Oddly, the ratification party—including Spalding and Anson—also went to Engel's place, where they were quickly ushered into a semiprivate back room. From the front came loud, off-key strains of "You Have Lost Your Popularity" and "My Good Old Friends Who Never Alter." The singers were the by-then well-oiled PL quartet. In between songs they reminisced, laughed, and toasted each other. Al Johnson kept lifting his glass toward Ward and saying, "Here's to you, my dear old pal."

"A gamer set of mourners never was," wrote a Philadelphia reporter.

They were aware they were licked, but they solaced themselves with the reflection that the other fellows knew that they had been in a muss. They no doubt felt a little sore down in their hearts over the collapse of the movement . . . but if they gave it any evidence it was only when the name was mentioned of some one whom they believed to have been traitorous to the lost cause.

The victors entered the main room of the restaurant, where the vanquished sat. There was "conventional cordiality" between the groups, and a "warm and dignified" debate about the just-finished rebellion. Remarkably, no one lost his temper. Both Anson and Spalding evidently kept in the background during the discussion.

"The Players' League is dead," Al Johnson said after the intruding party left. "And here in this place of good cheer, where it was born, we will bury it. Let the wine go 'round."

"We four are all that is left of the greatest base ball league that was ever formed," said Richter. "Let the wine go 'round."

They refilled glasses and sang "He's a Good Old Has-Been."

These four had stood by their honest convictions for a year. They had made the old League quail and created a revolution in base ball, and now they were beaten they had no regrets. Deserted by former comrades, betrayed by trusted friends, these four were left all alone. Beaten at last, they were consigning their idol to the tomb.

"Baseball will live, and live on forever," said Richter. "Here's to the game and its glorious future."

"Pass the wine around," said Ward, before standing to deliver the afternoon's grace cup: "The League is dead, long live the League."

Twenty-Five

She Turned on Ward with a Fury

O<small>N SATURDAY</small>, December 13, 1890, after the Players' League's collapse and before its formal demise and the ensuing wake at Nick Engel's, T. H. Murnane, a *Boston Globe* sportswriter, persuaded Ward to meet with Spalding at the Manhattan Athletic Club. Spalding, magnanimous in victory, greeted Ward and recalled that it was exactly two years ago to the day that the tourists had arrived in Melbourne.

Ward, in no mood to stroll down memory lane, corrected Spalding. "You are wrong, Al, it was the 14th of December." (Both men were right—Australia is across the International Date Line, so the 13th in New York was the 14th in Australia; and wrong—on the 13th/14th, the tourists had sailed into Sydney Harbor, not Melbourne.)

Ward was disgusted, disillusioned, and exhausted. Spalding praised Ward by saying that he alone had kept the PL alive.

"If you had died last June, the Players' League would have gone to rest."

"I was almost dead long before that," Ward replied, "but struggled along, thinking the other fellows were in a bad way."

Spalding then dismissed the fractious year with maladroit flippancy. "You gave us a hard battle. What amusement we could have had about that time comparing notes!"

Ward's reaction was not noted.

Why did Ward bother to break bread with his conqueror? It may have been a simple business matter. Spalding, rumor had it, wanted to place an Association team in Chicago for the 1891 season, with Ward as its captain-manager. Additionally, Ward must have felt a sense of duty, part of the code of manliness to which he subscribed, to be gracious, at least in appearance, in defeat.

After some pro forma disagreements about the reserve clause, Spalding deftly turned the subject to his philosophy of club management, pointing to Anson's near-total control of the Chicagos. Clearly Spalding was suggesting that, should Ward take over the rumored Chicago Association team, he would be given a free rein.

As Spalding suspected it would, the idea, at least abstractly, appealed to Ward, who suggested that the reason he had ended his own captaincy of the New Yorks years earlier had been because of continual interference—by a man "who had little knowledge of the game." (Ward might have meant Day. He might have meant Mutrie. More likely, it was a veiled attack on Buck Ewing.)

Spalding said he was looking forward to the new season, and made it clear that there would be no grudges held against the rebel players. In fact, there was no blackballing. Players returned to their 1889 clubs or, if those clubs no longer existed, were "distributed" by a central board.

Ward, his temper barely under control, answered rudely.

"It doesn't make a particle of difference to me personally what is done by the League. I am satisfied to go out of the business and may. I worked faithfully for principle, and don't know but now would be the best time to stop. I will enjoy a little country life from now until the first of the year and then go into a law office here in New York."

Spalding laughed avuncularly, predicting Ward would play for ten more years—he certainly had the talent.

Ward ignored the ingratiation and, icily, repeated himself. "I am not certain that I will remain in the business. I certainly will not unless I have something to say in the matter."

Retirement or a relocation to Chicago were only two of many publicly bandied rumors about Ward's future. The Cincinnati League team had been cozying up to him. So had Pittsburgh. Another strong possibility was Ward's remaining in Brooklyn—he had become a property owner there.

The wildest story had Ward returning to Day and Mutrie and the Giants. Not bloody likely, said Ward. Not only was Mutrie already installed as manager, but the New York roster included Jack Glasscock, Mike Tiernan, Mickey Welch, and Jerry Denny—the Brotherhood Judases.

Finally, in February, Ward announced that he had signed on as the player-manager of the new Brooklyn League team.

The sullen, bitter Ward who had spoken with Spalding in December was no doubt absolutely sincere in his intimations of baseball retirement. There is also little doubt that he had used the interview for his own purposes, making it clear to all that if he were to be wooed back to baseball, it would be on his own terms.

Nonetheless, it would have been perfectly understandable had he decided to retire and not become part of what he saw as an imperious, subjugating organization, one toward which he clearly felt not an atom of either loyalty or affection.

But he signed on with Brooklyn. Why?

He was only thirty years old, a highly competitive athlete in the prime of an exceptional career. He loved playing baseball—notwithstanding the cynical depictions of a ballplayer's life he had limned in his magazine articles. Like many performers, he enjoyed his place at center stage, the daily object of affection for thousands of fans. Ward agreed with the press's prediction that whatever team he played for, he would be its major attraction.

He would be able, for the first time in at least a couple of years, to concentrate fully on the game on the field, without the distractions of meetings, negotiations, proclamations, manifestos, denials, assurances, ledger entries, strategy meetings, and the thousand and one demands, complaints, questions, and comments of his fellow Brotherhood members.

His deal at Brooklyn would allow him to satisfy his appetite—whetted in 1890—for complete control of a team. He would be in charge of both field strategy and roster selection.

Possibly, as distasteful as it might have been to return to the National League fold, Ward may have felt it more distasteful to be seen a whipped dog who ran to a new and lesser kennel.

He might also have felt he owed his fellow Brotherhood members at least one more active year. No doubt he was not going to enter into any sort of sustained reigniting of hostilities—and he did not—but by his mere presence, his honorable, manly behavior in defeat, he would prove a tempering influence on the League executives and owners.

He might, in short, have felt that baseball—in his eyes, the greater good—needed him.

Ward also had practical reasons for returning. He had come to enjoy a high standard of living. He had lost money investing in the Players' League. In May of 1890, he had bought an "elegant homestead and a large tract of land" on Brooklyn's Cypress Avenue for $35,000—over three years' salary. He seems to have bought the land, which had evidently been eyed as a car barn for an elevated railway, as an investment, with thoughts of turning the property into some sort of athletic/country club. All that was fine, but even investment property requires mortgage payments. He could count on a large baseball salary. By contrast, a law career—even for someone as well known and connected as Ward—would not guarantee a steady income at first. He would, at the very least, be faced with building a practice, a long and expensive process.

There was also the formidable matter of Helen Dauvray, a woman who was expensive under any conditions. The first evidence of trouble in the marriage had appeared within fifteen months of their union. In November 1888, only a few hours before the baseball tourists sailed from San Francisco to Honolulu, Helen telegrammed Ward from Omaha, saying that urgent business—the nature of which was never disclosed—required her attention and prohibited her from accompanying Ward on the recently extended world tour. She had, however, traveled to Europe in November, while Ward steamed to Australia. Ward was reported, ambiguously, as receiving Helen's news in San Francisco with "incredulity."

After his return from the tour, Ward met with Helen. Their reunion was evidently not a tranquil one, for less than a month later, just after the 1889 baseball season had begun, the *Dramatic Mirror*'s "The Usher" column announced that Helen would return to the stage that fall, "in spite of Mr. Ward's protests." Four months after this news, however, the *Dramatic Mirror* announced that Ward had persuaded Helen to "[change] her mind again." The successful persuasion, the paper continued, was "another notable addition . . . to John Ward's brilliant record of short-stops."

The whole on-off affair, and its attendant announcements by Helen, was becoming something of a tiresome joke in theatrical circles. Toward the end of September, just above the news of a Japanese performer whose act was to walk barefoot up a ladder built of knives—their business edges uppermost—the *Dramatic Mirror* printed a few lines of verse:

> Just a little nerve-food,
> Just a little gall,
> Just a Giant husband
> Who understands base-ball;
> Just a rattled actor,
> Dateless—turns to drink;
> Just a twinkling starlet
> Never more to twink!

The doggerel was dedicated to "Dauvray-Ward Sufferers."

Toward the end of November 1889, when Ward was thick in Players' League business, a careful reader of the *New York Star* might have been able to predict the eventual turn of the Ward-Dauvray marriage. A reporter had seen Helen in the city,

> gazing into a shop window filled with lovely brocades. "Alas," she sighed. "How I would like to order ever so many yards of these beautiful fabrics. Why don't I? Ah, well. I have no place to wear them now. Mr. Ward positively will not let me act. Each season I think I can cajole him into letting me have my way about it, but it's no use. Of course I miss it. I, love the stage; it's my normal condition to act, and—well, I'm heartbroken about it.

"As she said this," the article continued, "with a twinkle of her bright eyes and a smile, she did not look very heartbroken. Mr. Ward must be an unusually devoted husband to induce her to change her purpose."

Evidently not devoted enough, however. Two months later, in January 1890, Ward and Helen were formally, though not legally, separated.

The news broke—at least in the sporting press—on April 19, 1890, opening day of the Players' League season, when Ward's Brooklyns were in Boston. What must have been known only within baseball and theatrical circles had become everybody's business. Helen had taken a room with her sister, Clara (Tim Keefe's wife), at the Vendome Hotel in Manhattan, while Ward had taken a room at the Clarendon in Brooklyn. Helen had also engaged a manager and a playwright—Sydney Rosenfeld—and planned to star in *The Whirlwind*.

Ward was irate. He told a friend that Helen "had to choose between me and the stage. She has made her choice." Helen, exhibiting more self-control than her husband, wrote a letter to the *World* decrying what she considered reckless and unsubstantiated media speculation.

> Perhaps because I declined to meet the reporter of a certain local morning journal . . . he saw fit to place me before the public in a false position and to deliberately accuse me of bad faith and broken promises to my husband.
>
> My domestic affairs are sacred to me, and therefore I have steadily refused to discuss them in public, but in justice to myself I cannot rest under the imputation published. I regret that this over-zealous reporter did not obtain an interview with Mr. Ward, for I am certain Mr. Ward would never have allowed such an undeserved accusation to be brought against me.
>
> It is true that Mr. Ward and I are living apart. It is true that I am going back to the stage, but that our separation is caused by my uncontrollable desire to return to the stage is absolutely false. I do love my art, but I loved my husband more and the stage has never in the past or in the present moment possessed for me charms as attractive as those of a happy home.
>
> I go back to the stage because I am separated from my husband. I am not separated from my husband because I want to go back to the stage. I have never broken a promise made to my husband. . . . I have now made all the statements in reference to any domestic affairs that I intend to make. My professional life belongs to the public; my private life . . . to my husband and myself.

Ward refused all comment.

On April 30, the two signed "articles of separation" at the offices of Ward's lawyer, H. E. Howland. Though terms were undisclosed—they would have concerned, no doubt, debt payment and other matter-of-fact details—the two were said to have parted "amicably," though reconciliation was "out of the question."

A week or so later Helen headed to California for six weeks. She planned to return to New York, where she "would be read" the new play, discuss script changes, then travel to Europe. Later that summer she would begin rehearsals in New York and open *Whirlwind* in early September.

In fact, though Ward's and Helen's differences about her stage life were real and serious, they were only secondary to the main, and much more sordid, cause of the marriage's failure. John Ward was an unfaithful husband. He had, in fact, probably been in the middle of an affair when the couple first got married. There is excellent evidence that he was having an affair only a few weeks after his wedding. Ward's pouting anger and self-pity about Helen's choosing the stage over her husband was, at the very least, disingenuous. Helen's most dramatic, "unwifely" act—her last-minute refusal, in 1889, to accompany Ward on the round-the-world tour—was, very likely, the result of another argument between the Ward-Dauvrays on the subject of infidelity. She had married, as she found out, a philanderer.

During the 1887 season, Ward had taken rooms in the house of a lawyer, George A. McDermott, at 155 East 46th Street, a respectable but hardly fashionable part of midtown Manhattan. How Ward met McDermott is unknown—most likely through mutual friends in the legal community or in the New York Democratic Party. The larger mystery is why the two became friends, for McDermott, a flashy, dishonest wastrel, was, in almost every way, Ward's opposite. McDermott was tall, florid, and red-haired. His notable presence was furthered by a dandyish, cheap fashion sense: four-in-hand ties with jewelled tiepins, fancy waistcoats, a cane, and a gray bowler "tipped boldly over one eyebrow."

McDermott had law offices at 5 Beekman Street, a stone's throw from that home-away-from-home of all good and decent men, New York City Hall. By 1887, though, his practice could best be described as nominal, because McDermott, long a gay blade, had succumbed to the lures of the city. For years he had rarely been seen without a "new and gorgeous" stage actress on his arm. As the years passed, though, he became a rather more familiar figure at vaudeville houses, race tracks, and men's clubs. He rarely, from all accounts, drew a sober breath.

McDermott's dissipation and greed must have been of heroic proportions, for he had the dubious distinction of being too crooked—or at least too carelessly crooked—to keep a municipal job for old New York's noto-riously corrupt Tammany Hall. After serving briefly for Mayor William Grace, McDermott "settled comfortably" with Grace's Tammany succes-sor, Franklin Edsel. McDermott was extraordinarily well placed within the machine. As first city marshall, he controlled a small army of under-lings whose job was to evict people for nonpayment of rent. Most of his office's responsibility, however, was devoted to awarding and renewing scores of city licenses for the likes of boardinghouses, express wagons, pushcart vendors, coach drivers, porters, pawnbrokers, cab drivers, junkmen, and any other profession the city could squeeze a few coins from. Needless to say, the position allowed McDermott ample opportunity for private enterprise.

In the summer of 1885, in the third year of his term, McDermott sud-denly quit his city job (and opened his Beekman Street office), telling everyone who would listen that he saw greener fields in private practice. In fact, he must have crossed his superiors. His successor, one Thomas Byrnes, noted that there was a rather conspicuous gap in McDermott's record keeping that preceded his departure. Whatever his trespass, McDermott was evidently liked enough, or feared enough, not to be prosecuted. In 1886, McDermott returned briefly to public disservice, appointed as Superintendent of Incumbrances—a sort of overseer of mortgage and license disputes. He was fired a year later, after numerous complaints, for taking bribes.

In 1884, the year before he entered private practice, McDermott had married sixteen-year-old Jessie Dermot.

When Jessie was born, in 1868 in Rockland, Maine, her father Tom Dermot was a successful sea captain. Ten years later, soon after Tom bought into a partnership in a new vessel, the ship was wrecked in a storm—still uninsured, as it had yet to weigh its maiden anchor. Tom fell into a deep depression and became a reclusive invalid.

Young Jessie was a beauty. She "astonished" people at first sight with her "brilliant black hair, ivory skin, and enormous eyes of a strange dark color that seemed to change from blue to brown to purple." At thirteen she was described as being "overripe" and having "a woman's bosom."

Evidently the teenage Jessie had an affair with a local playboy, twenty-three-year-old Art Hall. Possibly pregnant, or possibly, in her father's eyes, just needing some time away from Rockland, Jessie and her father took a "long voyage" to parts unknown. If Tom had ideas about taming Jessie they were ill-formed: the returning teenager startled Rockland with her earrings of Spanish gold and a bright, cawing parrot on her shoulder.

Her desperate father sent Jesse to Notre Dame Academy, a convent school, in Roxbury, near Boston. There she met Mary Kiernan, who invited Jessie to spend a vacation with the Kiernans, a "jolly, noisy, untidy" family who lived on East 36th Street in Manhattan in a respectable working-class neighborhood, close to Third Avenue, with its elevated railway, restaurants, and boardinghouses.

Teenage Jessie immediately fell under the spell of the urbane, entertaining George McDermott, a neighbor of the Kiernans. George, in turn, "found delight in taking the young beauty to parade before his cronies and putting despair into the hearts of his aging mistresses."

George and Jessie married and moved into new digs at 155 East 46th Street. At first the couple spent many romantic afternoons at home or in the country. Within a year, however, George became less and less reliable as a husband. He missed lunch and he missed supper, spending hours at the nearby Brunswick bar and stumbling home drunk in the wee hours. The couple were soon in serious debt. George began staying in bed instead of going to the office. His temper shortened. Violent arguments turned into beatings. Jessie put on a good front, but her friends soon recognized the cause of the bruises and welts that covered her arms and neck.

George had become a raging, drunken monster.

Jessie barred him from her bedroom. George, consumed with jealousy that had tipped into paranoia, had his thuggish former "deputies" tail his wife whenever she left the house on errands.

It was in this household that, for whatever reason, John Ward found himself a boarder. One morning in October 1887, a week or so before Ward and Helen's public marriage in Philadelphia—but actually about a month after their real marriage in New Haven—McDermott arrived home unannounced. According to a Philadelphia paper, "as a result of his unexpected coming he and Mr. Ward [entered into] a severe tussle, which lasted until both men, and particularly Ward, were pretty well 'done up.' " McDermott told Ward if he ever spoke to Jessie again he would "repeat the dose" of medicine he had already administered. Ward moved out.

McDermott went on a booze-and-brood bender. On Saturday, October 8, he lurched to the Polo Grounds to seek out Ward, who was playing the last game of the regular season. He arrived late. Two days later, he took up the search again, traveling to Jersey City, where New York was to play an exhibition with the Cuban Giants. Once again the befuddled McDermott missed confronting his enemy. (These Giants were blacks. They dubbed themselves "Cuban" to avoid being identified as Negroes, thereby antagonizing white baseball patrons, and to avoid any possible race-mixing controversies. The players took the charade so far as to speak cod-Spanish on the field.)

Ward's friends, who had evidently thwarted McDermott, were convinced that Ward's life was in danger. A *New York Times* reporter, learning of the situation, tracked the aggrieved husband down. McDermott denied wanting to kill Ward: "I have no such purpose. If I had I should have achieved it before this. My grievance will keep, but there is no danger of bloodshed."

The reporter noted, however, that McDermott's

words were calmer than his manner as he told this story. His eyes flashed, his lips quivered, and he seemed to be laboring under suppressed excitement. He refused, however, to specify the wrong he claimed that Ward had done him. When asked if it related to his family in any way he replied that it did not.

Three years later, in 1890, by lurid coincidence, on the same day that news broke about Ward and Helen's articles of separation, Jessie McDermott applied for a restraining order against George. The *Herald* played the McDermott affair prominently.

SEEKING TO ENJOIN A HUSBAND FROM SPYING
*Pretty Mrs. McDermott's Novel Application
to the Court to Avoid Being Bothered*

SHE OBJECTS TO EAVESDROPPING
*John M. Ward, One of the Objects of McDermott's
Jealousy, Chastised Him in the Street*

The article consumed most of a column. Immediately below the piece was a shorter item, announced in smaller headlines:

WARD AND HIS WIFE SEPARATE
The Ball Player and the Actress Sign
Articles of Separation

If the timing of the two events was coincidental, the typographical linking was not: Ward and Jessie's affair, in full bloom in 1887, had never, apparently, ended. Jessie's application summarized her life with McDermott, concentrating on the period after he left city government and entered private practice. He spent his days at the race track, losing so much money he began pilfering her bank accounts, pawning her jewelry, and missing rent payments. He began following her and having her followed, and eavesdropping on her conversations. Physical violence was, while not a regular occurrence, not a rare one either. Jessie said that once, when she and her sister had been invited to the theater by a friend, the enraged George had kicked her.

Then, on March 27, 1890, the drunken George, who had been following Jessie, confronted her as she left a Madison Square restaurant with Ward. The bloated, bleary McDermott began to "upbraid" his wife and tried to punch Ward, who retaliated with a "sharp blow," knocking George flat on the sidewalk. Jessie hailed a cab and escaped. Half an hour later, according to newspaper accounts, George came home, pointing to his swollen, blackening eye and shouting, "I got that for your sake." He then cursed "vilely" and struck her in the face.

Jessie gathered her possessions and left her husband. According to the *Herald* she moved first to 5 East 41st Street and then to more stately digs, at the corner of Madison Avenue and 39th. Diana Forbes-Robertson, in a biography of Jessie, *My Aunt Maxine*, elaborates and says that the humiliated and angry Jessie traveled with Ward to her childhood home, Rockland, Maine. There, defying convention, the two stayed together for several days in a boardinghouse—an arrangement, according to Forbes-Robertson, the town still spoke of sixty years later.

George was persistent, however. A few weeks after Jessie and Ward returned from Maine, George took to standing vigil in the shadows across from her 39th Street apartment, bothering any man who entered or exited the building and bribing the servants to let him eavesdrop in her parlor and hand over all her mail. He also followed Jessie. Finally, she went to a precinct station to see if she could have him arrested. He followed her and she changed her mind. As she left the building, he accosted her and called her "the vilest and filthiest names that a low and depraved nature could conceive or invent." He tried forcing his way into the apartment of one of Jessie's friends, and when rebuffed, screamed from outside the door that he would kill her and anyone who tried to interfere. When a policeman, alerted by a friend of Jessie's, accosted him on the street near Jessie's apartment, George identified himself as a private detective hired by George McDermott—"mayor's marshall and superintendent of the Bureau of Encumbrances." George evidently neglected to use the past tense, and the policeman let him be.

The next night, however, George was served with papers. From all accounts the harassment and stalking ceased. A month after the restraining order was issued, a Philadelphia paper reopened the story, adding many details. McDermott and Helen, furious at the public airing of their private affairs, abandoned all the discretion they had exercised to date.

McDermott went into detail to the newspapers about Jessie's infidelity and Ward's cuckoldry, saying that after his first discovery of them—*in flagrante delicto*, he all but shouts—he forgave her all.

> It was no use, however, for as soon as my back was turned she would continue on her own course . . . and I was obliged to leave her. It was in my house, when I was assisting [Ward] to fit himself for the Bar and doing all in my power to advance him in the world, that Ward proved to be a traitor to me and acted more villainously than any chance acquaintance would have done. I have nothing but the highest praise for Helen Dauvray, and am extremely sorry that she was so unfortunate as to marry John M. Ward.

Ward denied everything. Helen turned on Ward with a fury.

> She admitted that when she gave up everything to marry Ward she expected to find domestic happiness, and in the trouble which had come she had suffered the keenest disappointment of her life. For Jessie C. McDermott she felt nothing but contempt.

George McDermott disappeared from public notice. Given his penchant for belligerence and suicidal drinking bouts, it is difficult to imagine he lived to see much of the new century.

About the time of her separation from George, Jessie, on a friend's suggestion, had begun acting lessons with a renowned instructor, Dion Boucicault. Though Jessie originally had no grand theatrical or artistic aspirations—she saw the theater primarily as a method of financial self-support—Boucicault recognized her talent, or at least her potential appeal. He persuaded her to change her name. Asked the grandest name she knew, she said "Maximilius," the name of a friend's father. It was a man's name, though, so Boucicault suggested "Maxine," which, he pointed out, had the added attraction, without the *x*, of spelling her home state. She chose Elliott as her last name, the inspiration being some distant ancestors. She made her professional debut six months after her separation from McDermott with a small role in *The Middleman*. (Her first line was: "What a charming collection of people a political candidate gathers round him in the course of his career, Mr. Chandler.") Those critics who did mention her remarked solely on her beauty.

By 1896, having established a comfortable career in New York, she decided to move to California, with its more liberal divorce laws, to free herself legally from McDermott. By the time her divorce had become final, later that year, Jessie had already been involved in another scandal. She had been carrying on a torrid love affair with another married man—the famous stage comedian, Nat Goodwin, whom she later married and divorced.

Her star ascended quickly: *An American Citizen*, *The Rivals*, *Nathan Hale*, *The Cowboy and The Lady*, *The Merchant of Venice* (as Portia), and *Her Own Way*. Her last notable stage success came in 1903, when she was thirty-five, in *Her Great Match*. In 1908, extremely wealthy, she opened Maxine Elliott's Theatre. Though the theater itself was successful, her own plays were not, and she retired in 1911. (She would un-retire several times, for brief periods, both for the occasional play and, in 1917, for two movies for Goldwyn Pictures, *Fighting Odds* and *The Eternal Daughter*.)

She spent most of the last half of her life in England and France. Edward VII became infatuated with her and desperately wanted to have an affair. Elliott thought the whole notion scandalous, and refused. Later, at her villa in Cannes, she entertained friends and acquaintances, including Gene Tunney, Noel Coward, Douglas Fairbanks, Johnny Weismuller, and Tony Wilding. Winston Churchill often visited her, and used the villa's rocky shoreline as inspiration for some of his watercolors. She died in 1940.

After 1890 John Ward was no longer a part of her life. If the two had assignations, it is unknown.

Helen opened her 1890 season on September 29—just as her husband was ending his—at New York's Standard Theatre. Her vehicle was a complexly plotted light comedy, *The Whirlwind,* in which she played "a young woman of large fortune who is as sharp-witted and generous as she is rich."

The critics, as usual, *wanted* to like Helen, and were gentle. After her long absence her appearance was greeted with "cordial esteem." She was, as the play unfolded, "encouraged by keen and sympathetic attention" from the audience. She did, however, lack "that indefinable quality the critics call magnetism. . . . the technique of her acting is too evident. Her laughter has not the true ring of merriment and her emotion is too histrionic to deeply stir the sympathies." The same *Dramatic Mirror* critic then damned her with extremely faint praise: "Considering her limitations, Miss Dauvray made a very creditable effort." The *Clipper* agreed, though more bluntly: "In the technicalities of her art she is still amazingly crude." *The Whirlwind* closed in a month. Helen took the play to Boston, where it closed after a week.

In 1892, Helen appeared in London in a revival of *A Scrap of Paper* to favorable reviews. The critics, again, were gentle; they admired her intelligence and the self-awareness of her range: "While she cannot be greeted as a theatrical revelation, she is, at any rate, an actress who knows her business, and she can play a safe part with a point of discretion."

Fifteen months later, Helen played to little notice—she was "theatrically demure" (the *Dramatic Mirror*)—in a revival of *The Prodigal Daughter.* The "elaborate and pretentious" play took second billing at the new theater in which it opened, the American. Audiences, however, liked it, and it ran for nearly seven months, closing two days before Christmas 1893.

Halfway through the play's run, in early October, just before Ward left on an extended hunting trip to Canada, Helen sued for divorce, declining to elaborate for reporters. She hoped that the business would be over quickly and quietly, that Ward would agree to a dissolution by default. He decided, however, to oppose the suit.

Why Ward opposed the action is truly a mystery, especially in hindsight. Possibly he felt that Helen's settlement terms—whatever they were—were unacceptably harsh and that, by refusing to agree to them he could induce her to moderate them so as to avoid an extended hearing with its attendant publicity.

He gambled wrong. The divorce case moved from the initially tacky to the ultimately sordid—but there was little publicity, only a brief notice in most papers. The hearing, before a court-appointed referee, began on November 15, 1893, and ended the next day.

Under New York law, adultery was the sole grounds for divorce. The plaintiff, Helen, had to prove that the defendant, Ward, had been unfaithful without her consent, connivance, privity, or procurement and that the alleged act had taken place within the last five years.

This would not prove difficult.

Her attorneys relied entirely on two witnesses, Sherwood Gilbert and William Odosha, who roomed together at 19 Greenwich Avenue in Greenwich Village. Gilbert ran a lunch counter on Duane Street, just west of City Hall, and Odosha worked as a timekeeper on Greene Street, in present-day Soho. They also moonlighted as the dreariest sort of private detectives.

October 10 had been a lovely fall day in New York—the high temperature a refreshing 69 degrees and the skies clear, thanks to light, fresh breezes.

Ward, who after two seasons with the Brooklyn League team had returned to play for the Giants, was in Brooklyn's Eastern Park to play the second game of a post-season "Metropolitan Championship." New York lost, 5–4, before 1,500 people, and Ward went hitless. The game was over around five o'clock.

Gilbert and Odosha, who had been staking out Ward for several days, testified that at about 7:30 on that evening, Ward strolled into Nick Engel's saloon, where he was greeted warmly by name. After a half-hour or so, Ward left and walked to the St. James Hotel, near Madison Square. A few minutes later he walked one block north and a couple of blocks east and met a woman on the corner of 27th and Fifth Avenue. She was a stout brunette, about thirty years old, dressed in black. She wore a "turban" hat. Ward, coatless, wore a suit, a high-collared linen shirt, a derby, and black patent leather shoes. He carried a cane.

Ward and the woman in black walked a block north and two blocks east, where they caught the downtown Third Avenue El. They got off at the corner of Fulton and Pearl, the site of the United States Hotel. The hotel, opened in 1832 as Holt's, was a popular, boisterous, 165-room, middle-range hostelry. This bustling, generally unremarkable place was notable for two things: a rooftop dining-and-dancing pavilion and its huge dining room, which, open twenty-four hours a day and capable of seating 1,000, served some 2,500 meals daily. It claimed to "kill an ox" every day, and at any given time to have 700 pounds of meat turning on its kitchen spits.

The couple had a drink in the "ladies' parlour." Ward then went to the desk and registered as "J. M. Watson & wife, New Haven, Conn.," and paid the clerk—the single-room tariff at the United States ran from $.75 to $1.50. Ward's signature was thick-inked and awkward, absent its usual confident flourishes. He was either drunk, agitated, fearful of discovery, or, in some ham-handed way, hoping to cover his tracks by disguising his handwriting.

The couple were assigned Room 14. Gilbert and Odosha quickly rented Room 17, across and just down the hall. A hall boy brought two or three rounds of drinks to Ward's room over the next hour or so.

After deciding that the hall boy's duties had ended, Gilbert and Odosha crept to the door of Room 14. Gilbert, making a cradle of his hands, lifted Odosha to the open transom. The room's bed, however, was located to one side, in an alcove. Odosha could see nothing of interest. The men decided a chair more suited their purposes, and over the next two hours, peeped into Room 14 a half dozen times with no better luck.

Finally, their vigilance was rewarded. They saw Ward and the woman at the far end of the room, Ward in his underwear, shirtless, the woman, without corset, in a short petticoat and thin undershirt. The two spent some time contemplating a picture on the wall, Ward's arm around her waist. The couple dressed and left the hotel about 10:45.

Gilbert and Odosha were diligent detectives. Once the coast was clear, they entered Room 14 and noted some slight disorder—the bed turned, the pitcher removed from its bowl, the bowl filled with water, and used towels scattered about. They were sure of three things: the man they had seen in Room 14 was John Montgomery Ward, whom they had earlier seen playing ball with the New York Giants. The woman in Room 14 was the same woman Ward had met on the corner of 27th and Fifth Avenue, and that woman was not Helen Dauvray, who was seated not far from the witness stand. They did not know who the woman was.

The cross-examination by Ward's attorney challenged the witnesses' credibility in perfunctory and ineffectual ways—How could Gilbert and Odosha be sure about the sort of collar Mr. Ward wore?—that sort of thing. Gilbert and Odosha were unshakable.

Helen was granted her divorce. Ward was assessed $117.40 in court costs. It was further adjudged and decreed that Helen could marry again at any time and could immediately assume her maiden name. Ward, however, per custom in the divorce-unfriendly state of New York, was forbidden to remarry during Helen's life.

Helen continued to act, both in the New York metropolitan area and on the road. In January 1894 Helen and Maxine Elliott were, for five nights, on stage together, in a benefit revival of *The Prodigal Daughter* at Brooklyn's Amphion Academy. Their dual appearance was not noted by the press. Helen's career as a box office attraction was effectively over. Of that performance, one encyclopedic stage history recalls only that Helen was "a stranger to youngsters in the audience, [but] pleasantly remembered by older spectators . . . [though] alas! playing a low comedy part."

Over the next few years, almost the only time her name appeared in print was in connection with various lawsuits. Helen had always been litigious—when she married Ward she was suing the Pennsylvania Railroad for $3,600 in costumes and "theatrical paraphernalia" that had been burned in a railroad car fire between Cincinnati and New York. In 1893 she was in a running battle over a $500 dressmaker's bill. In that matter she had been cited for contempt of court—though the charge was the result of a misunderstanding and quickly dropped. In September of that year, a month before her filing for divorce, she was again in court about the bill. The judgment had gone against her, but Helen had not as yet paid. The question before the court was whether Helen was merely being petulant or was she, in fact, without means to pay.

Over the course of three years, beginning in 1899, a "Miss Helen D. Ward" was involved in a contentious lawsuit against New York's St. Vincent's Hospital. Miss Ward claimed that several years earlier, she had been "maimed for life" by an untrained nurse who, while Miss Ward was lying "insensible," scalded her with a hot water bag "uncased by flannel," leaving her "permanently crippled." Finally, after three trials ending in hung juries, a fourth panel found in her favor and awarded her $18,000. Oddly, "Miss Helen D. Ward" was described as the sister-in-law of Henry Howland—John Ward's lawyer in his 1890 case against the New York Giants.

In 1896, en route to Australia with her company, Helen met U.S. Navy Rear Admiral Albert Gustavus Winterhalter, who at forty was either one or five years older than Helen. They married within the year. Winterhalter had graduated "with distinction" from Annapolis in 1877. After commanding four different ships, he was assigned in 1884 to special duty with the Naval Observatory in America and Europe. He then commanded the battleship *Louisiana* from 1909 to 1911 and, after a short period on the navy's General Board, worked directly under the secretary of the Navy. In 1915 he was named commander-in-chief of the Asiatic Fleet. By 1917 he had returned to Washington and the General Board. When he died unexpectedly of lobar pneumonia three years later, he was eulogized as an officer of "wide and varied experience and exceptionally high professional attainments." His widow, the *New York Times* obituary noted, was "Mrs. Helene Winterhalter."

Helen returned briefly to the stage upon Winterhalter's death. She took ill in 1922 while working in a production of *The Bat* in Philadelphia, and died, of unknown causes, on December 7, 1923. She was buried at Arlington National Cemetery in a military ceremony. Her pallbearers included five rear admirals and one civilian. Her obituary named her Mrs. Helen Gibson Winterhalter. "A generation ago," the notice went on, "she was known throughout the United States as Helen Dauvray, the star of Bronson Howard's play [*One of*] *Our Girls* [which was] the chief source of her fortune." There was no mention of John Ward.

Twenty-Six

His First Ranch of Rest

WARD PLAYED FOR four years beyond the collapse of the Players' League—two years at Brooklyn and two years back with the Giants. He played shortstop in 1891 and second base until he retired after the 1894 season. He managed all four years.

In 1891 his Brooklyns finished sixth in the eight-team National League, twenty-five and a half games out of first. Ward batted .277, twenty-three percentage points above the League average. He stole fifty-seven bases, tying for fifth-best, and was the League's second-best-fielding shortstop.

In 1892 the League experimented with a "split season." Brooklyn did slightly better the first half than they did the second. Ward batted .265, twenty points above the League average. He led the League in stolen bases with eighty-eight. His fielding average was only eighth-best among regular second basemen.

In 1893, his New Yorks finished fifth out of twelve teams, nineteen and a half games out of first. Ward batted .328, forty-eight points above the League average. He stole forty-six bases. Only one regular second baseman fielded worse than he did.

In 1894, New York finished in second place, only three games behind Baltimore. Ward batted .265—fifty-four points under the League average. He stole 39 bases—Billy Hamilton led the League with 98 thefts, a number that would not be surpassed until 1962. Only one second baseman fielded more poorly than Ward.

Ward steered absolutely clear of baseball's ongoing political battles. The most significant of these was between the National League and the faltering American Association. To make a short story terse, by the end of the 1891 season, the Association—financially crippled by the 1890 war and weakened by defections of many of its stars to the Players' League and then the National League—had two teams fewer than it started the year with. Milwaukee played only 36 games of the 130-plus-game season, and Cincinnati only 100. After another "peace conference," the four strongest Association franchises—Baltimore, Louisville, St. Louis, and Washington—were incorporated into the National League; the others were dissolved.

The League, twelve teams strong, was now without competition. That is why, in the main, the League came up with its idea of a split season in 1892—to stimulate interest in what otherwise was a competitive dead end: one league, one champion, one yawn. Though the split-season concept was abandoned, other attempts to solve the dramaless one-league problem were made. In 1894, for example, Ward's New Yorks, the second-place team, played Baltimore, the first-place team, in a postseason series.

Ward had almost nothing to say, at least publicly, about the 1891 fracas, known as the Second Association War. Nor did he rise to the bait of the 1891 *Base Ball Guide*. Spalding's publication was spiteful, insistent, and inflammatory, graceless in victory. On the second page of the book's preface it reminded readers that the "revolt of 1890 . . . got away with hundreds of thousands of dollars of the capitalists' money—not that of the players, be it remembered." The success of the National League in 1888 and 1889, it went on, "aroused a feeling of self aggrandizement among the 'star' players . . . and out of this condition . . . the players' organization known as the 'Brotherhood' . . . was brought into play." It called the revolt of 1890 a "conspiracy," the manifesto a "revolutionary pronunciamento," and the 1890 season a "financial disaster" that caused "general demoralization." The rebel players were motivated solely by "selfish greed" and their business plan was a "fallacy."

Later, in a section entitled "A Suggestion To Professionals," the *Guide* asserted that among the prominent weaknesses of professional ball players in the matter of trying to better their pecuniary position each season is their great tendency to do as the greedy dog did in the fable, viz. "grasp at the shadow while losing the substance."

The "Suggestion" went on:

The sensible player will prefer the home position with a sure salary, even if it is not very large, to a mere stopping place for a temporary period at fancy figures.

A few pages later, in a compilation of "Editorial Comments," the *Guide* scoffed at anyone imagining that

the ball-players' strike was of a like character with that of the contest between underpaid operatives and grasping manufacturing monopolists. The absurdity of classifying professional ball players, earning from three to five thousand dollars for a season's services on the ball field three hours a day, either with the Southern slaves of old, or the overworked and underfed factory operatives of the present day, is one of the most glaring fallacies of the year.

Finally, in a low blow aimed directly at Ward, the *Guide* quoted a "noteworthy paragraph" that pointed out the "Benefit of the Reserve Rule."

"To the Reserve rule more than any other thing, does base ball as a business owe its present substantial standing. By preserving intact the strength of a team from year to year, it places the business of base ball on a permanent basis, and thus offers security to the investment of capital."

It then cited the source of the quote: John M. Ward.

Ward signed with Brooklyn to play and manage in 1891 for $7,000. He wintered in Europe and returned in April, ready to begin the new season. Interestingly, for a man who had made such a point of the dangers of authoritarianism—as it applied to the National League—and such a strong case for the advantages of cooperativism, Ward the manager was something of a tyrant. He believed that a team was a company with many departments. If a player—the head of his department—made a mistake, he and only he was to blame. That went for Ward as well, the head of all the departments. This was the same attitude that had caused friction through Ward's earlier captaincies—which were, effectively, managing positions. The term for a team's field boss had changed, not the duties or power. Not only did some players resent Ward's stern autocracy, but Ward resented anyone who interfered with that autocracy. He had said, when he handed in his captaincy years earlier, that he would never lead a team again unless he was given "full and free direction of the players and absolute authority."

He desperately wanted to show up the New York team, which, from his vantage point, was full of traitors, and he felt his Brooklyn team was capable of "easy sailing pennantward."

Though Ward fancied himself a good judge of baseball flesh—and he was not entirely wrong in that self-assessment—he occasionally made some whopping mistakes. In 1915, for example, he would go on record saying that Benny Kauff, a young flashy-fielding outfielder who had hit .370 the year before, was all but the equal of Tris Speaker and Ty Cobb. He wasn't. Ward would also trade future Hall-of-Famer Willie Keeler from New York, in 1893. The following year, Keeler hit .371. In the next five years he would hit .377, .386, .424, .385, and .379. He would play for nineteen years with a lifetime average of .341.

His first misjudgment of 1891 was to rely on the services of George Hemming, a young right-hander from Carrollton, Ohio, who had pitched decently for him in 1890. In 1891 he went 8–15. By the time he retired, after the 1897 season, Hemming's record was only 91–82. Another misjudgment that year was his signing of Hemming's battery mate, Tom Kinslow, who also played for the 1890 Players' League Brooklyns. Kinslow hit only .237 in 1891; by the time he retired, after the 1898 season, he had appeared in only 380 games, batting a polite .266. Kinslow's most spectacular performance in 1891 came before the season, when he got knee-walking drunk at a concert hall, fought people with a cane, and threw billiard balls across the room before leaving a step ahead of the cops.

Everything, it seemed, was snake-bit for the Brooklyns that year. Ward injured his thumb in Philadelphia in the second game of the season. In the ninth inning of the same game, with Brooklyn behind 3–1, left fielder Darby O'Brien lined out to third. The Philadelphia infielder stepped on the bag to double up the runner who had left for home, then threw to second to catch the runner there: triple play.

But the low point came between games of a Fourth of July double-header in Chicago. Catcher Tom Daly was catching forty winks on the outfield grass. Right fielder Oyster Burns, playing a practical joke of some sort, pricked him in the leg with a penknife. Daly started, rolled over, and severed a tendon.

Whatever the reason, Brooklyn stunk in 1891.

Ward spent January 1892 in Florida. Ostensibly, he was hunting and fishing, but in between times, he came up with a gloriously farsighted idea, one that has lasted to this day. While it is a matter of speculation as to which team first went south for the pre-season—another of baseball's many angels-on-the-head-of-a-pin debates—honors go to Ward for beginning the custom of having Southern towns *pay* to have Northern teams train within their boundaries. In the spring of 1891, Brooklyn had paid Ocala, Florida, about $350 for use of their baseball grounds. In 1892, Ward announced that not only would Ocala give Brooklyn free use of their field, but the city fathers would furnish the team with various free railroad tickets around Florida. The plan was for the major leaguers to play games against Florida State League teams. This modest inducement was, effectively, the beginning of a century-long bidding war among communities in Florida and later Arizona to host major league teams during spring training.

With these savings, Ward could adopt another innovation: he would bring south not only his expected starters, but any players who had not been absolutely released. His plan was to stage open competition, ensuring dedicated training as well as the opportunity to be pleasantly surprised (or disappointed) with various performances. He wanted to give players a "full, fair and final chance. . . . Any that have been found wanting will have no ground for complaint, and neither will those who shout for them, all criticism being disarmed." As extra insurance, Brooklyn made a quick and successful grab of Association players after that organization folded, securing heavy-hitting Dan Brouthers and slick-fielding, sign-stealing shortstop Tommy Corcoran—Ward moved to second base and never played shortstop again.

Toward the end of February 1892, just days before Brooklyn headed south, fire broke out in Ward's Brooklyn home. The *Clipper* reported he lost many effects, including a scrapbook. From the distance of nearly a century, this fire was disastrous. Ward had kept faithful journals and had dabbled in photography, bringing his camera south during the spring of 1890.

The 1892 voyage from Brooklyn to Jacksonville, aboard the *Algonquin*, was eventful. On the first night out, a storm split the topmast, nearly crushing several ballplayers busy watching a school of porpoises. A couple of nights later, M. J. Forrest, a passenger, "went insane."

> At midnight he became raving mad and in dishabille, with unkempt hair and eyes starting from their sockets, rushed into the passageway, trying the doors as he went. One door was unlocked, and the combined strength of two men was required to keep the maniac, for such he proved to be, from entering the room. The man held some sort of a heavy weapon [and] was possessed of the idea that the Brooklyn base ball players . . . were in league with the ship's men and conspiring to do him harm. . . . Burns and Terry of the Brooklyn team came to his assistance. The ball tossers' appearance crazed the man and four men were required to hold him down until an officer arrived. The appearance of the latter pacified the insane man. . . . He was at one time looking for matches, and the ship was never nearer to being burned than at that moment.

Ward's post-Brotherhood remove from the nonfield issues of baseball was never so apparent as during the 1892 and 1893 seasons. As might be expected, with the demise of the American Association, there was little competition for player services. This, coupled with the losses the National League had suffered during the Brotherhood War, brought back belt-tightening policies, including, of course, precipitous salary cuts.

The fourteen-man reserve limit was ignored: effectively every major league player fell under the shadow of the reserve rule. At the same time, the clubs reduced their rosters by two men, from fifteen to thirteen. Owners still kept large numbers of men on reserve—Cincinnati was reported to have thirty-three on its list—but "farmed them out" to minor league teams, where they could keep their skills sharp at a greatly reduced salary.

The most efficient cost-cutting measure, as usual, was salary reduction. Louisville, for example, reduced its payroll by half. Other teams followed suit, though to lesser extents. Players who had signed multiyear contracts found themselves fired (and sometimes rehired). Probably the best example of this was Tom Burns of Pittsburgh. He had signed a three-year contract at $4,500 a year. He was fired after two months of the first year and had to go to court for his back pay. In 1891, the average major league salary was about $3,500. By 1893 it had fallen to roughly $1,800.

There had been seventeen major league teams in 1891. In 1892 there were twelve. There had been two leagues. Now there was one. There had been hungry up-and-coming players in the minors; now there were former major leaguers, also quite hungry, joining their ranks.

Ward lectured his players before they signed their 1892 contracts. What a temptation for him to say, "I told you so." As a *Sporting Life* reporter wrote,

> [The prospective players] will be shown a mathematical picture, and conducted through the inner aisles of subtraction. They will be regaled . . . and when they have heard Mr. Ward through on the subject, they will . . . feel the force of his remarks, although possibly not endorse them in an alarmingly emphatic manner.

But beyond these Dutch-uncle reality lessons, Ward kept his counsel, letting the proof of magnate-dictated economic reality float on the meager pudding the players were served.

Only once did Ward vent his feelings publicly, and even then he did so wittily. In 1892, young third baseman Bill Joyce wrote Ward, asking him for a small advance so that he could "take the boil" at Hot Springs, Arkansas.

"Friend Bill," Ward wrote in reply,

> Your letter and telegram asking me to send you $200 advance were received on my return from the South. I have been wondering ever since whether you really meant it. Either you are joking,

William, or you are away behind the times. Haven't you heard yet of the consolidation of the League and Association . . . ? And if so, don't you understand that the days of advance money are past?

Why, my innocent William, hereafter it is the players who are paying advances to the magnates. . . . Your inning is over, my boy.

Wake up and thank your stars you got under cover this year before the consolidation was effected. I'm going to take the team South about March 1, and shall expect you here at that time. If you haven't the price perhaps you had better start at once. There's many a tie between St. Louis and Brooklyn. Get a move on you, William.

Brooklyn's unexpected success in the 1892 season—second place in the first half of the split affair and third place in the second half—was generally credited to Ward, his management deemed "clever."

Between the 1892 and 1893 seasons the mound was moved back five feet with hopes of firing up offense. It worked: the average number of runs per game in 1892 was a bit over ten, in 1893 a bit over thirteen, and in 1894 just under fifteen. Owners wanted the offense goosed up because, in their opinion, fans preferred higher-scoring games. And fans were in short supply in 1892. Teams were losing money hand over fist. The uninspiring 1892 Giants were reported to have lost over $32,000. By the end of the season the club, three months behind in player salaries, cut a deal with them: a quarter on the dollar and IOUs.

On June 13, 1892, the League allowed teams to limit their rosters. Salaries, which had been widely cut in December, were cut again, by up to several hundred dollars per man. In addition, the 1893 season was shortened by eighteen games a team, to 132.

Perhaps the lack of attendance was due to the low-scoring games. Perhaps it was widespread dissatisfaction with the split-season format and the ensuing lack of a true post-season championship between two leagues. Perhaps it was due to some abstract, general, delayed disenchantment with baseball in particular—for two years labor, not the game itself, had dominated the news. Certainly fans in New York had no special reason to come to the ballpark in 1892. Old favorite Roger Connor had gone to Philadelphia; Mickey Welch had been sent to the minors. The new players were, generally, uninspiring. The team finished tenth in the first half of the season and sixth in the second half. It had become unfashionable to go to the Polo Grounds. The high rollers from Wall Street and the theatrical crowd found it possible to miss games.

Adding to the owners' woes were their war debts, incurred in the wholesale buyouts of both the Players' League and the American Association. The teams had assessed themselves 10 percent to begin their payment. This soon rose to 12, and finally 16 percent.

Ward did not involve himself in these matters. He went hunting in Canada after the 1892 season, then to the South during the coldest months, and finally back to Bellefonte to hunt and work his dogs, whom he boarded with relatives during the season.

On February 10, 1893—to great newspaper fanfare—Ward announced his return to New York to manage the Giants. The *Times*, for one, hailed "the active little short stop"—though he had been an active little second baseman for the previous season—for his "daring slides, timely hits, speedy base running and scientific bunts."

Ward's 1893 baseball whereabouts had been the subject of much off-season speculation, and Ward himself had said, soon after the 1892 season's end, that if 1893 found him anywhere but New York, it would find him out of uniform for good.

The *Times* reported that Brooklyn let Ward go only when they realized that he was not bluffing: he would not stay in Brooklyn, or go anywhere but New York, as an active player. After the signing, however, Charles H. Byrne, the Brooklyn club president, told a different story: Ward's relocation was fine with him, and "in some ways the best" thing that could happen to the Brooklyn franchise. The reason for this was player resentment at his autocratic ways. He was popular with the public, Byrne said, but "not with the team. There was no companionship between him and any of the players."

Ward scoffed at this. He even dared Byrne to allow him to negotiate with those players with whom he was evidently so unpopular, confident he could "sign a number of them for New York at less than they will receive in Brooklyn."

He denied disliking Brooklyn, only saying that he had "more friends" in New York than in Brooklyn and that he played "better ball at the Polo

Grounds than anywhere else." Those were very good reasons, certainly. Reading between the lines, however, Ward might have been anxious all along to return to New York, both for the immediate pleasures of the theater and night life and with an eye to the future and his law career. Perhaps he had stayed in Brooklyn for a couple of seasons only to allow the wounds to heal between him and his former owners and the Manhattan cranks. Lastly, despite his challenge to Byrne, Ward acknowledged that there might be some bad blood in Brooklyn. His presence there had displaced three popular men, manager Bill McGunnigle, captain Darby O'Brien, and shortstop George Smith. He also denied his rumored 1893 salary, saying that while he would not divulge actual terms, it was nowhere near the $5,000 widely reported in the press. Not only was it less than he had received at Brooklyn, it would be considerably less—a "very moderate sum" in fact. Then, in a statement that does more than anything to prove the woeful finances of the League, he said, "I recognize the fact that all players must accept a reduction in salaries [so] that the game may again be put on its feet."

He looked forward to spring training and confirmed his reputation as a disciplinarian by warning players not to appear in camp carrying "fifteen to twenty pounds of superfluous flesh." For the moment, he was quiet about the presence of Buck Ewing on the New York roster.

Two weeks after Ward signed with New York, however, he traded Ewing to Cleveland for young infielder George Davis. When asked about the trade—which in pure baseball terms was a good one—he rose to the management occasion by characterizing the transaction as purely business. It is doubtful anyone believed Ward.

> I don't care to discuss the subject of the transfer, but will
> from a New York standpoint. . . . we have got the best of the
> bargain. . . . Davis would be a better man than Ewing. The latter
> is a great ball player when his arm is all right, but I don't think
> it is.

Maybe his arrival in New York happened to coincide with a general rekindling of enthusiasm for the sport. Maybe his exciting brand of play and the memories of earlier days of glory caused the rekindling. Or maybe, as some have stated, baseball is an example of an economic "countercycli-cal" industry—the country in 1893 suffered a brief but severe depression. Whatever the reason, baseball fever returned to New York with Ward.

DeWolf Hopper returned to the stands, as did Digby Bell and Nick Engel and the anonymous swells of Wall Street. Fifteen thousand, in fact, attended the 1893 opening day. Another 5,000 came on May 6 to watch the Giants—who started the season poorly—play the hapless Senators. On Memorial Day, 6,000 came for the morning game and an amazing 23,000 attended the matinee. In early June, DeWolf Hopper treated the Giants, as well as the Brooklyn, Pittsburgh, and St. Louis teams, to an evening of his current show, *Panjandrum*.

The New York management paid off its IOUs from the previous sea-son—$12,000—in June.

By late August the Giants were in fifth place, fourteen games out of first—more or less where they would end the season. But even the perfec-tionist Ward was pleased.

> I shall not tinker with [the team]. This has been our first year together . . . and it has taken the men some time to get accus-tomed to one another. [The teams ahead of us] are practically veterans, which have gotten team work down to perfection. The New Yorks are just beginning to strike their proper gait.

Ward had New York eating out of the palm of his hand. One day when the crowd was sparse because of torrential rains, Ward announced that there would be a game even if the men had to wear divers' suits. While the grounds crew set up a makeshift diamond in the outfield, the club organized watery running races for "the urchins" in the crowd, with a special prize going to the boy who could stand on his head underwater the longest. "Extra Bill," a well-known newsboy, claimed the prize.

Ward spent the fall with his dogs in Bellefonte, part of the winter in New York, and part of it in the South, hunting in Charlotte, North Car-olina, and playing the odd exhibition game for charity. After one such game, some of his Charlotte friends presented him with a "handsome gold-headed cane."

Ward gave occasional interviews. There was a movement to allow runners to overrun second and third base as well as first. Ward the base stealer thought the idea abominable: "The slide is one of the pretty features of baseball. . . . Do away with sliding and baseball wouldn't be in it with croquet."

Ward could smell success. He was, in general, excited about playing baseball in 1894, even to the point of casting off some of his ideological outerwear. He said the prospects of the new season—for the Giants and baseball in general—were good, because fan interest was reviving, an interest that was "partially killed by the Brotherhood movement."

He took the Giants to Florida for a week of limbering up, followed by a series of exhibition games with the Universities of Virginia and North Carolina. He conducted training with a "vim that will allow of no lagging." Ward, the *Clipper* went on, "doesn't sit by the fire and tell his men what to do, but instead sets the pace and expects them to follow."

He told New York fans not to "dispose of the pennant until the end of the season, as my team may wish to be heard on the subject as to where it is to go."

When two of his key players, pitcher Amos Rusie and catcher Duke Farrell, balked at signing contracts, Ward lashed out. He complained that Rusie had shown up for spring training the year before in such poor condition that he wasn't effective until nearly two months into the season. Ward offered him an 1894 contract for the same salary as 1893, but received in return a letter that, according to Ward, named a "perfectly absurd" sum. Ward dug his heels in even further when the New York club treasurer, E. B. Talcott, promised Rusie a bonus if he showed up for 1894 in good physical shape. "I suppose Mr. Talcott will make him a present, but that has nothing to do with me."

Ward said Farrell had left Pittsburgh, a contender, for lowly Washington, and demanded a raise for the sacrifice. Now that New York wanted him, Ward said, dripping with sarcasm, Farrell offers the same argument—but in reverse.

"We offered him the same money Washington paid him and I'll tell you frankly that if his Washington contract hadn't called for it I shouldn't have given it to him because I do not think he is worth it." Then, most startlingly, Ward objected to Farrell's asking for some of the sale money. "That is a matter between him and [Washington]. I don't see what I've got to do with it."

Farrell eventually signed, for less, he maintained, than he had been paid at Washington, and without receiving any percentage of the sale money. He wanted to play with a winner, and he knew, from the tone of the three letters Ward had sent him, that New York's terms were final. Farrell was ready to give his all for New York, but reminded the public—and John Ward—that by holding out he was asking "only what any businessman would ask."

Ward would make one other uncharacteristic move in 1894. He got rid of old Brotherhood member and friend Roger Connor, who, after returning to the Giants from Philadelphia in 1893, had been relegated to a substitute's role. Connor played out the season with St. Louis, but not without taking a parting shot at Ward.

> Treasurer Talcott has always treated me white. . . . When Ward laid me off, Mr. Talcott told me not to worry. . . . I could remain with the New York club for the balance of the season drawing my salary if I didn't play another game. . . . I shall never forget his kindness to me.

Ward was widely criticized for his release of the popular Connor. The criticism, coupled with New York's sputtering start—at the end of May the team was in sixth place—made him testy. He accused those who criticized the Connor move of suffering from "an attack of the big head." He followed with a labored analysis of his preference for Jack Doyle on first instead of Connor. His reasoning boiled down to this: Doyle hustled more, even though Connor was hitting well.

> I don't care two cents what the criticisms may be, for they cut no figure with me. . . . I am the manager of the New York team, and I will still hold the place the first of next October. Mr. Talcott is the only man in this club who has anything to say in the matter.

As the summer wore on and the team began playing well, the criticism stopped. By the end of July, New York was in third place, within five games of Boston. They moved into second the first week of September. New York went 20–6 that month, but fell behind Baltimore, which scorched September by going 20–3 and winning the pennant by three games.

There had been a dismal post-season championship in 1892, and none in 1893. In 1894, a Pittsburgh businessman donated a three-foot-tall, heavily ornamented cup—known as the Temple Cup—to be presented to the winner of a post-season series between the first- and second-place teams. The teams would share the gate after expenses, with the winning team taking 65 percent, the loser 35 percent.

Immediately an unattractive squabble broke out. Ned Hanlon, the Baltimore manager, wanted the split to be all or nothing. Temple said no. Then Hanlon and Ward came up with the idea of a 50-50 split—a bad idea, since, should the series go its entire seven games, the players would be vulnerable to charges of hippodroming. Finally, the teams agreed, officially, to the original terms, but rumors of private 50-50 splits made between individuals on each team abounded.

In the first game, New York beat Baltimore, there, 4–1, before 12,000 people. Baltimore third baseman John McGraw—who would become New York's most famous manager (and hire John Ward as his personal lawyer)—ran into Ward at second during the seventh inning. A brawl nearly erupted. Later, Steve Brodie, the Baltimore center fielder, and Dirty Jack Doyle, the New York first baseman, actually fought each other.

In the second game, Mike Tiernan of New York hit a bases-loaded triple in the ninth to break a 6–6 tie. The Baltimore crowd had been mercilessly heckling New York left fielder Eddie Burke. He said a few things back to the crowd, which responded by surrounding him in the field. Police broke up the mob.

The series then moved to New York, where the home team won its third straight, 4–1.

The *Tribune* was breathless in its coverage. "Never before in the history of baseball was a more striking picture presented than that seen at the Polo Grounds yesterday afternoon." It went on to describe the grandstands as "weighted down with pretty women" and the aisles as filled with "men prominent in the financial, social and political world." In addition to those who found seats, there was a "solid human wall" about the field. A group of Wall Street brokers and bankers, the "Jolly Jooggers," rode to the field on bicycles. The Catholic Protectory Band gave a short concert before the game and broke into "Hail to the Chief" when Ward led his team onto the field. In the seventh inning, a horse ran onto the field. A section of the right field bleachers gave way: twenty-five people fell to the ground, but no one was hurt and the game resumed.

> [In the eighth inning] the band struck up "John Brown's Body" and the crowd joined in in a mighty chorus and the "Glory! Glory! Hallelujah!" rang out resonantly from thousands of throats. It was a merry crowd and it must have been a severe blow to doctors. A mortal could not help being healthy and happy after a visit to the Polo Grounds yesterday.

The two teams met again on Monday, October 8, for what would prove to be John Ward's final game as a professional baseball player. It was a blowout, with New York winning in eight innings—on account of darkness—16–3. The crowd was in excellent spirits throughout the contest, waving hats and canes and handkerchiefs and blowing horns and ringing dinner bells. In the seventh inning, with New York ahead 11–3, two horses escaped and led police and their owners on a wild chase around the outfield.

Ward came up five times in that last game. He got one hit and was not a factor in the victory.

That night, the teams went to a gala at the Broadway Theatre.

> The outside of the theatre was decorated with flags and Chinese lanterns, while over the door hung in illuminated letters the words "Baseball Night." Inside the theatre flags and bunting hid the walls, balconies, and pillars, while over the boxes to be occupied by the two teams hung the New York and Maryland State ensigns.
> The street . . . was thronged with men and women, and at about 8 o'clock Capt. Ward was seen to alight from a Broadway cable car followed by the rest of the team. Capt. Ward's appearance was the signal for an outburst of applause, horn blowing and flag waving. A squad of police cleared the way for the players. . . . As the players passed into their boxes on the left-hand side of the house the band played "See the Conquering Hero Comes."

Digby Bell recited his familiar poem about a knotholer—"A Tough Boy on the Right Field Fence." DeWolf Hopper and his company performed "Dr. Syntax." Hopper, after a brief time backstage, returned, but the crowd clamored for Ward. "There was such an uproarious demand for him that Hopper had to come to the captain's rescue." Hopper promised that Ward would speak at the formal presentation of the Temple Cup, upcoming. He then recited "Casey at the Bat" and the crowd cheered itself hoarse.

On the following Sunday, October 14, again at the Broadway Theatre, after the usual interminable recitations and toasts and vocal solos and quartets, Ward was presented with the Temple Cup by one Miss Della Fox. Shouts of "Say, Johnnie, are you with us next year?" rang out. Miss Fox herself, after handing over the heavy silver cup, shook her "white fist in 'Johnny's' face and said: 'And now I want you to promise me that you'll play ball for us again next year.' "

Ward's immediate reply was unintelligible, as he had his back to the audience. He then turned and spoke

> of the dark hours of last spring when the team was losing, and of
> the encouragement of New York people, who had faith in the
> men, even in the face of their defeat. Now, he said, the Giants
> were glad that they had justified that confidence. He pledged the
> team to do their best next season, not only to win the pennant,
> but to retain the cup for another year. In this pledge he used the
> plural pronoun "we," which the audience took in its literal sense.

Athletes, like actors, often retire badly. Think of Helen, dragging herself and her second-rate troupe around western New York in 1894. Think of bloated, creaky Babe Ruth flailing away for Boston in 1935, hitting .181.

John Ward, however, retired brilliantly. He had been toying with the public for weeks—years, if we recall his 1890 meeting with Spalding. He had said in late September that he was "not prepared to say whether I will be with the New York club next season or not." He went on to obfuscate artfully, saying that if he retired as a player, he would also retire as a manager. But, he went on, he did not mean to imply that his playing days were over. If he could become part of an established law firm . . . If matters began to take shape . . . He would, however, make his intentions clear as soon as he could . . .

This was old stuff. The *Herald*, a fortnight after the Temple Cup gala, headlined a speculative article "Ward's Annual Farewell Lecture" and went on to call his threats "empty," nothing but "bluff," and suggested it would be foolish to "lose any hair this winter by worrying over Mr. Ward's probable disposal of himself next spring."

Then the paper became nasty, suggesting that if Ward gave up "bat and ball for Blackstone and briefs . . . the world will keep right on whirling upon its axis."

> 'Tis true "Johnnie" Ward has been a popular idol and a nervy, winning ball player, but he should remember Rip Van Winkle's philosophy: "how soon we are forgot when we are gone." We shall have Giants long after Counsellor Ward begins his arduous and ambitious task of untangling the minds of our eminent judges. . . . Don't pay any attention to what Ward is reported to have said. . . . Wait till the plans are put into practice. Then you'll know. Till then just keep on living.

Ward, meanwhile, had headed back to Bellefonte to gather his dogs and go hunting.

On November 28, 1894, the day before Thanksgiving, Ward announced to New York reporters that he had decided to retire from baseball and join Austin B. Fletcher's Manhattan law firm. The *Herald* received this news sniffily, primarily because its reporter was O. P. Caylor, long a Spalding intimate, and an opponent of everything the Brotherhood and Ward stood for.

> There will be one more thing for which New Yorkers may be thankful to-day, when they tackle, punt and slug their turkey. The dreadful uncertainty is over. "Johnny" Ward will not play ball next year. The Giants will have another captain and the New York Bar will have another shining light. Though no genuine crank will rejoice to hear the news, all must feel a grateful relief that the uncertainty is removed. It was "just awful"—this

guessing whether John would or would not. Now it is officially announced he will not. That ought to settle it. Goodby, John.

The *Clipper* was far more elegaic, calling Ward one of the most "prominent" players of the Giants: "a greater batting, fielding and base running combination than he could not be found anywhere." Ward, the paper went on,

> knew the game as thoroughly as any man that ever played it. . . .
> He had on many occasions turned an apparent defeat into a great
> victory, gaining for himself renown and making him popular
> wherever his team might happen to be playing. How many
> enthusiasts are there who can recall the times when Ward has
> snatched a victory out of the fire, as it were, by bunting the ball,
> and beating it out at first. Then, with a daring steal and a great
> slide to second, had come home from that point of the diamond
> on almost any kind of a hit.

Ward himself, though unapologetic when he spoke of his decision, was sentimental and witty.

> In the first place, let me say that, though I am now bidding
> farewell to the diamond, after seventeen years of it, there isn't a
> finer, squarer business in the world than baseball. . . . Well, I'm
> going to retire, and put in two years of hard work batting Black-
> stone, Chitty, Metcalf, Bishop, and a good many other legal
> pitchers of tough curves for the mind to get onto. . . . I can make
> a home run with the judges as umpires. But, having worked so
> severely for seventeen years, I'm going to take a little rest and
> recreation before buckling down to my law studies.

He would be returning to New York in the early spring. But, he concluded, his immediate plans included a hunting trip to Montana. "There," he said, "I shall be seven days in the saddle before reaching my first ranch of rest."

Part III

It ain't what it used to be, but what the hell is?

—Dizzy Dean

Twenty-Seven

Batting Blackstone

WARD BEGAN his law career at 29 Broadway, near Bowling Green in New York's financial district, where his office was neighbor to the magnificent new Standard Oil building. By the turn of the century, he had moved north to 96 Broadway, near its intersection with Wall Street. Two years later he was farther north still, on the eleventh floor of 277 Broadway—the northwest corner of its intersection with Chambers Street, hard by City Hall—in the just-completed Cass Gilbert Renaissance-revival structure known as the Broadway Chambers Building.

As a lawyer, Ward was "shrewd, quick-witted and humorous; smiling and sarcastic," in other words, much like Ward the Brotherhood president, Ward the ballplayer, Ward the captain-manager, and Ward the author. His practice, as was common at the time, was an eclectic one, encompassing everything from contractual disputes and personal injury cases to dreary estate parsing. The only sorts of cases he avoided, evidently, were those involving criminals or patents.

His practice was, as well, mercenary. In one breath he defended players against owners and League shenanigans, while in the next he was counsel for the Brooklyn League club, fighting against players. Depending on the circumstances of the individual personal injury cases, Ward pleaded for workers who had been injured on the job or defended employers sued by injured workers. In *Wenzel* v. *Patrick Ryan Construction Corpo-*

ration, for instance, Bill Wenzel, a laborer, was crushed as he uncoupled railroad cars filled with cement on a railroad bridge being built across the East River. Wenzel's widow sued, alleging unsafe working conditions. Ward, as counsel for the construction firm, argued that Wenzel, negligent and careless, had only himself to blame for his death. Ward won the case.

In *Larkin v. New York Telephone Co. et al.*, however, a case involving Michael Larkin, a telephone lineman who was electrocuted while repairing shorted power lines in Queens, Ward pled for Larkin. Larkin, during the summer of 1911, had climbed a pole and, without using rubber gloves or rubber boots, opened a terminal box, removed a clamp, and began cutting insulation with a pair of splicing scissors to expose the live wires. His assistant heard a snapping sound. Larkin called out, "My God, John, I got it," and fell dead. The case swam up the legal stream of trials, appeals, and reversals like a determined salmon. Finally, five and one-half years after Larkin's death, Ward won a judgment for his widow.

As busy as he was building his practice, and despite his avowal that he rarely even thought about baseball and rarely attended games, Ward hardly severed his connection with the sport. His baseball compass, in the first twenty years after his retirement as a player, took a pronounced swing toward management's pole. Because of the long and circuitous path that legal cases sometimes take, however—and because of Ward's twin loyalties to his old Brotherhood comrades and his new corporate clients—the compass swing is best described as irregular. During the last decade or so of his life he once again became a strong—though barely listened to— advocate for players and their freedom of movement and economic independence.

In 1895, Ward took on the case of Amos Rusie. The two men were, at first glance, strange bedfellows: Rusie had supported neither the Brotherhood nor the Players' League and in fact had been a teammate of the hated "Judas" Jack Glasscock, arriving with him from Indianapolis to play for the 1890 New York NL team. Rusie and Ward, however, had evidently made amends. Rusie, whose fastball was, legend has it, the inspiration for one of baseball's oldest saws—"You can't hit what you can't see"—won 33 games for Ward's Giants in 1893 and 36 in 1894. In all likelihood, Ward's willingness to become Rusie's advocate was encouraged by personal spite against Andrew Freedman, the New York owner and the target of Rusie's legal action.

In 1895, Rusie won twenty-three games—over a third of all that season's wins—for the ninth-place Giants. To his suprise and consternation, when he opened the last of his season's paychecks, he found that Freedman had deducted $200 from it: half for missing curfew, half for an "indifferent" attitude during his last game. Rusie refused to sign his contract for the 1896 season until the fines were rescinded. The pitcher was an extremely popular player and the public outcry against his treatment was long and loud. A grass-roots campaign backing Rusie took hold. Some Wall Street brokers hung a large sign in a tobacconist's urging their fellow citizens to boycott the Giants. The supportive crowd that gathered by the sign grew so boisterous that police had to be called. *The Sporting News,* among others, also backed Rusie's case, saying, "Every independent fair-thinking man is with Rusie. . . . Every ball player of standing is with him."

Freedman was as reviled as Rusie was loved: though the competition is fierce, he must be awarded laurels as the most loathsome team owner in baseball history. Freedman, born in 1860, had made a fortune in the real estate and insurance industries—he would be a major financial backer of New York's first subway, the IRT—thanks in equal parts to his business acumen and his close friendship with Tammany Hall chief Richard Croker. (Even the *Dictionary of American Biography* throws up its hands when it comes to Freedman's business dealings, calling them "devious" and "no longer traceable.")

In 1894, Croker and company had been temporarily displaced from influence by the election of reform mayor William Strong. Croker hied to England to escape the long arms of Strong and his gangbusters. Freedman found himself at loose ends and, for $54,000, bought 1,200 shares of stock in the New York Giants, a slight majority.

The previous owner, E. B. Talcott, had for most of 1894 made it clear he wanted out of the baseball business. Among the many rumors swirling around New York was one that had the just-retired John Ward returning to baseball. Officially he would become team treasurer. The position would be, in fact, an apprenticeship of sorts until such time as Ward could buy Talcott out and become the team owner. Talcott, however, wanted to sell immediately, not finance "Ward's fling at baseball management."

As these things go, the Ward-as-treasurer rumor was an odd one in that it understated the actual case. Ward's friends had, during the 1894 season, been urging him to buy the team from Talcott. In fact, Ward already owned some stock in the team—he had won twenty shares in a bet with Talcott in 1892—and, with his reputation and connections throughout the city, $50,000-odd dollars would not have been difficult to raise. Ward finally decided to stick with his decision to practice law, a decision, he told *Sporting News* writer Joe Vila years later, that was a huge mistake. "Yes," Ward said, "I was wrong! I should have bought the Giants in 1894. But I never dreamed that the National League would develop into such a bonanza."

Freedman began alienating much of the known world—including John Ward—within weeks of his takeover of the Giants. He cut back on the number of complimentary tickets allotted for each game; he tried to throw his weight and opinions around in meetings with other owners; he punched Edward Hurst, an *Evening World* sportswriter whose copy displeased him, and demanded that the paper fire Hurst; he barred other sportswriters from the Polo Grounds, including Sam Crane, who had bought a ticket. Crane wrote his game story with help from his colleagues, and included a report on Freedman's ban. Crane then hired John Ward as his lawyer in a suit against Freedman. (Nothing came of this.) At one point, Freedman himself had filed twenty-two libel suits against the *New York Sun*.

Ward may have been seething privately already at the lost opportunity of team ownership. He must also have been embarrassed and angered at seeing the Giants being run by a monster; but he had another reason as well to despise the niggardly, litigious Freedman. At the November 1895 League meetings, Ward demanded that the Giants—and Freedman—publicly, officially release him from reservation. Ward's request placed the National League between a rock and a hard place: if they refused, they could count on Ward taking the matter to court, where all the issues of the validity of League contracts and the reserve clause would be sure to be raised; if he was granted his release, it could set a troubling precedent, giving lots of other players ideas. There was a third consideration: Ward, despite all his denials, might be setting himself up to return to baseball as a free agent.

Ward got his release in February 1896, but only after much wrangling with owners, Freedman foremost among them. Ward's official position was that the reserve clause he had played under in 1894 had expired, because he had not been offered a contract for the 1895 season. Suppos-edly Talcott had made him an offer—which, under existing baseball law, would cause the clause to roll over—but no one could prove it. It is entirely possible that the owners could have produced a document, had they not been so afraid of an ensuing legal battle over the validity of the reserve clause. Ward, once again, had let the owners see the stalking horse of the reserve clause grazing outside their windows. It was a clever and successful move on Ward's part. But it was, as well, either a very selfish move or a too-clever move. That is, Ward may have outsmarted himself: perhaps he was *hoping* the League would refuse him—so he could take the contract to court and this time, unlike his and Ewing's battle in 1890, have the reserve clause declared illegal. Instead, the League submitted, losing the battle but winning the reserve clause war by keeping it out of court.

At one point during the negotiations, Freedman had offered Ward his release on the condition he sign a guarantee not to play with another club without New York's consent. Ward laughed out loud, saying "he did not care to accept as a courtesy from the club what was due him as a right."

In fact, Ward's request for release was entirely symbolic, as he had no immediate plans to return to baseball.

> I am not as yet making a baseball salary as a lawyer, but I am
> doing better every month. I am entirely satisfied, and shall not
> return to baseball unless my circumstances change materially. I
> broke a record to-day, for I am the only player ever released from
> reservation by the National League.

So, when Ward was approached by Rusie, he must have rubbed his hands in glee to go after Freedman. Ward took the case before the League board, arguing that the fines were unjust. Unsurprisingly, the board ruled in favor of the Giants. Rusie then did the unimaginable: he refused to play for the entire 1896 season. Even the fact that the Giants without Rusie improved slightly (from ninth to seventh place) did not silence the pub-lic, which continued to pummel Freedman with insults. But their grum-bling probably had less effect than did Ward's legal strategy. Having been rebuffed in the court of baseball law, he would take the case to extra-baseball court. He filed suit against Freedman, asking for $5,000 and Rusie's unconditional release.

The other owners blanched: once again, they feared Ward would argue that Rusie's contract—and by implication, all major league contracts—was invalid. Outside the courtroom stalked the pale horse: the fragile reserve clause.

The other owners finally persuaded Freedman to settle out of court. Rusie got $5,000, paid by a consortium of owners, and agreed to play for the Giants in 1897 for a salary of $3,000. Rusie laughed that he had received $2,000 more for not playing than he had for playing. Ward may well have hoped Rusie would not settle, but ultimately he had to respect the wishes of his client. Once again, the reserve clause escaped legal scrutiny.

With the collapse of both the Players' League and the American Association, the National League was, once again, a monopoly. As such, the League quickly instituted measures to increase profitability.

The National Agreement, signed in March of 1892, among other things allowed League teams to draft players from upper echelon minor leagues at predetermined and artificially low prices: a player from a Class A league could become a League team's property for $1,000, a player from a Class B team for $500—the money going to the minor league club's owner, not the player.

Though League clubs, theoretically, were limited to fourteen reserved players each, the number was ignored, and virtually all players were reserved. Some of these players, though, were not playing for the League club—rosters had been pared to thirteen per team. The "extra" players, who did not draw League salaries, played for minor league teams, in "cold storage," to be brought up to the League team only as needed. With the roster reduction, the number of League playing jobs had dropped to 156 from 180. There was, simply, a baseball labor glut. Salaries quickly fell. The average major league salary in 1891 was $3,500. By 1894 the figure had dropped by 50 percent—to the same level as 1883 salaries. In this context, the Rusie settlement was an aberration. Players not of Rusie's stature had to take pay cuts or find themselves replaced by hungry minor leaguers, willing to play for as little as $600 a year.

Not surprisingly, players began to explore avenues of recourse. In 1894, several players began meeting with *Sporting Life* editor Frank Richter and drawing up plans for a new rival league—which they planned to call the American Association.

The League reacted swiftly and forcefully. It said that any player who deserted would be blackballed for life. The threat—whether or not it would hold up in courts, and whether or not it was, as Richter called it, a "tremendous bluff"—worked, and the new organization barely got beyond the blueprint stage.

One of the primary organizers of the stillborn rival league was Fred Pfeffer. A fervent Brotherhood activist, Pfeffer, like Ward, was a smart, base-stealing, flashy-fielding infielder as well as author—his book *Scientific Baseball* was published in 1889, the year after Ward's book. The League, hoping to show that it had not been bluffing, branded Pfeffer and two others—Billie Barnie and Al Buckenberger—ingrates and anarchists, and suspended them until they could prove themselves innocent of treachery.

Buckenberger quickly surrendered: he signed a League-approved affadavit declaring his innocence. Barnie stood firmer. He appeared before a League board and testified at length. He was then offered a "loyalty oath" to sign, one that included a "promise of future allegience." Barnie refused, but the League, unable to build a strong case, reinstated him anyway, after issuing a stern warning that Barnie was on an extremely short leash as far as his future with the League was concerned.

Pfeffer, however, adamantly refused to sign anything, appear before any board, or apologize. Further, he said, the League had no control over him, because when he had been injured toward the end of the 1894 season, he had effectively secured his release from his team—Louisville—because he had forgone his salary during his recovery. The League ignored his petition.

Pfeffer signed on to coach baseball at Princeton, but let it be known he did so reluctantly. A grass-roots movement of fans—10,000 strong by some reports—threatened a League-wide boycott if Pfeffer was not reinstated.

Meanwhile, the League was tripped up in the same way it had always been tripped up, by one of its own magnates. The Louisville club broke ranks and mailed Pfeffer a contract for 1895, even though the League-proclaimed deadline for Pfeffer's signing of a "loyalty oath" had passed. The League then backed down. So did Pfeffer. The League fined him $500 and Pfeffer signed his pledge. Pfeffer's friends paid the fine and he was reinstated. The League issued a proclamation that in the future, any player, manager, or club official found guilty of organizing a rival league would be banned forever.

Pfeffer's flame of activism had not been doused, however. In 1896 he went from Louisville to New York, where he played only four games before he was suspended without pay "until such time as he was in fit condition to play ball."

Pfeffer was bought by his old team, Chicago, where he finished the season, but he quickly engaged Ward to fight for his back pay. The case was interesting, turning less on whether Pfeffer had been able to play than whether the club had to prove that Pfeffer was able to play and whether the contract allowed for such indefinite suspensions. There was, of course, every possibility that the high-profile Pfeffer was being punished, by colluding team owners, for his original sins against the League in 1894.

Not until 1907 was Pfeffer's success in the lower courts upheld by the New York Court of Appeals. He received $800 in back pay, and costs. The relatively small amount involved and the fact that the case took eleven years to resolve suggest that for both Ward and Pfeffer, the fight was one of principle rather than capital.

By 1899 Ward was counsel for the Brooklyn League club. In a case that had begun a year earlier, Ward was put in the awkward position of fighting against a former Brotherhood member, Michael Griffin, in Griffin's contract dispute with the Brooklyn club. Griffin had signed to play for and manage the Brooklyns in 1899. He was to be paid $3,500. Before the season began, Brooklyn and Baltimore had combined their clubs and Brooklyn wanted the Baltimore manager, Ned Hanlon, to manage the new team. They offered Griffin a $300 raise as compensation for not managing. Griffin refused the offer and refused to report to Brooklyn. The Brooklyns sent him to Cleveland, which quickly sent him on to St. Louis. Griffin had refused to play for either team, on the grounds that neither was offering him $3,500—as his original Brooklyn contract specified.

He quit baseball and returned to his native Utica, where he became a successful businessman and filed suit against Brooklyn, claiming the club had failed to honor his contract. The suit, with Ward arguing for Brooklyn, was finally decided in 1903. Griffin was awarded $2,349.47.

Ward very deliberately removed himself from any public discussion of the 1894 American Association revival plans. He did the same six years later, when players, weary of their declining stock in the League monopoly, formed a protective organization.

By the turn of the century, though the clubs were generally profitable and had been so for several years, salaries remained depressed. The average League salary, about $2,000—still four times the average American worker's wages—stood nearly exactly where it had been in 1878, and about 40 percent lower than the peak wage season of 1890–1891.

There had been, as well, continuing cases of owner capriciousness. Clark Griffith, who won 137 games for Chicago between 1894 and 1899, never saw his salary grow beyond $2,500. He nearly led a strike of his Chicago teammates in 1897 for better pay, and kept up a constant stream of invective against the owners. In a more striking example, Cap Anson, in 1897, after 27 years in the major leagues, 22 of them with Spalding's Chicago team, was fired. According to Anson's account, he was badly cheated by his lifelong associate, Spalding, who, after Anson publicly criticized the Chicago team, refused to renew his contract. To say that National League player morale was bad at the end of the last century would be massive understatement: if one of the League's premier pitchers and one of the League's most venerable personalities could be treated so badly, what did that mean for the rest of the players?

In the spring of 1900, Griffith and two other players, Charles "Chief" Zimmer and Hughie Jennings, announced the formation of the Protective Association of Professional Baseball Players. Samuel Gompers, president of the American Federation of Labor and a baseball fan, was wildly enthusiastic, and delivered a long statement to the press about the excellent prospects for a ballplayers' union. In the course of his statement, he gave a brief history lesson:

> I have been told that since the failure of the Brotherhood in
> 1890 the players are chary of trusting each other in proposed
> similar movements. The Brotherhood was practically a fight of

capital against capital; the present movement has simply in view the formation of an organization of a self-protection and benevolent character. The Brotherhood was also handicapped by a few unfaithful leaders and the fact that it was not affiliated with any national labor body. Conditions are different now. Personally I would like to see the players organize with officers from their own ranks; they have plenty of good, honest men on the retired list.

Clearly Ewing was the "unfaithful leader" and Ward a "good, honest man" on the retired list. But Ward had no intention of leading another player organization, and in fact warned players against aligning themselves with organized labor. Ward's single comment on the Protective Association was detached and aphoristic.

> I have little opportunity nowadays to keep myself informed of what the players are doing. It is as much as I can . . . to get time occasionally to witness a game. I believe that the players ought to have an organization, not for the purpose of fighting with any one, but to protect themselves. . . .
> . . . I believe now, as I believed and said in the days of the Brotherhood that the players themselves can, through an organization of this kind do more to help baseball than any other influence. . . . I think they should go very slowly.

In July 1900, over one hundred players met to discuss grievances and strategies. Again, the players were initially cautious—strikes were far down the list of proposed actions. Had the owners acted with any moderation, the players would probably have been satisfied with a modest reform of the reserve rule or even a general salary hike, as they were willing to cede the rule's necessity in the unique world of baseball.

The group's president was Harry Leonard Taylor, a lawyer and former ballplayer. He suggested such other reforms as a ban on trades and sales of players; an equalizing of the ten-day dissolution clause, which said that a player was linked to a team for life, but a team could release a player with ten days' notice; an impartial arbitration board; and some form of medical insurance—clubs would pay for medical expenses, or at least physicians' fees, for field-related injuries.

The National League owners reacted badly. So did John Day, who said he would raze his ballpark before he'd negotiate with any player organization. But the Protective Association died a quick death less because of owner opposition than because of the formation of a rival baseball organization: the American League. Clark Griffith, for example, redirected his energies from the Protective Association toward getting players to jump to the new league.

The American League was the brainchild of Ban Johnson, a college-educated former semipro ballplayer and sportswriter for the *Cincinnati Commercial-Gazette*. Johnson became president of the Western League in 1894. Through his astute leadership, the league—with teams in towns such as Grand Rapids, Indianapolis, St. Paul, Minneapolis, Columbus, and Detroit—prospered. The level of play was high, only a few steps below that of the National League. Johnson was ambitious and smart. He envisioned the Western League as a major league on a par with the National League, and he slowly built his hand. When the NL dropped four clubs after 1899 as part of a general housecleaning of the unwieldy twelve-team circuit, Johnson's Western League took over the vacated Cleveland franchise. He also managed to persuade the Chicago NL owner, Jim Hart, to allow Johnson to move his St. Paul club to the city's South Side.

Johnson changed the name of his league from Western to American. Pointing to the threat to his circuit from yet another rumored American Association startup, he asked the NL if he could expand into Washington, Baltimore, and Philadelphia. Unwisely, the NL did not deign to reply. The enraged, willful Johnson made his move: he refused to sign the National Agreement after the 1900 season and, in effect, declared that his new league was not only the equal of the National League but that it would welcome and sign any players who cared to leave the "senior circuit."

Players, as they had every time a rival league seemed viable, flocked to Johnson's fold, which offered attractive salaries, recognition (at least initially) of the Protective Association, and the prohibition of "farming" players to the minor leagues without their consent. Players were interested in jobs, and suddenly there were eight new teams offering them. The American League (AL), with 111 of its 182 players former National Leaguers, began play in 1901 and was barely outdrawn by the National

League, 1.6 million to 1.9 million. The very next year, the AL outdrew the NL 2.2 million to 1.7 million. The average major league salary rose 50 percent, from $2,000 to $3,000, from 1900 to 1902.

By the end of the 1902 season, the National League surrendered, and both leagues signed another National Agreement, with the now-familiar mutually protective policies such as honoring each other's contracts. The reserve clause was reinstituted. Salaries leveled off after dropping 16 percent from their 1902 peak. As had been the case with the earlier peace treaty with the American Association, the only difference between the major league structure of 1900 and that of 1903 was that the new monopoly had two heads. Ban Johnson was only briefly an advocate of players' rights.

The Protective Association had withered during the American League's courting, and was powerless to make any demands for the players. At one point, in 1901, several minor leagues, sensing the National League's weakness, reared up and formed their own organization, the National Association of Professional Baseball Leagues. John Ward was the group's attorney. With the 1903 peace agreement, however, the power of the minor leagues, despite their brief revolution, had waned dramatically. So promising was the new agreement between the NL and the AL that Ban Johnson, the AL president, felt secure in branding Chief Zimmer of the erstwhile Protective Association "one of the worst characters in baseball."

During the period after the formation of the AL and before its National Agreement with the NL, Ward once again was drawn into a contractual interleague dispute. Ironically, hypocritically, he argued on the side of management: the Brooklyn NL team.

After the 1901 season, James McGuire, a catcher, signed with Brooklyn for 1902. He then decided to jump and sign with Detroit of the fledgling AL. Ward, arguing for Brooklyn, said that, while the AL, having created itself "without permission" from the NL, was in fact free to sign players, it could not sign McGuire because he had signed an NL contract.

Tough, said McGuire's lawyer. The Brooklyn contract was invalid because it lacked "mutuality"—it held the rights to McGuire's services in perpetuity, but could release him with only ten days' notice. Ironically, this was the same argument Ward's and Ewing's lawyers had made in 1890.

McGuire won. Ward lost. Again, the decision seemed to condemn the reserve rule—a large reason the contract was considered not mutual. However, once again—as with both the Ward and Ewing cases—the case, which was tried before a federal judge, revolved around issuing an injunction and did not set precedent.

Ward would, ultimately, become deeply involved in the NL-AL National Agreement. His legal advice to a single player—infielder George Davis—came precipitously close to unraveling the entire peace treaty. Ward's work in the Davis case—like his work in the McGuire case—was not, by any stretch of the imagination, his finest hour.

George Stacey Davis was born near Albany, New York, in 1870. He entered the major leagues in 1890, replacing Ward as manager of New York in 1895—on Ward's recommendation.

After the 1901 season, Davis jumped from the New York NL team to Chicago of the new American League. The perspicacious Davis had hired Ward as a legal consultant to vet the new contract. Ward assured him it was binding and that, since the AL was not a signatory to any agreement with the NL, New York had no hold over him.

Davis played well for Chicago in 1902. As the season ended, however, he was contacted by the Giants, who badly wanted him back on their roster. Davis wanted back as well. Over the winter, the two leagues signed their peace agreement. Part of that agreement included the formation of a joint committee to decide on the placement of "disputed" players—those who, like Davis, were claimed by more than one team. It was, as it turned out, one of the new agreement's thorniest problems.

Although the peace treaty still stands today, during the first year or so of its existence, both leagues slept with one eye open. Enter Davis and John Ward.

Both Chicago and New York claimed that their contracts were binding. Davis wanted to return to New York, which was offering him a substantial raise.

In effect, Ward argued that Davis had the legal right to jump to Chicago *and* return to New York. Ward had assured Davis that New York had no hold over him. But when Davis returned to New York, Ward made the argument that Davis could collect a salary from the Giants without breaking his Chicago contract.

As it turned out, Chicago sued to keep Davis, and won, though Davis drew his New York salary until he returned to Chicago.

Though Ward prevailed legally, it seemed to many baseball observers and legal laymen that Ward was engaging in double-faced technicalities, the sort that turns "lawyer" into a four-letter word. Ward and Davis, it seemed, wanted to have their cake, eat it, and demand seconds.

The NL, anxious to placate the AL, agreed that Davis would, in fact, play for Chicago.

Six years later, Ward paid dearly for his involvement in the Davis case and Ban Johnson enjoyed a cold meal of revenge. Ward had, during the Davis case, so angered Ban Johnson that the AL threatened to seek Ward's disbarment for "unprofessional advice." Johnson told *Sporting Life* that Ward was "as crooked in regard to breaking contracts as any base ball player that ever jumped his agreement." Additionally, though the AL had won the Davis case, Johnson was infuriated that the victory had cost the Chicago team nearly $3,000 in legal expenses.

In July 1909, Harry Pulliam, the NL president, shot himself in his room at the New York Athletic Club. John A. Heydler, the league's secretary-treasurer and interim president, was the logical choice as successor. But after some furious backroom politicking, the competent but unimpressive Heydler was pushed out of the picture.

August Herrmann of Cincinnati nominated Robert W. Brown, editor of the *Louisville Times*. Countering Herrmann was a bloc of owners, including Charles Ebbets of Brooklyn, Charles Murphy of Chicago, John Brush of New York, and Horace Fogel of Philadelphia, who distrusted Herrmann and were convinced that he and Brown were far too chummy. This second bloc nominated John Ward.

Realistically, Ward was a protest candidate, or at least an "anti-Brown" candidate, and his election chances were slim. As Harold Seymour, in *Baseball, The Golden Age*, has pointed out, though Ward's day as a "revolutionary" was almost twenty years past, electing him president would be "comparable to electing John L. Lewis or Walter Reuther as chairman of the board of a corporation."

Herrmann and Pittsburgh owner Barney Dreyfuss declared themselves so opposed to Ward that they would bolt to the AL if he were elected. Ban Johnson, who had no business at all butting into NL affairs, brought up the Davis case, calling Ward a "trickster" and his advocacy of Davis six years earlier "clearly conspiracy." Johnson also announced that, should Ward be elected, he would resign from the National Commission (the two leagues' governing board). Finally, Johnson issued a barely veiled threat of interleague war:

> It is far from our purpose to say, or even suggest, who the National League should select as its President, but common sense, and the interests of other parties to the National Agreement should be considered if the present cordial relations are to continue.

At one point, Ward, who had generally held himself above the fray, lashed out publicly:

> I am willing to submit the question as to my action in that [Davis] case to any reputable attorney he may have. If Mr. Herrmann's selection says that I did anything contrary to right I will withdraw at once from the race for president of the league, provided Mr. Herrmann will withdraw that objection to me if the decision is in my favor.

After eight deadlocked ballots, Charles Ebbets read to his fellow owners a letter from Ward. Ward "deeply appreciated" the support of Ebbets, as well as that of Brush, Murphy, and Fogel. But, he continued, "the time has arrived when I owe it to you to relieve the existing situation" by withdrawing his name from consideration. Thomas J. Lynch, a former umpire, was quickly elected as a compromise candidate.

Ward sued Johnson for libel. During the trial, Johnson's attorney asserted that Johnson had merely spoken the truth about Ward's dealings in the Davis case, and at one point read sections of the "lawyer's code of ethics," to which Ward subscribed.

Ward, meanwhile, dug himself into several large holes. He said he did not know that Davis was under contract with the Giants (certainly a lie). Further, he said he had advised Davis to sign with Chicago only *if* he could get out of his agreement with New York. Finally, he said, he had acted as a legal advisor, not a "keeper of the moral character of his clients. . . . When a client was between 'two horns of a dilemma,' " he would give him his "best advice and nothing more." Ward also pointed out that he had received only $250 in legal fees.

The trial lasted three days. On May 13, 1911, the judge ruled in favor of Ward on a single count of libel (he had sued on five counts of slander and libel) and ordered Johnson to pay Ward $1,000 (Ward had asked for $50,000).

Johnson's counsel moved for a new trial. The judge denied the motion, saying "I think it's a light verdict and that you ought to be satisfied." Ward, for his part, insisted that all he had ever wanted was a retraction. "I have already said that I didn't want Johnson's money. What I wanted was to clear my name and I think the verdict has done that."

Twenty-Eight

Machine Play

N LATE 1911, a group of New York City investors, including Ward, bought the Boston National League Club. These Bostons were one of early baseball's embarrassingly bad teams: in the previous nine seasons, they had finished in sixth place twice, in seventh place three times, and dead last four times—including the previous three seasons. During that nine-year span they had lost at least one hundred games six times. In 1906 and 1909 they finished 66½ games and 65½ games out of first place, respectively—two of the five most distant finishes in baseball history. (In 1889, Louisville of the American Association finished 66½ games out, as did the 1890 Pittsburghs of the National League. Honors, however, for the most Plutonian team in baseball's solar system go to the 1899 Clevelands, who finished 84 games behind Brooklyn.)

Ward, the impetus behind the formation of the investment group and the only member experienced in the ways of professional baseball, assumed the Boston club presidency on December 19. His original strategy seemed to be one of patient and major rebuilding of his woeful new acquisition. In one letter to August Herrmann, who had opposed his candidacy for the NL presidency, Ward admitted to needing, for a start, "several pitchers and at least one infielder." His recruiting record was spotty. He re-signed forty-five-year-old pitcher Cy Young. Young had won 511 games, far and away the most in baseball history, but had had a losing record the last two years: he didn't appear in a single game in 1912. On the other hand, Ward discovered and signed a minor league shortstop, twenty-year-old Rabbit Maranville, whose brilliant fielding over his twenty-three-year career would lead him into the Baseball Hall of Fame.

It is impossible to judge, however, whether Ward's rebuilding plan was solid or not, as he was evidently the victim of a cabal of other NL owners—led in all likelihood by August Herrmann—who colluded to prevent Boston from acquiring promising players. Ward, in keeping with the "open tryout" he had developed during his management years at Brooklyn and New York, was interested in taking a look at as many players as possible. For several years, baseball had had in place a system of waiver rules. Essentially, a club could send a player down to the minors only after all the other clubs had "waived" claim to him. Ward, as often as possible, would refuse to waive on players. As soon as the other owners realized Ward had some interest, they would remove the player from the waivers list. *The Sporting News* noted that "the new Boston owners have not been treated as friendly as [they] were led to believe they would be." Ward agreed wholeheartedly, and told the newspaper, "It looks like a case of every man for himself, and the Old Boy take the hindmost."

The 1912 season began badly for the Bostons and never improved—they ended the year in last place, fifty-two games behind the first-place Giants. Ward, however, did not last to see the season end. On August 5, he resigned his presidency and sold his interest in the club to his fellow investors.

Ward's hasty and frustrated retreat from club ownership was understandable, but his performance as an executive was hardly exemplary. If his old ally *The Sporting News* is to be believed, no one—not other owners, Ward's fellow investors, or the Boston players—was exactly heartbroken at his departure. In a series of short articles, Tim Murnane—a former player (and 1878 teammate of Ward) turned sportswriter—viciously attacked Ward.

"Lawyers make very poor magnates," Murnane began.

> The brainy ballplayer developed into a fine attorney, but when it came to handling base ball of the up-to-date brand, the old Brotherhood leader was a pronounced failure. . . .
>   There are a number of men who fought under the Brotherhood banner still in the game, but I can't find one who lost a

night's sleep over Johnny Ward's failure to make good in the old game.

Ward never found a place in the players' hearts. He disposed of players without first gaining the consent of [field manager John Kling]. . . . Though once a player, he had no heart for the men that he employed—no sentiment but cold business.

Murnane then went on to compare Ward with his American League counterpart in Boston, James R. McAleer, also a former Brotherhood member, whom he called "just the opposite from Mr. Ward. McAleer is impulsive, kind hearted, a maker of friends."

Ward was not only arrogant, autocratic, and critical, he was cheap, according to Murnane.

As a club president he wouldn't even pay for the drinking water with which the players . . . refreshed themselves between innings; nor, did accident befall, would he even provide lint or liniment for torn flesh or bruised muscles. . . . to the pampered players of these degenerate days he is now a shattered idol.

Murnane's assessment of Ward is so harsh that it suggests an enmity between the two men; certainly, Ward may have, at some point in 1912, rebuffed Murnane in some particularly hurtful way. On the other hand, Murnane's opinion cannot be dismissed, as he was in many ways a kindred spirit of Ward: as a player he was hustling and hardnosed; he revered the "old school" of ballplayers (as opposed to the "pampered" one of the degenerate teens) such as George Wright, Ned Williamson, and Mike Kelly. Additionally, the two had similar politics: Murnane had played for and managed a Union Association team, and in 1901 founded the short-lived minor league counterbalance to major league power, the National Association of Professional Baseball Leagues, the same group that hired John Ward as its legal counsel.

As brief and maladroit as Ward's association with the Boston NL team was, in one way, his legacy still echoes. Before Ward's tenure, the club, one of professional baseball's original organizations, had been known by a variety of names: Nationals, Red Stockings, Red Caps, Beaneaters, Doves, Pilgrims, and Rustlers.

Ward's 1912 investment group consisted almost entirely of members and associates of New York's Tammany Hall, the New York Democratic Party political machine. The story goes that Ward puckishly suggested to his primary fellow investor—James E. Gaffney, a "politician contractor" and brother-in-law of Tammany sachem Charles B. Murphy—that the team, located in Republican Boston, adopt the symbol of Democratic Tammany Hall: the Delaware Indian chief, Tammamend, in "full head-dress." The alliterative name took immediate hold during the 1912 season. Ever since then—through the franchise's flush years and lean years and in-between years, the years of Babe Ruth, the years of Hank Aaron, the years of Ted Turner, the moves from Boston to Milwaukee to present-day Atlanta—the team has been known as the Braves.

Two years later, in 1914, Ward became business manager of the Brooklyn Brookfeds or Tip-Tops, of the newly formed Federal League, the last viable organization to compete with the two established major leagues.

Baseball in the teens was generally very successful, so much so that there were several attempts to create a third major league. In 1912, William Abbott Wittman, of Reading, Pennsylvania, formed the United States League. This was an "outlaw" league—that is, a nonsignatory to the National agreement (like the Union Association, the Players' League, and, briefly, the American Association and the American League before it). Wittman's league was an inferior one, composed mostly of semipro players, former amateurs with dim professional prospects, and former major or current minor leaguers. The league folded by mid-June.

About the same time, plans for another independent, potentially "major" league were under way. The Columbian League, brainchild of John T. Powers of Chicago, planned to place teams in Cleveland, Chicago, and St. Louis. The proposed league died aborning early in 1912, when its primary financial backer, St. Louis brewer Otto Steifel, backed out.

In 1913, Wittman reorganized the United States League. Opening day was May 10. By Monday, May 11, the league "collapsed" because of sparse attendance. *Sporting Life* called the USL the "quickest and most ridiculous failure in the long history of base ball."

John Powers, like Wittman, was not discouraged by his earlier failure. In 1913 a reorganized Columbian League, now called the Federal League, began a 120-game schedule with teams in Chicago, Cleveland, Indianapolis, Pittsburgh, St. Louis, and Covington, Kentucky/Kansas City. That first year the new league, like the short-lived United States League, was a mix of hot former amateurs, semipros, minor league footnotes, major leaguers in decline, and the occasional novelty item (like Cy Young, the winningest pitcher in baseball, who roused himself from retirement to manage the 1913 Clevelands).

However successful the Federal League was in 1913—exact figures are impossible to come by—it was successful enough to attract new capital. The new capital in turn attracted new leadership and the new leadership led to serious muscle flexing, some franchise realignment (the 1914 league would have franchises in four NL cities and two AL cities), and a unilateral declaration of "major" league status.

Declarations are one thing; major league–caliber players are another. But in fact the new league began attracting these almost immediately, with offers of generous contract terms. In place of the reserve clause, players were offered long-term contracts and guaranteed 5 percent raises. Paychecks would begin when players reported to spring training, not on opening day. Most enticing, ten-year veterans would become "free agents"—they would be able to negotiate contracts on the open Federal League market, with any league team.

The trickle of American and National Leaguers who signed with the Federal League soon became a brook. Among the higher-profile signers were shortstop Joe Tinker; pitchers Three-Finger Brown, Chief Bender, and Eddie Plank; future Hall of Fame outfielder Edd Roush; briefly phenomenal outfielder Benny Kauff; premier first baseman Hal Chase; and infielder and Hall of Fame manager Bill McKechnie. Among others who almost signed, did sign and jumped back, or had their contracts invalidated were Johnny Evers, Walter Johnson, and New York Giants left-hander Rube Marquard.

As in all the previous baseball trade wars, players jumped leagues, some players jumped more than once, breach-of-contract lawsuits sprouted like spring grass, and the players benefited financially, though only briefly. Generally, whether they jumped to the Federal League or used the new league as a stalking horse, players saw their salaries grow during the Federal League's three-year existence, from about $3,000 in 1913 to an average of $5,000 in 1915.

The rise was even more precipitous for stars: Ty Cobb's American League salary rose from $12,000 to $20,000; Ward's find, Rabbit Maranville, earned $1,800 in 1913 and $6,000 in 1915. On and on it goes, though just as telling is the fact that by 1918, with the Federal League three years in its grave and the number of long-term 1914 and 1915 contracts down to a handful, the average major league salary had tumbled from $5,000 to about $3,600.

Ward's tenure with the Brooklyn Federal League team was brief but controversial. Rube Marquard, coming off three sizzling seasons for the New York Giants, signed with Ward's Brooklyns for two years at $10,000 a year. Ward, who later denied having signed Marquard at all, required all new Brooklyn players to sign affidavits that they were not bound to previous teams. (This policy was less honorable than smart—legal contract battles, as Ward well knew from the Davis case, could be prohibitively expensive and spiritually draining.) Marquard, who in fact was bound to the Giants, signed the affidavit anyway. When Ward found out, he sent him packing.

Ward resigned from Brooklyn in January 1915, the Federal League's last season. He was immediately descended upon by reporters, eager to hear the reasons for his latest departure from baseball, his opinions on the present and future of the Federal League, and his view of baseball in general.

Ward had always been a pundit, a very quotable favorite of reporters, a man who loved to see himself in print. He was also a man who had from very early on shrewdly used the press for his own purposes. After his retirement his quoted remarks gradually became less immediately analytical and more and more reminiscent and prognosticatory. As a storyteller and prophet he was neither especially interesting nor accurate. Nor was he immune from the virus of nostalgia.

In 1903, he declared to *Sporting Life* readers that modern baseball had become debased. It was no longer a sport, but a mere exhibition "of the ability of a clever manager, with more money and more tact in managerial council, to get together the best players in the market." That said, he did not think the status quo permanent. He prophesied a return to baseball's preprofessional era, in which teams filled with "local talent" would play a "locally patriotic game for blood." He went on to say, without offering examples, that such a movement was, in fact, under way. Of course there were problems, large ones, to be addressed:

> New York . . . by virtue of its size would have the advantage of a smaller city like Boston . . . and to even up matters it would be necessary for the committee to give the smaller towns enough territory to make all available population the same.

No one mentioned the apparent contradiction between Ward's vision of "the future of the game of base ball" and his long-held beliefs about player autonomy. Would players be forced to stay in service to their hometown teams?

In 1906, Ward was reported busy writing a chapter about baseball for a sporting book, among whose contributors would be Theodore Roosevelt. In a short but wide-ranging interview, Ward was condescending toward current ballplaying and current ideas about the origin of certain practices, including the squeeze play, the sacrifice bunt, and the suicide bunt. Ward reckoned there was nothing new under the sun; that the champion Providence team of 1879 had perfected all "modern" tricks; and that there was no element of surprise in the current game, which was nothing but monotonous "machine play."

He was optimistic about the Federal League, he told reporters during the winter of 1915. The only reason he had left was that he had sorely neglected his law practice, not because he feared for the Federal League's future. In fact, he said, the Federal League was proving much more resilient and successful than the American League had been in its fledgling years. Then, dipping into hyperbole, he said the new league had gained a secure foothold after "the most remarkable fight against tremendous odds that was ever chronicled in the history of the sport."

Ward was just warming up. In response to those who said there was no room for a third major league, he said there was not only room for a third, but "plenty of room for a fourth . . . and in time the public will have its eyes opened" to that very fact. He began rambling, saying that the biggest losers in the current trade war were the minor leagues, who had their best players taken up to the majors without recompense. And minor leaguers, because of the self-limiting policies of the National and American Leagues, were being forced to toil in tank towns, even though there was "brilliant . . . crackerjack talent all around the minors," talent, he implied, of major league caliber.

He likened the minors and their relation to the major league clubs to "Belgians drawn into the fight between the big fellows." He suggested that the Federal League develop a system of minor league aid. Climbing up on his activist's soapbox, he declared that any magnate's cry of financial pain should be received with laughter. He said that owners contributed, at best, 25 percent to the game's success, while players contributed the other 75 percent. Finally, he said that baseball had not amounted to "a hill of beans" until the New York National League team was established and New York reporters took a serious interest in the game. "From that moment [baseball's] future was established as a signal success."

Twenty-Nine

None of the
Spice of Baseball

H E GOLFED. He fell in love. He remarried. He practiced law. He golfed. He moved to the country. He hunted, fished, golfed. He traveled back to Bellefonte to hunt and fish and visit his relatives. He continued to go to the theater. He and his second wife took extended trips to the South and the Caribbean most winters, to fish, hunt, and golf.

Before all this, in the 1890s, he was a bicyclist. He was not alone. Becoming a bicyclist then was the thing to do, just like becoming a skier in the 1950s and 1960s or playing tennis or jogging in the 1970s and 1980s. Americans were mad for the sport.

In 1896, over 120,000 people attended a bicycle exhibition at Madison Square Garden. In 1893 there were an estimated one million bicyclists in America; by 1896 there were more than four million. People joined bicycle clubs—there were 53 in New York and over 500 in America by the turn of the century. People attended bicycle races in velodromes. People stood at roadsides and cheered bicycle road racers. Bicyclists were a powerful lobby: they demanded that politicians pave roads and open park lanes to bicyclists. When Carter H. Harrison II ran for mayor of Chicago in 1897, he decided to become a cyclist so he could win the bicyclist vote.

Not everybody rode bikes, though. They were expensive, costing anywhere from $50 to $100. Before long, bicycling became a symbol of class struggle and resentment.

Lawyers, stockbrokers, even businessmen would ride their bikes to work or during their lunch hours or home from work. They were ur-yuppies, in business clothes, bicycle dusters, or club uniforms—ur-Lycra—and they liked to explore different routes. To poor people, who were stuffed into unspeakable tenements without light or indoor plumbing and who used the streets to visit and shop and whose children used the streets to play, these bicyclists were despicable. They seemed to have all the leisure time in the world and, in an age when the only methods of individual mobility were a horse or shank's mare, they might as well have been riding on magic carpets.

More importantly, the bicyclists quickly decided that the streets were made for their convenience, and there were many accidents and near-accidents. (Bicycle hot-rodders were called "scorchers.") The bicycles on those crowded streets must have been as annoying as skateboarders now and even more dangerous. At the same time bicyclists were clamoring to have streets paved, or paved with asphalt instead of cobblestones or bricks, some poor people and social advocates were lobbying to keep the streets unpaved, so poor people could claim a little territory for their own. Often, poor people and street merchants terrorized bicyclists by strewing glass, vegetables, and stones along the streets, or parking carts and wagons at wild angles to turn the roadways into obstacle courses.

Ward, for most of a decade after his 1894 retirement from baseball, lived in Brooklyn. Until 1905, his address was 86 Livingston, though he briefly lived on nearby Montague Street and, for about a year, he lived several miles to the east of Brooklyn Heights, on Crescent near Fulton. He probably took a ferry to work in Manhattan, but he might have ridden his bike over the Brooklyn Bridge, or put his bike on a streetcar. Or—and this is most likely—he kept his bike at home, and rode it after work and on weekends. Though Brooklyn was a large city in the 1890s, a short trolley or rail ride took one to open spaces such as Coney Island, Canarsie, Jamaica Bay, or the rural westernmost towns of Long Island's Sussex County.

Ward was a perfect candidate for bicycling: he had always earned a good salary, and had never been anything approaching profligate in his spending, so cost was not a consideration. He was a professional, setting his own hours, so he had, in addition to discretionary income, discretionary blocks of time. Plus he was young, athletic, and fit.

There were relatively few participatory sports for the recreational athlete such as Ward. Hunting, fishing, and ice skating were seasonal pursuits. Croquet was likely too sedate to keep his interest for long, and tennis, though more of a democratic and class-spanning activity than is usually imagined, was generally associated with the new, highly exclusive, and very expensive gathering places known as country clubs.

But Ward had to do something. For American men in the latter part of the nineteenth century, the world was an uneasy place. The American male was obsessed with manliness—in the same way that Americans today are obsessed with weight and cholesterol. American men were, by and large, convinced that they were racing toward a special, jelly-bellied hell in a newfangled handcart.

By today's standards, of course, life was brutish in the nineteenth century but by yesterday's standards, men felt emasculated, overcivilized, and generally about as lionhearted as manatees. Blue-collar workers had lost control of the workplace; had become mere replaceable cogs in a huge machine. Their tasks—wheelwrighting, say—had become ritualized, less strenuous. Wheels rolled toward them on an assembly line, they didn't have to be hefted (or hefted as far, high, or often). Bureaucrats and artisans, as well, felt stripped of their independence and creativity. The world, in short, did not require as much muscle and brawn and sinew as it once did, nor, in many instances, as much brain. The world, many men thought, was becoming feminized and overcivilized.

Reactions to this perceived slipping away of manliness were varied. Some had all the sophistication of college fraternity high jinks: sheer physical bulk was admired, as was enormous consumption of both alcohol and food, as was brute strength and endurance—in, for example, the boxing ring. So too were the making of enormous amounts of money, and the conspicuous, extravagant spending of that money, considered manly and admirable.

So John Ward, who had proved his manliness on the baseball diamond a thousand times over (and who did it so well that he did not feel compelled to booze or smoke or overeat), must have felt himself—stripped of his uniform, shuffling papers in an office—at a terrible loss, back at manliness square one.

Bicycling, for a while, was the answer: it was acceptably rugged; it put him outdoors and enabled him to "keep in shape." It would not hold his interest for very long, however, because, essentially, at least outside of the velodrome, it was noncompetitive.

During the summer of 1897 Ward would find the perfect complement to the aesthetic and spiritual rewards of hunting and fishing and bicycling: golf. On vacation near Hyannisport, he happened by some golfers. Although he had undoubtedly seen golfers before, something about that day, that setting, that unknown foursome, the game, struck him—as it has struck millions since—as delicious and formidable and miraculous. Ward was "soon busy with a cleek."

Golf in America at the turn of the century was, and would remain for decades, the near-exclusive domain of the upper classes. The game requires a large and intricate physical plant, and before long golfers joined resources to form private clubs.

At first Ward was undoubtedly a guest at friends' clubs—his social status a bit "mean" for the club standards of the time. In 1898, a friend, Mortimer Singer, managed to nominate Ward, successfully, for membership in the Lawrence Harbor Club, in Morgan, New Jersey. Soon enough, Ward was playing regularly at Lawrence Harbor, and competitively, *for* Lawrence Harbor, at other courses. In short order, he became a member of clubs in Hollywood, New Jersey; Montclair, New Jersey; Fox Hills, Staten Island; Westbrook, Connecticut; and finally, about 1909, Garden City, on Long Island. Garden City would become his home club.

To modern eyes, full membership in so many clubs is astonishing, if for no other reason than the expense. At the turn of the century, however, multiple club memberships were not uncommon. A system of "linked privileges" was in place, and, perhaps more importantly, membership costs were a fraction of today's. At one Long Island course, for example, what we would call a resort course or a semipublic course, guests at the nearby hotel could play eighteen holes for a dollar (caddies were an extra $.30 plus tip) and nonguests could buy a season pass for $15.

But then, as now, membership in private clubs was self-regulating. One had to be invited to join by a member, and one had to have the spare time: a round of golf can take four hours, and in those days, merely getting to various clubs, far out on the end of Long Island or in the wilderness of

New Jersey, would make eighteen holes a day's excursion—something quite out of the realm of possibility even for most of the middle class.

Ward was, as well, a popular man on the links. From all accounts he was a wonderful golf partner—educated, a good conversationalist, well behaved (neither boisterous nor a social climber), ethical, a stickler for the game's etiquette, and a ferocious competitor. He was also an excellent golfer. In those days, the professional game was, if not an afterthought, far less important in the public eye than the amateur game. Professionals were basically instructors, and considered a rough-hewn lot of scapegraces. Interclub competition was extremely important. Ward was, therefore, likely courted by many clubs. So, ironically, in the seemingly genteel world of amateur golf, Ward finally found himself a free agent in a truly open market—a situation beyond his most fanciful baseball dreams.

His final choice of Garden City as a home club was telling. Of course the club was convenient—he had moved to nearby Babylon, Long Island, around 1907—but more importantly, Garden City was not a country club: it was a golf club, created *by* serious golfers *for* serious golfers. The course was long—6,000 yards in 1899—and rugged and treacherous, enough so to attract the world's best golfers. Garden City was the venue for the 1902 U.S. Open, and the 1900, 1908, 1913, and 1936 U.S. Amateur Championships.

Women were welcome, or at least not overtly forbidden, at Garden City. But the difficulty of the course led it to become known as an "Eveless Eden."

How avid was Ward the golfer? As avid as he was a baseball player, scraping together a winning run with a mad dash to home from second on a teammate's infield single. (Though he did not think golf was a game for the young: "While I think [it] is a great game . . . there is none of the spice of baseball in it for the boy.") As avid as he was a law student, burning the midnight oil on those endless train trips while his teammates played cards and drank and whored. As avid as he was a baseball manager, a lawyer, a bicyclist. Avid enough to move for a year or so, in 1906, to Montclair, New Jersey, home of his favorite club at that time. Avid enough, soon after that, to move to Babylon, on Long Island, to be closer to Garden City. Avid enough, despite the pressures of a successful law practice in the heart of the heart of the city, to golf three and four times a week.

How good was Ward the golfer? Excellent. He hovered between scratch golf and a five handicap. He was the best golfer in the club and one of the best golfers in the state. In 1909 he was described, matter-of-factly, as one of the "first ten players in the amateur lists." He was a good enough golfer, on the right day, to beat some of the best players in the world; good enough to play winning golf against the visiting Oxford-Cambridge Golfing Society in 1904; to win the New Jersey state championship in 1905; to be a member of the New York team in the prestigious Lesley Cup championships (later known as the Tri-City—New York, Boston, and Philadelphia—Championships) for thirteen years.

In 1907, in the Tri-City, he teamed up with Findlay S. Douglas, two-time runner-up in the U.S. Amateur Championships. The two best-balled themselves to a 77 for eighteen, beating Walter J. Travis and his partner. Walter Travis had been the U.S. Amateur Champion in 1900, 1901, and 1903 and the British Amateur Champion in 1904. Ward and Douglas also beat Jerry Travers and his partner in 1907; Travers was a four-time U.S. Amateur champion, as well as the 1915 U.S. Open champion.

In 1911, in the Metropolitan (New York) championship qualifying round, Ward shot a 156—five strokes better than Travers, five strokes better than Travis.

In 1915 and 1916 he won the Garden City Club Championship, a competition that Walter Travis had won seven of eight previous times and would win again in 1918.

In 1907, 1908, 1910, 1913, and 1916, Ward made it to the round of thirty-two—the first "championship" round—of the U.S. Amateur Championship, beating out about 120 of the country's best golfers before being eliminated. In 1908 he made it to the round of sixteen before elimination.

On and on it goes: prizes from Ekwanok (ten), Montclair and Fox Hills (eight each), Shinnecock (four), Lawrence Harbor (three). In 1922, when he was sixty-two years old, he won the Nassau (Long Island) championship. He founded the Long Island Golf Association, was its first president, and organized that association's father-and-son tournament, donating a prize—the John M. Ward Cup—to the winners.

In 1905 or 1906, he traveled to Europe. There he played at St. Andrews, Troon, Muirfield, and Prestwick. He played with Ben Sayers, former British Open runner-up; with Harry Vardon, 1900 U.S. Open champion and four-time British Open champion; with Arnaud Massy, 1907 British Open champion; and with Robert Maxwell, two-time British Amateur champion. He played in Paris, in Baden-Baden, at St. Moritz.

Ward's house "bristled" with trophies: "book shelves, tables, brackets, sideboards, mantels and window sills are loaded with reminders of his prowess: cups, umbrellas, clocks, chafing dishes, vases, and medals."

In late August or early September 1903, Ward applied for a modification of his 1893 divorce decree from Helen, which had prohibited him from marrying again during her lifetime. He stated that during the past decade his life had been "uniformly good." Two friends, Thomas Gooderson and Ned Hanlon (a former outfielder, Brotherhood member, and Baltimore manager, at the time managing the Brooklyn NL team), presented affidavits stating that Ward had, for the last five years, led an "irreproachable life." Within two weeks of the application, Justice Herrick of the New York Supreme Court relieved Ward of the marriage-prohibition injunction.

On Thursday, September 17, Ward married Katherine Waas, the daughter of Mr. and Mrs. John Waas, of Brooklyn. The Reverend Dr. Newell Dwight Hillis of Brooklyn's Plymouth Church—where Henry Ward Beecher had preached for forty years—performed the ceremony. *Sporting Life*, under the headline "Ward's Venture," carried news of the marriage and extended to its "old friend . . . heartiest congratulations and [wished] him and his bride long life, good fortune and unmeasured happiness."

Katherine—twenty-six when she married Ward—was, in many ways, Helen's opposite. She was five feet six and trim; the family remembers her "wonderful figure." She had a wide mouth, a strong chin, very large, round, dark eyes, and a thick, flowing mane of bright brown hair. The few pictures of her that have survived show her smiling as if she just couldn't help herself.

She was headstrong and athletic—Ward met her on a golf course—and a thoroughly modern woman, even a bit of a tomboy. She shot skeet, hunted, and fished. She likely played golf with Ward on their tour of the great courses of Europe. She probably played billiards and lawn tennis as well and without qualification endorsed the thoughts of John Gilmer Speed, who wrote in an 1894 issue of the *Ladies' Home Journal*:

With golf links in every neighborhood there is no reason why the middle-aged woman should fasten herself in a rocking chair and consent to be regarded by youngsters around her as antiquated at forty-five. Instead of that, she can, with her golfing club, follow her ball from link to link, renewing her beauty and her youth by exercise in the open air.

After Ward died, Katherine, who was a favorite of Ward's extended family, regularly visited Bellefonte. Katherine still golfed—at least through the beginning of World War II, when she was in her mid sixties. She had a perpetual tan and had become something of an eccentric. She packed very lightly (her raincoat doubled as her robe) and was something of a health fanatic. During one visit she would eat only protein. During another visit she would eat only carbohydrates. One of the Bellefonte relatives found her a bit exasperating: "I can't stand to sit at the table with her," he said. "She's so observant of what everyone is eating." For her part, Katherine said, "I don't want to live forever, I just want to be healthy when I die."

Not much of Katherine's life after the death of Ward is known. She moved to Florida, and every Christmas sent the Bellefonte relatives a box of oranges, signing her card "Aunt Katherine." In 1964, toward the end of her life, Katherine began corresponding with Lee Allen, the Baseball Hall of Fame historian, who was gathering biographical information prior to Ward's induction into the Hall later that year.

"I did not meet Mr. Ward until after he had retired from baseball and [was] already practicing law and playing golf," Katherine wrote Allen from her winter home in St. Petersburg, Florida.

> It was on a golf course that I met him. . . . Mr. Ward was very loyal to baseball and took me to many games. He even showed me the Polo Grounds, which he said had been named for a wonderful old hunting dog that he had. . . . Mr. Ward was an all-around active sportsman [who] liked to fish for trout during the short season in the lake on our place in Babylon. Mr. Ward was married to a Helen Gibson when he was twenty-seven years old. . . . Mr. Ward told me all about it before we were married, and after, we never spoke of her again.

Katherine apologized to Allen for being unable to attend the Hall of Fame induction ceremonies that summer. "A few years ago I had a bad fall in the mountains, so I travel little now."

Over the years of her visits to Bellefonte, she sometimes brought some of Ward's things with her, leaving them with the distant kin who remained around the Bellefonte area: a polar bear rug, stuffed animals, sterling silver plates, a three-handled loving cup that Ward had won in 1903 at a golf tournament in Pinehurst, North Carolina. Though she was a practical, unsentimental woman, during one visit, in the course of describing one of their winter trips south, she paused and said simply, "God, how I loved that man."

There were little disappointments and setbacks during Ward's and Katherine's twenty-two years together. Ward hurt his back in an automobile accident in 1913. During World War I he volunteered to close down his law practice and go overseas as a YMCA fitness instructor, but, much to his dismay, never received a call. Generally, however, life was very good for the Wards.

In 1906 the couple bought about 200 acres, formerly a rod and reel club, in North Babylon, Long Island, then about an hour's travel east from the Brooklyn Bridge. Ward would attend to business a few hours a day a few days a week at his Manhattan office—he had moved to 36 West 44th Street, a block whose tenants included the Harvard Club and the New York Yacht Club—but most of his time was spent either on the golf course or on his land.

The land included a twenty-seven-acre pond, fed by three creeks that flowed year around and were, according to Ward, "almost as wild in their upper reaches as the most obscure leads I ever encountered in excursions into the Everglades." In the winter, the pond served as a source of ice for Ward's local business interest, the Babylon Fuel and Supply Company, on Carll Avenue.

On the land's "tangled thickets" were squirrels, wild ducks, quail, raccoons, pheasants, blue herons, mink, grouse, foxes, skunks, and a large variety of songbirds. Ward also raised livestock: he had ten cows, three horses; and 500 "pedigree" chickens. He also had pigeons, a pack of hunting dogs—his favorite was a golden retriever named Bob—and a cat: Evelyn Nesbit Thaw Ward.

The animals, excepting the birds, all had names. One of the cows was named Klondike. Ward had bought the animal from a crew of sandhogs building a railroad tunnel under the East River. Klondike, evidently, had fallen from a barge or steamer, and was swimming down the East River by Hell's Gate when the men rescued her, keeping her as a good-luck mascot.

Ward cultivated most of his land, the fields "mapped off like a checkerboard in squares, on which various fertilizers and combinations have been tested on cereals, vegetables, alfalfa, etc." He received varieties of seed from "Uncle Sam" and in turn supplied extension agents with exact reports on their viability.

The farmhouse was wired for electricity, but Ward had a small acety-lene gas plant installed for emergencies.

When asked if he ever got lonely, Ward howled with laughter.

There's something doing every minute on a farm. One day the Irish terrier has puppies under the house piazza and I have to crawl in on my stomach and pull them out with a rake. . . . The next day the servant girl sprains her ankle. . . . Another day I have to attend to the squirrels' commissary department because they are getting so lazy they won't pick up nuts under the clump of chestnuts in which their winter hoarding is placed.

Probably the best indication of Ward's contentment came to light in an article written not long before his death. Ward, in what would be his last published interview, roamed far and wide down memory lane, talking about the good old days and Polo Grounds crowds of 20,000. He spoke fondly of old teammates and even brought up his old enemy Buck Ewing without rancor. "Buck . . . had come to New York from Troy," Ward said. "[He] was the captain and did nearly all the catching. Poor Buck—he's dead."

Thirty

He Wore a Uniform for Seventeen Years

N 1921, at the annual May invitational at Garden City, the sixty-one-year-old Ward eclipsed 105 other golfers with a bright qualifying round of 75. His performance was "extraordinary . . . considering the blustery breezes" that day.

That winter, he contracted pneumonia, after which he was never again in "robust health." His illness, however, did not keep him from his appointed rounds. He continued to golf—though his days of formal competition were effectively behind him—work his land and stay active in the Elks and Babylon Masonic Lodge 793.

Returning to New York after a brief Bahamas golfing and fishing trip, Ward, on February 2, 1925, attended the National League Jubilee, held to celebrate forty-nine years of existence, at the Broadway Central Hotel, the site of the organization's founding.

The world was there: John Heydler, the League president, club owners, sportswriters, and players galore—such an "outpouring of old and new timers," in fact, that the occasion, which included a buffet and the usual endless succession of speeches, had to be moved from the small parlors of the original 1876 meeting to the hotel's grand ballroom.

Billy Sunday, an old-timer who had left the ballfield to become America's most famous evangelist, sent a telegram that said that he loved the game "with every drop of blood" in his body, and that every time he saw a grandstand of a base ball diamond, the blood surged through his veins "like a fire pressure."

The men honored the dead, including A. G. Spalding, William Hulbert, Nick Young, and Morgan S. Bulkeley, the founders of the National League, and then settled in for a long afternoon of platitude and hearty self-congratulation. Christy Mathewson, the celebrated New York Giants pitcher, spoke, as did Barney Dreyfuss, the Pittsburgh NL team owner who had so opposed Ward's candidacy for NL president. Others stood and were recognized: Tom York, Ward's old Providence teammate from whom he had bought his ill-fated Baseball Emporium; Jim Mutrie, Ward's old manager; and many others. The multitude cheered themselves to the echo. All was well in baseball America.

At long last John Ward spoke. He made a joke at the expense of Ban Johnson, about a dust-up the previous fall in which Johnson had demanded that baseball commissioner Kenesaw Mountain Landis call off the World Series in light of some New York Giants being accused of gambling and game-throwing. It was impossible, Ward said, "to change human nature." But, he went on, "I want to say that I wore a uniform for seventeen years and I am proud that never in that time did I see a move that looked to be anything but straight."

Ward waited for the applause to die down and launched into delicate—perhaps, considering the occasion, indelicate—territory. He may have been tipsy; he may have taken umbrage at the love feast that had been going on. Or he might have felt a premonition of his own death—he had been feeling under the weather for some weeks. Whatever the reason, as he spoke, the event's organizers must have gagged on their cigars and cursed the fool who had invited Ward, that damned troublemaker, to speak.

Looking out over the owners past and present—among them Dreyfuss and the miserly Soden of Boston—Ward did not evoke memories of the golden days of yore; he did not trace the outline of League progress, or expound on the cleverness of all present. Instead, he mounted a spirited defense of both the Brotherhood and the Players' League, which included a brief but pointed explanation of why, fully thirty-five years earlier, the players had been right and the owners—some of them still alive, some of them in that very room—wrong. He detailed the working conditions of the times, and many of the players' gripes big and small. Pausing again, he brought up the straw that had broken the camel's back—the long-forgotten-by-almost-everyone-but-him Brush classification scheme.

> This salary [system] was based on what the weakest club in the
> league could afford, and it was this leveling process which drove
> the players into a brotherhood.

There was no report of the reaction to Ward's remarks, but the *Times*, slyly, printed its banquet story on the same page as an item about a bill introduced by New York City congressman Fiorello La Guardia. La Guardia's bill (which never passed) would have levied a 90 percent federal tax on the sale of professional baseball players whenever the selling price exceeded $5,000. The proposal was tempered by mercy: the tax would not be assessed if the player received an amount equal to the purchase price. La Guardia noted that professional baseball was unique, an enterprise in which "an individual failed to profit through improved ability and transfer of his services." John Ward, reading the paper at breakfast that morning, must have howled with glee.

Twenty-eight days later, at 4:35 on the afternoon of March 4, 1925, at University Hospital in Augusta, Georgia, John Ward died of acute lobar pneumonia. Katherine was beside his bed. Ward had turned sixty-five years old the day before.

Two weeks earlier, he and Katherine had headed south again, to winter with their friends, Mr. and Mrs. Alfred Bourne, at the Bourne winter home in Pinehurst, North Carolina. Alfred was the son of Frederick Gilbert Bourne, financier, yachtsman (he was best known as Commodore Bourne of the New York Yacht Club), clubman, and former president of the Singer Sewing Machine Company. Alfred was twenty-five years younger than Ward and one of his Garden City golfing partners. When he died in 1956, he was described as an "athletics patron."

While hunting with Bourne in Georgia, Ward had fallen ill and was taken to the hospital. Katherine, at Pinehurst, rushed to Augusta. Ward lay in bed five days, without noticeable improvement, before he died. On the transit permit, which allowed the body to be sent north, Ward's name was mistyped. It read: Mr. James Montgomery Ward.

On Saturday, March 7, Ward's funeral took place at West Islip Christ

Episcopal Church on Long Island. More than two hundred people attended, including state senators, New York City judges, the former president of the Brooklyn & Coney Island Railroad, the deputy fire chief of New York City, and Charles Stoneham, owner of the Giants. The Professional Golfers Association sent a wreath, as did the National League, the Brooklyn NL team, several local baseball clubs, the Giants' manager John McGraw, and "many other" prominent baseball people.

Ward was not buried that day. The body remained in a vault until Katherine decided that instead of taking her husband back to Bellefonte, she would bury him on Long Island. He is in Lot 185, Section 2 of the Greenfield Cemetery in Hempstead. Katherine, who died in 1966, lies beside him. Their gravestone is a handsome rectangle, guarded on either end by bushes and engraved with the couple's names and dates. An easy throw west sits a school and a baseball diamond.

You might visit there late on a cool December weekday afternoon, with the sun low and bright, shooting through bare-branched trees onto the cemetery greensward. The ballfield is deserted, the two-lane not far from John and Katherine's graves mostly free of traffic, free enough anyway to hear the busy twitter of small birds in leafless trees. Ward, Katherine once said, wanted to lie where "a pheasant might run over my grave once in a while."

The sun is almost gone; it's time to leave. As you head to the car you look south, across the cemetery. Some Canada geese—there are one hundred or so—are busy going about goose business, walking toward you in their fat-hipped, preposterous, proprietary way. Geese'll do fine, just fine.

On July 27, 1964, Ward was inducted into the Baseball Hall of Fame in Cooperstown, New York, with five others, including Tim Keefe, Ward's old teammate and former brother-in-law.

The day was humid and hot, 93 degrees in nearby Albany. Mrs. Babe Ruth was there, as well as many other earlier inductees and their wives. Many of them were old and tottered about on canes. One fainted in the heat. Representing Ward were William J. Watson and Barbara Fleming Watson, the great-grandchildren of Ward's cousin Isabella; Winifred Fleming Watson, William's and Barbara's mother; John Montgomery Fleming, Winifred's brother; Ruth Koenig, Ward's brother Charles's granddaughter; and Maria Koenig, Ruth's eleven-year-old daughter.

Baseball commissioner Ford Frick did not dispel his reputation as one of the sport's blandest men. He virtually repeated what is carved on Ward's ghastly Hall of Fame plaque: "He played a key role in establishing the patterns of baseball as we know it."

Then came lunch at a lakeside inn, a generous buffet: chicken salad, tuna salad, potato salad, macaroni salad, shrimp salad, ham, turkey, baked beans, roast beef, relishes, hot dogs, hamburgers, fruit salad, fresh fruit, cakes, pies, and, most spectacular of all, a huge centerpiece ice sculpture of a baseball player. Photographers frantically herded elderly ballplayers and their relatives to pose for commemorative shots.

The crowd then moved to nearby Doubleday Field for the annual game. The teams were two of the major leagues' worst: the New York Mets, twenty-eight games out of first with a record of 30–70, and the Washington Senators, twenty-five and one-half games out of first and 38–65. The Senators won 6–4, in a dull game that took two hours and twenty-three minutes to play. Attendance was 9,791.

The Koenigs, Watsons, and Flemings, suffering from the heat, left before the game's end. Winifred—a lifelong baseball crank—wrote her mother that the Mets had played "their usual . . . Little League baseball."

Winifred had sat next to Lola, her brother John's wife. Lola had attended many minor league games back in Arkansas, but never a major league game, and Winifred told her mother that she regretted the choice of teams in Cooperstown that day. "I do wish Lola could have seen a real demonstration of big league ball," she wrote. "Lola said, and it was true, 'They don't look as good as the Little Rock Travelers.' "

Afterword and Acknowledgments

DURING THE NEARLY FOUR YEARS I've spent researching and writing this book, a few things happened: I sneezed repeatedly in dusty archives; went half-blind in front of microform machines; badgered librarians, court clerks, baseball experts; checked and rechecked conflicting accounts of events major and minor, and spent sinful scores of hours playing solitaire on my laptop. (Which, in a fit of writerly despondency, I almost threw against my office wall. But only once.)

All this hoping to bring to life, with at least a semblance of accuracy and measure, a man too long overlooked.

Things got a little goofy at times out there brushing the back trails of twelve states. One day, after many hours in the Pennsylvania State University library, I walked to a complex of science buildings where, I had ascertained, John Ward had once played ball with his scofflaw schoolmates. Students were still in the labs, packing things into their backpacks, or seated at benches pouring things and wearing safety glasses. There was a hallway display entitled "The Common Ion Effect: A Small Scale Approach." I found the explanation very confusing. I walked around and around, and finally found myself, I decided, on the site of Penn State's original baseball diamond. It had become a parking lot. I stood in the middle of the mostly empty lot, closed my eyes, and tried to—this is a little embarrassing—*feel* John Ward's spirit there, hoping that, somehow, it would well up through the asphalt and wish me luck, point me in the right direction, give me a pep talk or some kind of damn sign that I was worthy. About twenty seconds into my unsuccessful conjuring, a car—it was a silver Honda Civic—honked its horn behind me. I dropped my briefcase and jumped two feet into the air. I tried to explain myself to the alarmed driver but finally gave up—the more I babbled the more the driver, I could tell, became convinced I was a lunatic.

A few days later, I was driving around campus and came upon the football stadium: Beaver Stadium. I could hardly miss it. In the middle of those soft, humpy hills, Beaver is a profanity. It could have been an aircraft carrier in some unimaginably dry dock. From afar it had a semblance of integrity—smooth, beveled, contained, balanced, gable-like with its press-box superstructure. But up close it was grim and industrial and mean. Like a cathedral, its purpose seemed to celebrate something far larger than mere man, but Beaver was more like an anti-cathedral, its purpose not to uplift, inspire, instill awe, but instead to grind one down, to scold: you were part of a mass, an atom, a visitor at best, mortal and puny. Giants play here; you watch. It was an abrasive, belittling holding pen. Across the street was the current baseball diamond—you could have dropped it into Beaver Field whole and no one would have noticed. Some young men were playing ball—no crowds, no uniforms, no boosters, no television. How quaint. How calming. How wonderfully, innocently opposed it was to big bad Beaver.

I spent a lot of time in the Centre County Historical Museum and Library in Bellefonte across from a guy who was, like me, using a laptop computer. Mine, however, was not stamped with an identification number and a tag reading "Property of City of Cupertino, California."

In a bistro in Great Barrington, Massachusetts, where I had dinner one night with my niece, there hung, just behind our table, a photo of John Ward and the 1885 New York baseball team. Maybe that was Ward's nod to me.

In Ellensburg, Washington, a fellow came up to me at the microfilm machine and asked the nature of my research. I told him. He shook his head sadly, told me I was barking up the wrong tree, that the story needing telling was the long relationship between baseball and world domination. Baseball players, he said, travel everywhere in the world. Wherever they go, women are attracted to them. Women who tell them things and women to whom the players tell things. State secrets. Then what happens to baseball players after their careers on the field are over? They become corporate vice-presidents. Don't get me started, he said. I heeded his advice.

Somewhere along the line, I got this notion that James Joyce had maybe attended a baseball game in Dublin during the Chicago/All-America tour of 1888–1889. (I didn't know it at the time, but Ward had already left the tour.) I was beside myself with some weird hope-against-hope that two fascinating men whose paths, by all rights, should never have crossed, were in the same place at the same time. Was it possible?

No help came from combing biographies or newspaper accounts. Finally, a friend suggested I "do," or whatever the verb is, the Internet. Someone found a Joyce discussion group and entered my queries. I got two replies. One saying that Joyce's attendance at the baseball game could be ruled out "authoritatively," since Joyce was barely seven years old at the time and the distance from his school to the baseball grounds would have required a trolley trip, with transfer, or a long omnibus ride, and besides, there was no record of a school field trip, and, most importantly, it was "not the sort of field trip you'd expect a Jesuit boarding school to undertake."

The other reply suggested—rather adamantly—that I read the Cyclops chapter of *Ulysses*

> . . . where there is a clear exchange of secret signals as the Citizen greets newcomers to the pub. The signals remind me of those between catcher and pitcher, between first base coach and runner . . . rubbing hand up inside of thigh, slapping knee, etc. My suspicion is that the signals went from Ireland to baseball rather than from baseball to Joyce . . .

Now, I've never seen a catcher *slapping* his knee, and I hope never to see a base coach rubbing the inside of his thigh. Without putting too fine a point on it, I thought the "Citizen" theory about the most curious thing I'd heard in ages. The writer concluded, huffily, that she had "suggested this baseball connection before, with absolutely zero response."

I know this guy in Ellensburg, Washington, you may like to speak to, I thought.

Every biographer—or everyone who writes a biography—I imagine, yearns for the unattainable. If the subject lived before photographs— Genghis Khan, say—the writer might like to see a photograph. If there were photographs but no recordings of the subject—Abraham Lincoln, say—he might yearn for a sample of his voice. What I came to want, over the years, was a moving picture of John Ward. Not necessarily of him playing—that I can imagine—but of him walking. Down the street maybe. Across a field with his shotgun, looking for birds; across the out-field toward home plate with his teammates, before a game; toward the green after his approach shot on a par four; from his office to a restaurant. I've written that Ward was obsessed with his size, that he spent much of his life among bigger boys, bigger men. I guess the reason I'd like to see him walk is to verify my opinion. Did he stride long, playing catch-up, keep-up? Or was he possessed of that curious gait of so many extraordinary athletes—a mincing, pigeon-toed, double-time, almost hobbled-looking thing—with every step ending in an aggressive heel-lift? Now I'm tall. Now I'm tall. Now I'm tall.

But there are no moving pictures of Ward, relatively few stills, to date almost no discovered correspondence beyond a few business letters, and no journals. So I made do, imagining myself as John Ward. I did this most fervently in Bellefonte. I stood in front of Ward's boyhood homes, wandered down to the old fairgrounds, walked outlying fields.

In general I liked Bellefonte. After a couple of days there, people began to recognize me. They'd greet me, ask what I thought of their town. After a couple more days, people in restaurants had begun greeting me by name. After a couple more days, people I had never met would stop me on the street and ask how the book was going. One day—it was a bright, warm, breezy autumn Sunday—I took a long walk. The center of town was quiet, the streets all but empty. Two women carried boxes of canning supplies from G. C. Murphy's variety store—the only downtown business I saw open. Three boys on fat-tire bikes whizzed past me. A man with an untucked shirt and white socks and blue jeans and scuffed shoes sat on some stairs—I could feel his hangover from across the street.

I walked to the old train station and the nearby greensward, a lovely commons reclaimed and groomed by the city fathers. A man read a book on a bench. A couple sat—his arm around her shoulder—and talked about the next day and the next and the rest of their lives. Birds chirped. Had a small boy in a sailor suit run by worrying a hoop with a stick, had a woman walked by shading her pale skin with a parasol, had Mole and Rat drifted down Spring Creek with a picnic basket—I doubt I'd have blinked an eye.

But even time-travelers get hungry. The waffle shop was closed; Schnitzel's Tavern and Kaffee Haus was closed. So was the Chinese, and the Diamond Deli, and the Italian tucked away near the Catholic church, and the Gamble Mill Tavern. Someone told me Bonfatto's—near the site where the Mills Brothers' grandfather had had his barber shop—was open, but I couldn't find it. I decided to go to a nearby convenience store and get a sandwich and a beer for a solitary picnic. Bellefonte, the clerk told me—a little sniffily, I thought—doesn't sell alcohol on Sundays.

"Go to State College"—twelve miles southwest, home of Penn State University—"you can get anything there," she said.

So I drove, into traffic, past major malls, warehouses, franchise joints, muffler shops and motor inns, to the college town, where the modern world, as characterized by brutal, boring youth, was in full weekend bloom: the very air shook from monstrous car stereos; a couple terminated a fearful argument by screaming filthy names at each other; a crying coed was comforted by a dry-eyed coed: "He's not worth it, I say that as your friend." Everywhere, ridiculously swaggering Betas and Kappas and Alphas and Sigmas and Phis leaned on car hoods and burped the night-before's beer. In a private parking lot, bright Notices of Violation flapped like tournament pennants; a shattered beer bottle lay on the pavement next to a diner; the main supporting industry seemed to be Penn State souvenirs.

I found a sports bar. I ate a hamburger and drank a couple of beers. The place was ringed with televisions and thick with overweight males— their faces bland and indistinguishable as police sketches—who wore Penn State sweatshirts and baseball caps and drank pitchers of beer and grazed on platters of french fries and made notation after notation on their football fantasy league scoresheets and brayed with joy or frustration as scores of other games appeared under the featured contest.

I felt old and vastly superior: these louts are they, I decided, who will grow up to attend professional athletic contests with painted faces and no shirts and almost-clever signs they hope will be featured on SportsCenter.

I drove back to Bellefonte, wishing I had some Trollope to read, but the earlier spell had been broken: the afternoon warmth had fled and the light had turned flat, and everyone, I imagined, was eating Sunday supper, surrounded by family, while I was a lonely traveler far from home. I went to my motel to wallow in self-pity. It's part of a writer's job.

By the next morning I had decided, should anyone ask, that both Bellefonte and State College seemed grand and true and desirable places. Me? I'd prefer to grow up in the bustle and excitement and seethe of State College. Then I would move to Bellefonte, soak up its cloistered, calm rectitude, its Edwardian gentility—as many State College visionaries are doing now—but only after I had matured, become tasteful, and had twice my fill of low, drastic fun.

Just up the road, Renovo, where Ward played his first officially professional game, was miles removed from comfortable, bourgeois, prosperous Bellefonte. There seemed little work there in that old railroad town, with its many boarded-up businesses. Lots of Renovo's residents are forced to drive to work in Lock Haven each day along a twisting, riverside highway that can be an icy, puckering piece of work in winter. But despite Renovo's lean and meager state—signs for its annual Flaming Foliage Festival lined the highway like so many beaks of hungry nestlings—it also seemed a decent, sturdy place.

Until I met some living, breathing Renovans. They—the ones I met—were young men, working on curbside cars. When I asked them for directions to the library (That way.) or if they had ever heard of John Montgomery Ward (Is he black?), they looked at me, as they answered, as if I had instead asked if any of their sisters were for rent. When Ward hopped off the caboose there in 1877, bustling Renovo's premier nine called themselves the Resolutes, and its muffins the Actives. If the town had teams today, I would name them the Sinisters and the Surlys.

But mostly I had a good time on the road, and occasionally I experienced delightful, dizzying coincidences that made me feel that, somehow, John Ward and I were meant to be distantly linked.

In Harrisburg, Pennsylvania, at the airport car-rental counter a large sign informed all that not only was this the Thrifty franchise, but as well the agency for Montgomery Ward car rentals. Later, driving around town, I saw an old man shambling along a riverside road: he was a deadringer for one of my favorite minor characters in American literature: Kerouac's

Ghost of the Susquehanna: "Can't tell me I don't know my way around here . . . I'm headed for Canady."

I discovered that John Ward's last Manhattan law office, on Forty-fourth Street, was only a couple of doors away from the north entrance to a building where I had worked several years ago.

When I was writing about John Ward's retirement, I blew out my last good knee playing softball, trying to stretch a double into a triple. Soon after I underwent my fourth knee operation in eighteen years and retired from organized ball. By the time I came to write about John Ward's golf career, I, too, had found that new sport and was whacking and hacking away with the unreasonable passion of the newly converted.

Lastly, I once, as a teenager, struck out (on three pitches) against Gary Sutherland, the brother of Darrell Sutherland, the Mets' starting pitcher in the Hall of Fame game in Cooperstown in 1964, the year John Ward was inducted. This tickles me, but I do not mean to suggest even the slightest sort of athletic bond between John Ward and me. To do that would be ludicrous, like a barn painter greeting Paul Cezanne with a hearty "Bon ami! Let us talk of things, my brother of the pigment!"

Without librarians and friends and experts and expert friends, a biographer's word-flight would be impossible. He might *want* to arrive at a distant, new place, but he might as well be sitting in a quarter-a-ride red jet in front of a supermarket. Without a quarter.

I thank the following: Don Spritzer and Vaun Stevens of the Missoula City-County Library; Holly Laslovich, Amanda Ward, Shawn Lake, Dorenda Berry, Kathy Ford, Patricia Collins, Shannon Seltzer, Doug Booth, Julia Jackman-Brink, and Rod Tschida of the University of Montana Mansfield Library, who, despite the neglect of the governor, the state legislature, and the board of regents, somehow maintain their enthusiasm and good cheer; Alice Walker of the Augusta, Georgia, public library; Joyce Adgate and Gladys Murray of the Centre County Library Historical Museum; Adrien Taylor and Barbara Thimsen of Boise State University's Albertsons Library; Brian Bach, Mae Marey, Kirsten Tozer, and Thomas Yeh of the Central Washington University library; Whitney Bagnell of the Columbia University Law School Library; Rhea Pliakis of the Columbia University Archives and Columbiana Library; Rick Ewig of the University of Wyoming American Heritage Center; Robert K. Lacerte and

Nancy Bunker of the Whitworth College (Washington) Library; Anne Ostendarp of Baker Library, Dartmouth College; Nancy Markee, Joan Adams, Marcy Bouton, and Jeanne Hatch of the Baker Library Jones Microtext Center; Jackie Esposito, Michelle Dyzak, and Lee Stout of Penn State's Pattee Library; Marjorie Hinman and Charles Browne of the Broome County, New York, Historical Society; John Santos of the Providence Public Library; Christine Hastreiter of the Rhode Island Historical Society; Alfred Thomas, librarian of the Arkansas *Democrat-Gazette*; Patty Moran of the United States Golf Association; Ruth Albin of the Babylon Historical Society; Louisa Bann of Tiffany and Co.'s archives; Geoffrey Sumi of Mt. Holyoke College Classics Department; S. Queak, of the Evans Memorial Library, Missoula; and Tim Wiles, Jim Gates, Milo Stewart, Darci Harrington, Bruce Markusen, and Scot Mondore of Cooperstown's National Baseball Library.

Many Society for American Baseball Research members gave generously of their time and expertise, including Mark Alvarez, Dennis Bingham, Larry Bowman, Rob Elias, Frederick Ivor-Campbell, Pete Palmer, Tom Shieber, and John Thorn.

In the greater central Pennsylvania area, the following folks were my guides and hosts: Mark Amdahl, Mike Bezilla, Catherine Brown, Charles Brown, Steven Furst, Roxie Ishler, Joan McMullen, Romayne Naylor, and Ronald A. Smith. I'd especially like to thank Hugh Manchester.

Thank you, as well, to Julia Mitchell, Maria Sinn, William Wharton, Mary Fleming, and Evelyn Beem. I hope I did well by your distant kinsman.

Jerry Shea made sense of old Denver real estate records; Lee Lowenfish and Cynthia Bass recognized Ward's place in history many years before anyone else. Mike Lynch, in New Haven, found vital records. Bruce Abrams, Assistant Archivist in the New York Supreme Court, provided me, thanks to his persistent, enthusiastic research, with one of the best days of this project. Bob Gelzheiser passed me his invaluable master's thesis.

Thanks to Andrew Wylie and Jin Auh of the Wylie Agency.

Leonor Lange Morton leads a busy life. Nonetheless, several times she dropped all and ran down lead after lead on Long Island, amplifying her findings wonderfully with an artist's eye for texture and details. Mike Lancaster helped with medical research. Larry Howell translated, and put in context, one seemingly indecipherable court document after another.

David Meggyesy of the National Football League Players Association was the first guy to twist my mind about both the business and the deep, strange grandness of sport.

John Whiston was my designated reader, and a very good one.

Walter Havighurst, the copy editor of this book, re-tarped a loose and flapping cargo with consummate skill.

Thanks to Bill Finnegan, Shan Guisinger, and James Welch for leading me on. Thanks especially to my mom and dad, Dorothy and Vincent Di Salvatore.

Steve Meyers, my friend since nursery school, picked up many loose research ends for me down in Boise. He died suddenly in 1997. Rest in peace, SW. I wish you were around to read this.

Finally, without the help of my wife, Deirdre McNamer, this book wouldn't exist and I'd be a babbling idiot. Not only did she read the manuscript and read it again, and edit it, and make invaluable suggestions, but she stuck by me and loved me and believed in me—even on those extremely rare days when I was an operatically insufferable jerk.

Appendix I: Players' Salaries vs. Average American Wage, 1876–1920

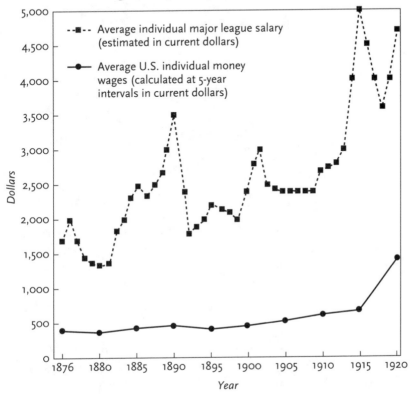

From *Never Just a Game: Players, Owners, and American Baseball to 1920* by Robert F. Burk. Copyright © 1994 by the University of North Carolina Press. Reprinted by permission of the University of North Carolina Press.

Appendix II: John Montgomery Ward Career Statistics

Minor League Batting and Fielding Record

Year	Club	League	G	AB	R	H	2B	3B	HR	RBI	SB	BA	Pos	FA
1877	Athletic	—	6	27	3	7	2	0	0	—	—	.259	p	.846
"	Philadelphia	—	3	10	1	2	0	0	0	—	—	.200	p	.825
"	JanesvMutual	—	14	61	4	14	—	—	—	—	—	.230	p	.860
"	Buffalo	—	10	26	2	5	—	—	—	—	—	.192	rf-p	.667
1878	BghtCrickets	IA	30	107	11	21	2	0	0	—	—	.196	p-rf	.821

Major League Batting and Fielding Record

Year	Club	League	G	AB	R	H	2B	3B	HR	RBI	SB	BA	Pos	FA
1878	Providence	NL	37	138	14	27	5	4	1	15	—	.196	p	.866
1879	Providence	NL	83	364	71	104	9	4	2	41	—	.286	p-3b	.938
1880	Providence	NL	86	356	53	81	12	2	0	27	—	.228	p-3b	.983
1881	Providence	NL	85	357	56	87	18	6	0	53	—	.244	of-p	.887
1882	Providence	NL	83	355	58	87	10	3	1	39	—	.245	of-p	.824
1883	New York	NL	88	380	76	97	18	7	7	54	—	.255	of-p	.859
1884	New York	NL	113	482	98	122	11	8	2	51	—	.253	of-2	.847
1885	New York	NL	111	446	72	101	8	9	0	37	—	.226	ss	.904
1886	New York	NL	122	491	82	134	17	5	2	81	36	.273	ss	.870
1887	New York	NL	129	545	114	184	16	5	1	53	111	.338	ss	.919
1888	New York	NL	122	510	70	128	14	5	2	49	38	.251	ss	.857
1889	New York	NL	114	479	87	143	13	4	1	67	62	.299	ss	.890
1890	Brooklyn	PL	128	561	134	188	15	12	4	60	63	.335	ss	.878
1891	Brooklyn	NL	105	441	85	122	13	5	0	39	57	.277	ss	.878
1892	Brooklyn	NL	148	614	109	163	13	3	1	47	88	.265	2b	.920
1893	New York	NL	135	588	129	193	27	9	2	77	46	.328	2b	.918
1894	New York	NL	136	540	100	143	12	5	0	77	39	.265	2b	.924
Major League Total			1825	7647	1408	2104	231	96	26	867	540	.275		.885

Minor League Pitching Record

Year	Club	League	GP	IP	W	L	Pct	ShO	R	H	BB	SO	ERA
1877	Athletic	—	6	54	5	1	.833	0	17	33	—	—	—
"	Philadelphia	—	3	27	2	1	.667	1	5	15	—	—	—
"	JanesvMutual	—	14	—	7	7	.500	0	74	91	—	—	—
"	Buffalo	—	3	16	0	3	.000	0	13	19	—	—	—
1878	BghtCrickets	IA	30	286	14	16	.467	4	165	252	—	—	—

Major League Pitching Record

Year	Club	League	GP	IP	W	L	Pct	ShO	R	H	BB	SO	ERA
1878	Providence	NL	37	334	22	13	.629	6	151	308	34	116	1.51
1879	Providence	NL	70	587	47	19	.712	2	270	571	36	239	2.15
1880	Providence	NL	70	595	39	24	.619	8	230	501	45	230	1.74
1881	Providence	NL	39	330	18	18	.500	3	183	326	53	119	2.13
1882	Providence	NL	33	278	19	12	.613	4	141	261	36	72	2.59
1883	New York	NL	34	277	16	13	.552	1	165	278	31	121	2.70
1884	New York	NL	9	60⅔	3	3	.500	0	43	72	18	23	3.41
Major League Total			292	2461⅔	164	102	.617	24	1348	2317	253	920	2.10

Minor league statistics courtesy of Robert Tiemann. Major league statistics courtesy of John Thorn and Pete Palmer, editors, *Total Baseball*, fifth edition. Copyright © 1999 by John Thorn and Pete Palmer. Reprinted by permission of The Viking Press, a division of Penguin Putnam, Inc.

Notes

Chapter One. *A LIGHT BIT OF A BOY*

page

3   *In all sizes:* Richard Topp, in his essay "Demographics," on page 410 in the 1989
    edition of *Total Baseball*, edited by John Thorn and Pete Palmer (New York:
    Warner Books), writes that between the years of 1880 and 1889, the average
    major league rookie stood a hair under five feet ten inches and weighed 170
    pounds. (The average major leaguer in 1989 stood a hair taller than six feet one
    inch and weighed 210.) In the 1995 edition of *Total Baseball*, Ward is listed at
    five feet nine inches and 165 pounds. These figures in Ward's case are unreli-
    able: they were gathered from second- and third-hand sources, the most likely
    being John Fleming, a distant cousin of Ward's who was a boy when Ward died.

    The only firsthand notations on Ward's vital statistics come from the April
    27, 1878, *Binghamton* (New York) *Daily Democrat*, which lists Ward as five feet
    eight inches and 140 pounds, and the March 25, 1885, *Sporting Life*, which lists
    him as five feet seven-and-one-half inches and 158 pounds. In team photos
    during his first few years in the National League, Ward, compared with team-
    mates Joe Start (listed at five feet nine inches) and Mike McGeary (listed at
    five feet seven inches) is clearly shorter than the former and imperceptibly
    taller than the latter. Start is listed in *Total Baseball* (4th ed.) at 165 pounds,
    McGeary at 138. Ward looks, if anything, even thinner than McGeary.

    If Ward's vital statistics are unreliable, so might be those of many nine-
    teenth-century ballplayers, including Start and McGeary. I have assumed here
    an "equality of unreliability."

    The nicknames and vital statistics of Ward's colleagues come from *Total
    Baseball* (4th ed.), *Nineteenth Century Stars*, and *Baseball's First Stars*.

    Except as noted, I have relied on *Total Baseball* throughout the book for base-

415

ball statistics, even when they are in contradiction with "firsthand" sources such as the Spalding *Base Ball Guide*. Over the years researchers have tracked down discrepancies—usually minor—in individual statistics. Record keeping in the nineteenth century was a much more informal affair than it is today. The summary of Ward's statistics includes a slight adjustment from the fourth edition of *Total Baseball*: Ward had 188 hits and a .335 batting average in 1890, and lifetime hits numbering 2,104. This adjustment has been incorporated into the book's sixth edition.

5   *Base-ball cannot be learned: Base-ball: How to Become a Player*, p. 41

5   *Frank Knoche, whose father owned a music store:* Ward's letter to Ridge Riley, a publicist for Pennsylvania State College in 1923, reprinted in a *Rambling Thru* column by Jerry Weinstein, source unknown. Centre County Library Historical Museum vertical files.

8   *A thin, nervous person:* The first two quoted paragraphs are from pp. 43 and 44. Ward devotes a chapter to each fielding position.

10   *After his death:* See Ward vertical file, Baseball National Library.

10   *Baseball cards were invented:* See Thorn, *Treasures of the Baseball Hall of Fame*, chapter 13.

12   *Between the 1881 and 1882 baseball seasons:* On Ward's trip west, see *New York Clipper*, April 8, 1882; on mustache, see Perrin, p. 16.

Chapter Two. NOT A SUMMER SNAP

page

14   *15,000:* The number of ballplayers was supplied by Pete Palmer. Ward's rankings, the essays, and the various formulas are taken from *Total Baseball*.

    Ward's base-stealing numbers deserve comment. During his first eight seasons, stolen bases were not an official statistic. Beginning in 1886, scorers credited a runner with a stolen base for every base he advanced on his own initiative—if he "stretched" a single into a double, or advanced two bases on a batter's single, or advanced on a sacrifice fly—unlike the modern definition, which credits a player with a stolen base only if he advances "unaided by a hit, a putout, an error, a force-out, a fielder's choice, a passed ball, a wild pitch or a balk." So Ward had eight "lost" years of credited stolen bases and nine seasons of "padded" theft numbers.

15   *Pacer Smith:* Charles N. Smith was hanged in Decatur, Illinois, on Friday, November 29, 1895. He had shot his young daughter, Louise, and his sister-in-law. Smith, who showed no emotion during the trial and gave no reasons for his actions, asked that, if possible, his execution take place on February 16, 1926—his murdered daughter's birthday. The judge denied Smith's request. Upon hearing the sentence, Smith's wife cried out, "Oh, the slayer of my child has got what he deserved. Thank God, he has got his dues. I am so glad! I am so glad!" *Sporting News*, October 12, 1895.

17   *Summer snap: New York Clipper*, December 26, 1896.

Chapter Three. AN *UNFAVORABLE IMPRESSION*

page

19 *Worshipped, blazing star:* In 1890, Ward's fame was such that he was the easily recognizable hero of an allegory, "The Enchanted Baseball: A Fairy Story of Modern Times," published in the April issue of *The Cosmopolitan*. Ward was called Algernon de Witt Caramel. He was conversant in all the modern languages and had mastered Greek, Latin, and Hebrew "with the utmost ease." He was a "veritable Adonis . . . a graceful dancer, a fearless swimmer, a daring equestrian, a brilliant conversationalist and . . . the best-dressed man in town." He was also a baseball player—the "Champion Short-Stop of America"—for the Brobdignagians, who were about to do battle against the Bridegrooms of Brooklyn. In the stands was Caramel's fiancée, Miss Violet Veronica Van Sittart. The story was written by Sydney Cowell, an English-born New York actress who died in 1925. See Bowman, "John Montgomery Ward and the Enchanted Baseball."

19 *Family lore:* See John Fleming–Lee Allen correspondence, 1963–64. Fleming, great-grandson of Ward's uncle Philo writes on January 13, 1964: "I have a faint recollection of my grandmother telling me that Uncle Monte resented the effeminate implications of the name and had many fights over it. According to Grandmother Fleming he was pugnacious. . . ." National Baseball Library.

20 *Irish surnames:* See Burk, p. 131.

20 *This odor:* See Seymour, *Early Years*, chapter 26; Reiss, *Touching Base*, chapter 6, and *City Games*, chapter 2; Adelman, chapters 6 and 7; Kirsch; Isenberg. Reiss and Adelman are especially good on ballplayer demographics and social mobility.

The January 4, 1879, *New York Clipper* complained bitterly of the "rowdyism or rollicking, skylarking way of some of the teams when traveling. . . . The minority behaved like gentlemen, orderly, quiet and unobtrusive; but the majority seemed to think—judging from their actions—that the moment they got on a train or on a steamer, or entered a hotel, then and there commenced their license to indulge in questionable [behavior]."

20 Buffalo Times *survey:* See Seymour, *Early Years*, p. 336.

21 *Robert Todd Lincoln:* See Reiss, *Touching Base*, p. 156.

22 *Baseball's agrarian roots:* Reiss, *Touching Base*, p. 153, points out that approximately 62 percent of major league professional baseball players during the years 1871–75 were from urban areas, and that nearly 40 percent of those were from four cities: Philadelphia, Brooklyn, Baltimore, and New York.

22 *Two other John Wards:* See Thorn and Palmer, *Total Baseball*, Player Registry and Pitcher Registry.

23 *Aaron Montgomery Ward:* See *Ward and Allied Families*, pp. 21–41. Maps and genealogical records from the Broome County (NY) Historical Society and the Tioga County (NY) Historical Society; other Ward family records are in the Centre County Historical Museum.

The Wards came from England. The first American Ward, Lieutenant John, settled in Branford, Connecticut, about 1648 and signed the Plantation and Church covenant there in 1667.

John Fleming's recollection that Ward's name came from other Montgomery families in the Bellefonte area cannot, of course, be proven, but Centre County (PA) Grantee Index (1800–1935) lists well over a score of individuals and families with the Montgomery surname.

23 *No end of confusion:* See Allen–Fleming letters. To add to the confusion of nomenclature, a February 1, 1912, *Sporting News* article by Tim Murnane says that when Ward signed with the Janesville, Wisconsin, minor league club in 1877, the "president of the club was surprised to learn that Ward was without a middle name, so as not to make it look as if they were short on names, Ward put John in front of the Montgomery." Murnane goes on to say that Ward himself is the "authority" for this statement. Ward was, evidently, taking the mickey out of Murnane.

24 *Algernon:* There are two major pitfalls for the writer of nonfiction: One is not enough information; the other is too much. Algernon Fleming Ward, unfortunately, must be relegated to a footnote. Ward's stage and screen name was Fleming Ward. He was born in 1887 and died August 3, 1962. His *New York Times* obituary recalled his "featured roles" in Broadway hits such as *Pal Joey, Three Men on a Horse,* and *Room Service.* He began his career with Minnie Maddern Fiske's company, and later appeared regularly in George Abbot productions. *New York Times Theatre Reviews* 1920–1970, vols. 9–10 (New York: New York Times and Arno Press, 1972), lists Ward in twenty separate productions and two revivals. He also appeared in at least two movies: *When Men Desire* (1919) and *The Invisible Bond* (1919). *American Film Institute Catalogue: Feature Films* 1911–1920, Patricia King Hanson, ed. (University of California Press, 1988).

Algernon's family nickname was Uncle Babadee. Ward–Fleming family lore maintains that he played Mr. De Haven, the high school principal, on the long-running and popular radio serial "The Henry Aldrich Show." No cast listings mention Ward, but John Dunning, in *Tune in Yesterday* (New York: Prentice-Hall, 1976), points out that the show, a light comedy revolving around teenager Henry Aldrich, had, during its 1939–53 run, "one of the highest turnover rates in the business."

Algernon never married, according to the family. He had one son, Michael Wardell.

Chapter Four. EVERY WINDOW-PANE BLAZED WITH GOLDEN LIGHT

page
28 *Back in the days of the Ward brothers:* See Naylor, ed., *Bellefonte Bicentennial Celebration.*
29 *Philo['s obituary]: Democratic-Watchman,* July 15, 1904.
29 *James's life:* Centre County Library Historical Museum genealogical records.

29   *Mary Caroline:* Tioga County Historical Society; interviews and correspondence with Evelyn Beem, Ozawkie, Kansas.

29   *The Binghamton spa:* See Lawyer, *Binghamton,* np.

30   *"Being of a delicate constitution":* Democratic Watchman, December 11, 1874. (Hereafter *DW.*)

30   *James and Ruth had three children:* Centre County Deed Book B2, p. 73.

31   *"Every window-pane":* New York Times, March 4, 1860. (Hereafter *NYT.*)

31   *Typhoid fever:* DW, March 22, 1860; *Bellefonte Central Press,* various 1860 dates; NYT, March 3, 1860.

34   *On the surface:* 1860 census.

34   *But a cloud hung over:* Centre County court records: January 1853, term #62; April 1855, term #86; August 1857, term #38, August 1862, terms #49 and #50; August 1865, term #194; August 1866, term #161.

35   *So, by 1862:* Philo's obituary (in *DW*) mentioned his career as a machinist. James's, on May 12, 1871, did not. The Bayard–James Ward partnership comes from the Hugh Manchester files, as does the Priscilla–Ruth transfer.

35   *The buyer, John Hoffer:* Hoffer was part owner of the Hoffer & Kline general store. He died December 8, 1885. *DW.*

Chapter Five. GOD KNOWS SHE WAS A GOOD WOMAN

page

37   *In the fall of 1873:* 1873–74 Pennsylvania State College Catalogue.

38   *Lop off a portion:* Quoted in Rudolph, *The American College and University,* p. 249. See also Rudolph, pp. 240–65, 286–95, and Veysey, pp. 28–39.

38   *"Hog cholera":* See Rudolph, ibid., p. 256.

38   *"First day of March":* Ibid., p. 260.

38   *Horace Greeley:* Quoted in *DW,* March 22, 1860.

39   *"Come, and we will do what we can":* See Rudolph, p. 260.

39   *Enrollment at Penn State:* Telephone interview with Mike Bezilla, Penn State University, 1997.

40–41 Almost all the specific information about Penn State curricula, prices, etc., is taken from Penn State catalogues of the period. Ward's grades come from grade books and attendance records; the disciplinary proceedings are from the faculty minutes. There is a summary of Ward's grades at the Centre County Historical Museum. Although generally accurate and helpful, it does misstate Ward's dates for his first two semesters: they should read "p. 4, 1874–75" (not 1875–76) and "p. 11, December 15, 1875" (not 1876). Also, Ward took Greek, not French, the first semester of his sophomore year; he received an 85 in Military Efficiency his second sophomore semester, and the December 15, 1876, semester indicates Ward's efforts in his junior, not sophomore, year.

42   *Death of Mrs. Ruth A. Ward:* DW, December 11, 1874. In my searches of the *DW,* I found no obituary whose length approached that of Ruth Ward's.

Chapter Six. IT WAS KNOWN THAT THEY TOOK CHICKENS

page

49   "Wrestling with Greek grammar": See Vescey, p. 28.

49   "Oral quiz": Ibid., p. 37.

49   Men are in demand: "President Hulbert" of Middlebury College; quoted in Vescey, p. 29.

51   By 1875: See Ronald A. Smith, Sports and Freedom, pp. 55–66, 95–99, and 165–90. The anecdotes about early college baseball are found in many places, including Seymour, The People's Game, pp. 131–43. To fully understand college ball in the nineteenth century one must see the bigger picture of amateur baseball and American attitudes toward sports in general. The subject is massive. I suggest Kirsch, Adelman, A Sporting Time, Riess, Touching Base, and especially, Goldstein.

52   No "regular baseball organization": See John Montgomery Ward letter to Ridge Riley. Penn State archives.

55   Williamsport pinned Lock Haven: Clinton Democrat, October 5, 1875; PSU faculty minutes.

57–58 [Orvis letter]: Penn State archives, February 19, 1877.

Chapter Seven. TO TRAVEL HAD BEEN HIS DREAM

page

59   "Some local reputation": See Ward, "Note of a Base-ballist."

59   "Persisted in running away": "Ramblin Thru," Penn State archives.

60   It seems that hazing: Fleming–Allen correspondence.

60–61 "To travel"; "Civilization"; "Find other employment": Ward, "BaseBallist."

61–62 [Ward's letter to Calder]: March 30, 1878, Penn State Room.

62   [Williamsport team names]: Williamsport Daily Gazette and Bulletin, various dates, Summer 1877.

The first mention of Ward the baseball player appeared in an August 3, 1876, Clinton Democrat, story of an 11–1 Lock Haven loss to Chester on July 31: "Kelly, Ward, Satterlee and Poorman filled vacant places in the Lock Haven Nine and did excellent service."

64   "Neglected to leave his address": See Ward, "Base-ballist."

Chapter Eight. CRICKET IS A SPLENDID GAME—FOR BRITONS

page

65   Plain as the nose on your face: See Guttman on "American Exceptionalism" in From Ritual to Record, pp. 91–94; also Kirsch, pp. 91–108.

67   National game: Kirsch, p. 92, points out that the phrase was in common use, at least in the sporting press, as early as the late 1850s.

67   *I claim that Base Ball:* See Spalding, pp. 4–9. Spalding's autobiography, while fascinating and revealing, must be read with skepticism because it is extremely self-serving. Levine's detailed and evenhanded A. G. *Spalding and the Rise of Baseball* is a necessary and soothing counterbalance to Spalding's chest-beating.

68   *"National character":* I have shamelessly cribbed the cricket–baseball analysis from Kirsch, pp. 91–110. His book details the formative American years of both sports. See also Sullivan, p. 20, "The Growing Popularity of Baseball in New York," and p. 25, "A Defense of Cricket as a 'National Game.' " Adelman, pp. 97–119, is especially concise and generally concurs with Kirsch with one important difference: he thinks the importance of the relative brevity of a baseball game overstated. Adelman points out that Americans played "one-day" cricket regularly, for example, and suggests that the relative time needed to play the two games only applied to "formal" competitions, and that for years baseball was thought of primarily as a recreation. For a weirdly contrary view about which game was most popular in America, see the *New York Times*, August 30, 1881.

69–71 *The controversy about baseball's origins:* No serious historian credits the Cooperstown–Doubleday myth. See Spalding, pp. 17–21. Sullivan wisely devotes an entire chapter to Spalding's commission, pp. 279–95, letting the documents speak for themselves. See also Seymour, *The Early Years*, pp. 4–12; Goldstein, pp. 10–11; Kirsch, pp. 50–53; Burk, pp. 4–5, and especially Henderson, pp. 170–94. Ward's stubborn take on the matter appears in his *Base-Ball: How to Become a Player*, pp. 9–23. Finally, see Alvarez, *The Old Ball Game*.

71–76 *He then cites Herodotus:* The subject of ur-baseball and, by extension, all primitive games of ball, remains for the most part virgin territory, if not for scholars—anthropologists, archaeologists, art historians, and crypto-linguists among them—then for the willing and able generalist. My brief discussion, which at best is a sort of "greatest hits" album, relies entirely on the scholarship of others. Nearly all baseball historians, professional and amateur, including Ward, discuss the matter. See Seymour, *The Early Years*, and Sullivan (especially for pre-Cooperstown American documentary evidence and a reprint of an 1867 *Ball Players' Chronicle* article, "The Ancient History of Base Ball," by Henry Chadwick, who differed vehemently with Spalding, Ward, et al. on the origins of baseball).

The most captivating and rigorous book to date, however, is Henderson, *Ball, Bat and Bishop*—and it is on him, as well as Strutt, that I have relied most heavily. Henderson's basic thesis is, I think, a bit overstated: that formal ball games can be traced back to Egyptian-Arabic fertility rites. But his wide-ranging scholarship is convincing, and his bibliography impressive. H. A. Harris, in *Sport in Greece and Rome* (New York: Cornell University Press, 1972) has an accessible, sensible chapter on ball games, pp. 75–111. Harris suggests that most Greco-Roman ball games were forms of "keep-away," and "ball-playing" mostly fitness exercises. Morse, pp. 4–7, briefly discusses the ancients.

71   *The Strutt citation is fitting:* Compare Ward, *Base-Ball: How to Become a Player*, pp. 9–10, with Strutt, p. 158. Herodotus, while a convenient and obvious

source, must be disregarded as the final word. Athenaeus, in *The Deipnosophists*, Book I, 19, says flatly, "Herodotus is wrong in saying that games were invented in the reign of Atys when there was a famine. . . ." G. S. Farnell, in *Tales from Herodotus*, 61, also discourages a too-literal reading of Herodotus, but does so affably: "As a matter of fact, most of the games [Herodotus] mentioned were of much greater antiquity than is implied; but Herodotus very properly abstains from spoiling a good story by disputing the accuracy of its details."

72   *"Bat and bares and suche play"*: Henderson, p. 75, discusses one theory: that "Bittle-Battle," mentioned in the Domesday Book, was a form of stoolball brought to England by the troops of William the Conqueror.

72   *"Down in the vale"*: See Henderson, p. 71. This is from D'Urfey *Wit and Mirth, Or, Pills to Purge Melancholy* (London, 1719), vol. I, p. 91. D'Urfey says the verse is from a play, *Don Quixote*, first staged in Dorset in 1694. Henderson does not cite the source of the "Easter Diversion."

73   *If, as seems likely*: Henderson, p. 128, mentions another theory, that cricket itself was "invented" in France. He begins his discussion by quoting a 1478 manuscript, translated by Du Cange in the nineteenth century: "The suppliant came to a place where a game of ball (*jeu de boule*) was played, near to a stick or *criquet*."

73   *Thomas Wilson:* Ibid., p. 132.

73   *"The Ball once struck* off": Ibid., p. 133.

73   An *1874 letter:* See Ward, *Base-Ball: How to Become a Player*, p. 19. Henderson, p. 134, strongly suggests that it was still primarily a children's game.

74   La balle empoisonnée: See Henderson, pp. 139–43.

74   Henderson, pp. 156–57, displays the Clarke and Boston books' rules side by side.

76   *Olympic Base Ball Club:* See Sullivan, pp. 1–11.

76   *Lurch toward modernity:* See Guttman, *Ritual to Record,* for a discussion of modern versus primitive sport.

76   *The Knickerbockers:* For further discussion of baseball up through the formation of the National League and beyond, see Kirsch; Seymour, *The Early Years*; Burk; Reiss; Goldstein; Adelman; and Sullivan. For summaries and discussions of early rules, see Ivor-Campbell, "Ballparks," pp. 15–69 in *Total Baseball*; Shieber, "The Evolution of the Diamond," pp. 113–24; Thorn, Palmer, and Joseph M. Wayman, "The History of Major League Baseball Statistics," pp. 642–56; and Bingham and Heitz, "Rules and Scoring," pp. 2426–81. Also, *Spalding's Official Baseball Guide, 1876–99,* and Nemec, *Great Encyclopedia* and *Rules of Baseball.*

77   *"Once there we were free":* Dr. Daniel Adams, *Sporting News*, February 29, 1896, reprinted in Sullivan, p. 14.

77   *"Voluntary association of sober":* See Burk, p. 6.

78   *Constant struggle:* See Adams in Sullivan, p. 15.

79   Burk, *Never Just a Game,* p. 9.

79   *Baseball spread:* See Seymour, *The Early Years,* 24ff.

80   *The Civil War:* See Dyja for a fictional account of wartime baseball.

80 The odd team names come from the *New York Clipper* and *Sporting News* (see Seymour), and in the case of the KKK v. "*Nine Carpetbaggers,*" Kirsch, p. 202.

81 For extended accounts of two "odd games," see *NYT*, June 30, 1886, p. 3, and August 3, 1886, p. 8.

82 *Huge sporting goods industry*: See Levine and *Spalding's Official Baseball Guides*.

82 *The Oscar Wildes*: Oscar Wilde's enormously popular American tour was in 1881. Wilde had not yet become dangerously scandalous, merely wittily outrageous.

83 "*Colored person*": See Sullivan, pp. 68–69; also pp. 34–36, for the "First Reported African American Baseball Games (1859 and 1862)."

84 *15,000*: See Kirsch, p. 83.

84 *Jim Creighton*: The Excelsiors were composed of merchants and clerks. They "bought" Creighton from the Niagara Stars.

84 "*Sniff of aristocratic odor*": *New York Clipper*, March 26, 1859. Hereafter *Clipper*.

84 "*Class stability*": See Burk, p. 29.

85 *Big-time college athletics*: See McQuilkin. Collegiate athletes of the 1880s and 1890s were "employed" as waiters, etc., in resort hotels, but actually received their money for playing baseball.

85 *Albert Spalding*: See Spalding, pp. 115–26.

85 *$600 and $2,500*: See Burke, p. 30; Adelman, p. 160, says *NYT* is responsible for the upper-end figures. The paper estimated the salary range for "all" ballplayers as between $1000 and $2500. Adelman thinks these figures inflated by $500. In a long footnote, he points out the difficulty of accepting contemporary figures. The figures, as Adelman points out, are of secondary concern: the main point is that for some baseball had become a lucrative profession.

86 *Obscure league in Iowa*: See Kirsch, p. 240.

86 "*Hippodroming*": Sullivan, pp. 49–53, reprints the *Clipper* account of November 11, 1865. In ancient Greece and Rome, a hippodrome was an oval for horse- and chariot-racing. By the nineteenth century, however, a hippodrome referred not only to racing tracks but to any number of enclosed venues for circuses and other large-scale entertainments. Since hippodrome activities were rehearsed, and staged—i.e., their "outcome" predestined—the term came to be applied to "fixed" games—i.e., those with orchestrated outcomes.

86 "*I Can assure you*": Sullivan, pp. 101–9, reprints the *Louisville Courier-Journal*, November 3, 1877, account of the affair. See Seymour, *The Early Years*, p. 87, for the letter and Ivor-Campbell, *Nineteenth-Century Stars*, for a brief biography and haunting photo.

87 *Wildly cheering citizens*: An account of the 1869 Cincinnati tour has been retold in many baseball histories. For a ripping good time, read Darryl Brock's novel, *If I Never Get Back*.

87 "*Sine die*": See Seymour, *Early Years*, p. 59. Sullivan, pp. 82–88, is more informative, reprinting the 1870 NABBP convention debate on professionalism and the *Clipper*, March 25, 1871, story on the formation of the NAPBBP. For detailed overviews of the formation of the National League, see Burk, pp. 50–60, and Seymour, *Early Years*, pp. 75–93.

89   *"Make it impossible for any . . . to leave"*: See Spalding, p. 210.
89   *"Flabby federation"*: See Turkin and Thompson, p. 385.

Chapter Nine. WE TRUST HE WILL PAUSE AND RECONSIDER

page

92   *"Twilight era"*: The term is Seymour's; see *Early Years*, p. 47.

94   *"An inshoot with a perpendicular twist"*: Kofoed, pp. 55–57; Alvarez, various places; *Spalding's Official Baseball Guide* 1876–83; Seymour, *Early Years*, pp. 62–63. For a typical article on the curve's physics and its demonstration, see *Buffalo Morning Express*, September 26 and 27 and October 24, 1877. See also a *Clinton Democrat*, June 14, 1877, reprint of a *Lewisburg* (PA) *Chronicle* article about Thomas Poorman performing a feat "hitherto supposed to be impossible, of sending a ball through a horizontal curved line. . . . This he did repeatedly in the presence of College professors and other men well versed in the science of lines and angles." These "exhibitions of the curve" appear regularly in scores of local papers. For Ward's Penn State exhibition, see Dunaway, pp. 446–47. For a capsule on Cummings, see Ivor-Campbell, pp. 43–44. Morse, pp. 32–40, provides a contemporary overview.

95   *Kelly could not curve*: Ward's version is in NBL vertical files. Poorman, of Lock Haven, played for Buffalo, Boston, and Chicago of the National League and Toledo and Philadelphia of the American Association. Poorman's lifetime pitching record was 3–9.

95   Democratic-Watchman's *revisionism*: DW, November 3, 1893. It is possible that the High Boys were Bellefonte's town team, either in addition to the Bellefonte Academy team, or composed primarily of Academy players and grads. The "local snippets," from *DW*, August 8, 1876, are typical.

96   *WARM: Clinton Democrat*, August 9, 1877.

97   *We played*: "Ramblin' Thru," Penn State Room.

98   *[DW's fair coverage]: Democratic-Watchman*, August 18–October 6, 1876.

99   *"Intelligent, well educated"*: DW, February 27, 1882.

99   *Straight and muscular*: DW, December 24, 1880.

99   *Monte Ward, youngest son*: DW, July 13, 1877.

Chapter Ten. HIS PITCHING IS SIMPLY IMMENSE

page

100 *"I had seen"*: See Ward, "Notes of a Base-Ballist."

101 *Ward came*: The *Philadelphia Times* account is undated; reprinted in *DW*, August 21, 1877.

102 *Ward's version*: During the summer of 1877, baseball news in Williamsport stopped suddenly and did not resume for weeks, so there is no way of knowing when, exactly, Ward left for Philadelphia. His debut against Hartford, played

in Brooklyn, took place on July 2, 1877, so we must assume that he left Williamsport before the manager absconded with the till—if we also assume that the manager would wait until *after* the Independence Day game, with its big gate, to leave town. If Ward left Williamsport—i.e., went AWOL—before the official pay day, his case of economic poor-mouthing is weakened considerably.

102   *Winning 66 of them:* See *Spalding's Baseball Guide,* 1878.

102   For an account of Ward's performances in Philadelphia, his move to Janesville, and his performance there and with Buffalo, see *Clipper,* June 30; July 21; August 4, 11, 16; and October 1, 3, 13, 18.

103   *They eventually did:* See *Spalding's Baseball Guide,* 1878.

103–4   The telegrams are courtesy of Joseph Overfield, Buffalo, New York. For more information on Buffalo baseball, see Overfield, *100 Seasons of Buffalo Baseball.*

104   *"Peanuts and gingerbread":* See Ward, "Base-Ballist."

105   *They began their season:* The Crickets, and other International Association teams, were well covered by various league city newspapers.

Chapter Eleven. A GENUINE MUFFING EXHIBITION

page

113–14   These *Clipper* items are culled from issues 1876–92, not just 1878. Many of the advertisements ran for years virtually unchanged.

116   The July 1878 items are taken from various papers, especially the *NYT* and the *Cincinnati Enquirer.*

119   *Had there been such an award:* Ward's baseball statistics, from here on, are culled from *Total Baseball,* fourth ed. For the history of the Providence Grays, see Perrin, Carson, Hancock, Stinson and Waldbauer.

120   *"Troublesome for the opponents":* **Clipper,** February 12, 1880.

121–22   Frederick Ivor-Campbell pointed out the sun's position. Pete Palmer, of *Total Baseball,* provided the number of regular season games and pitchers since 1871. Don Larsen's perfect game is not included because it occurred after the regular season.

Chapter Twelve. THE HIGHLAND FLING

page

123   See Brock and Dyja for extended nineteenth-century "insider" experiences.

123   *["Cranks" (also kranks)]:* The *Oxford English Dictionary* allows that the use of "fan" as a truncation of fanatic is an American invention. Its first citation for a "keen and regular spectator of a (professional) sport, orig. of baseball" is the *Kansas Times and Star,* March 26, 1889: "Kansas City base-ball fans are glad they're through with Dave Rowe as a ball club manager." While taking issue with the *OED* is risky business, I doubt that this was the first occasion of the

word's appearance in American print. The further matter of when "fan" over-
took "crank" in common parlance is even more in question, but certainly Lawson was using the latter, and most common, word when he published his 1888
book, *The Krank*.

Crank, in America, originally meant an insane person, or one possessed of
irrational or uninformed views. The word evolved to mean, as the *OED* more
elegantly puts it, "a person with a mental twist; one who is apt to take up eccentric notions or impracticable projects especially one who is enthusiastically
possessed by a particular crotchet or hobby . . . a monomaniac." American
though this particular usage may be, George Bernard Shaw, in 1889, according
to the *OED*, wrote: "I move amidst cranks, Bohemians, unbelievers, agitators
and riff-raff of all sorts."

On a far more ghastly fetch across time, "crank" derives from an Old English
word form which meant "to fall in battle," of which the ancient meaning
appears to have been "to draw oneself together in a bent form, to contract oneself stiffly, to curl up."

I think "crank" a marvelous word, and wish it were still in use because of its
connotation—on the part of the observer—of long-suffering affection, which
"fan" lacks. Clearly, "crank" was an appellation to set a crank's own heart
abeaming, as suggested by a modern equivalent: "Oh, that George, he's such a
golf nut."

124 *The 1882 season:* See *Total Baseball*, fourth ed: Shieber, pp. 113–25; Bingham
and Heitz, pp. 2426–81; Nemec, *The Rules of Baseball*; and *Spalding Baseball
Guide*, 1876–1893. Dennis Bingham carefully reviewed this chapter.

126 *The Highland fling:* See Shieber, *Total Baseball*, p. 117.

127 *Pitching descriptions:* Shieber, in a letter to the author (December 10, 1996)
quoted unknown sources from volume 2 of the Chadwick Scrapbooks
(National Baseball Library).

127 *Ward's style:* See Perrin, *Providence Journal*, July 24, 1928; also *Cincinnati
Enquirer*, July 16, 1878. During the 1888–89 World Tour, there occurred a dust-
up between the two touring nines in Adelaide. The center of controversy was
Ward's delivery: Was he or was he not facing the batter when he threw the ball?

Chapter Thirteen. THE GREAT FAVORITE

page

130 Most of the details of the Providence franchise during Ward's years come from
Perrin. For Providence demographics and baseball attitudes, see Carson, Hancock, Stinson and Waldbauer.

130 *"Best general players":* From the *Boston Journal*, quoted in the *Providence Evening
Star*, October 10, 1882.

130 *"Great favorite . . . no man of the nine":* Providence Sunday Star, October 15,
1882.

130 "*Ball of yarn*": *Providence Daily Journal*, September 30, 1881.

130 *Rhode Island years:* Bass first pointed out Ward's curt attitude toward his Providence years.

131 Charles Brown, of Bellefonte, has several original advertisements for the Emporium. The ownership/address information is from the Providence city directory. I was unable to track down any financial records.

132 "*Become conversant*": See Perrin, p. 12.

136 *$3,100: Spalding's Official Base Ball Guide*, 1890, p. 19.

Chapter Fourteen. HE RAN LIKE A DEER

page

137 See Nemec, *The Beer and Whisky League*, for a full treatment, lavishly illustrated, of the American Association. See also Seymour, *Early Years*, pp. 135–71. Burk, pp. 69–80, is mostly interested in the American Association's economic impact on the National League and its players. See especially Burk's appendixes, figures 1, 4, and 5, pp. 243–47. *Reach's Base Ball Guide* was the "official" guide of the American Association through the 1891 season. Sullivan, pp. 119–21, reprints the *Cincinnati Enquirer* account, November 3, 1881, of the Association's founding.

138 Keefe played with the AA Mets, 1883–84.

138 *What a day May 1 was:* Clipper, April 19 and May 5, 1883. See also *NYT* for day-after coverage.

142 "*In 1884, I injured my shoulder*": Vertical files, NBL.

142 "*Already gone back on him*": *Sporting Life*, April 30, 1884.

Chapter Fifteen. OUR PLAYERS

page

144 *League membership varied:* See *Total Baseball*, p. 2552; see also Seymour, *Early Years*, pp. 86–87, for financial details.

145 "*Eighty percent*": See Seymour, *Early Years*, p. 119.

146 *The potential size of its daily gate:* One of baseball's most hoary and cherished myths is the class-blindness of its devotees: in the stands the banker sits next to the baker, the financier next to the fishmonger. However true this became as the twentieth century rolled along, it was most decidedly untrue—at least as far as physical presence at games is concerned—during the nineteenth century, especially in the National League. The fifty-cent admission was a goodly portion (one-third to one-half) of an average wage-earner's daily income; games were, of course, always played during the daytime. Because there were no Sunday games, and work-weeks were, in the 1870s, six-day, ten-and-one-half-hour per-day affairs—even twenty years later, the typical work week exceeded sixty

hours (Reiss, *Touching Base*, pp. 30–31)—most "working class" cranks, even those willing to shell out four bits, simply could not attend games except on holidays.

Most fans, then, as now, followed the game vicariously: through newspaper accounts, or telegraph- or runner-produced scores at the local saloon. League and team officials' seemingly benevolent and progressive ideas, such as "ladies' day" and free ducats for the clergy, were in fact part of an ongoing crusade to woo the middle class and make baseball respectable. On an equally cynical note, politicians were aware of the advantages of being seen as "one of the people"—hence, perhaps, their high-profile attendance at games.

By far the best analysis of baseball's self-serving mythology is in Reiss, *Touching Base*. In his first chapter, he discusses the "construction of baseball reality," including its insistence on its "agrarian roots" (both the sport's origin and the birthplace of many of its players), as well as its "democratic" essence and its "integrative" power for those hundreds of thousands of "new Americans." Baseball also appealed to the majority of Americans who were nostalgic for an "idealized, pristine" past. Reiss also posits that baseball was in some way the "moral equivalent of the frontier," exuding the frontier qualities of "courage, honesty, individualism, patience, temperance and . . . teamwork."

Reiss also, on pages 153–219, discusses baseball as a "source of social mobility," with invaluable charts of baseball players off-season and post-career employment. See also p. 18 for the importance of "localism."

I found that the most accessible and informative survey of American workers in the nineteenth-century was Laurie, *Artisans Into Workers*. See p. 128 for baseball/other wages (see also Burk's appendixes); pp. 133–34, for management attitudes toward workers; and p. 35 for an insight into the changing attitude, in America and baseball, toward "worker" control versus management control of the workforce. All in all, Laurie makes abundantly clear the mind-boggling changes at work in industrial America during Ward's era.

I would be remiss if I did not mention two other books that emphasize baseball's place in the larger world: Burk, entirely, and Adelman, especially pp. 92–145.

146 *Owners also began to reduce on overhead:* See Burk, pp. 61–64.

148 *Ned Williamson:* See Tiemann and Rucker, p. 139; Joe Vila file, NBL.

150 *Spalding, on hearing of his death:* See Vila file. Also in the file is a letter, dated January 6, 1972, from Stephen H. Jambor, vice-president of Chicago's Rosehill Cemetery Company, to a reporter at the *Cleveland Plain Dealer:* "[Williamson's] remains are interred in an Adult Grave described as Grave No. 19 in Section 6. We have searched our files and have had no correspondence from any one since the year 1910, with regard to the aforesaid Mr. Williamson. At that time a Mrs. Nettie Lena Goodman . . . who we understand was formerly Mrs. Nettie Williamson, wife of Edward N. Williamson, wrote us in connection with a lot owned by her mother. . . ."

151 *"Higher degree of perfection":* Spalding's *Official Baseball Guide*, 1880.

151 *"War upon crooks and knaves":* Spalding's *Guide*, 1890.

151   *A sober player:* Ibid., 1882.

151   *"Dizzy summits of morality":* See Seymour, *Early Years*, p. 129.

151   *"At that hour in my life":* See Spalding, p. 184; see also Appel for a book-length treatment of Kelly.

152   *"As an artist on the diamond":* See Spalding, p. 193.

153   *Armour transformed:* See Laurie, pp. 116–17.

153   *Jumped to twenty in thirty years:* Ibid.

154   *"Playing of the game":* See Spalding, p. 193.

154   *"At the same time":* Ibid.

156   *The International Association:* See Burk, pp. 58–9, 61–2, 69, 94.

156   *Salaries jumped by about* 15 percent: Ibid., p. 243.

156   *"State of the League" address: Clipper,* October 11, 1879; Sullivan, pp. 113–15.

157   *6–8 percent:* See Burk, p. 62.

157   *Large personal loss: Clipper,* October 11, 1879.

157   *Braying in the barnyard:* See Burk, p. 243.

Chapter Sixteen. THE AIM OF THE LEAGUE

page

158   *"In support of the sport":* The quote is from H. A. Hulbert. See Sullivan, pp. 113–15, for reprints of the *Buffalo Commercial Advertiser,* September 30 and October 3, 1879.

158   *"To some extent for* 1880": See Sullivan, ibid.

158   *The undersigned . . . :* See Gelzheiser, appendix 2, p. 291. The *Buffalo Commercial Advertiser* printed the outline of the plan, with a hypothetical example of how it might work with the Buffalo team. The *Clipper* printed the news on October 25, 1879. The 1880 *Spalding's Guide* does not mention the reservation system. Lowenfish follows the reserve clause from its inception through the twentieth century. See Dworkin, and Berry, et al. for general discussions of labor relations in professional sports. Burk begins his reserve clause discussion on p. 62; see also Seymour, *Early Years,* p. 104.

158–61   These examples come from Burk and Seymour.

161   Lowenfish's book—the only one devoted entirely to the reserve clause—is especially valuable for its discussion of various players who felt strongly enough about the injustices of the reserve system to fight it in court. The most touching of these is the story of Danny Gardella, p. 155.

161   *Feet, pounds, and gallons:* In 1975, the reserve clause finally met its match when two pitchers, Andy Messersmith and Dave McNally, won a grievance before a three-man arbitration panel. Peter Seitz, the lawyer and professional arbitrator who cast the panel's swing vote in favor of the pitchers, wrote that the baseball owners' claim that not only could they reserve a player but could do so in perpetuity, was analogous to

> the claims of some nations that persons once its citizens, wherever they live and regardless of the passage of time, the swearing of other allegiances, and

other circumstances are still its own nationals and subject to the obligation that citizenship in the nation imposes. [This theory] is incompatible with the doctrine or policy of freedom in the economic and political society in which we live and of which the professional sport of baseball . . . is a part.

Interestingly, the reserve system was never destroyed, but only made impotent. After the 1975 decision, owners read the writing on the wall—that the courts would sustain the arbitration panel—and worked out, with the players' union, a complex, annually changing and precarious agreement. But even today, while players do in fact become "free agents," they must earn that status through longevity formulas. Lowenfish begins his book with the 1975 decision; see also Dworkin and Berry.

162   *The following opinion:* Sporting Life, October 28, 1885; reprint from *Buffalo Commercial Advertiser* (no date).

164   *American Association:* See Nemec, *The Beer and Whisky League;* Seymour, *Early Years,* pp. 135–48; and Burk, pp. 50–81.

164   *"Battle of the champions":* See Burk, p. 71.

164   *"Club property":* Ibid., p. 70.

164–65   *Allegheny Base-Ball Club v. Bennett:* Federal Reporter, vol. 33, pp. 257–61; also *Pittsburgh Legal Journal,* vol. 14, nos. 5–17.

165   *League's most popular team:* See Burk, p. 72; Seymour, *Early Years,* p. 143.

166   *Reserve lists, and blacklists:* The Northwestern League was a minor league with teams in Toledo, Peoria, Fort Wayne, Grand Rapids, East Saginaw, and Springfield, Illinois. The league wanted to prevent the National League and American Association from raiding its rosters. The National League, by entering into a preliminary "cooperation and reciprocity" pact with the Northwestern, used the latter as a stalking horse, causing the American Association to fear that the two leagues would "lock up" potential expansion territory as well as developing players.

166   *The Union Association:* See Pietrusza, pp. 80–99; Burk, pp. 74–77, 79–84, 86, 89, 92, 110; and Seymour, *Early Years,* p. 123, 148–62, 168–69, 171, 212, 229, 271.

167   *As one writer:* See Pietrusza, p. 83.

167   *"Regarded as a high salary":* Ibid., p. 85.

168   *During the Association's:* See Burk, p. 243.

Chapter Seventeen. A VAMPIRE KEEN FOR HIS PREY

page

170   *"A little misunderstanding":* Clipper, September 24, 1884.

170   *[Ward's salary]:* Spalding's Guide, 1890, p. 19.

171   *"Prominent place":* See Ward, *Base-Ball: How to Become a Player,* pp. 98–99.

171   *New York's decision:* Clipper, January 31, 1885; *Sporting Life,* February 14, 1885. *Clipper* said Ward "dropped in" its offices on January 24.

171 *"As eating does . . .": Sporting Life,* June 3, 1885.

171 *"Ward's fielding": Clipper,* November 7, 1885.

174 *"Beyond the bounds": Spalding's Guide,* 1884, pp. 7–10 and 41–45.

175 *A capital idea: Sporting Life,* November 11, 1885.

175 *It [was] rather tough: Sporting Life,* November 4, 1885.

176 *The Brotherhood [oath]:* See Pietrusza, pp. 99–102.

176 *The Brotherhood constitution's: Players' League Baseball Guide,* 1890.

177 *"On a small notice . . .": Clipper,* January 30, 1886.

178 *Only 115 men: Spalding's Guide,* 1886.

178 *Like-mindedness:* See Burk, p. 90, quoting Allen notebooks, NBL.

180 *[Letter to Calder]:* Penn State Room.

180 *Spring of that year:* Ward evidently did not attend classes in Hanover. He did, however, turn around, to some extent, the fortunes of the then-moribund Dartmouth nine. The high point of his tutelage came in the spring of 1879 when Dartmouth beat its traditional rival, Brown, 4–3. Lee Richmond, who would pitch major league baseball's first perfect game on June 12, 1880, only five days before Ward, pitched for Brown (see the *Dartmouth,* March 17, 1925). There is no evidence that Ward ever considered attending Brown—as he may have Dartmouth—which would have been a logical choice during his Providence years. It is possible that he had applied, but was rejected—which may have been another source of his bitterness toward Providence.

    The captain of the Dartmouth team during Ward's brief stay there was Webster Thayer. Thayer, according to his obituary in the June 1933 Dartmouth Alumni magazine, was dubbed the "Father of Baseball at Dartmouth." In an odd coincidence, Thayer demonstrated to one "Professor Emerson the possibility of delivering a curved ball, which the Professor had insisted was an impossibility." Thayer was appointed justice of the Massachusetts Superior Court in 1917, and in 1921 presided over the trial of Sacco and Vanzetti.

    At least one obituary, from an unknown paper (Columbiana Library, Columbia University), states that Ward coached the Princeton University baseball team during the late winter and early spring of 1884. One intriguing detail in the obituary—that during the winter practices at Princeton Ward injured his arm—has a whiff if not of the truth then of John Ward's occasionally impish imagination.

180 *Ward ultimately enrolled:* Stevens, pp. 21–95, provides an excellent survey of legal education before and during Ward's time. Goebel is rigorously detailed. Other sources for Ward's Columbia years include the 1885 yearbook *The Columbiad;* a scrapbook, "Ephemera"; the law school's twenty-sixth catalogue; *Handbook of Information,* 1884; the 1885–86 *Annual Register;* the *General Catalogue* 1754–1916; and the *Columbia Alumni Register* 1754–1931.

182 *Second-class status:* See Stevens, p. 37. Stevens relates two telling anecdotes: Hugo Black, when a young man, did not "qualify" for the University of Alabama College of Arts and Science, but easily qualified for law school there; meanwhile, at Georgetown, potential law students did not even need to have a

high school degree, and a "disproportionate number" of Georgetown athletes were law school enrollees.

182   *School of Political Science:* See Goebel, p. 89.

184   *Angel visits:* References include "Like Angel visits, short and bright," John Norris, "The Parting," c. 1700; "[Visits] Like those of Angels, short and far between," and Robert Blair, "The Grave" (1743) Pt. ii, 586. The "hungry face" might be a reference to *Julius Caesar.*

184   In general, daily newspaper reports ran the day after the game. The weeklies, depending on the day of the week of the game in question and the newspaper's publication day, ran their shorter reports either a week or two after the game date.

186   *Dead certainty: New York Daily Tribune,* October 11, 1885.

190   *Abolish this abuse of power: Clipper,* December 25, 1886.

191   *"Successful baseball player of today": New York Daily Tribune,* July 14, 1887.

191   *"A strong feeling in this city": Clipper,* March, 26, 1887.

191   *"And was drowned": Sporting Life,* July 20, 1887.

191   *"Fiction twang":* Ibid.

191   *"Brainy little fellow": New York Herald,* July 14, 1887.

192   *"For $50,000": Sporting Life,* July 27, 1887.

192   *Like a fugitive-slave law: Lippincott's,* August 1887, pp. 310–19.

193   *"Contracts for the season": Clipper,* September 3, 1887.

193   *"Interests are also mutual":* Ibid.

194   *Ward had overstepped: Clipper,* September 10, 1887.

194   *I expressed the opinion: Clipper,* October 1, 1887.

194   *"No objection": Clipper,* Ibid.

195   *Mr. Ward's last letter: Clipper,* October 15, 1887.

Chapter Eighteen. HER TINY HANDS BEAT EACH OTHER RAPTUROUSLY

page

196   *Helen Dauvray:* The *Clipper,* January 1, 1886, has Nellie, San Francisco, and 1857. The October 14, 1887, *New York Herald,* quotes the marriage license as Helen, Cincinnati, and 1861; O'Dell, vol. XII, p. 437, cites T. Allston Brown as saying her name was Ida Louisa Gibson.

196   *"Informed"* . . . *"cultured,"* . . . *spoke "five or six languages":* NYT, October 12, 1887. Helen's hyperbole is interesting. Actors were at the time, even if popular, looked upon by the majority of Americans as less than respectable citizens who were more than capable of living dissipated, decadent, and complicatedly spurious lives. The fact that actress Helen seems to feel the need to trumpet her husband's social and educational bona fides would strongly suggest that professional baseball players' place in proper society was looked upon even more skeptically.

196   *Ward's hunting dogs:* See Katherine Waas letter (Ward vertical file, Coopers-

town). Ward had a singular talent for these fibs. John Fleming, in his 1963–64 correspondence with Baseball Hall of Fame historian Lee Allen, suggests that Ward, his great-grandfather Philo's nephew, told the family that he had "invented" the pitcher's mound, either at Penn State or soon thereafter. He did not. He also suggested that he was responsible for the Penn State college colors (*Rambling Through*, Centre County Historical Museum). While Ward did evidently come up with white and "blue trimmings" for his 1875 team, his musing is disingenuous. In 1887, the student body "unanimously" adopted dark pink and black as the school colors (see Brown, *Penn State Centennial Histories*, pp. 64–65). The pink was "deep pink—really cerise." The colors were not fast—and faded within a few washings—so dark blue and white were adopted instead. Another version has the school, during the pink and black days, creating a school yell: "Yah! Yah! Yah! Yah! Yah! Yah!/Wish-whack! Pink, Black!/P! S! C!" Then, after Dickinson College, during a PSC/Dickinson baseball game in 1888, came up with a parody—"Yah! Yah! Hay! Yah Yah Yeh!/Bees wax! Bees Wax!/A!B!C!"—the humiliated Penn State students changed their yell. Dunaway credits the former version as "more reliable."

196   *"Nervous constitution"*: *New York Herald*, October, 13, 1887.

196   *"Is a French idea"*: *Dramatic Mirror*, April, 18, 1885.

197   *"Brilliant and alert"*: NYT, April 12, 1885.

197   *"To suit an artist"*: NYT, April 28, 1885.

197   *[Helen's early years]*: *Clipper*, January 1, 1886.

198   *"I knew hardly a word"*: NYT, January 4, 1885.

198   *He could not restrain himself*: Ibid.

199   *"Stocked with valuable horseflesh"*: NYT, April 12, 1885.

200   *"I only play here four weeks"*: *Dramatic Mirror*, April 18, 1885.

200   *Mona opened*: In general, reviews appeared in daily newspapers the morning after an opening, and in the weeklies, especially the *Clipper*, depending on the day of the week, in the issue immediately following the opening or the week after.

201   *Bronson Howard*: See Mary C. Henderson, *Theatre in America* (New York: Harry N. Abrams, 1986).

202   *"Gallant a man"*: *Dramatic Mirror*, January 1, 1887.

202   The reviews of *Scrap of Paper* are December 21–25, 1886, in the *Dramatic Mirror*, the *Herald*, and the *Tribune*, respectively.

204   *Joseph Golding*: *Herald*, March 9, 1887; also NYT, March 9, 1887.

205   *In late May 1887*: *Herald*, May 19, 1887.

206   *Watching baseball games*: NYT, August 20, 1887.

207   *Dauvray Cup*: See Bowman, "The Dauvray Cup."

207   *The Tiffany Company*: From an unknown newspaper (probably Philadelphia) under the headline "Baseball and Drama United." The article was probably printed the week of the Ward–Dauvray marriage.

208   *Two crossed bats*: Two of these medals survive in the Baseball Hall of Fame and Museum collection. One is on permanent display. The *Kansas City Star*, October 8, 1893, printed an illustration of the Dauvray Cup.

208   National Police Gazette: October 8 and July 2, 1887. According to Bowman, the Dauvray Cup was retired after National League Boston took permanent possession, having won the league title for a third consecutive year. (After 1891, the American Association was absorbed into the League, and the League champion, rather than the post-season interleague champion, received the trophy. The Cup was presented to the Bostons in Kansas City, where the club was playing an exhibition game. It later disappeared, and its whereabouts are unknown.

208–9   *[Early September]:* The NYT followed Helen closely, on September 4, 7, 9, and 11. The *Tribune's* financial article ran October 23, 1887.

210   *"Contract for life":* Tribune, October 16, 1887.

210–11   *"Handsome catch . . . base-stealing,"* Clipper, October 22, 1887.

212   *[Annie Allen and Adolph Gibson]:* NYT, October 15, 1887; *Tribune*, October 15, 1887; suit's withdrawal, NYT, March 12, 1888.

214   *August 31 [1887]:* New Haven Court Records; also NYT, November 30, 1893, and Superior Court of New York, *Helen Dauvray Ward v. John Montgomery Ward;* action was filed October 11, 1893, and the divorce granted November 29, 1893.

214   *"Thermocautery":* From a telephone interview with Bob McCoy (Museum of Questionable Medical Devices; quack@med.org).

Chapter Nineteen. *What in Thunder Cross-Eyed Men Were Made For*

page

215   *Larger incidents of public unrest:* Los Angeles Times, November 13, 1887.

215   *Bad coons:* Ibid.

215   *Ward, nominally in charge:* Chicago Tribune, November 3, 1887, ran reports of heavy drinking. Ward's replies appeared in many papers, including the *Chicago Tribune*, November 4, and the *Los Angeles Times*, November 5, 1887.

216   *"Puerile in the extreme":* The meetings were November 16, 17, and 18. *Clipper* coverage followed. The NYT had day-after coverage.

216   *"St. George of baseball":* Quoted in Burk, p. 97.

216   *"Prosperous looking":* Sporting Life, November 30, 1887.

217   *Ward and Helen:* Clipper, December 31, 1887.

218   *Salaries:* Spalding's Guide, 1890, p. 19.

218   *Rule changes:* See Burk, p. 56, on rule changes and salary inflation.

218   *Fiction of the salary limitation rule:* A November 25, 1888, *Chicago Tribune* piece (unsigned, but possibly written by Ward) detailed some types of side payments: a player signs a contract; the owner then makes a "fictitious" deal with the player on the side; for example, "buying an old pair of shoes or a photograph for a fabulous price." Also common were "private contracts"—some of them performance bonuses, some of them performance bonuses in name only: the bonus might be paid, say, if the player showed up on the first day of the season.

218–19 [Keefe/Ward holdout]: NYT, April 13, 20, and 28, 1888; Clipper, May 5 and 12, 1888. Ward said that Pittsburgh, at the end of the 1887 season, had offered New York $10,000 for his release.

219 Fred Boldt: See Hardy, p. 80.

219 "Supernatural intervention": See Bowman, "Baseball Mascots."

220 Daily Examiner, November 25, 1887. Moore and Vermilyea, p. 221, write that California cranks called the tourists the "joints."

221 "Road uniforms": See Seymour, Early Years, p. 336.

221 I wish you would step: New York World, June 21, 1890.

222 In early June: The lampoon took place June 8, 1888.

222 The house was packed: New York World, August, 15, 1888. Moore and Vermilyea's Casey at the Bat is, essentially, a biography of Ernest L. Thayer rather than a biography of the poem. (See SABR's Nineteenth Century Committee's "Nineteenth Century Notes" (Summer/Fall 1995, pp. 3–4) for William Curran's review of the book.)

If "Casey" is generally considered verse, as opposed to poetry, it does have a somewhat rarefied pedigree. Thayer was elected president of the Harvard Lampoon. His staff included Owen Wister, William Randolph Hearst, and George Santayana. Moore and Vermilyea's book is exhaustive, although, as Curran points out, the authors' penchant for literalism is unfortunate; for example, their theory that Thayer, instead of relying on "signifying" names (especially those sounding "Irish" and "English") and instead of thinking of the contest in which Casey met his downfall as Anygame, played Anywhere, used actual Stockton, California, players and set the poem in Stockton itself.

Moore and Vermilyea's chapter, "Will the Real 'Casey' . . . ," p. 275, is entertaining and straightforward. (See also Gardner's The Annotated Casey at the Bat and Hopper's memoirs Once a Clown Always a Clown.) Thayer himself wrote to Lee Allen, who reprinted the letter in his Hot Stove League, that the "verses owe their existence to my enthusiasm for college baseball . . . [and] has no basis in fact," although, he went on, there was a Daniel Henry Casey, a "big, dour Irish lad" of Thayer's high school days who may have influenced the poem.

One of the several "flesh and blood" contenders for Casey was Daniel Maurice Casey, a pitcher for Philadelphia's National League team in 1887, who remembered, after a sharp blow to his head in 1900, an August 20, 1887, game against Ward and his New Yorks in which he (Casey) hit a dramatic, late-inning home run. Then, Casey went on, in a game on August 21, he struck out just as dramatically. If this was the inspiration of Thayer's poem, John Ward would have been in the field, for both the home run and the next-day strikeout. Casey's story is, as Moore and Vermilyea point out (see p. 210), full of holes. Among other things, the twenty-first was a Sunday—and no games in the National League were played on Sundays.

223 "Talked of more than": Sporting Life, August 17, 1887.

223 [Post-season series]: See Lansche, Glory Fades Away and The Forgotten Championships.

Chapter Twenty. VEDI NAPOLI E POI MORI

page

225   *Vedi Napoli e Poi Mori:* "See Naples and then die."

225   *Spalding:* Levine's biography is authoritative.

226   *In 1888:* See Spalding, p. 251.

227–28   The tour was widely covered by local papers in Colorado and California, especially the *San Francisco Daily Examiner*, as well as the *Clipper*, *Sporting News*, *Sporting Life*, and the Chicago and New York dailies. See also Spalding and Anson. By necessity, the American papers' accounts are delayed, sometimes by days, sometimes by a fortnight or more.

228   *Local tax base: Denver Daily News*, October 29, 1888, pp. 2 and 3. The property was no longer in the Wards' hands as early as 1893, and likely earlier. The November 24 *Clipper* was a bit sharp in its reporting of the Ward acquisition, writing that because Ward was a Denver property owner, "What is the matter with Johnny organizing a team in that city and infusing his ideas into it?"

228   *"Old trick": Daily Examiner*, November 12, 1888. The paper, in a column of miscellany entitled "Bunched Hits," noted that the Chicago Negro mascot, Clarence Duval, was "on the blacklist."

228   *In general:* Ibid.

229   *Terrapin á la Ward:* See Anson, p. 169.

229   *"Local leaguers": Daily Examiner*, November 19, 1888.

230   *Fear of injury: Daily Examiner*, September 9, 1888.

230   *"Baseball and the ladies": New York Herald*, April 7, 1889.

231   *[Ward's dispatches]: Chicago Tribune*, November 11, 1888.

232   *"No inducement . . . was necessary": Chicago Tribune*, November 18, 1888.

232   *The inducements: Chicago Tribune*, April 7, 1889.

232   *One evidently unanticipated result: Chicago Tribune*, December 9, 1888.

233   *Gray-colored paste: Chicago Tribune*, December 30, 1888.

233   *"Laden with gentlemen and ladies":* See Anson, p. 193.

233   San Francisco Daily Record: *Clipper*, January 25, 1889.

234   *"Oil on troubled waters": Chicago Tribune*, April 4, 1889.

234   *Era's context:* For a specific baseball/black context, see Zang, upon whom I relied for the Walker–Anson account.

236   *Walker, the coon catcher:* See Zang, p. 54.

236   *Voted, six to four:* Ibid.

236   *"Anson's . . . slight with Walker":* Zang, p. 59.

237   *The supposed offer was rescinded:* My search of the sporting weeklies and daily papers, including the *New York Herald*, which covered the game in some detail, failed to unearth any such offer. Zang, p. 55, cites Jerry Malloy's essay "Out at Home" in *The Armchair Book of Baseball II* (John Thorn, ed., New York: Charles Scribners Sons, 1987) and Timothy Michael Matheney's undergraduate thesis for Princeton University, "Heading for Home: Moses Fleetwood Walker's Encounter With Racism in America" (1989), as well as the *Newark Daily Journal*, April 8, 1887. Ribowsky, p. 25, quotes only "the sporting press" as

having an account of what he terms the "highly dubious scenario" that Ward and company wanted Walker and Stovey. Ribowsky's book is, generally, indignant at the treatment of black players and skeptical of any white overtures. He may be right, but his book's inexcusable lack of either bibliography or notes renders it, finally, unreliable.

During the waning days of the 1890 season, *Sporting Life* (September 13) interviewed John and his brother Charles, who was the Brooklyn Players' League team business manager. Ward, the paper said, was informally trying out a couple of "smoked Italians" at Brooklyn's Eastern Park. The men were almost certainly black, because Ward, the writer remarked, also called them "Cubans." Ward went on to say that there were many fine players in Cuba, including the pair in question who, he said, were "corkers at juggling the leather," and that he might bring some of them to play in the big leagues.

In 1892, the *Clipper* (January 16) and *Sporting Life* (January 9) printed stories about Ward's winter trip to Enterprise, Florida. (The *Sporting Life* piece is actually a letter from Ward, and the *Clipper* account is an abridgment of the letter.) Ward wrote that chances for his "merry Christmas Friday looked very slim" because his hunting partner was ill, his hunting dogs lame, and the fishing impossible because the boatman, having overcelebrated, had not gathered in any live bait. Ward took in a baseball game instead—as a player—between Enterprise and Garfield, two "colored" teams.

Ward said it was a true "country" field, with a stump in front of second base, the position he played, and gopher holes that swallowed balls. Ward called the occasion a game only out of "courtesy" because it was instead a "kicking" (beefing about rules and plays) contest. He says that one of the "gem'men" could, in the kicking department, give Mr. Anson "cards and spades."

Ward indulges himself in blatant stereotyping, mentioning that one of the players carried a razor. A long story is told in "dialect" about a disputed strike call: Ward's captain said the ball was high and told the umpire, "Say, man, dat boy isn't seben feet high, he's only four." The umpire replied, according to Ward, that "I know dat, but you must reckon I'm not 'sponsible for dat boy's height." This "dialect" may have been Ward's doing or the result of the newspapers' poetic license.

237   *Color line:* See Zang, p. 56.
237–38   *[Mullane/Walker]:* See Zang, p. 43.
238   "*A madder little coon*": See Anson, p. 220.
239   "*A queer sort of people*": *Chicago Tribune,* January 27, 1889.
239   "*He's a goner*": See Carlson, p. 39.
239   *To the minds of the unsophisticated:* See Anson, p. 232.
239   *(Years later, Ward:* Sporting News, October 27, 1894.
240   *Where they use a stick for a plow:* See Carlson, p. 39.
241   "*Life insurance policy*": *Chicago Tribune,* March 17, 1889.
241   *Ward later revealed: Chicago Tribune,* April 7, 1889.
241   *After an eight-hour train trip:* The state of the Colosseum comes from Scherer, pp. 80–89, and a phone conversation with Geoffrey Sumi, of the Mt. Holyoke

College Department of Classics. The $5,000 offer is an item taken from Carlson, p. 39.

242   *"Well, rather"*: *Sporting News*, March 30, 1889.

243   *The Frenchman*: See Carlson, p. 40.

245   *Fred . . . Pfeffer*: See Gelzheiser, pp. 163 and 193.

245   *Operator at Alexandria*: My notes say *Clipper*, December 10, 1888. This notation may be a slight error—a week or two off—because I may have transcribed the date of the tourists' arrival in New Zealand with the issue in which I found the description of the cable.

246   *The Americans, without Ward*: *Clipper*, April 6, 1889.

246   *"Stick of licorice"*: *New York Herald*, April 7, 1889.

247   *Delmonico's*: *New York Tribune*, April 9, 1889.

247   *Groaned under*: Ibid.

247   *"Well-meaning potentates"*: Ibid.

247–48   *[Menu]*: *Clipper*, April 13, 1889.

248–49   *[Remarks]*: Ibid; *New York Tribune*, April 9, 1889.

250   *"Rather uninteresting"*: See Anson, p. 281.

250   *"Particularly off"*: April 13, 1889.

Chapter Twenty-One. *A LOOK OF EXPECTANCY ON HIS FACE*

page

251   *A look of expectancy*: *Clipper*, November 9, 1889.

252   *Not expected to survive long*: Ibid. and August 18, 1889.

253   *Our twenty Americans*: *Chicago Tribune*, March 11, 1889.

253   *Welcome, boys*: Ibid. and April 9, 1889.

254   *But even in New York's*: *Clipper*, November 17 and December 8, 1888; January 5, 1889; *Chicago Tribune*, February 3, 1889.

256   *Kelly was scheduled*: *Chicago Tribune*, March 17, 1889.

256   *"Whatever differences"*: *Clipper*, April 6, 1889.

258   *On several occasions*: See Ward, *Baseball*, pp. 119–20.

258   *Occasionally*: Ibid., p. 105.

259   *"The standard authority"*: *Clipper*, April 6, 1889. In early 1888, Mike Kelly came out with a book (most likely ghostwritten) titled *Play Ball: Stories of the Ball Field*. The book was part autobiography, part baseball primer, and part series of secular homilies. Another book, *Sphere and Ash*, by Jacob Morse of the *Boston Herald*, was cumbersomely subtitled: "History of Base Ball. Notable Record by Primitive Clubs. Contests for Supremacy in the Sixties. Remarkable Tours of the Early Organizations. Games Conspicuous for Extra Innings. Complete review of All Championship Series." In addition, many short primers on batting, fielding, and pitching had been published, as well as a full-length work, *Batting and Pitching, with Fine Illustrations of Attitudes* (1884), by Boston

infielder Honest John Morrill. The first baseball novel was Noah Brooks's *The Fairport Nine*, published in 1880. See Seymour, *Early Years*, pp. 356–58.

261   *"Demands will be made"*: *Clipper*, April 26, 1889.

262   *"In categories to correspond"*: Ibid. and June 24, 1889.

263   *A few weeks later*: The meeting took place May 19. *NYT*, May 20, 1889; *Clipper*, May 25.

264   *The salary limit law*: *Clipper*, June 1, 1889.

264   *The rule was passed*: *Clipper*, June 8, 1889.

264   *Detroit, he continued*: Ibid.

266   *"If rare on one side"*: Gustav Axelson, *"Commy"*: *The Life Story of Charles A. Comiskey* (Chicago: Reilly, 1911), p. 48; quoted in Pearson, p. 58.

266   *"Such an invitation"*: *Clipper*, June 8, 1889. The benefit game was played on July 13.

266   *"Like Bre'r Fox"*: *Sporting News*, May 11, 1889.

266   See Pearson, pp. 38–40, for the Robinson story.

266   *Thrown ball*: *Clipper*, July 1, 1889.

267   *"Sell my carcass"*: Seymour, *Early Years*, p. 225.

268   *Each man told me*: *Clipper*, September 28, 1889.

268   *"Syndicated Baseball"*: *Sporting Life*, February 5, 1890, quoting the *Pittsburgh Despatch* (no date).

Chapter Twenty-Two. A MAGNATE BEE IN THEIR BONNETS

page

270   *On Sunday night*: *New York Herald*, October 21, 1889.

271   *"Our John" Ward*: *NYT*, October 26, 1889.

272   *Arthur "Hi Hi" Dixwell*: *NYT*, October 31, 1889; Pearson, p. 182.

272   *After the clubhouse formalities*: See Pearson, p. 183.

272   *"Tinge of sadness"*: *Clipper*, November 2, 1889.

273   *"Un-American"*: *Sporting Life*, October 23, 1889.

273   *The players may have some fault*: *Clipper*, October 19, 1889.

273   *At 1:20 P.M.*: *Sporting Life*, November 13, 1889.

275   *I have seen streetcars*: See Gelzheiser, p. 196. The organizational details of the Players' League are in Seymour, *Early Years*, Burk, and Gelzheiser.

277   *In a pair of less controversial decisions*: See Shieber, *Total Baseball*, p. 118. The ball also caused no end of fielding problems; see *Sporting Life*, January 28, 1912.

278   *[Reactions]*: *Free Press*, November 6, 1889; *Sporting Life*, November 13, 1889; *Herald*, November 24, 1889; *Enquirer*, quoted in Seymour, *Early Years*, p. 232.

278   *"That's so, Mr. Spalding"*: *NYT*, November 5, 1889.

279   *The* Times *soon*: December 13, 1889.

279   *Over the next year*: Among the dailies, the *New York Mercury*, *New York World*, *Pittsburgh Dispatch*, and the *Chicago Tribune* supported the players. The *New York Sun*, *Star*, *Tribune*, and *Journal Herald* began the season, at least, in the

National League camp; see Gelzheiser, p. 221. The *Mercury* "exhorted the players to 'rise up in their manhood and rebel.' "

279 *"Brotherhood players withdrew": Clipper*, November 23, 1889.

280 *All I know: Sporting Life*, November 13, 1889.

281 *I did not believe:* See Spalding, pp. 270–71.

281 For the Brotherhood's context in the world of organized labor, I relied heavily on Braverman, Gelzheiser, Golb, Laurie, Montgomery (see him especially on Taylorism, chapter 1), and, via phone conversations and correspondence, John Whiston of the University of Iowa Law School.

281 *Though the decade:* See Laurie, p. 156.

282 *Samuel Gompers: Sporting Life*, April 7, 1900.

282 *"Disruptive and dogmatic":* See Grob, p. 41.

283 *Laboring men: Sporting Life*, January 22, 1890.

283 *Powderly was disdainful:* Quoted in Grob, p. 77.

283 *[Assembly #2583/Chicago carpenters/Yale/Elks]:* See Gelzheiser, pp. 232 and 233.

284 *Vigilant spirit:* See Laurie, p. 185.

286 *Ward was furious: Clipper*, December 12, 1889. The January 30, 1948, *NYT* obituary of Jacob L. Jacobs, a retired New York City clothing manufacturer, described him as the "Man Who Saved The National League in 1890." Jacobs gained the title after Arthur Daley, the *Times* sportswriter, wrote a 1944 column under that heading. According to Jacobs, his shop on Lafayette Street had become an unofficial hangout for infielder Charles Bassett, Jacobs's childhood friend, and several of Bassett's Indianapolis teammates. One day, a "committee" of undecided players, including Bassett, Amos Rusie, Crab Burkett, and Glasscock, asked Jacobs about his thoughts on "deserting" the league. When Jacobs asked the men if, in general, they had been treated fairly and paid regularly, they nodded. He then advised them to stay where they were. (Joe Peters, of Plandome, New York, brought the obituary to my attention.)

287 *[League desertions]: Sporting Life*, January 8, 1890; *Spalding's Guide*, 1889, 1890; Burk, p. 108; Seymour, *Early Years*, p. 233.

287–89 *A few . . . typical . . . headlines: Clipper; The Sporting News*, and *Sporting Life*

289–90 *[Spalding and Kelly]:* See Spalding, pp. 295–97.

290 *In early August: Sporting Life*, August 2, 1890; Spalding's comments, *Sporting Life*, August 16, 1890; on Ward's "deserting the Brotherhood," *Sporting Life*, August 16, 1890.

291 *Privately, however: Clipper*, January 10 and 17, 1891; *Sporting Life*, January 17, 1891. The *Clipper* also quotes the *NYT*.

292 *It also suggests: Boston Herald*, October 6, 1890.

293 *"Seldom, if ever": Sporting Life*, March 19, 1890.

294–95 *[Allegheny Base-ball Club v. Bennett]: Pittsburgh Legal Journal* 14, nos. 5–17; *Metropolitan Exhibitition Co. v. Ward*, 9 N.Y.S. 779 (1890); *Metropolitan Exhibition Co. v. Ewing*, 42 F. Supp. 198, 199 (S.D.N.Y., 1890); Richard L. Irwin, "A Historical Review of Litigation in Baseball," *Marquette Sports Law Journal* 1, no. 2 (Spring 1991), 283–300. Hardy, pp. 115–20, is also helpful.

295 *Wheelbarrow full:* See Tiemann and Rucker, p. 12.

296 *"Mortifying":* February 5, 1890.

Chapter Twenty-Three. SO CHEER THEM TO THE ECHO, LADS

page

300 *"Break not bend":* Sporting Life, May 24, 1890.

301 *They have one great advantage:* Sporting Life, March 26, 1890.

301 *Two men shared a laugh:* New York Herald, March 28, 1890. *Sporting Life,* on July 12, halfway through the season, punned on the phrase, calling out "Where are the people?"

302 *[The Brooklyns/New Yorks]:* Clipper, May 3, 1890.

302 *Hurrah for the gallant lads:* Clipper, May 10, 1890.

303 *In place of powder and shell:* See Spalding, p. 285.

304 *Pittsburgh Press:* Sporting Life, July 19, 1890.

304 *Attendance:* Total Baseball, p. 106, has the National League drawing 776,042.

305 *"Extinct as the dodo":* NYT, May 31, 1890.

305 *"Campaign purposes":* Clipper, July 26, 1890.

305 *Nonpayment for bats:* Clipper, September 20, 1890.

305 *1,727 fans:* See Hardy, p. 122.

306 *Professional gambler:* See Burk, p. 111.

306 *I want to say right here:* Clipper, October 4, 1890.

307 *"Permanent figure":* Sporting Life, September 27, 1890. The preceding headlines/rumors were culled from the daily papers and sporting weeklies.

308 *Before he left:* Clipper, October 11, 1890.

309 *"The greatest war in base ball history":* Ibid.

Chapter Twenty-Four. A SUDDEN TUMBLE INTO A DEEP AND WIDE PITFALL

page

312 *"Stupidity, avarice and treachery":* Clipper, December 6, 1890.

314 *"Bearing a flag of truce":* See Spalding, p. 288.

314 *"Found only a nugget":* Sporting Life, October 18, 1890.

315 *I do not begin:* Ibid.

316 *Vote of six to three:* Sporting Life, October 25, 1890. *Sporting Life, The Sporting News,* and *The Clipper,* as well as the New York dailies, covered the demise of the Players' League in great detail.

317 *[Keefe suit]:* Clipper, December 20, 1890.

317 *Dave Orr:* Orr returned from Arkansas in May; Fogarty died May 20; Corcoran died February 1891.

318 *Worse than any of the deserters:* Clipper, January 17, 1891.

319 *"We have won the fight":* Sporting Life, October 4, 1890.

319   *"Showed their hand"*: Sporting Life, February 17, 1891.

320   *They were aware*: Sporting Life, January 24, 1891, quoting Frank Hough of the *Philadelphia Press*.

321   *These four*: Ibid., quoting H. H. Diddlebock of the *Philadelphia Inquirer*.

Chapter Twenty-Five. SHE TURNED ON WARD WITH A FURY

page

322   *[Ward/Spalding]*: Clipper, December 20, 1890.

324   *Major attraction*: Sporting Life, January 24, 1891.

325   *Cypress Avenue*: Centre County Library Historical Museum, vertical file; unknown newspaper, May 24, 1890.

325   *"Brilliant record of short-stops"*: Dramatic Mirror, September 9, 1889.

326   *Just a little nerve-food*: Dramatic Mirror, September 21, 1889.

326   *Gazing into a shop window*: New York Star, vertical file; unknown newspaper, November 22, 1889.

327   *Ward was irate*: Sporting Life, April 19, 1890.

327   *Perhaps because*: Sporting Life, April 19, 1890, and New York World, April 17, 1890.

327   *"Amicably"*: NYT, May 1, 1890.

327   *Out of the question*: New York Herald, May 2, 1890.

328   *Whirlwind*: Dramatic Mirror, May 10, 1890.

328   *155 East 46th*: One unknown Philadelphia paper says 36th Street.

328   *"Tipped boldly over one eyebrow"*: See Forbes-Robertson, p. 50.

329   *For taking bribes*: New York Daily Tribune, January 13, 1887.

330   *"As a result"* . . . *"repeat the dose"*: Centre County Library Historical Museum vertical file; unknown Philadelphia paper, June 7, 1890.

331   *Cod-Spanish*: See Zang, p. 52.

331   *I have no such purpose*: NYT, October 13, 1887.

331   *SEEKING TO ENJOIN*: New York Herald, May 2, 1890.

332   *March 27, 1890*: Ibid; the article states that the two were "chatting."

332   *Struck her in the face*: Ibid.

333   *It was no use*: Centre County Library Historical Museum; unknown Philadelphia paper, May 7, 1890.

334   *[Elliott's stage career]*: This part of her career is widely documented. The detailed story of her time in France and the Edward VII non-affair is in Forbes-Robertson.

335   *Helen opened*: Dramatic Mirror, October 11, 1890.

335   *"Sympathetic attention"*: Clipper, October 11, 1890.

335   *[London review]*: NYT, February 28, 1892.

335   *"Theatrically demure"*: Dramatic Mirror, May 27, 1893.

336   *Decided . . . to oppose the suit*: NYT, November 3, 1893.

336   The Ward–Dauvray divorce was conducted in the Superior Court of New York. Judge David McAdam decided, but August C. Nanz acted as the arbiter at

the actual hearing. Ward was served with the papers on October 12, 1893. The hearing took place on November 15 and 16. The arbiter gave his report to the judge on November 17, and the decision was filed on November 29, 1893.

336–37 *She was a stout brunette:* There is no way of knowing whether or not this woman was Maxine Elliott, but the age is about right. The stoutness would seem to eliminate her, but Elliott may have been in disguise. The best evidence against Elliott is that at the time she was appearing at the American Theatre's production of *The Prodigal Daughter.* October 10, 1893, was a Tuesday. At 8:15 — the approximate time of the meeting—the play would be in full swing.

337 *The United States Hotel:* See Batterberry, pp. 58 and 191. The divorce record includes a tariff card, a photo of Ward, and his registration signature.

338 The Prodigal Daughter, See Odell, vol. 15, 812.

338 *"Low comedy part":* Ibid., p. 343.

338–39 *[Helen's suits]: New York Herald,* October 14, 1887, and July 29, 1893; *Dramatic Mirror,* January 11 and July 29, 1893.

339 *"Miss Helen D. Ward": New York Tribune,* December 21, 1899, January 1, 1900, and March 22, 1902.

339 *[Winterhalter's obituary]:* NYT, June 6, 1920.

339 *[Helen's obituary]:* NYT, December 7, 1923, and *Variety,* December 13, 1923. The latter states she met Winterhalter in 1896.

Chapter Twenty-Six. *His First Ranch of Rest*

page

340–41 All numbers are from *Total Baseball* except for fielding stats, which are from *Spalding's Guide.*

343 *Faltering American Association:* See Nemec, *Beer and Whisky League,* and Pietrusza, *Major Leagues.*

343 *"Absolute authority"/"easy sailing pennantward": Sporting Life,* January 31, 1891.

343 *Benny Kauff:* See Ward vertical file, NBL.

343 *Tom Kinslow: Sporting Life,* January 31, 1891.

344 *But the low point:* NYT, April 25, 1891.

344 *"Any that have been found": Sporting Life,* February 2, 1892.

345 *Toward the end of February 1892:* The *Brooklyn Daily Eagle,* February 29, reported the fire was in the Smith, Gray & Co. building where Ward stored his "furniture, bric a brac, etc." and "trophies" from the 1888–89 world tour.

345 *At midnight: Sporting Life,* March 12, 1892.

346 *Tom Burns:* See Burk, p. 124.

346 *Salary:* Ibid., p. 243.

346 *[The prospective players]: Sporting Life,* February 16, 1892.

346 *"Friend Bill":* Ibid.

347 *"Clever":* The first half of the season ended July 13.

347 *Lost over $32,000:* Clipper, October 29, 1892, and Hardy, pp. 144–45.

348 *"Scientific bunts":* NYT, December 11, 1893.

348 *"In some ways the best"*: Clipper, March 8, 1893.

348 *Ward scoffed:* Ibid.

348 *"More friends" in New York:* Clipper, February 18, 1893.

349 *[Salary, etc.]:* Ibid.

349 *"Superfluous flesh":* Ibid.

349 *I don't care to discuss:* Clipper, February 25, 1893.

350 *"Countercyclical":* Hardy, p. 148, makes much of this.

350 *Panjandrum:* Ibid., p. 150.

350 *I shall not tinker:* Clipper, date unknown.

350 *"Extra Bill":* NYT, August 25, 1893.

351 *"With croquet":* Clipper, February 3, 1894.

351 *"Killed by the Brotherhood movement":* Clipper, February 2, 1894.

351 *"Expects them to follow":* Clipper, March 31, 1894.

351 *"Nothing to do with me":* Clipper, March 24, 1894.

351 *"We offered him the same money":* Ibid.

352 *"What any businessman would ask":* Clipper, April 14, 1894.

352 *Never forget his kindness:* Clipper, July 16, 1894.

352 *I don't care two cents:* Clipper, June 2, 1894.

353 *Rumors of private 50-50 splits:* See Hardy, p. 152.

354 *A visit to the Polo Grounds:* New York Daily Tribune, October 7, 1894.

354 *The outside of the theatre:* New York Sun, October 9, 1894. The *Sun* said Hopper recited "Casey" before rescuing Ward; the *Clipper*, October 13, says the rescue preceded the poem.

355 *On the following Sunday:* Sun and Herald, October 15, 1894.

355 *"Not prepared to say":* Clipper, September 29, 1894.

356 *'Tis true "Johnnie":* New York Herald, October 31, 1894.

356 *On November 28, 1894:* New York Daily Tribune, November 29; also the *Herald*.

357 *Knew the game as thoroughly:* Clipper, December 26. This was more a retrospective than a news story.

357 *"Seven days in the saddle":* Clipper, November 3, 1894. This seeming "scoop"— more than three weeks before the dailies announced Ward's decision—was effectively, but not officially, a formal retirement announcement. The popular spelling of ranch at the time was "ranche."

Chapter Twenty-Seven. BATTING BLACKSTONE

page

361 *"Shrewd, quick-witted, and humorous":* See Jack Kavanagh, *The Ballplayers*, p. 1143; Mike Shatzkin, ed. (New York: Arbor House, 1990).

361 *Wenzel v. Patrick Ryan Construction:* 223 NY 610 (119 NE 1085); 169 App-Div 357 (154 NYS 809).

362 *Larkin v. New York Telephone:* 220 NY 27 (114 NE 1043); 158 AppDiv 357 (143 NYS 578); 169 AppDiv 162 (154 NYS 804).

362   *"You can't hit what you can't see"*: See Richard Puff, in Ivor-Campbell, Tiemann, Rucker, p. 143.

362–63   The Rusie case was widely covered in the sporting press until its conclusion on April 12, 1897. For Freedman, see Hardy, pp. 154–91; and Seymour, *Early Years*, pp. 296–98, 303–06, 309, 317–22.

363   *"No longer traceable"*: See Seymour, *Early Years*, p. 296.

363   *"Ward's fling at baseball management"*: See Hardy, p. 154.

364   *"Such a bonanza"*: *Sporting Life*, March 12, 1925.

365   *Ward laughed out loud*: NYT, February 25, 1896.

365   *I am not as yet*: Ibid.

367   *A "tremendous bluff"*: See Seymour, *Early Years*, p. 272.

367   *Fred Pfeffer*: Ibid., pp. 272–73; William McMahon, p. 102, in Tiemann, Rucker.

368   *Pfeffer's flame of activism*: *Sporting Life*, December 20, 1902.

368   *Michael Griffin*: See Puff and Rucker, p. 55, in Tiemann, Rucker; *Sporting Life*, April 18, 1903.

369   *Peak wage season of 1891*: See Burk, p. 243.

369   *[Griffith/Protective Association of Professional Baseball]*: See Seymour, *Early Years*, pp. 307–24; Burk, pp. 142–77; *Sporting Life*, April 7, 1900–December 1901.

369   *I have been told*: *Sporting Life*, April 7, 1900.

370   *I have little opportunity*: Unknown paper, May 22, 1900.

371   *The city's South Side*: See Burk, p. 135, for discussion of National League's vulnerability.

372   *The AL outdrew the NL*: See Pietrusza, p. 164; Burk, p. 150; and Burk, p. 243, for salaries.

372   Lowenfish discusses the Protective Association, the National Association of Professional Baseball Leagues and other organizing efforts throughout the twentieth century.

372–73   *[McGuire case]*: *Sporting Life*, June 28 and July 5, 1902.

373   *George Davis*: See Joseph M. Overfield, in Tiemann, Rucker, p. 36, for autobiographical and legal summary. William F. Lamb has a much more detailed profile in *The National Pastime* 17 (Spring 1997). (Davis was elected to Baseball's Hall of Fame in 1998.) The case occupied a high-profile position in the weekly sporting press during the entire 1903 season. The Davis case is ferociously complicated, and I have risked blurring nuance by summarizing it. See Seymour, *Golden Age*, pp. 12–13, for a further explanation, as well as for the Johnson–Pulliam "Kid" Elberfield wrangle.

374   *"Unprofessional advice"*: *Sporting Life*, July 18, 1903.

374   *"As crooked in regard"*: *Sporting Life*, April 7, 1903.

374   *[Pulliam suicide]*: NYT, July 29–30, 1909.

374   *Electing John L. Lewis*: See Seymour, *Golden Age*, p. 28.

375   *It is far from our purpose*: NYT, December 14, 1909. Generally, the *Times* reports on the December League elections are clearer, if slightly less detailed, than those of the sporting weeklies.

376   *[Johnson/Ward verdict]*: NYT, May 13, 1911.

Chapter Twenty-Eight. MACHINE PLAY

page

378   *Letter to August Hermann:* December 20, 1911. See Ward vertical file, NBL, Cooperstown, N.Y.

378   *"The new Boston owners":* Sporting News, February 8, 1912.

378   *"Old Boy take the hindmost":* Ibid.

378   *"Lawyers make very poor magnates":* Sporting News, August 8, 1912. Murnane, by 1912, had become a baseball political conservative. He praised a 1912 Protective Association, but saw its role as a complement rather than an adversary to the leagues and the ruling body, the National Commission, which, he said, had done "splendid work . . . in protecting the rights of the ball players . . . and has never been appreciated by many of the men" (*Sporting News*, August 8, 1912).

380   *In "full headdress":* See Leonard Koppett's letter to the editor, NYT, June 26, 1893.

380   *Federal League:* See Okkonen; Pietrusza, pp. 183–252; Seymour, *Golden Age*, pp. 196–244; and Burk, pp. 194–212, 216–17, 220–35.

380   *"Quickest and most ridiculous failure":* See Pietrusza, p. 207.

381–82   *[Salaries]:* See Burk, p. 243.

382   *Rube Marquard:* See Mansch, pp. 152–54.

382   *In 1903:* Sporting Life, April 11, 1903.

383   *New York . . . by virtue of its size:* Ibid.

383   *"Machine play":* Unknown paper, March 31, 1906, in Ward file, NBL.

383   *"The most remarkable fight":* Ibid.

384   *"Established as a signal success":* See vertical file, NBL, unknown paper, February 6, 1915.

Chapter Twenty-Nine. NONE OF THE SPICE OF BASEBALL

page

385   *[Bicycling]:* Encyclopedia of New York; Riess, *City Games*, pp. 62–65, 114, 192, 209, 296, 273.

387   *But Ward had to do something:* See Isenberg, pp. 38–81. His biography of John L. Sullivan discusses manliness and American attitudes toward many sports, not only pugilism. Riess, *City Games*, is also invaluable, as well as Kirsch, Adelman, and, more abstractly, Oriard.

388   *"Busy with a cleek":* See Harry Smith, *Golf Illustrated*, April 4, 1925.

389   *"Eveless Eden":* See Martin, p. 20, and Fulkerson and Thacher.

389   *"None of the spice of baseball":* New York Herald-Tribune, December 7, 1924.

390   *Scratch golf and a five handicap:* Spalding Official Golf Guide, 1907.

390   *"First ten players":* Golf, February 1909. Much of the following tournament information came from the United States Golf Association Library and from golf magazines during the years 1903–23.

390–91   The tournament information and the trip to Europe and his playing partners comes from an article by "Jigger" in an unknown magazine, March 16, 1916 (vertical file, NBL).

391   *"Dishes, vases and medals"*: Ibid.

391   *"Irreproachable life"*: *New York Tribune*, September 18, 1903.

391   *"Unmeasured happiness"*: *New York Tribune*, September 26, 1903.

391   Ladies' Home Journal: Date unknown.

391–92   *[Katherine Waas]*: From an interview with Mary Fleming, September 1995.

392   *[Katherine's letters]*: Ward vertical file, NBL, January 22, February 7, 1964.

393   *"How I loved that man"*: From the Mary Fleming interview, September 1995.

393   *Little disappointments and setbacks*: *Babylon Leader*, March 6, 1925.

393   *Babylon Fuel and Supply Company*: Ibid.; see also the "Jigger" article, Ward vertical file, NBL. Harry C. Smith, in "An Intimate Sketch of John M. Ward," *Golf Illustrated*, April 1925, seems to have borrowed liberally from Jigger, assuming the authors are not one and the same.

394   *[Life on the farm/Klondike]*: See "Jigger" article; also Smith, ibid.

394   *"Poor Buck—he's dead"*: Ward vertical file, NBL.

Chapter Thirty. *He Wore a Uniform for Seventeen Years*

page

395   *"Considering the blustery breezes"*: *New York Evening Telegram*, May 13, 1921.

395–96   *[Jubilee]*: NYT, February 3, 1925.

396   *Ban Johnson*: See Seymour, *Golden Age*, p. 378.

397   *This salary [system]*: NYT, February 3, 1925.

397   *Acute lobar pneumonia*: Georgia State Board of Embalming, Original Transit Permit.

398   Obituaries ran in the sporting weeklies and many other papers, including the NYT, *Augusta Chronicle*, and *Babylon Leader*.

399   *Ford Frick*: NYT, July 28, 1964.

399   *[Menu, details]*: From a letter from Winifred Watson, courtesy of Mary Fleming.

Afterword and Acknowledgments

page

403   *James Joyce*: See *Finnegans Wake*, p. 197.6–197.26, for Joyce on baseball.

Bibliography

ARCHIVES AND LIBRARIES

Babylon Historical and Preservation Society, Babylon, N.Y.
Broome County Historical Society, Binghamton, N.Y.
Centre County Library Historical Museum, Bellefonte, Pa.
Columbia University, Law School Library/University Archives and Columbiana Library, New York.
Dartmouth College Library Archives/Special Collections, Hanover, N.H.
August "Garry" Herrmann Papers, National Baseball Library, Cooperstown, N.Y.
Abraham G. Mills Papers, National Baseball Library, Cooperstown, N.Y.
Museum of Questionable Medical Devices, Minneapolis, Minn.
Penn State Room, Pattee Library, University Park, Pa.
Rhode Island Historical Society, Providence, R.I.
Albert G. Spalding Collection, National Baseball Library, Cooperstown, N.Y.
Tiffany & Co. Archives, Parsippany, N.J.
Tioga County Historical Society, Owego, N.Y.
United States Golf Association Library, Far Hills, N.J.
Vertical Files, National Baseball Library, Cooperstown, N.Y.
Aaron Montgomery Ward Papers, American Heritage Center, University of Wyoming, Laramie.

UNPUBLISHED AND MISCELLANEOUS MATERIAL

Bowman, Larry G. "John Montgomery Ward and the Enchanted Baseball." Denton, Tex., 1998.

Brown, Charles H. *Centennial Histories*. Penn State Room, Pattee Library, Pennsylvania State University, College Park.

Carson, Tom. "Major League Baseball's First Post-Season Champions: the Providence Grays." Dept. of Philosophy, Virginia Polytechnic University. Undated. Rhode Island Historical Society, Providence.

Elias, Robert. *The National Pastime & the American Dream: Baseball as Cultural Mirror*. Class Syllabus, Politics Department, University of San Francisco, 1998.

Gelzheiser, Robert Paul. *The Great Baseball Rebellion: The Brotherhood of Professional Baseball Players and The Players' League: A Labor/Capital Perspective*. Master's thesis, Trinity College, Hartford, Conn., 1991.

Hancock, Robert. "Providence and the Providence Grays." Society for American Baseball Research (SABR) Research Papers Collection. Cleveland, Ohio, 1992.

Koenig, Karl F. Personal papers/Ward research. Courtesy of Julia Mitchell, Olympia, Wash.

Stinson, Fred, and Richard Waldbauer. "The Providence Grays as a Franchise." SABR Research Papers Collection, 1984.

NEWSPAPERS

Augusta (Ga.) *Chronicle*
Babylon (N.Y.) *Leader*
Bellefonte (Pa.) *Democratic-Watchman* and *Central Press*
Binghamton (N.Y.) *Daily Democrat, Daily Leader, Morning Republican, Morning Republican and Morning Times*, and *Republican-Times*
Boston Globe
Brooklyn Eagle
Buffalo Morning Express
Chicago Tribune
Cincinnati Enquirer
Clinton (Lock Haven, Pa.) *Democrat*
Denver Daily News
Dramatic Mirror
Los Angeles Times
National Police Gazette
New Orleans Picayune
New York American, Clipper, Daily Graphic, Daily Tribune, Herald, Star, Sun, Times, and *World*.
Providence Daily Journal, Evening Press, Evening Star, Journal, and *Star*.
Rocky Mountain News
San Francisco Daily Examiner
Sporting Life
The Sporting News
Williamsport (Pa.) *Daily Gazette and Bulletin*

ARTICLES

Adelman, Melvin L. "Baseball, Business and the Work Place: Gelber's Thesis Re-examined." *Journal of Social History* (Winter 1989): 285–301.

Bass, Cynthia. "The Making of a Baseball Radical." *The National Pastime* (Fall 1982): 63–65.

Bowman, Larry. "Baseball's Intriguing Couple." *The National Pastime* (Fall 1998): 69–72.

———. "Baseball Mascots." *The National Pastime* (1999): np.

———. "The Dauvray Cup." *The National Pastime* (Spring 1997): 73–76.

Carlson, Lewis. "The Universal Athletic Sport of the World." *American History Illustrated* (April 1984): 36–43.

Cowell, Sydney. "The Enchanted Baseball: A Fairy Story of Modern Times." *Cosmopolitan* (April 8, 1890): 659–68.

Gelber, Steven M. "Working at Playing: The Culture of the Workplace and the Rise of Baseball." *Journal of Social History* (Summer 1983).

Hall, Donald. "The Look of Old Baseball." *Yankee* 52 (July 1988): 62–68.

"Hot Dogs, Homers and Hinkey: A History of Baseball at Penn State." *The Penn Stater*. 81:6 (July/August 1994).

Kofoed, J. C. "Early History of Curve Pitching." *Baseball* (August 1915).

Lamoreux, Dave. "Baseball's Late 19th-Century Appeal." *Journal of Popular Culture* 11 (Winter 1977): 597–613.

Lowenfish, Lee. "The Later Years of John M. Ward." *The National Pastime* (Fall 1983): 67–69.

McQuilkin, Scott A. "Summer Baseball and the NCAA: The Second 'Vexation.'" *Journal of Sport History* 28: 1 (Spring 1998): 18–42.

Perrin, William D. "Line Drives Then and Now," *Providence Journal* (June–July 1928). Collected as *Days of Greatness*. Society for American Baseball Research, 1988, Cooperstown, N.Y.

Pierce, Edward. "What They Wrote About Monte Ward." *Baseball Digest* (May 1964): 69–75.

Smith, Don. "Strike Didn't Always Mean Gold." *Montana Magazine of Western History* (July 1970).

Smith, Harry C. "An Intimate Sketch of John M. Ward." *Golf Illustrated* (April 1925).

Ward, John Montgomery. "Is the Base-Ball Player a Chattel?" *Lippincott's* 40 (August 1887): 310–19.

———. "Making a Baseball Team." *Collier's* 45 (May 14, 1916): 28–29.

———. "Notes of a Base-Ballist." *Lippincott's* 38 (August 1886): pp. 212–20.

———. "Our National Game." *Cosmopolitan* 5 (October 1888): 443–55.

BOOKS ON BASEBALL

Adelman, Melvin L. *A Sporting Time: New York City and the Rise of Modern Athletics 1820–1870*. Urbana: University of Illinois Press, 1986.

Alexander, Charles C. *John McGraw*. New York: Viking, 1988.

Allen, Lee. *The National League Story*. New York: Hill and Wang, 1962.

Alvarez, Mark. *The Old Ball Game*. Alexandria, Va.: Redefinition, 1990.

Anson, Adrian C. *A Ball Player's Career*. Chicago: Era Publishers, 1900. Reprint: Mattituck, N.Y.: Amereon House, nd.

Appel, Marty. *Slide, Kelly, Slide*. Lanham, Md.: Scarecrow Press, 1996.

Brock, Darryl. *If I Never Get Back*. New York: Crown, 1989.

Burk, Robert F. *Never Just a Game*. Chapel Hill: University of North Carolina Press, 1994.

Dworkin, James B. *Owners Versus Players—Baseball and Collective Bargaining*. Dover, Mass.: Auburn House, 1981.

Dyja, Tom. *Play for a Kingdom*. New York: Harcourt Brace, 1997.

Frommer, Harvey. *Primitive Baseball*. New York: Atheneum, 1988.

Gardner, Martin, ed. *The Annotated Casey at the Bat*. 3d ed. Mineola, N.Y.: Dover Publications, 1995.

Goldstein, Warren. *Playing for Keeps*. Ithaca, N.Y.: Cornell University Press, 1989.

Hardy, James D., Jr. *The New York Giants Base Ball Club 1870–1900*. Jefferson, N.C.: McFarland, 1996.

Helyar, John. *Lords of the Realm—The Real History of Baseball*. New York: Villard, 1994.

Ivor-Campbell, Frederick, Robert L. Tiemann, and Mark Rucker, eds. *Baseball's First Stars*. Cleveland: Society for American Baseball Research, 1996.

Kirsch, George B. *The Creation of American Team Sports: Baseball & Cricket 1838–1872*. Urbana: University of Illinois, 1989.

Lansche, Jerry. *The Forgotten Championships—Postseason Baseball, 1882–1981*. Jefferson, N.C.: McFarland, 1989.

———. *Glory Fades Away—The Nineteenth-Century World Series Rediscovered*. Dallas: Taylor Publishing, 1991.

Lawson, Thomas W. *The Krank, His Language and What It Means*. Boston: Rand Avery Co., 1888.

Levine, Peter. *A. G. Spalding and the Rise of Baseball: The Promise of American Sport*. New York: Oxford University Press, 1985.

Lowenfish, Lee. *The Imperfect Diamond: The Story of Baseball's Reserve System and the Men Who Fought to Change It*. Rev. ed. New York: Da Capo Press, 1991. (Originally, with Tony Lupien. New York: Stein & Day, 1980.)

Mack, Connie. *My 66 Years in the Big Leagues*. Philadelphia: John C. Winston, 1950.

Mansch, Larry D. *Rube Marquard*. Jefferson, N.C.: McFarland, 1998.

Moore, Jim, and Natalie Vermilia. *Ernest Thayer's "Casey at the Bat."* Jefferson, N.C.: McFarland, 1994.

Moreland, George L. *Balldom*. New York: Balldom Publishing Co., 1914. Reprint: St. Louis: Horton Publishing Co., 1989.

Morse, Jacob. *Sphere and Ash: History of Baseball*. Boston: J. F. Spofford & Co., 1888. Reprint: Columbia, S.C.: Camden House, 1984.

Murdock, Eugene. *Ban Johnson: Czar of Baseball*. Westport, Conn.: Greenwood Press, 1986.

Nemec, David. *The Beer and Whisky League*. New York: Lyons & Burford, 1994.

———. *The Great Encyclopedia of 19th Century Major League Baseball*. New York: Donald L. Fine Books, 1997.

———. *The Rules of Baseball*. New York: Lyons & Burford, 1994.

Okkonen, Marc. *The Federal League 1914–15*. Cleveland: Society for American Baseball Research, 1989.

Orem, Preston D. *Baseball 1845–1881*. 341 E. Calaveras St., Altadena, Calif.: 1961.

Overfield, Joseph. *100 Years of Buffalo Baseball*. Kenmore, N.Y.: Partners Press, 1985.

Palmer, Harry Clay. *Athletic Sports in America*. Philadelphia: 1889.

Pearson, Daniel M. *Baseball in 1889—Players vs. Owners*. Bowling Green, Ohio: Bowling Green State University Popular Press, 1993.

Pietrusza, David. *Major Leagues: The Formation, Sometimes Absorption and Mostly Inevitable Demise of 18 Professional Baseball Organizations 1871–Present*. Jefferson, N.C.: McFarland, 1991.

Players' National League Official Base Ball Guide. Chicago: F. H. Brunell, 1890. Reprint: St. Louis: Horton Publishing Co., 1989.

Reach's Official Base Ball Guide. 1889–1891, 1895. A. J. Reach Co. Reprints: St. Louis: Horton Publishing Co., 1988–1989.

Ribowsky, Mark. *A Complete History of the Negro Leagues 1884–1955*. New York: Birch Lane Press, 1995.

Riess, Steven A. *City Games: The Evolution of American Urban Society and the Rise of Sports*. Urbana: University of Illinois Press, 1989.

———. *Touching Base: Professional Baseball and American Culture in the Progressive Era*. Westport, Conn.: Greenwood Press, 1989.

Selzer, Jack. *Baseball in the Nineteenth Century: An Overview*. Cleveland: Society for American Baseball Research, 1986.

Seymour, Harold. *Baseball, The Early Years*. New York: Oxford University Press, 1960.

———. *Baseball, The Golden Age*. New York: Oxford University Press, 1971.

———. *Baseball, The People's Game*. New York: Oxford University Press, 1990.

Smith, Myron J. *Baseball, A Comprehensive Bibliography*. Jefferson, N.C.: McFarland, 1986.

Smith, Robert. *Baseball*. New York: Simon and Schuster, 1974.

Spalding, Albert G. *America's National Game*. New York: American Sports Publishing Co., 1911. Reprint: Lincoln: University of Nebraska, 1992.

Spalding's Official Base Ball Guide. 1876–1895. A. G. Spalding & Bros. Reprints: St. Louis: Horton Publishing Co., 1988–1989.

Spink, Alfred E. *The National Game*. St. Louis: The National Game Publishing Co., 1910.

Sullivan, Dean A., ed. *Early Innings: A Documentary History of Baseball 1825–1908*. Lincoln: University of Nebraska, 1995.

Thorn, John. *Treasures of the Baseball Hall of Fame*. New York, Villard, 1998.

————, and Pete Palmer, eds. *Total Baseball: The Official Encyclopedia of Major League Baseball*. New York: Viking, 1995.

Tiemann, Robert L., and Mark Rucker. *Nineteenth Century Stars*. Cleveland: Society for American Baseball Research, 1989.

Turkin, Hy, and S. C. Thompson. *The Official Encyclopedia of Baseball*. New York: A. S. Barnes & Co., 1951.

Voight, David Q. *American Baseball: Gentlemen to Commissioner*. Norman: University of Oklahoma Press, 1966.

————. *America Through Baseball*. New York: Nelson-Hall, 1976.

Ward, John Montgomery. *Base-Ball: How to Become a Player, with the Origin, History, and Explanation of the Game*. Philadelphia: Athletic Publishing Company, 1888. Reprint: Cleveland: Society for American Baseball Research, 1993.

Zang, David W. *Fleet Walker's Divided Heart*. Lincoln: University of Nebraska, 1995.

BOOKS ON SPORTS

Ball, Donald W., and John W. Loy, eds. *Sport and Social Order: Contributions to the Sociology of Sport*. Reading, Pa.: Addison-Wesley, 1975.

Berry, Robert C., William Gould IV, and Paul D. Staudohar. *Labor Relations in Professional Sports*. Dover, Mass.: Auburn House, 1986.

Fulkerson, Neal, and John T. Thacher. *The Garden City Golf Club*. Garden City, N.Y.: 1974.

Guttman, Allen. *From Ritual to Record*. New York: Columbia University Press, 1978.

————. *Games and Empires: Modern Sports and Cultural Imperialism*. New York: Columbia University Press, 1994.

————. *Sports Spectators*. New York: Columbia University Press, 1986.

————. *A Whole New Ball Game: An Interpretation of American Sports*. Chapel Hill: University of North Carolina Press, 1988.

Henderson, Robert W. *Ball, Bat and Bishop: The Origin of Ball Games*. New York: Rockport Press, 1947.

Isenberg, Michael T. *John L. Sullivan and His America*. Urbana, Ill.: University of Illinois Press, 1994.

Kyle, Donald G., and Gary D. Stark, eds. *Essays on Sport History and Sport Mythology*. College Station, Tex.: Texas A & M University Press, 1990.

Mandell, Richard D. *Sport—A Cultural History*. New York: Columbia University Press, 1984.

Martin, H. B. *The Garden City Golf Club*. Garden City, N.Y.: 1949.

Meggysey, David. *Out of Their League*. Berkeley: Ramparts Press, 1971.

Mrozek, Donald J. *Sport and American Mentality 1880–1910*. Knoxville: University of Tennessee Press, 1984.

Noll, Roger G., ed. *Government and the Sports Business*. Washington, D.C.: Brookings Institution, 1974.

Oriard, Michael. *Sporting with the Gods: The Rhetoric of Play and Game in American Culture*. New York: Cambridge University Press, 1991.

Simon, Robert L. *Sports and Social Values*. Englewood Cliffs, N.J.: Prentice-Hall, 1985.

Smith, Ronald A. *Sports and Freedom: The Rise of Big-Time College Athletics*. New York: Oxford University Press, 1988.

Spivey, Donald, ed. *Sport in America: New Historical Perspectives*. Westport: Greenwood Press, 1985.

Staudohar, Paul D. *The Sports Industry and Collective Bargaining*. 2d ed. Ithaca, N.Y.: ILR Press, 1989.

Strutt, Joseph. *The Sports and Pastimes of the People of England*. London: Chatto & Windus, 1897.

GENERAL

Allen, Oliver E. *New York, New York*. New York: Atheneum, 1990.

The Amazing Pennsylvania Canals. York, Pa.: Historical Society of York County, 1965.

Barth, Gunther. *City People: The Rise of Modern City Culture in Nineteenth Century America*. New York: Oxford University Press, 1980.

Batterberry, Michael and Ariane. *On the Town in New York*. New York: Scribners, 1973.

Birmingham, Stephen. *Life at The Dakota*. New York: Random House, 1979.

Bishop, Joel Prentiss. *New Commentaries on Marriage, Divorce and Separation*, vol. 1, T. H. Flood & Co., 1891.

Boyer, Paul. *Urban Masses and Moral Order in America 1820–1920*. Cambridge, Mass.: Harvard University Press, 1978.

Braverman, Harry. *Labor and Monopoly Capitalism*. New York: Monthly Review Press, 1974.

Brody, David. *Steelworkers in America: The Non-Union Era*. Cambridge, Mass.: Harvard University Press, 1960.

Brown, Henry Collins, ed. *Valentine's Manual of Old New York*. No. 7, New Series. Hastings on Hudson: 1923.

———. *New York in the Elegant Eighties*. Hastings on Hudson: 1926.

———. *New York in the Golden Nineties*. Hastings on Hudson: 1928.

Bushman, Richard L. *The Refinement of America: Persons, Houses, Cities*. New York: Alfred A. Knopf, 1992.

Chandler, Alfred D., Jr. *The Visible Hand*. Cambridge, Mass.: Belknap Press, 1977.

Cook, Ann, Marilyn Gittell, and Herb Mack, eds. *City Life, 1865–1900*. New York: Praeger Publishers, 1973.

Dunaway, Wayland Fuller. *History of The Pennsylvania State College*. Lancaster, Pa.: Lancaster Press, 1946.

Forbes-Robertson, Diana. *My Aunt Maxine*. New York: Viking, 1964.

Goebel, Julius, Jr., ed. *A History of The School of Law, Columbia University*. New York: Columbia University Press, 1955.

Grob, Gerald. *Workers and Utopia: A Study of Ideological Conflict in the American Labor Movement, 1865–1900*. Evanston, Ill.: Northwestern University Press, 1961.

Haber, Samuel. *Efficiency and Uplift: Scientific Management in the Progressive Era, 1890–1920*. Chicago: University of Chicago Press, 1964.

History of Tioga, Chemung, Tompkins and Schuyler Counties, New York. Philadelphia: Everts & Ensign, 1879.

Hoy, Suellen. *Chasing Dirt—The American Pursuit of Cleanliness*. New York: Oxford University Press, 1995.

Huizinga, Johan. *Homo Ludens*. Boston: Beacon Press, 1955.

Jackson, Kenneth T., ed. *The Encyclopedia of New York City*. New Haven, Conn.: Yale University Press, 1995.

Knobel, Dale T. *Paddy and the Republic: Ethnicity and Nationality in Antebellum America*. Middletown, Conn.: Wesleyan University Press, 1986.

Laurie, Bruce. *Artisans into Workers: Labor in Nineteenth-Century America*. New York: Noonday Press, 1989.

Lawyer, William S., ed. *Binghamton: Its Settlement, Growth and Development—1800–1900*. Binghamton, N.Y.: Century Memorial Publishing, 1900.

McArthur, Benjamin. *Actors and American Culture 1880–1920*. Philadelphia: Temple University Press, 1984.

Mathews, Brander. *Vignettes of Manhattan*. New York: Harper & Bros., 1894.

Montgomery, David. *The Fall of The House of Labor: The Workplace, the State, and American Labor Activism 1875–1965*. New York: Cambridge University Press, 1987.

Morris, Lloyd. *Incredible New York High Life and Low Life from 1850–1950*. Syracuse, N.Y.: Syracuse University Press, 1951.

Moss, Frank. *The American Metropolis*. 3 vols. New York: Peter Fenelon Collier, 1897.

Nasan, David. *Going Out: The Rise and Fall of Public Amusements*. New York: Basic Books, 1993.

Naylor, Romayne, ed. *Bellefonte Bicentennial Celebration*. Bellefonte, Pa.: Bellefonte Bicentennial Committee, 1995.

Odell, George C. D., *Annals of the New York Stage*. Vols. 9–15. New York: Columbia University Press, 1942.

Phillips, Roderick. *Putting Asunder: A History of Divorce in Western Society*. New York: Cambridge University Press, 1988.

Rudolph, Frederick. *The American College and University: A History*. Athens, Ga.: University of Georgia Press, 1962.

Sante, Luc. *Low Life*. New York: Farrar, Straus & Giroux, 1994.

Scherer, Margaret R. *Marvels of Ancient Rome*. London: Phaidon Press, 1956.

Schouler, James. *A Treatise on the Law of the Domestic Relations*. Boston: Little, Brown, 1889.

Simon, Kate. *Fifth Avenue: A Very Social History*. New York: Harcourt Brace Jovanovich, 1978.

Stearns, Peter N. *Be A Man!: Males in Modern Society*. New York: Holmes and Meier, 1979.

Stevens, Robert. *Law School: Legal Education in America from the 1850s to the 1980s*. Chapel Hill: University of North Carolina Press, 1983.

Taylor, Frederick Winslow. *The Principles of Scientific Management*. New York: Harper & Bros., 1914.

Veysey, Laurence R. *The Emergence of the American University*. Chicago: University of Chicago Press, 1965.

Ward and Allied Families: A Genealogical Study with Biographical Notes. New York: American Historical Society, 1930.

Wiebe, Robert H. *The Search for Order 1877–1920*. New York: Hill & Wang, 1967.

Willensky, Elliot, and Norval White. *AIA Guide to New York City*. 3d ed. New York: Harcourt Brace Jovanovich, 1988.

Williams, Marilyn Thornton. *Washing The Great Unwashed: Public Baths in Urban America 1840–1920*. Columbus: Ohio State University Press, 1991.

Index

About the Author

Bryan Di Salvatore's work has appeared in *The New Yorker*, *The New York Times Magazine*, and *Outside*, among other publications. He lives in Missoula, Montana.